The Sandalwood Mountains

檀香山先輩華人史

謝廷玉編著

The Sandalwood Mountains

Readings and Stories
of the Early Chinese in Hawaii

Compiled and edited by Tin-Yuke Char

The University Press of Hawaii
Honolulu

Copyright © 1975 by The University Press of Hawaii
All rights reserved
Manufactured in the United States of America

Library of Congress Cataloging in Publication Data

Char, Tin-Yuke, comp.
    The Sandalwood Mountains.

    Includes bibliographical references and index.
    1. Chinese in Hawaii—History—Sources. I. Title.
DU624.7.C5C45   919.69'06'951   74-76375
ISBN 0-8248-0305-1

To Wai Jane,
my wife,
who assisted me in
research and writing

Contents

Illustrations   x

Preface   xi

Acknowledgments   xv

I. Historical Background of Nineteenth-Century China
Imperial China's Policy of Self-Imposed Isolation   1
Manifest Destiny Meets the Mandate of Heaven   2
Foreigners Segregated in Canton   6
Impact and Disintegration in China   8
Ban on Emigration   12
China Lifts Emigration Ban to America, 1868   14
Ethnographic Background of Chinese Migrants   16
Two Country Tours in China, 1884   23

II. Early Relations between Hawaii and China
Hawaiians Visit China, 1787   33
Chinese Visit Hawaii, 1788–1789   36
A Chinese Woman in Hawaii, 1837   42
King Kalakaua's Visit to China, 1881   44
Hawaiian Students in China   51

III. Contract Labor System and Immigration Problems
Chinese in Sugar, 1802–1852   54
Economic Basis for Contract Labor   57
First Contract Laborers Arrive, 1852   60
Local Chinese Petition for Free Immigration, 1869   63
Further Legislation on Contract Labor   66
Chinese Stories from Grove Farm Plantation   69
Protests and Complaints, 1891–1897   74
Conditions of Labor in Hawaii, 1899   82
Two Stories from Kohala   85

IV. Economic and Social Development

Chinese Residents before 1852	88
Chinese Ball for King Kamehameha IV, 1856	90
Rice Industry, 1857–1929	91
Bubonic Plague and the Chinatown Fire, 1900	101
Kula Chinese and Homestead Leases	110
Occupational and Educational Adjustments	113
Changing Family Relations	119
Chinatown Stores in the 1930s	126
Some Old Chinese Customs in Hawaii	131
Summary of Social Progress	138

V. Chinese Organizations in Hawaii

Chinese Tongs and Societies	145
Fraternal Societies	159
The Thirty-Six Oaths of Hoong Moon Societies	163
Inventory of Fraternal Societies, Past and Present	167
Chinese Cemeteries	171
Tong Wo Society in Kohala	176

VI. Religious Faiths and Practices

Chinese Religion and Chinese Temples	181
Kohala Sugar Hires Christian Worker for Chinese, 1878	192
Early Christian Arrivals, 1878	194
Basel Mission Work	197
Christian Hawaiian Family Stranded in China, 1879	198
Tours to Call on Chinese in Plantation Camps, 1882	199
Frank and Mary Damon's Work among the Chinese	218

VII. Family Histories, Lineage, and Genealogy

Family Organization	223
Chinese Genealogies	227
Biography of the Reverend Woo Yee-Bew	230
The Chun Afong Story	236
Ninety-One-Year-Old Rice Planter	243
From Slave Girl to Respected Grandmother	247
Autobiography of Chung Kun-Ai	253

Appendixes

A. Keoni Pake Sugar Agreement, 1839	267
B. Chinese Sugar Plantation Inventory, 1848	270
C. Labor Recruitment Contract, 1865	275
D. Labor Contract, 1870	278
E. Labor Contract, 1890	280
F. Labor Import Declaration, 1890	285
G. Chinese Mass Protest, 1894	287
H. Claim for Loss of Property, Chinatown Fire, 1901	293
I. United Chinese Society Petition to Congress, 1916	296
J. Chinese Population, 1853–1960	308
K. Arrivals and Departures, 1879–1898	309
L. Chinese Laborers on Sugar Plantations, 1882–1924	310
M. Age and Sex Distribution of Chinese in Hawaii 1910, 1920, 1930	312

Notes 313

Glossary 333

Index 351

Illustrations

Map of Chungshan Hsien	17
Map of Kwangtung Province	18-19
Menu of Dinner for King Kalakaua	45
Map Showing Destruction Caused by Chinatown Fire	104

Preface

With increasing interest in ethnic history, there is need for more pertinent and provocative materials on the various groups that make up the broad spectrum of America's people. One aspect of this vast subject is that of the Chinese in the Hawaiian Islands. In order to initiate a comprehensive approach to this subject, a variety of readings were selected and compiled, many of which are not easily available. Included are excerpts of printed articles, extractions from books, government documents, and a few news stories, each preceded by interpretative comments.

The readings were chosen principally from primary or older sources. A broad sweep of writings about the immigration period up to World War II was made before selection. The selection was made from the point of view of historical perspective. Some describe the experiences of the community into which the Chinese were thrust. Some lighter stories have been added for atmosphere rather than for their objectivity.

To broaden the scope of historical records, it is currently being suggested that oral histories of the immigrant generation or their earliest descendants be tape-recorded. Such oral histories, documented, are not yet available to complete the ethno-cultural picture of the Chinese in Hawaii. An editorial in *The Sunday Advertiser* expresses the need for such local history.*

> Have some of Hawaii's non-haole [i.e., non-Caucasian] racial groups dealt themselves out of meaningful future identity by not taking enough interest in their history?
>
> The question comes up in relation to a story last week by *Advertiser* writer Tom Kaser telling of the work of a historian

---

* "Completing Hawaii History," *The Sunday Advertiser* (Honolulu), 18 October 1970.

and a retired speech professor in collecting oral history interviews with significant people, both well-known and unknown.

These important efforts have been under way for a number of years. They deserve increased support.

It is very much a race with time to gather the impressions of older people involved in significant events or important periods of Hawaii's history. Bits of meaningful, unrecorded history die or fade from memory every year.

The oral history situation is part of a larger point about Hawaii's history—that it is quite incomplete in racial terms.

It is natural that the early writing of history of Hawaii was by haoles for haoles; some of it is very good from that viewpoint.

Still, as one authority points out, "Histories are generally the history of the power elite. And historians, like doctors, bury their mistakes."

In Hawaii's case it might have been more omission or preoccupation; but whatever the case, the Islands' history is said to need more multi-racial perspective both in terms of material available and those who present it.

This is of special importance here, of course, since our history is one of ethnic groups.

Various departments at the University of Hawaii and the Bishop Museum have been working to collect historical source material from racial groups.

But what's needed is a greater degree of private citizen awareness of the value of historical materials and viewpoints to the writing of future histories.

Various ethnic civic groups, for example, might do well to set up historical committees.

One aim would be to cooperate with University programs in seeking meaningful historical materials that might otherwise be lost. Fortunately, such programs are already under way in the labor unions.

History seems somewhat out of style with activist American youths these days.

But even in that context Hawaii may be something of an exception: many local youths appear increasingly interested in the Islands' racial history. Ethnic studies are a popular topic at the University, for example.

Preface

Some of these youths, with their unique perspective and chance to talk with older immigrant family members, may be our historians of tomorrow.

But for now it will take an active interest from all citizens to insure that the records all historians work with are as complete and representative as possible.

This work is meant to fulfill some of the historical background necessary to an understanding of the Chinese in Hawaii and thus to provide a basis for a meaningful oral history program of one of Hawaii's ethnic groups.

The first Hawaii-China contacts occurred soon after the discovery of Hawaii by Captain James Cook on 18 January 1778. A few Chinese adventurers—seamen, artisans, and traders on European and American vessels—stopped in the islands during the early period 1788 to 1852. Some stayed and established themselves in the islands. From 1852 on there was an influx of workers for the sugar plantations. Coffee, rice, and pineapple plantations also welcomed agricultural laborers. They were needed for a greatly expanding economy, and their immigration was actively solicited by government and planters. The migrants' original goal of returning home was often laid aside because of intermarriage with native Hawaiians or because of a liking for the way of life in Hawaii or because of news of turmoil in the homeland. Immigrant Chinese and their families lived side by side with people of many racial origins, absorbing some of their traditions as well as maintaining the customs brought from China. By World War II, the approximate cut-off point for the selections included here, many Chinese had already moved into the mainstream of American life. It is this story that I wish to document.

In this book there are many variations in the English spelling or romanization of Chinese words. They vary according to individual preferences, dialectal usages, and methods of romanization. A modified Wade-Giles system was used in some instances. Romanization of Cantonese dialects follows no consistent system. The many writers of the different selections in this book used what they thought were the best transliterations. I have referred constantly to the classical *Chinese Dictionary of Words and Phrases (Tz'u-Yuan)* and Dr. Lin Yutang's *Chinese-English Dictionary of Modern Usage (Tang-Tai Han-Ying Tz'u-Tien)* to verify meaning and usage.

Preface

For a ready reference to other data, see *The Chinese in Hawaii,* an annotated bibliography compiled by Dr. Nancy Foon Young, published with the support of the Hawaii Chinese History Center and by the Social Science Research Institute, University of Hawaii, 1973.

Acknowledgments

The editor is grateful to the Hawaii Chinese History Center, a community organization that participated by securing support from the following financial sponsors:

    Chung Kun-Ai Foundation
    Louise and Y. T. Lum Foundation
    Chun Hoon and Lee Oi Chun-Hoon Memorial Fund
    Mr. and Mrs. Ellery J. Chun
    See-Yick Char and Chong-Fo Char Memorial Fund
    Mr. and Mrs. Leong Hop Loui
    Arthur Y. Wong and Margaret Au Wong

The library and archives staffs at the University of Hawaii (Hamilton and Sinclair Libraries), Archives of Hawaii, Hawaiian Mission Children's Society and Hawaiian Historical Society Libraries, Hawaii Bureau of Conveyances, Hawaiian Sugar Planters' Association Library, Hawaii Tax Map Division, and Hawaii State Library System have been helpful in many ways.

Chinese calligraphy is by Mrs. Chau-mun Lau, Asia Collection, University of Hawaii.

I am very appreciative of the skillful assistance from the editorial and production staff of The University Press of Hawaii. Dr. Bernhard L. Hormann, retired Professor of Sociology, University of Hawaii, read the preliminary draft and gave encouragement together with extensive and helpful suggestions as to contents and interpretations.

Permission and approval, where necessary, have been received for the use of other authors' works, for which I acknowledge my indebtedness.

I. Historical Background of Nineteenth-Century China

IMPERIAL CHINA'S POLICY OF SELF-IMPOSED ISOLATION

A study of the history of the early Chinese immigration into Hawaii and other overseas areas begins with China's political and social climate in the nineteenth century and the Imperial Government's policy on emigration of her subject people. The Manchu Ch'ing rulers were then facing pressure from foreign powers to open up trade and diplomatic relations and to permit Chinese emigrants to be recruited in large groups for Western colonies.[1]

At this time, China's attitude in foreign relations was one of self-styled cultural superiority, of egocentrism with little interest in territorial occupation and economic exploitation of neighboring "tributary states." China was the Middle Kingdom ("Chung Kuo") surrounded by "barbaric, culturally inferior" neighbors. Emperor Ch'ien Lung's mandates in 1793 were in keeping with this viewpoint of cultural superiority and self-sufficiency.

In 1793 a British mission headed by Earl Macartney reached Peking. The Chinese considered this a "tribute-bearing" mission. They received the foreign visitors with utmost courtesy; the ceremony of the kowtow was waived in deference to Earl Macartney's objections. The Emperor granted an audience at his summer resort in Jehol, outside Peking.[2]

As a result of the mission, the Chinese Emperor prepared a message to his British counterpart.*

You, O King, live beyond the confines of many seas, nevertheless, impelled by your humble desire to partake of the benefits of our

---

* Harley Farnsworth MacNair, "Ch'ien Lung's Mandates to King George III, 1793," in *Modern Chinese History: Selected Readings* (Shanghai: Commercial Press, 1933), pp. 2–3.

civilisation, you have dispatched a mission respectfully bearing your memorial. Your Envoy has crossed the seas and paid his respects at my Court on the anniversary of my birthday. To show your devotion, you have also sent offerings of your country's produce.

I have perused your memorial: the earnest terms in which it is couched reveal a respectful humility on your part, which is highly praiseworthy. In consideration of the fact that your Ambassador and his deputy have come a long way with your memorial and tribute, I have shown them high favour and have allowed them to be introduced into my presence. To manifest my indulgence, I have entertained them at a banquet and made them numerous gifts. I have also caused presents to be forwarded to the Naval Commander and six hundred of his officers and men, although they did not come to Peking, so that they too may share in my all-embracing kindness.

As to your entreaty to send one of your nationals to be accredited to my Celestial Court and to be in control of your country's trade with China, this request is contrary to all usage of my dynasty and cannot possibly be entertained. It is true that Europeans in the service of the dynasty have been permitted to live at Peking, but they are compelled to adopt Chinese dress, they are strictly confined to their own precincts and are never permitted to return home. You are presumably familiar with our dynastic regulations. Your proposed Envoy to my Court could not be placed in a position similar to that of European officials in Peking who are forbidden to leave China, nor could he, on the other hand, be allowed liberty of movement and the privilege of corresponding with his own country; so that you would gain nothing by his residence in our midst.

Moreover, Our Celestial dynasty possesses vast territories, and tribute missions from the dependencies are provided for by the Department for Tributary States, which ministers to their wants and exercises strict control over their movements. It would be quite impossible to leave them to their own devices.

MANIFEST DESTINY MEETS THE MANDATE OF HEAVEN

In 1971 President Richard M. Nixon made his historic trip to Peking to normalize relations with the People's Republic of China. This event brought forth an article about another kind of exchange between an American president and the Emperor of China.

Emperor Ch'ien Lung's edict in the previous selection can be

Historical Background of China

contrasted with an exchange between President John Tyler and the Chinese Emperor Tao Kuang fifty years later. It is discussed in an article written by Norman Geschwind of the faculty of Leeward Community College in Hawaii.*

An American President did not visit his Chinese counterpart in the 19th century, but he did exchange letters with him. The first such exchange of diplomatic notes was made between President John Tyler and the Emperor of the Tao-kuang period.

In 1844, two years after the formal end of the Opium War, Caleb Cushing, the first U.S. envoy to China, carried a letter to the Chinese Emperor, part of which reads:

> I, John Tyler, President of the United States of America which States are . . . [there follows a list of the 26 states then in the Union], send you this letter of peace and friendship, signed by my own hand.
>
> I hope your health is good. China is a great empire, extending over a great part of the world. The Chinese are numerous. You have millions and millions of subjects. The twenty-six United States are as large as China, though our people are not so numerous. The rising sun looks upon the great mountains and great rivers of China. When he sets, he looks upon rivers and mountains equally large in the United States. Our territories extend from one great ocean to the other; and on the west we are divided from your dominions only by the sea. Leaving the mouth of one of our great rivers, and going constantly toward the setting sun, we sail to Japan and to the Yellow Sea.
>
> Now my words are, that the governments of two such great countries should be at peace. It is proper, and according to the will of Heaven, that they should respect each other, and act wisely. I, therefore, send to your court Caleb Cushing, one of the wise and learned men of this country. On his first arrival in China, he will inquire for your health. He has then strict orders to go to your great city of Peking,

---

* Norman Geschwind, "America and China: A Nineteenth Century Exchange," in *Notes on Asian Studies,* University of Hawaii Newsletter no. 2, April 1972.

and there to deliver this letter. He will have with him secretaries and interpreters. . . .

Written at Washington, this twelfth day of July, in the year of our Lord one thousand eight hundred and forty-three.

Your good friend,
John Tyler

How should the Chinese word their reply to Tyler's letter? The chief Chinese negotiator advised the Emperor:

> Your slave begs to note that the location of the United States is in the Far West. Of all the countries, it is the most uncivilized and remote. Now they hope for the Imperial favor of a special Imperial Mandate which can be kept forever. We have both commended the sincerity of their love of justice and strengthened their determination to turn toward culture. The different races of the world are all grateful for Imperial bounty. It is only that the said country is in an isolated place outside the pale, solitary and ignorant. Not only in the forms of edicts and laws are they entirely unversed, but if the meaning be rather deep they would probably not even be able to comprehend. It would seem that we must follow a rather simple style. Our choice of words and use of expressions should in general show that the constitution of the Heavenly Court is to be respected. . . .
>
> It is noted that the executive of the said country is called *Po-li-ssu-t'ien-te;* translated into Chinese this means president. Besides this he has no other designation. It would seem proper, therefore, to use this term to address him. . . .

[The Emperor replied]:

> The Imperial Majesty hopes the President is well. Since receiving the mandate to rule over China WE have regarded (the countries) within and beyond the seas as one family. Early in the Spring the Commissioner of your honorable country, Caleb Cushing, presented his credentials. He came from a great distance to Our Province of Kwangtung, passing through many seas and suffering many hardships before arriving at his destination. WE could not

FOREIGNERS SEGREGATED IN CANTON

Trying to limit foreign intrusion, China at first restricted foreign trade to one seaport, Canton. The foreign traders there were strictly supervised. Wives of the traders who came to the Far East had to remain behind in Macao. Macao was the Portuguese trade settlement that had been set up as early as 1557 and was ceded to Portugal in 1849.

The trading season lasted six months, and foreigners were permitted to reside only in *hongs* ("trading stations") which were located outside the city walls. They were forbidden to go inside the walls of the city or to carry firearms into the *hongs*. Twice a month they were allowed to leave their premises for exercise or vacation but had to be accompanied by an interpreter to act as their guide and protector.[4] Thus, Canton had its little haole town. The Chinese argued that the foreigners were of different languages and culture from themselves. When anti-Chinese agitations started against Chinese immigrants in America, the same argument of differing language and culture was used by Westerners. As it turned out, the European area developed into a most desirable residential and commercial settlement in Canton. The foreigners, backed up by gunboats and overwhelming military power, put up signs and posted guards in parks and public areas restricting Chinese from entering or using the facilities.

The regulations governing the actions of foreigners were codified in the eighteenth century.*

The authorities framed eight regulations for the especial government and control of these divers people from afar. They date from the year 1760, and are curious enough to recall. Never having been abrogated, they were assumed to be in force always. They were confirmed by an edict of the Emperor Kea-King in 1819, after a revision in 1810. Some of them came to be disregarded by the foreign community. . . . The chief sufferers in the event of a disregard of any important item of the regulations would of course be the Hong merchants. The 'Eight Regulations' were now and then brought to the Factories by a Linguist, as an intimation that they were not to be considered a 'dead letter.' Translated into English they read thus—

* John Robert Morrison, "Eight Regulations," in *Modern Chinese History: Selected Readings,* ed. H. F. MacNair (Shanghai: The Commercial Press, 1933), pp. 46–47.

bear to order him to submit to the hardships of further travel (and thus) he was prevented from coming to Peking and being received in audience. WE specially appointed as Imperial Commissioner Ch'i Ying (Kiying), an Imperial Clansman, to receive him and to negotiate all business. Subsequently the Imperial Commissioner submitted your letter for examination. Its sincerity is of the highest order, its sentiments well-expressed. After opening and reading it WE were very much pleased. The regulations of trade which have been agreed to have received OUR careful consideration. They are carefully and minutely drawn up and are satisfactory. They are to be eternally respected. Citizens of the United States are permitted to proceed to Canton, Amoy, Foochow, Ningpo, and Shanghai and are free to engage in trade at these places in accordance with the articles (of the regulations). . . . This will promote friendly relations for all time and be of mutual benefit to the peoples of our two countries. It is expected that the President will also be much gratified.

Tao Kuang 24th year, 11th moon, 7th day (Dec. 16, 1844)

The young State Department clerk [who translated the reply] noted that "the characters for 'President' are used without honorifics while those for 'Emperor' are preceded by the character 'Great.' The importance of the Emperor is emphasized by the position of the three characters for 'The Great Emperor (His Imperial Highness)' at the beginning of the letter." He also revealed for the first time, more than eight decades after the letter was written, that the "opening sentence is in colloquial Chinese, as if addressed to an illiterate person."

The Emperor was less than candid in claiming that the reason for his refusal to allow Cushing to travel to Peking was to avoid the hardships of further travel. A Chinese official writing in 1853 touched upon the American problem. "Besides never having been in the class admitted to audience, the United States ordinarily has no official costumes, and still they claim equal rank for themselves and ignorantly puff themselves up."

Thus began the first chapter in Sino-American relations which provided the background for inter-relations between China, Hawaii, and the United States.[3]

Regulation 1.—All vessels of war are prohibited from entering the Bogue. Vessels of war acting as convoy to merchantmen must anchor outside at SEA till their merchantships are ready to depart, and then sail away with them.

Regulation 2.—Neither women, guns, spears, nor arms of any kind can be brought to the Factories.

Regulation 3.—All river pilots and ships' Compradores must be registered at the office of the 'Tung-Che' at Macao. That officer will also furnish each one of them with a license, or badge, which must be worn around the waist. He must produce it whenever called for. All other boatmen and people must not have communication with foreigners, unless under the immediate control of the ships' Compradores; and should smuggling take place, the Compradore of the ship engaged in it will be punished.

Regulation 4.—Each Factory is restricted for its service to 8 Chinese (irrespective of the number of its occupants), say 2 porters, 4 water-carriers, 1 person to take care of goods ('go-down coolie'), and 1 *mā-chen* (intended for the foreign word 'merchant') who originally performed all the duties of the 'House Compradore,' as he is styled to-day.

Regulation 5 prohibits foreigners from rowing about the river in their own boats for 'pleasure.' On the 8th, 18th, and 28th days of the moon 'they may take the air,' as fixed by the Government in the 21st year of Kca-King (1819). All ships' boats passing the Custom-houses on the river must be detained and examined, to guard against guns, swords, or firearms being furtively carried in them. On the 8th, 18th, and 28th days of the moon these foreign barbarians may visit the Flower Gardens and the Honam Joss-house, but not in *droves* of over ten at one time. When they have 'refreshed' they must return to the Factories, not be allowed to pass the night 'out' or collect together to carouse. Should they do so, then, when the next 'holiday' comes they shall not be permitted to go. If the ten should presume to enter villages, public places, or bazaars, punishment will be inflicted upon the *Linguist* who accompanies them.

Regulation 6.—Foreigners are not allowed to present petitions. If they have anything to represent, it must be done through the Hong merchants.

Regulation 7.—Hong merchants are not to owe debts to foreigners. Smuggling goods to and from the city is prohibited.

Regulation 8.—Foreign ships arriving with merchandise must not loiter about outside the river; they must come direct to Whampoa. They must not rove about the bays at pleasure and sell to rascally natives goods subject to duty, that these may smuggle them, and thereby defraud His Celestial Majesty's revenue.

IMPACT AND DISINTEGRATION IN CHINA

The nineteenth century was one of foreign impact and resulting disintegration of China. For the Chinese, it was a period of over one hundred years of national humiliation and frustration at the hands of foreign powers. Unsatisfactory relations between China and Great Britain led to the "Opium Wars" of 1839 and 1858. On the British side, the avowed intention was to expand trade and diplomatic relations. The British were buying more Chinese goods than they were selling to China. The balance of trade favored China and the British had to pay the difference in silver. In order to redress the imbalance, the British East India Company began to export opium to China, receiving silver taels from the Chinese which were spent by the British to pay for their Chinese purchases. In 1839, commissioner Lin Tse-hsü in Canton seized and destroyed 20,000 chests of opium. The British opened fire and easily won the resulting engagement. This began a troublesome period that culminated in a series of "unequal" treaties that were forced on China. The 1842 Treaty of Nanking that ended the First Opium War included:

1. The ceding of Hong Kong to Great Britain. Hong Kong replaced Macao as the sea "door" of Chinese trade with the Western nations and became the port of embarkation for emigrants recruited as laborers for European colonies.

2. Opening of four additional ports to foreign trade and residence— Shanghai, Amoy, Ningpo, and Foochow.

3. The payment of an indemnity of $21,000,000 of which $6,000,000 in silver taels was for destroyed opium.

The opium trade continued to flourish, contaminating more and more Chinese to whom opium had previously not been so readily available.

China increasingly tried to adapt herself to the Western world. At the same time, internal affairs deteriorated and discontent proliferated. *Tin joy yan wo* ("heaven-brought disasters and man-made catastrophes") plagued China. In the period between 1846 and 1878 it is estimated that human lives lost from famines and floods and from internal rebellions numbered over 44,000,000.[5]

Hunger and general discontent with the Manchu rulers sparked the Taiping Rebellion (1850–1864) which began in Kwangsi province, adjoining Kwangtung.[6] This outbreak started with a group of religious fanatics who had adopted some Christian concepts. It was led by Hung Siu-chuan, an unsuccessful scholar who had repeatedly failed in the Imperial examinations. As a result, he had had to remain in his native Hakka village of Fah Hsien, Kwangtung, where he earned a meager living as a village schoolmaster. He became acquainted with evangelistic Christian teachings and was converted.

The movement developed a strong revolutionary army which swept northward as far as Nanking. After fourteen years of bitter struggle, the rebellion was crushed in 1864 with the help of Western mercenaries, including an American, General Frederick Ward. Sixteen provinces were ravaged and an estimated twenty million lives were lost.[7] Some rebels fled and accepted recruitment as contract laborers for oversea colonies.

Professors Ssu-yu Teng and John K. Fairbank of Harvard University have summarized the conditions in China leading to the rebellion thus: " . . . Western contact, lent impetus by the industrial revolution, had the most disastrous effect upon the old Chinese society. In every sphere of social activity, the old order was challenged, attacked, undermined, or overwhelmed by a complex series of processes—political, economic, social, ideological, cultural—which were set in motion within China as a result of this penetration of an alien and more powerful society."[8]

It was from this kind of situation that Chinese emigrants left for Hawaii.*

The impact of war broke down all political barriers which had previously closed "The Celestial Empire" to the outside world. With these barriers gone, China was wholly exposed to the cultural invasion of Western Civilization. In the field of economic enterprise, the invasion greatly stimulated her trade and commerce with other countries. Between 1867 and 1905 her foreign trade registered marked increases

* C. K. Cheng [Ch'eng-k'un Cheng], *The Dragon Sheds Its Scales* (New York: New Voices Press, 1952), pp. 94–105; reproduced by kind permission of the author.

with a tendency for imports progressively to exceed exports. Following trade and commerce came Western systems of banking, manufacturing, communication and transportation. Foreign banks, tobacco and cigarette factories, telegraph companies and electric power plants rose to change the skyline of many Chinese cities. Foreign post-offices established mail services between many points in China and between China and foreign countries. Foreign steamships plied in and out of Chinese waters and foreign railways were constructed amidst loud protests from the Chinese government.

In the field of culture, the invasion was mainly perpetuated by agencies of the Christian Missionary Movement in China. While the success of the movement is still debatable, its importance in the introduction of Western culture to the Chinese people cannot be underestimated. Christian missionary activities in China have a rather long history. Before the 16th century, Nestorian and Franciscan fathers had set foot on Chinese soil at different times, but they failed in their attempts to preach the gospel of Christianity to the "heathen" natives. . . .

Western medicine entered China as a vital part of the programs of the Christian Missions, especially the Protestant Missions. In the middle of the 19th century, many missionaries found that effective medical treatments could often break down Chinese prejudices against Christianity, so great attention was paid to the organization and development of their medical services. . . .

Another characteristic feature of the missionary movement was the organization of welfare and philanthropic agencies. Included in this sphere of activity were care and education for the orphans, the blind, and the deaf; reform of opium addicts; and relief for those who suffered from poverty or natural calamities such as floods and famines. In addition, some Christian missionaries adopted positive measures against the evil practices of concubinage and foot-binding. Foot-binding for women was introduced in the 10th century, presumably to improve the feminine gait. For one thousand years, it was very popular among the Chinese people, particularly of the middle and the upper classes. About 1867 a mission school for girls in the city of Hangchow in Chekiang Province ordered all its inmates for whom it provided board and clothing to unbind their feet. A Methodist girls' school in Peking in 1872 made foot-unbinding a prerequisite for entrance. In 1874, at the inspiration of missionaries, Chinese women converts in Amoy in the southern part of Fukien Province organized an anti-foot-binding association. [Hawaii passed a law in 1895 banning foot-binding.]

The cultural invasion of the West was also perpetuated by Chinese emigrants who had the opportunity to see for themselves the Western systems of organization and administration. Of course, the bulk of them were laborers. But in 1846, a missionary named Samuel M. Brown took three young Chinese with him to the United States where they entered the Academy of Monson, Massachusetts. Later one of them [Yung Wing] went to Yale College where he graduated in 1854. On his return to China, he was instrumental in persuading the Chinese Government to send the first Educational Mission of one hundred and twenty students to America between 1872 and 1875. Toward the end of the 19th century, however, an increasing number of students were sent by the various Christian Missions and the government. After the humiliating war with Japan in 1895, many of the students who returned to China rose in prominence in the reform movement which was gathering force in that ancient land. More and more students were sent to the United States, Japan, England, France and other European countries. In 1908, U.S. Congress waived its claim "to the remainder of what was due of its share of the Boxer Indemnity" and this sum was set aside by the Chinese Government to cover expenses of preparing and sending students to the United States.

Under all these military, political, and cultural impacts, the old Chinese system of organization and administration began to disintegrate. At first this process was slow because the resistance of inertia was great. But at the end of the 19th century, it was clear to many educated Chinese that the traditional monarchy must be scrapped if the existence of China as a political entity was to be preserved. . . .

The history of the international relations of China in the one hundred years before 1930 was essentially a record of conflict between two civilizations. It was also a record of conflict between two different stages of cultural development. At the beginning of the 19th century, the West had just entered an era of industrial and technological progress. This progress gave many Western nations the productive power which pushed their seamen and merchants to the four corners of the world in search of markets. In Asia, China was an unexploited market with tremendous potentialities. But the Chinese authorities wanted to preserve their agricultural economy which, in their eyes, had adjusted satisfactorily to their social and political organizations. They could not see why they should make any new adjustments, especially when these adjustments were alien to their tradition. Neither could they understand why they should open their gates for trading activities profitable to the "barbarians" from across the sea and detrimental to the welfare of their own people.

Insistence on conflicting claims based on conflicting standards naturally resulted in clashes of arms. The wars which followed proved conclusively that an agricultural nation was no match for an industrial one. The impacts of military, political and cultural invasion humbled the Chinese Empire, exposed the weaknesses of her system of organization and administration and awakened her from her state of dormancy. The disintegrating effects on her political and social institutions in the two decades after the Chinese Revolution might appear slow and superficial. But they were the beginnings of a gigantic process of adjustment which held promises for the ultimate transformation of China. . . .

BAN ON EMIGRATION

Besides adopting a closed door policy in discouraging foreigners from entering China for trade and cultural exchange, in 1712 China also put a ban on her people migrating abroad. What happened to any who slipped by and made it overseas was officially ignored by China. These emigrants were prohibited by law from returning home. Many left anyway with hopes of returning undetected due to poor administration of laws. An edict of 13 September 1893, urged on China by foreign powers, finally granted the right of return of her nationals.

Section 225 of the 1712 law (Ta Tsing Leu Lee or Fundamental Law of the Ch'ing Dynasty) detailed the restraints on emigration.*

All officers of government, soldiers, and private citizens, who clandestinely proceed to sea to trade, or who remove to foreign islands for the purpose of inhabiting and cultivating the same, shall be pun-

* H. F. MacNair, *The Chinese Abroad* (Shanghai: The Commercial Press, 1924), pp. 1–11. (The Chinese text is available in Huang Fu-luan, *The Oversea Chinese and the Revolution in China* [Hong Kong: Asia Press, 1955], p. 27.)

ished according to the law against communicating with rebels and enemies, and consequently suffer death by being beheaded. The governors of cities of the second and third orders shall likewise be beheaded, when found guilty of combining with, or artfully conniving at the conduct of such persons. When only a neglect of their duty, in not taking measures to prevent the same, is the offense imputable to them, they shall not suffer death, but be degraded and dismissed forever from the public service. Governors of cities of the first order, and other officers having the same rank, when guilty of a similar neglect, shall be degraded three degrees and removed from their stations. Viceroys and other great magistrates of provinces shall, in similar cases of imputed neglect, be degraded two degrees, but retain their offices. Nevertheless, the neglect of all such officers shall be pardoned, if they afterwards succeed in securing the offenders, and in bringing them to condign punishment.

The Chinese attitude is further exemplified by a dialogue between Captain Samuel F. Dupont, representing the U.S. plenipotentiary William B. Reed, and Commissioner Tan of the metropolitan province of Chihli who were negotiators for the Tientsin Treaty of 1858 which opened further ports to foreign powers. Captain Dupont suggested to the Viceroy that China send consuls to the United States to look after the Chinese immigrants there.*

Viceroy. It is not our custom to send officials beyond our own borders.
Dupont. But your people on the farther shore of the Pacific are very numerous, numbering several tens of thousands.
Viceroy. When the emperor rules over so many millions, what does he care for the few waifs that have drifted away to a foreign land?
Dupont. Those people are, many of them, rich, having gathered gold in our mines. They might be worth looking after on that account.
Viceroy. The emperor's wealth is beyond computation; why should he care for those of his subjects who have left their home, or for the sands they have scraped together?

* Ibid., p. 11. (The Chinese translation is available in Chen Li-teh, *History of Chinese Emigration* [Shanghai: Chung Hua Publishing Co., 1946], p. 54.)

CHINA LIFTS EMIGRATION BAN TO AMERICA, 1868

In the Burlingame Treaty of 1868 China changed her official policy toward emigration of her people. U.S. diplomat Anson Burlingame initiated the negotiation for China to join with America in recognizing "the inherent and inalienable right of man to change his home and allegiance, and also the mutual advantage of free migration and emigration of their citizens and subjects respectively from one country to the other for purposes of curiosity, of trade, or as permanent residents."

This wording reflected more the political philosophy of the United States than that of China. It was obviously dictated by the American ideal of democracy and not by the Chinese tradition of absolute monarchy. It was merely a concession by China to the United States which was anxious to secure an abundant supply of cheap labor for the development of her western areas.[9]

As it turned out, in a few years the United States had to change its policy of free migration. The influx of Chinese immigrants lead to anti-Chinese agitation and legislation. In 1880, the United States negotiated another treaty (presented below) with China giving America the right to limit or suspend the immigration of Chinese laborers.* Thereafter, from 1882 to 1924, Congressional legislation, instead of treaty agreements, regulated the entry of Chinese by race into the United States."[10]

ARTICLE I

Whenever in the opinion of the government of the United States the coming of Chinese laborers to the United States, or their residence therein, affects or threatens to affect the interests of that country, or to endanger the good order of the said country or of any locality within the territory thereof, the government of China agrees that the government of the United States may regulate, limit, or suspend such coming and residence, but may not absolutely prohibit it. The limitation or suspension shall be reasonable, and shall apply only to Chinese who may go to the United States as laborers, other classes not being included in the limitations. Legislations taken in regard to Chinese

* Eliot Grinnell Mears, "The Chinese-American Treaty of 1880," in *Resident Orientals on the American Pacific Coast: their Legal and Economic Status* (New York: Institute of Pacific Relations, 1927), p. 433.

laborers will be of such a character only as is necessary to enforce the regulation, limitation, or suspension of immigration, and immigrants shall not be subject to personal maltreatment or abuse.

ARTICLE II

Chinese subjects, whether proceeding to the United States as teachers, students, merchants, or from curiosity, together with their body- and household servants, and Chinese laborers who are now in the United States shall be allowed to go and come of their own free will and accord, and shall be accorded all the rights, privileges, immunities, and exemptions which are accorded to the citizens and subjects of the most favored nation.

ARTICLE III

If Chinese laborers, or Chinese of any other class, now either permanently or temporarily residing in the territory of the United States, meet with ill treatment at the hands of any other persons, the government of the United States will exert all its power to devise measures for their protection and to secure to them the same rights, privileges, immunities, and exemptions as may be enjoyed by the citizens or subjects of the most favored nation, and to which they are entitled by treaty.

ARTICLE IV

The high contracting powers having agreed upon the foregoing articles, whenever the government of the United States shall adopt legislative measures in accordance therewith, such measures will be communicated to the government of China. If the measures as enacted are found to work hardship upon the subjects of China, the Chinese minister at Washington may bring the matter to the notice of the Secretary of State of the United States, who will consider the subject with him; and the Chinese Foreign Office may also bring the matter to the notice of the United States minister at Peking and consider the subject with him to the end that mutual and unqualified benefit may result.

In faith whereof the respective plenipotentiaries have signed and sealed the foregoing at Peking, in English and Chinese, being three original of each text of even tenor and date, the ratifications of which shall be exchanged at Peking within one year from date of its execution.

Done at Peking, this seventeenth day of November, in the year of our Lord, 1880. Kuangshu, sixth year tenth month, fifteenth day.

James B. Angell (Seal)
John F. Swift (Seal)
Wm. Henry Trescot (Seal)
Pao Chun (Seal)
Li Hungtsao (Seal)

ETHNOGRAPHIC BACKGROUND OF CHINESE MIGRANTS

The two southeastern maritime provinces of Kwangtung and Fukien[11] provided the greatest number of emigrants seeking their fortunes overseas. Chinese who went to Hawaii, the United States, Canada, Cuba, Peru, and Australia generally came from Kwangtung and were called Cantonese. In southeast Asian areas such as the Philippines, Thailand, Malaya, and Indonesia there were chiefly Fukienese migrants from Amoy, including the Hoklo people from the Swatow area in northeastern Kwangtung who spoke a southern Fukienese dialect.

The people who migrated to Hawaii were Cantonese of the Pearl River delta areas near the cities of Canton, Macao, and Hong Kong. Those calling themselves Punti were from the county of Heungshan now known as Chungshan in honor of a native son, Dr. Sun Yat-sen, father of the Chinese Republic.[12] (Sun Yat-sen adopted the name Chung-shan while living in Japan.) The rest of these immigrants to Hawaii were recruited from the See Yup subdialectal group living in the counties of Toishan, Yan Ping, Hoi Ping, and Sun Wui and from the Sam Yup subdialectal group of the counties of Pun Yu, Shun Tak, and Nam Hoi.

Another dialectal group in Hawaii, the Hakka, came from the counties of Pao On, Fa Yuan, Waichow, Tungkun, Ka Ying Chow, and Chungshan. Some Hoklo,[13] the third dialectal group, also came to Hawaii. Hoklo were relatively few in number and too scattered, while in the islands, to form fraternal or home village (*ka heung*) organizations.

There were a few immigrants who had come from the northern province of Shantung,[14] birthplace of Confucius. In addition, the Royal Hawaiian Agricultural Society sought laborers from as far away as Siberia where they brought out two thousand Russians through the river port of Harbin, Manchuria.[15]

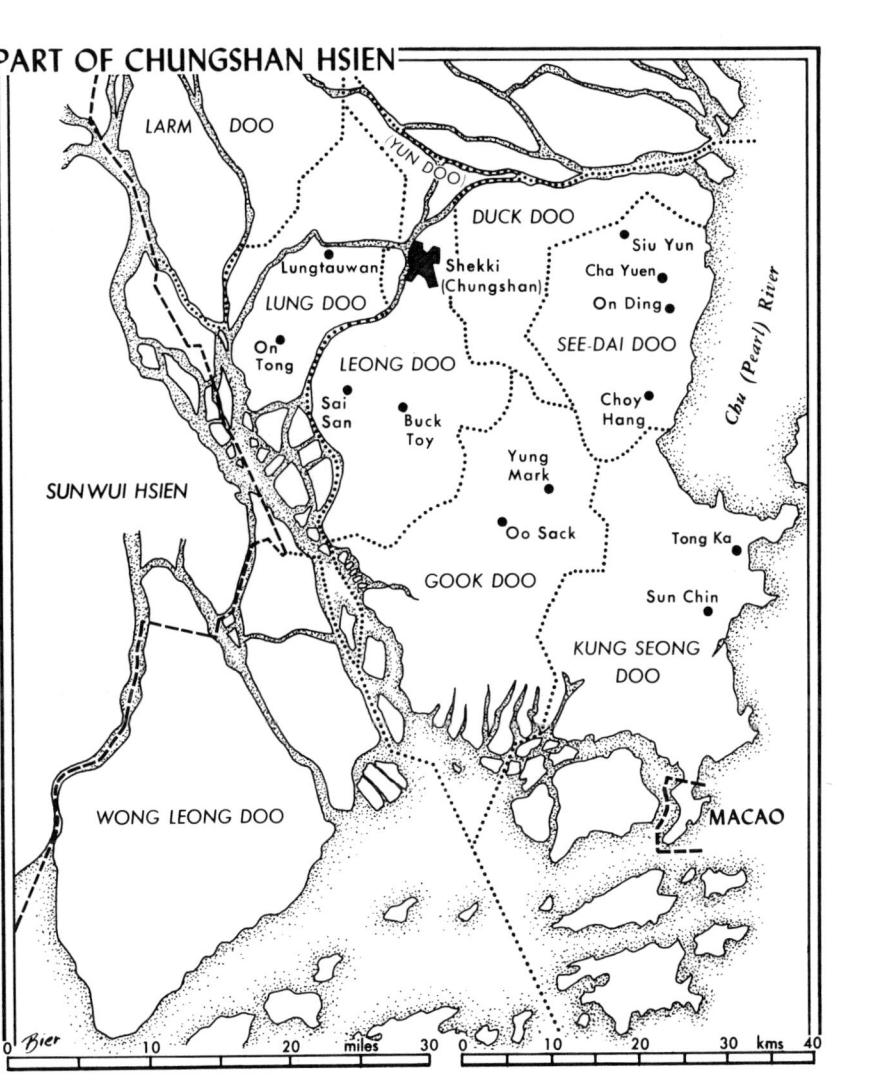

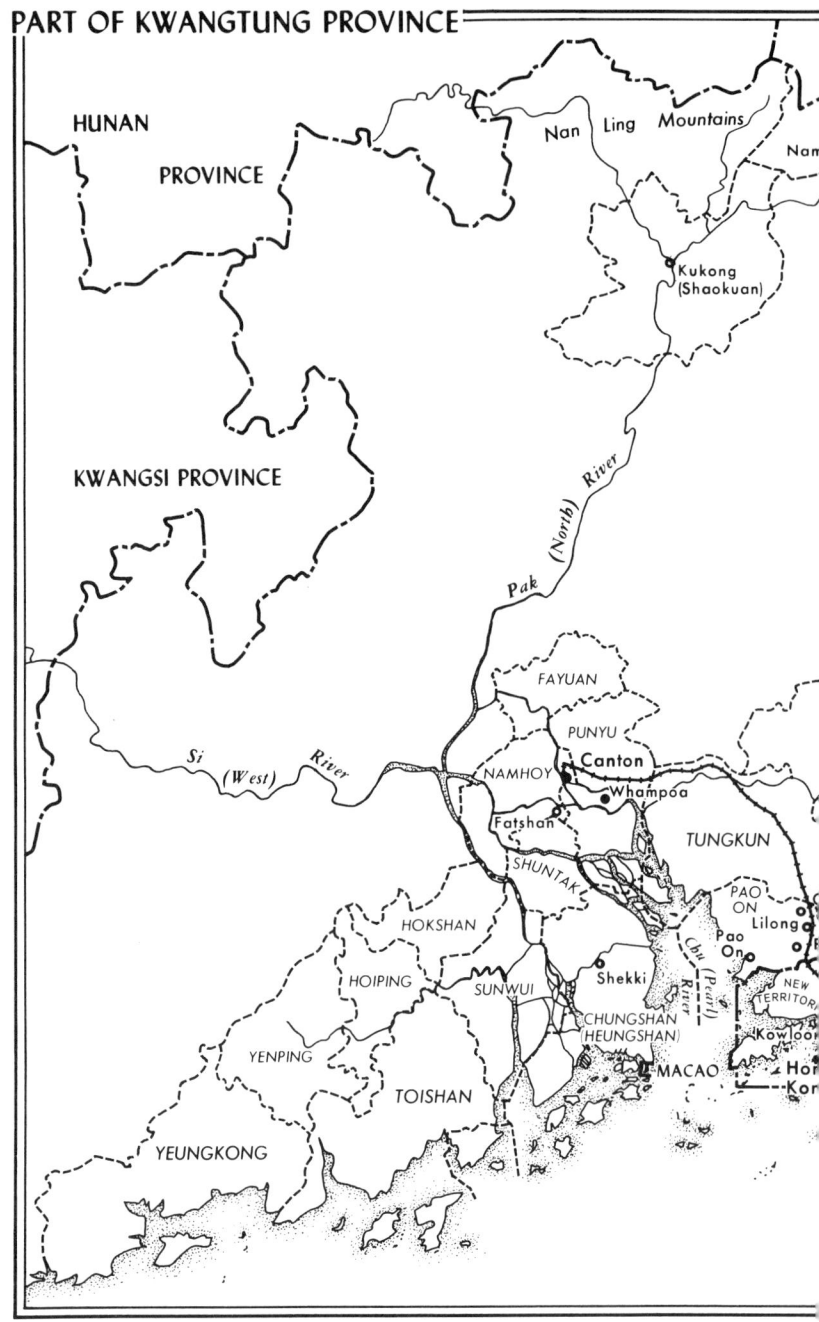

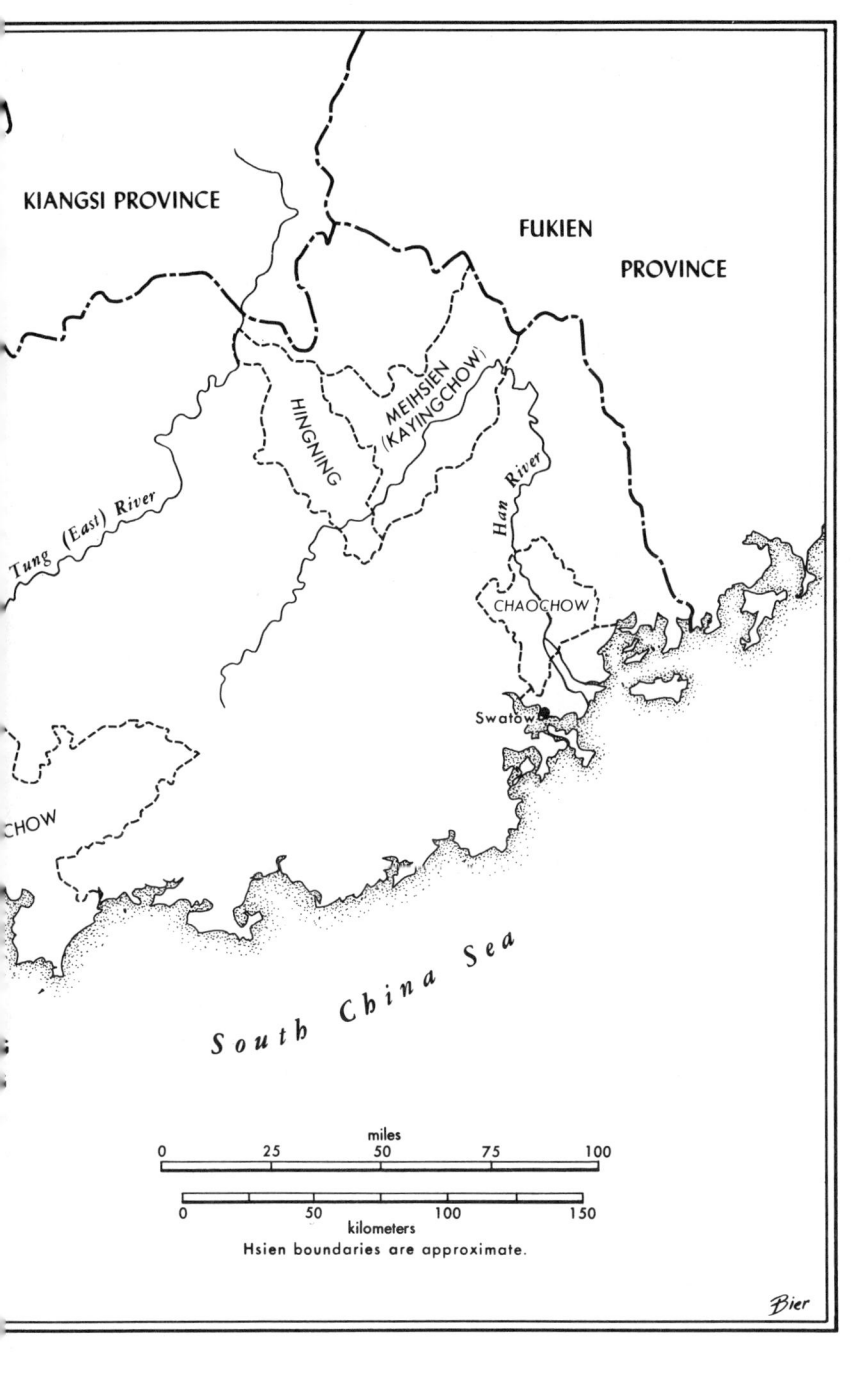

Natural barriers in China that separated different groups of people contributed to dialectal differences. The written language is, however, the same for all. The universal pictorial and phonetic characters helped keep the Chinese as one nation.

The standard speech of China is *Kuo Yu* or Mandarin. In the province of Kwangtung, Cantonese is spoken for business and socially while subdialects are used at home. *Kuo Yu* is taught in the schools and is being used more and more. Thus, the people of Kwangtung have become trilingual in speech.

The dialect spoken in Shekki, the county seat of Chungshan, became the standard speech of the Chinese inhabitants of Hawaii, regardless of the subdialects they spoke at home—Lung Doo, Nam Long, Sam Heung, or Hakka.

The following geographic account of Kwangtung will help in understanding the ethnographic background of the Chinese who came to Hawaii. It was written about the immigrants to Canada but is equally pertinent to those who came to Hawaii, for the geographic origins were the same. The official provincial and district gazetteers (*tung chih*) were used as sources. The overseas Chinese from Canton still call themselves *Tong yan* ("people of the T'ang [Tong] dynasty"), as the reading will elucidate.*

The province of Kwangtung has an area of about one hundred thousand square miles and a population of nearly thirty million. It is bounded north and west by other provinces and south and east by the China Sea. It extends six hundred miles from east to west and about four hundred twenty miles from north to south. The chief mountain range in the province is the Nan Ling Mountains, which, extending several hundred miles on its northern border, make communication with the northern provinces difficult. The principal river of the province is the Si-kiang (the West River, its lower part being called the Pearl River), which comes down from the plateau in Yunnan and has a length of over a thousand miles. It is one of the three famous rivers in China, the others being the Hwang-ho (the Yellow River) and the Yangtze-kiang and is of great commercial importance. The coast line of Kwangtung extends well over a thousand miles, with many islands dotting the sea. . . .

* T'ien-fang Ch'eng, *Oriental Immigration in Canada* (Shanghai: Commercial Press, 1931), pp. 4–9.

Historical Background of China

The climate of Kwangtung is varied. The mountainous region in the north is covered with snow in winter and is extremely hot in summer. In the central plain and along the coast it is very warm in summer; but being cooled by the sea breeze, it is rarely so hot as to be unendurable. In winter, it seldom snows, and the temperature rarely goes down below 30°F. In fact, the southern part of the province falls into the tropical zone, and we find in it such tropical products as coconuts, pineapples, palm trees, etc. Most of the soil in the province is extremely fertile and produces two or three crops annually. . . .

Historically, Kwangtung is one of the latest developed provinces in China proper. The earliest civilization of China was founded along the banks of the Hwang-ho in the present provinces of Honan, Shantung, Hopei (formerly Chihli), and Shansi. When that part of China was in a highly civilized state, and when Confucius, Lao-tse, Moh-tse [Mo Tzu], and others were establishing their schools of philosophy in northern China (550–250 B.C.), Kwangtung was still inhabited by barbarians. When the famous Ch'in Shih Huang (reigning from 249 B.C. to 210 B.C.) abolished the feudal system and brought the whole of China under his rule, Kwangtung for the first time accepted governors appointed by the Emperor of China. Yet for eight centuries after, it never played any important part in Chinese politics and never was an integral part of the Middle Kingdom in the sense in which Honan or Shantung was. Whenever China was ruled by a strong emperor, it obeyed his rule; but as soon as the power of the central government weakened, it was usually the first province to break away and establish a sort of independent state. It did not even produce great scholars or statesmen who could influence the thought and actions of the peoples in other provinces. It was not until the famous Tang dynasty (A.D. 618–907) that the people of Kwangtung attained a high stage of civilization, and even to-day these people still call themselves men of Tang (*T'ang jen*), which fact clearly denotes that their real civilization began with the Tang dynasty.

The main reason for this slow development was its geographical situation. Canton is sixteen hundred miles away from Peking . . . and eight hundred miles from Nanking, the present [1931] capital of China. To-day these distances may seem short, but fifty years ago it was usually a six months' journey from Peking to Canton, and a three months' journey from Nanking to Canton. Besides, the Nan Ling Range made traveling extremely difficult. Consequently, with the exception of government officials and merchants, very little traveling was done between Kwangtung and the northern provinces. Kwangtung thus developed more or less as an isolated community within the empire.

But this same geographical situation which retarded its development at first was to be in its favor at a later stage. When modern European intercourse with China began at the beginning of the sixteenth century, it was at Canton where the East and the West met. The Portuguese arrived in 1517, and forty years later they were permitted by the Chinese government to stay at Macao, a place about one hundred miles southwest of Canton. Canton was then the only port open to foreigners. Thus the Kwangtung people were the first to do business with Westerners. Later, Macao was ceded to Portugal; and from that time down to 1840, it was the headquarters for all Westerners who came to China for commercial, political, or religious purposes. The trade was then mainly in the hands of the Portuguese, the British, and the Dutch. . . .

The people of Kwangtung may be classified into two groups: the Punti or the natives; and the Hakkas, or the strangers. The Punti is a mixed race of the original tribes and people from central China. There is no doubt that before the Han dynasty the people in Kwangtung had an ethnological descent different from that of the Chinese in northern China. This explains why they were barbarians when northern China was highly civilized. Then "during the Han dynasty . . . people from northern and central China went beyond the Nan Ling Mountains, and their descendants have since made their permanent homes there." (Translation of the *Kwangtung Tung Chih,* Vol. 37, Book 92, p. 40) A fusion of race gradually took place between these people and the native tribes, and the process was completed during the Tang dynasty. Thus we have the so-called Punti people. The Hakkas also came to Kwangtung from northern and central China through Fukien. The date of their coming was probably between 1250 and 1300 and again between 1650 and 1700. While intermarriage between Hakkas and Puntis took place occasionally, yet the two have not quite assimilated. The Puntis spoke a dialect so different from those in other provinces as to be nonunderstandable, while the dialect of the Hakkas is not very different from those of the northern provinces. Most of the Hakkas are living east of Canton to the Fukien border, while the Puntis live in the northern and western parts of the province. . . .

Historical Background of China

Due to their long contact with foreigners, the Cantonese are more ready to adopt Western ideas and modes of living; but, on the other hand, their national consciousness is more developed. Due to development of commerce and emigration, Kwangtung probably is the richest province to-day; and the standard of living in Canton is higher than in any other city.

History tells us that peoples living on the seashore are more adventurous than peoples living inland. China is no exception to the rule. . . . It was only the people in Fukien and Kwangtung who had a chance and who succeeded in colonizing oversea lands.

TWO COUNTRY TOURS IN CHINA, 1884

Frank Damon[16] visited China in 1884. He made two field trips and wrote as a Hawaiian observer familiar with the Chinese in Hawaii. One trip was to the countryside northeast of Hong Kong where the people were predominantly Hakka, and the other to the Chungshan area north of Macao where the people were largely Punti.

At the time of Damon's trip, his father, the Rev. Samuel C. Damon,[17] edited *The Friend,* a monthly published in Honolulu between January 1843 and June 1954. It was the "oldest paper published in the Pacific" and was devoted to moral and educational interests in the Hawaiian Islands. The concern of its editor for all the peoples of Hawaii led it to print much of historical interest, including the article below.

Frank Damon and his wife were highly respected by the Chinese who knew them in Hawaii. As will be recounted below, Damon had the interesting experience of finding two Hawaiian women living in a Chinese village.

A few geographical names as romanized by Damon have been changed to more popular versions. Very long paragraphs have been divided, and obvious typographical errors have been corrected to avoid the distraction of editorial notations.*

By this time anyone on our islands who has had anything to do with the Chinese, must know that there are two distinct clans or

* Frank Damon, "Rambles in China—Two Country Trips," *The Friend,* June 1884, pp. 41–45.

classes among the immigrants who flock to our shores. These are the *Hakkas* and the *Puntis,* both Chinese, but speaking different dialects, and differing from each other in certain other respects. The name of the former signifies "stranger" and that of the latter "native of the soil." The Hakkas came down from the northern and central parts of China, probably a few centuries ago and hence are regarded by the Puntis as intruders. There are estimated to be about nineteen millions of inhabitants in the province of Kwangtung and of these it is thought, about six millions are Hakka, the remainder being Puntis, and a still third class called *Hoklos,* residing in the vicinity of Swatow, of whom however, only a very limited number have ever come to our islands. The Hakkas occupy a number of districts in the neighborhood of Canton and Hongkong, in the eastern and northeastern parts of the province. Their most important center is in the prefecture of Ka Ying Chau above Swatow. Most of the Hakka people who immigrate to us come from the districts lying near the ocean and not far from Hongkong.

A most successful mission work is being carried on among these people by two European societies, whose headquarters are in Basel, Switzerland, and Berlin, Germany. The former of these has a line of stations starting from Hongkong and its neighborhood and running up through the province in a northeasterly direction. The readers of the *Friend* are undoubtedly already familiar with the name of the head of the Basel mission in China, Mr. Lechler, who for nearly forty years has labored so earnestly and successfully here. This gentleman has been my companion and guide in a recent and most interesting trip I have been privileged to make among the Hakkas. We were able to visit three flourishing stations of the Basel mission. . . .

Leaving Hongkong one breezy morning, in the early part of this month, . . . we left British rule and foreign civilization behind us. After a few words and a cup of tea in the shop of a man who has a brother in Kohala, we prepared to cross the mountain. The "chair" which took me over was borne by two Coolies,[18] and a most primitive affair and tested all the joints and muscles of my body in a most searching way. My bearers had straw sandals on their feet, which reminded me of those one sees on the statues of Grecian heroes, but there was very little else about these men to suggest a likeness to the warriors of classic days. We were fairly now among the Hakkas. The Cantonese dialect which I have been hearing in this city is rarely spoken in the region where we now are. Truly this is a land of "burden bearers." Men and women and children passed us in a continuous stream bearing great baskets and bales and parcels of every description. But they all seemed cheerful and always looked up with a pleasant word and smile.

Passing the crest of the mountain and descending on the other side, we found ourselves in a hilly country stretching away in long blue reaches, with still bluer bays running in here and there. . . .

A little boat takes us off to the awkward old junk lying in the still waters of the bay. . . .

A man hears I am from "Tan Heung Shan," the "Fragrant Sandal Wood Hills" (the name which the Chinese gave our islands) and immediately establishes a friendly conversation. He has lived seven years at Ewa, Oahu, and thinks of going back there again and has much to relate of the land which has a climate where one need not fear the heat nor the cold.

Early the next morning we are making our way up from the white sandy beach where we have landed, to the interior. On the shore we notice a temple to the "Goddess of Mercy," which Chinese fishermen and sailors are accustomed to worship. . . .[19]

A Country Mission Station

In the neighboring district difficulties had arisen between the mandarins and the people, some of whom were in open revolt. Reports had reached the valley where our friends reside that an armed force, formed of members of the revolutionary "Triad Society" was soon to march through their region. The Chinese were much terrified and the native Christians and attendants were anxious. . . .

The houses are of brick and stone; narrow passages serve for streets. Signs of heathenism may be seen at every turn. At the doorways are often shrines. In the principal room is the ancestral tablet, which receives the worship of the family. . . .

Fire-vermilion or orange colored papers over the doorways call down the "five blessings," (health, wealth, many children, long life, and peaceful death) on the inhabitants of the dwelling. Often we may see a stone of a curious form, set up to be worshipped, before which incense sticks are lighted. Here, using the lower part of this dwelling as a chapel, the faithful missionary gathers together his congregation. . . .

In a walk off among the hills we noticed a large number of huge jars scattered here and there over the hillsides. These contain the bones of the dead, awaiting final entombment. First the body is buried for three years. Then the bones are taken and placed in jars until some "lucky place" is pointed out where it will do to bury them. This important and delicate task is entrusted to the geomancer, or "Wind and Water Professor" who cheats the poor people as much as possible and gets all the money he can out of them before he hits upon an auspicious site. The hills all over this part of China are cut up with tombs of stone and mason-work, built in the form of an immense horse-shoe. . . .

Near the mission house is an immense great quadrangular building inhabited by the man called Pao. It is quite the custom in China for a family thus to live together for generations in one vast establishment if they have the money.[20] This building had four towers, and presented something of the appearance of an ancient castle. Within, it was in the most deplorable and dilapidated condition. The family seem to be in reduced circumstances, but desire to keep up the name of being the great people of the district. In one of the towns, we found two of the family who were "literary graduates," and who have become Christians. Nearby is the ancestral hall of the family. . . .

Lilong and Its Schools

From here our way lay over the hills, past villages and towns of the Hakkas. It is a struggle for existence, and the people have but little on which to live; and yet the homes and streets are full of healthy children, paradoxical as it may seem. The women work side by side in the fields with the men, and are strong and energetic. I asked them if they would like to go to the islands with the men if they could get free passage, and I received a most hearty affirmative reply.

I have now been over the principal districts of China, from which our labor comes, and I am convinced that a fair proportion of able-bodied, healthy women, would gladly avail themselves of the opportunity to come, if aid could be given them and their children. As it is, the men get together with considerable difficulty the fifty dollars which is necessary for the passage money, and which is a great sum here. Then to pay in addition sixty dollars for the wife and a number of dollars more for the children is, in many cases, an impossibility.

Historical Background of China

The present policy of allowing great companies of men to come in upon us without their families is most unwise and short-sighted. The married man with wife and children is the only normal colonist! . . .

The village of Lilong, nestling among the hills of the Sin-on district, is one of the most important stations of the Basel Mission. Here are a flourishing Theological Training School, with some twenty young men, instructed by Rev. Mr. Schaub, and a fine Boys Boarding School, at present in care of Rev. Mr. Piton. If any one needs to have his faith in mission work strengthened, he should read the story of the struggles of the early Basel missionaries to get any foothold in this region. . . .

We spent a Sabbath in this delightful place. The people gathered from the neighboring village for worship, and the church was well filled. Nearly all had friends in the Hawaiian Islands, and came to greet me most cordially. In the village we made many visits. In one house we found an old Chinese woman, over ninety, who, for years, has been a true and consistent Christian. She has a grandson at Kohala. We stopped at one house after another to take messages for husbands, brothers and sons in the faraway "sandal-wood hills". . . .

In Chong Hang Kang, a comfortable looking home, which one sees on coming into the village, has just been built by a man who has recently returned from Honolulu. An old blind woman, with wrinkled face asks me about her boy in that far land. A young mother, with a brood of little ones, wants me to take her out to her husband living there. We went to our house, where a pretty little Chinese woman has brought joy and happiness. A young man, who not long since returned from our part of the world, chanced to meet a young woman, of whom he asked the way, or some similar, simple question. So much did this Chinese damsel please him, that he takes many a hard-earned dollar which he has brought back with him, and pays it down for the object of his choice, and with her family's permission gains her hand to reign in his house a happy wife. It seems to have been quite a case of love at first sight. A very unusual thing in China—when the whole affair is generally managed by a "go between." Here at Chong Hang Kang is another mission-house chapel, where a company of Christians gathers.

Primitive Sugar Making

We had some delightful walks through the farming country. I remember one day on our way homewards, we passed through great spreading fields, with here and there clusters of ancient trees, banyans, I think. The land was most carefully tilled. From time to time, we passed patches of sugar-cane, which is raised here in this part of China, both for the sugar and for eating. The cane, all which I have seen, is as a general rule, small and poor-looking, but quite sweet. By the wayside as we saw one of the sugar mills in operation we stopped to examine this most primitive method of making sugar. The "hands" received us most courteously and we were allowed to inspect everything. The cane was piled up in great heaps ready for the "grinders." These were under a mat-shed, and were worked by four oxen or buffaloes, who patiently marched round and round in a circle, running the rude frame work which kept in motion two huge stones which ground and crushed the cane. The juice was then taken to the boiling-shed, when it passed through a considerable boiling process, in the last kettle being rigorously "beaten" by a Chinaman, who had a hot and trying place, I thought, calling for no little muscular effort. Clean-looking mats were spread at one side and here the hot syrup was poured-in very thin layers, and allowed to cool. The great sheets of sugar were then cut up into regular little squares and packed neatly away into jars. We received a liberal supply of this Chinese sugar, and I must confess, that it tasted far better than I had expected. The gulf, which separates this ancient process from the methods adopted in some of our splendid mills in the Islands, seems very wide indeed!

In Hongkong

The last night of the journey we spent at a Chinese store, which is mainly carried on by the Hakka Christians in a large market-town. They have a sort of branch-business in Honolulu. We were most kindly entertained.

The District of Heung Shan

Following quickly upon the trip of which I have spoken above came another into the Heung Shan district from which I returned only a day or two since. This fertile and populous region lies to the south of Canton City, bordering upon the ocean. At its southern most point is the Portuguese colony of Macao, on land ceded long ago by the Chinese to that nationality, which was for many years the only point where foreigners in China were allowed to live. The people of Heung

Shan are [predominantly] Puntis [and] are very energetic and enterprising. Large numbers have emigrated to America, Australia and to our own islands. The majority of Chinese scattered over our group are Heung Shan men. Most of the leading Chinese merchants in Honolulu are from this region. In Hong Kong many wealthy shopkeepers and compradores have come from there. Though they have for generations had to do with foreigners, there has been scarcely any Christian work among them. That terrible evil, the Macao Coolie Trade, though now removed, has caused a hatred and distrust of foreigners which will not for a long time be eradicated. Agents used to be sent through the district to lure the simple country people down to Macao, where they were kidnapped and sent off to distant lands, as laborers. The horrors of the long ocean voyage, where they were treated rather like brute-beasts than rational beings, the dreary years of exile and of enforced labor, made a sad page in the history of human suffering and wrong.

The upper part of the district is intersected by numberless river-branches and canals which renders travel here exceedingly easy. Towards the southern point it is more hilly. . . .

We found the country beautiful with the coming of spring. The jute-fields of mulberry shrubs were mantled in tender green. Busy workers filled the rice-swamps, preparing for the fruit crop. The orange trees, which we saw, were white with blossoms and full of sweetness. Birds sang brightly among the trees, and animated the advent of this most beautiful of the seasons. Our way led through the heart of a vast population, where men till the soil here as for long generations, their ancestors have done.

It was an especially interesting trip for me, because I saw so many Chinese friends whom I have either known before, or to whom I was known, or who were in some way linked to our Islands. I shall always find a deeper sympathy for the thousands of Heung Shan people, who dwell among us, because I have seen their homes here, and know something of their life from which they have come.

We directed our boat man to take us first to the District City, called Shekki, a large and flourishing place—lying along the river bank and at the foot of a hill, from which rises a lofty pagoda,—which can be seen from a considerable distance and makes an excellent land mark. These pagodas are thought a great deal of by the Chinese, who appear to believe that they will bring good luck in some way or other.

At this place there is a chapel, and a little company of native Christians, under the charge of the English Church Mission. I think it is the only Christian station in all this populous region.

Shekki is the principal point to which the Chinese return from our Islands, and then branch off to their native villages. Great passenger-junks ply between here and Hongkong and Macao.

One of my Chinese friends had given me directions how to find him. So I despatched my letter to him. Through the rain and darkness, he came a number of miles to find us and the next day guided us to his native village among the hills. Since his return from Honolulu lately—he has put up a nice new home for his old parents and his family where they live most comfortably.

I was interested to see here and there how foreign ideas had crept in. In one of the rooms he had a good, generous window, which is unusual in Chinese homes, where it is feared such an aperture will make a good place of entrance for evil spirits. He had framed photographs to ornament his walls; among them I noticed a very elaborate frame, containing the pictures of King Kalakaua, and the great Chinese statesman Li Hung Chang. We were treated with the utmost kindness and cordiality. My host's father was a reverend and courteous old gentleman of some eighty years, who seemed very bright and alert, and impressed me much by his gentle and refined manners. My friend belongs to the Au Young clan, whose ancestral tablets to the 24 generations could be seen in the spacious Ancestral Hall in the village. Nearly all the people of the village belong to this clan. The present Chinese consul in New York is perhaps its principal representative just now. His house stood near my friend's.

Crowds of people came to see us and stare at the foreigners. The majority of them had never seen white men before. Everything about us seemed to interest them even to the gold filling in our teeth which seemed especially to impress them. Followed by a chattering throng of boys, inquisitive but good natured, we made the turn of the village, and visited the old Ancestral House where bright eyed lads were studying the classics of Confucius and Mencius and shouting at the top of their voices—with the tablets of their forefathers looking down upon them. Back of the village rises a hill, covered with beautiful trees. On all sides stretch away vast rice fields, from which the people obtain the "staff of life."

A dinner was served up for us in fine style, one Chinese dish being

Historical Background of China

especially good, duck stuffed with lotus seeds and pearl barley. After exchanging many friendly expressions, we parted from our kind friends, taking with us the memory of a very pleasant visit.

An Interesting Walk

One long day's walk of many miles, enabled us to pass through village after village from which people have gone out to the Hawaiian Islands or other parts of the world. It was very strange every now and then to have a man look up from his work in the field, or run out from a shop to greet us in English or Hawaiian, and to ask us where we were going.

Many new homes at different points had been built by these returned laborers who had earned enough abroad to give their family thus a decent home. The dwellings are all of one story with a main room in the center where the family all gather and side rooms where they sleep. There is very little that is attractive about these villages, and you wonder sometimes how human beings can live, as some do here. Those who go abroad get many ideas, which in time cannot fail to be felt here.

Our way lay through great rice districts with distant glimpses of hill and woodland, and at one time we sighted the open sea along the coast. I was touched by the cordiality of the reception which these friends returned from the Islands gave me. Just at the present time when there is considerable opposition manifested to foreigners here in China, it was doubly pleasant to find the people so glad to see us. As we entered a village some one would shout, here is the "man from the fragrant Sandal wood hills" . . . and people would run from all sides to have a look. Of course they would sometimes call us "foreign devils." But then one gets used to that here.

We were into the homes of the people, and had a capital opportunity of talking with them. The country seems most fertile, but the population is immense and has to overflow, as we see, into other countries. We visited the homes of some of our well-to-do Honolulu merchants, whose families are here, and were most courteously received. Altogether it was a "red letter day" in my travels in China.

Light in the Darkness

During this same day's excursion we saw two Hawaiian women who are living here, married to Chinese. They were delighted to see me and I was equally glad to say "aloha" to them. One of them spoke English excellently which she said she had learned in a Honolulu school. They both were dressed in Chinese fashion and looked well and healthy and told me that their husbands were kind to them. But one especially longed to get back to the islands. She comes from Ka'u where she said she was a member of the church.

I was very much touched with a little incident which occurred during our visit in the village where she is living. I heard there was one Hawaiian woman there and sent for her to come and see me. We had a little talk in the street and I was preparing to say "good-bye" and go on my way, when she asked me if my friend and I would be willing to go to her house and offer a prayer. I need scarcely say that we readily complied.

We were followed by a crowd of curious Chinese who must have wondered at it all. The woman took down a large Hawaiian Bible, which she had brought with her across the ocean, and read in her own musical Hawaiian language, part of the 14th chapter of the Gospel of John,[21] while the tears gathered in her eyes, and I felt something of the same kind coming in mine, as I listened to her. Then Mr. Noyes[22] [who accompanied Damon] offered a prayer in Chinese, and I followed in Hawaiian and, as we finished, a Chinaman, her husband, who had just come repeated the Lord's prayer in English, to our great surprise.

F. W. DAMON
Canton City, March 28, 1884

II. Early Relations between Hawaii and China

HAWAIIANS VISIT CHINA, 1787

During the late eighteenth century Hawaiians and Chinese started to visit each other's country. After Captain James Cook's discovery of the Hawaiian Islands in 1778, many European and American ships on the China trade began to stop in Hawaiian waters for provisions, to winter over, and to trade. Hawaiians were taken on some ships for their superior seamanship. While in China, Chinese were put on as carpenters, cooks, and crew.[1]

The earliest known contact between Chinese and Hawaiians occurred in 1787 when Chief Tyaana[2] (Kaiana) of Atoui (Kauai) left with English Captain John Meares on the ship *Nootka* bound for Canton. Kaiana stayed in Canton and visited Macao as well. He was described by Captain Meares as being over six feet in stature, "and the muscular form of his limbs was of an Herculean appearance. His carriage was replete with dignity." Chief Kaiana hoped to continue his journey to Pretane (Great Britain) but instead was taken to America in 1788 and returned to Hawaii later that year. Captain Meares bought two vessels while in China—the *Felice* and the *Iphigenia*—and sailed them to Nootka Sound, off Vancouver Island in northwest America, to collect more furs and to build another ship. Nootka Sound was for many years the general rendezvous for fur traders.[3]

The excerpt is from the journal of another sea captain, Nathaniel Portlock, who had frequently visited Hawaii and knew Kaiana. Portlock tells of his unexpected meeting with his Hawaiian friend in a foreign land in 1787.*

Soon after my arrival at Canton I took an opportunity of paying a

* Nathaniel Portlock, "Voyage Round the World," *The Friend,* March 1861, p. 18.

visit to Mr. Cox, an English gentleman resident there; and I was much surprised to see my old friend Tyaana, whom the reader may recollect I met with at Atoui on my second visit to the Sandwich Islands. Tyaana immediately recollected me; and so sensibly was he affected with the interview, that he clasped his arms about me in the most affecting manner, reclined his head on my shoulders, tears ran unheeded down his cheeks, and it was some time before he became calm and composed enough to utter the name of his old acquaintance Popote [Portlock]; but when the first transports of joy, which so unexpected a meeting excited, had a little subsided, he seemed happy in making every inquiry that could please or afford satisfaction respecting his friends at the Sandwich Islands; and on my inquiring how he came to China, I found that Captain Meares had touched at Atoui in his passage from the coast of America to China, and Tyaana expressing a wish to accompany the captain to Pretane [Great Britain], he had taken him on board and brought him to Macao; at which place he left him in the care of Mr. Ross, his chief mate, of whom Tyaana was remarkably fond. They remained some time at Macao; and Tyaana was generally indulged in walking about wherever his inclination led him; and on these occasions he constantly wore a beautiful feathered cap and cloak, and carried a spear in his hand to denote himself to be a person of grandeur and distinction; nor did he like to wear any other dress, except the *maro* ["loin-cloth"], which is always worn by the Sandwich Islanders about the waist: such an appearance however being scarcely modest in a civilized country, Mr. Ross got a light satin waistcoat and a pair of trousers made for him, and which he was prevailed upon to wear, but not without great seeming reluctance at first but with which he was better pleased after they became familiar and habitual to him.

Tyaana, though *no professed papist,* would frequently go to the places of divine worship at Macao, and always observed the manner, motions, and attitudes of the congregation, standing or kneeling, and as they did, so did he, appearing very studious to imitate them, by an exact conformity to all their actions, gestures, and behaviour.

His noble and generous spirit visibly discovered itself on various occasions. One time he went up to an orange stall, and picking out half a dozen oranges, gave the woman who sold them a couple of nails for them, which in his estimation was a very ample, and indeed a superabundant compensation for her oranges and made her a present beside; but the good woman was by no means satisfied with such payment, and was about to raise a disturbance, by a loud, rude, offensive clamour of her not being paid; when some gentleman luckily happening to be with Tyaana at the time, readily pacified her complaint, by paying her to her satisfaction.

When the *Queen Charlotte* arrived in Macao Roads, Mr. Ross and Tyaana often went with Captain Dixon to Whampoa. During this short passage Tyaana often expressed his dislike of Chinese, particularly that custom of shutting up and excluding the women from the sight of strangers. And he seemed likewise to have contracted a prejudice, as well, against the form, shape, and manner of their persons, as against their practices and customs; and carried it even to hatred and antipathy, insomuch that he was once going to throw the pilot over-board for some trivial matter of offense.

When he arrived at Canton he was particularly noticed by the gentlemen of the English factory, from whom he received invitations, and every mark of civility which could testify their respect and regard to his rank and dignity; nor was he less caressed and admired by all classes of people at Canton.

A Captain Tasker, of the *Milford,* from Bombay, gave a sumptuous entertainment to a number of English gentlemen, and of course Tyaana was among the rest. After dinner, being upon deck, a number of poor Tartars [Tankas (boat people), not Tartars] in small sampans, were about the ship asking alms, as is customary there on such occasions of entertainment and festivity. Tyaana immediately inquired what they wanted, and being told that they were beggars who came to supplicate the refuse of the table, he expressed great concern, saying that he was very sorry to see any persons in want of food, and that it was quite a new scene to him; for that they had no people of that description at Atoui; he seemed to be under great impatience to procure them relief, and became a very important solicitor on their behalf. The captain's generous disposition readily co-operated with his importunities, and he ordered all the broken victuals, being a large quantity, to be brought upon deck, and Tyaana had the distribution of it among the poor Tartars [Tankas], which he did, observing the most equal, impartial division he was able to make of it; and his pleasure and satisfaction in the performance of that task were not less visible in his countenance than his actions.

I asked him if he was willing to go to Pretane; but he told me that he expected to have been there in twelve moons, but that now he should be glad to return to Atoui. It seems Captain Mears [*sic*] had engaged in a Portuguese expedition to the coast of America, and promised to leave Tyaana at Atoui in his passage thither. The gentlemen at Canton, desirous to give him lasting proof of their friendship and esteem, furnished him with whatever could be useful or acceptable; such as bulls, cows, sheep, goats, rabbits, turkies, &c with oranges, mangoes, and various kinds of plants; so that his safe arrival with his cargo would prove of the utmost value to his country, and an honourable testimony to his countrymen of the distinguished esteem and regard with which he had been treated, and his very name revered by all ranks and conditions of the people of Canton.

CHINESE VISIT HAWAII, 1788–1789

In 1778 and 1779 when Captain James Cook discovered and revisited the Hawaiian Islands, he did not find any non-Hawaiian inhabitants. He named the islands the Sandwich Islands after his patron, the Earl of Sandwich, first lord of the British Admiralty.

In 1787 and 1788, the British Captain John Meares was in Hawaiian waters. He brought with him fifty Chinese carpenters and artisans returning to China from northwest America.

When Captain Meares on the *Felice* and Captain William Douglas on the *Iphigenia* left Canton in January, 1788, they carried with them their Hawaiian passengers Kaaina, "Wynee,"[4] and a man and boy from Maui who were not further identified. The sailing vessels generally followed the China coast northward to Japan to take advantage of favorable winds and currents to cross the Pacific to northwest America. On the return trip to Canton, the ships took the southern route and stopped over at Hawaii for water and provisions.[5]

When the two English ships reached Nootka Sound, work was begun building a new forty-ton schooner, the *North West America*. Kaiana was intensively interested in the new vessel and spent most of his time with the Chinese carpenters and smiths whom Captain Meares had brought over.

In the fall of the same year, Captain Meares started off again, with the *Felice, Iphigenia,* and the new *North West America* taking the fifty or so Chinese workmen back to Canton by way of Hawaii.[6] This

Early Relations between Hawaii and China

was the thirteenth European vessel to land in Hawaii. King Kamehameha visited the *North West America* in Kealakekua Bay on the island of Hawaii and asked that a carpenter be left behind to assist in building another similar ship. There is reason to suppose that some of the Chinese workmen remained in Hawaii in 1788. At least, they were the first Chinese to see Hawaii. Other writers used 1789 as the probable date of the first Chinese residing in the islands.

In 1789 an American trader, Captain Simon Metcalf,[7] sailed from Macao for northwest America on the *Eleanora*. A stop was made in Hawaii for the winter to rest the crew of forty-five Chinese and ten Americans. This was among the first American vessels on the China trade to stop over in Hawaii. It is surmised that one or more Chinese remained in the islands, probably coming off the *Eleanora* with John Young, British boatswain detained here by the King and who later was the King's adviser.

The Chinese community here used the 1789 date in celebrating, in 1939, the 150th anniversary of the first Chinese arrival in Hawaii.[8]

In 1791 British Captain William Douglas of the schooner *Grace* left two of his men on Maui to collect sandalwood.[9] This fragrant wood was traded to the Chinese in Canton to be used for incense, for making fans, carved boxes and other *objets d'art*. This was probably the first trade relation between Hawaii and China. It introduced the wonderful gamut of "China goods" to the islanders, and King Kamehameha I learned the intricacies of customs and port duties from China. But irreparable damage was done to the flora of Hawaii for the hills were denuded by indiscriminate felling of sandalwood trees. Native Hawaiians suffered greatly from the forced labor of gathering logs of sandalwood; their Polynesian lifestyle and ecology was upset. However, to the Chinese, Hawaii continues to have the romantic name of the Sandalwood Mountains (*"Tan Heung Shan"*).

Early in 1794 when Captain George Vancouver[10] came for the fifth time, he saw one Chinese among other adventurers on Oahu and Edward Bell who was with Vancouver recorded into his "Log of the *Chatham*" Chinese among the eleven foreigners seen with Kamehameha at Kealekekua Bay of the island of Hawaii in 1794.[11] This gave credence to the story that the first Chinese came in 1789 at the time of "John Young, Isaac Davis, and a Mr. Boid" and stayed on in the islands.

Loraine Kuck describes the circumstances of the first Chinese visit to Hawaii.*

The year was 1788. In America, the thirteen colonies had recently won their revolution against England and shortly would elect George Washington the first president. In China the Emperor Ch'ien Lung was approaching the end of his long reign, one of the great periods of Chinese history and art. In Hawaii, the young high chief, who was to be known as Kamehameha the Great, had just entered on his conquest of all the islands.

There was a haze over the ocean on October 16 of that year. It is so recorded in the diary of Captain John Meares, master of the ship Felice which was approaching the Sandwich Islands after a long spring and summer spent along the northwest coast of America. The captain, who had visited the place the year before, remarks that in clear weather "the high land of Owhyhee can be seen at a distance of twenty leagues." Because of this haze it was not until five o'clock the next morning that the landfall was made and "to our infinite satisfaction we discovered land . . . at a distance of six leagues."

As far as any records go, this was the first time that natives of China saw Hawaii. For the crew of the Felice was made up of Europeans and Chinese, in about equal proportions.

Ten months before, the Felice had left China, to trade knives and trinkets with the Indians of northwest America for the furs of that vast, wild region. These furs brought pleasantly high prices from the hong merchants of Canton, for the wealthy Chinese loved, as they still do, the soft luxuriance of fur linings to their silken robes during the winter. After so many months at this business of gathering furs, even the monotonous "stores" which fed an 18th century ship's company were running low. Captain Meares notes in his diary that to the men aboard the Felice "the idea of that plenty and those comforts which awaited our arrival filled every heart with joy and gladness."

The approach of the ship was a matter of mutual excitement aship and ashore. It was only the thirteenth time that a European vessel had

---

* Loraine E. Kuck, "The First Chinese to See Hawaii," *Paradise of the Pacific*, December 1946, pp. 33–35; reproduced by kind permission of the author.

touched at the islands. The native people knew now that what they saw was not a floating island bearing gods as they had thought the first ships had been, ten years before. Many of the Europeans on board must have felt considerable interest in these new islands, discovered by Captain Cook so long after most of the other South Sea archipelagos had been found. The interest of the Chinese crewmen, however, would have been rather [indifferent]. To them it would have been just another land of outer barbarians, like everything else which surrounded their country, the Middle Kingdom, the only civilized country in the world.

Afterward the Captain wrote: "On the 18th at daybreak, we bore up, and proceeded under a gentle sail to close in with the land, which we accomplished about nine o'clock; when the late barren and unfriendly prospect was succeeded by a scene which might suit the fablings of poetry and romantic fiction. The haziness of the morning did not obscure the varied landscape before us. The great mountain Mouna Kaah (Mauna Kea) which is situated on the northeast part of the island, was clothed in clouds, which seemed, as it were, to be falling down its declivity; while its summit towered above the vapours, and presented a sublime object of nature; from its base to the sea was a beautiful amphitheatre of villages and plantations, while the shore was crowded with people, who, from the coolness of the morning, were clothed in their parti-colored garments. Some of them were seated on the banks to look at the ship, while others were running along the shore toward the little sandy patches where their canoes were drawn up, in order to come off to us . . . nor was it long before a considerable number of canoes came off to the ship, with hogs, young pigs, taroroot, plaintains, sugar cane and a few fowls."

The visiting and trading for these provisions went on all day. It is easy to picture the scene, the native people smiling up from their canoes. . . . Some of the women were allowed to come on board, but the number of men was limited, since the Europeans had not forgotten that Captain Cook had been killed in a brawl with these people.

"By sunset," the Captain continues, "we had purchased a sufficiency of fresh provisions to last us to China; we, therefore, prepared to make sail . . . but the number of natives, and the women in particular, were so great, not only covering the decks, where there was any room, but even clinging to the rigging, that we were under the necessity of bribing them with presents of some kind or other to procure their departure. Some of the women took to their canoes, but the greater part plunged into the sea and swam ashore."

The Felice visited the other islands briefly, Maui, Oahu, Kauai and Niihau, then went on to China with its cargo of furs. It had sailed from China with a consort ship, the Iphigenia, and a few weeks later this ship, which remained a little longer off the coast of America also arrived off Hawaii. It was followed by a little schooner of only forty tons, named the North West America which had been built by the carpenters aboard the two vessels during the summer ashore. The arrival of these two ships brought up to fifty the number of Chinese to touch the islands, for this number had been among the crews of the Felice and the Iphigenia when they left China.

Picking up a crew partly of native Chinese was an experiment initiated by these two vessels. They had been purchased in India for the purpose of going to Alaska for furs hence they were under the necessity of finding crewmen wherever they could. There were evidently some European sailors available, but not enough so that Chinese were recruited.

"The Chinese were, on this occasion, an experiment." Meares states. "A much greater number of Chinese solicited to enter into this service than could be received; and so far did the spirit of enterprise influence them, that those whom we were under the necessity of refusing, gave the most unequivocal marks of mortification and disappointment. From the many who offered themselves, fifty were selected as fully sufficient for the voyage. They were . . . chiefly handy-craft men of various kinds with a small proportion of sailors who had been used to man the junks which navigate every part of the Chinese seas."

The experiment proved a success, as he commented later. "During the whole of the voyage there was every reason to be satisfied with their services." It is easy to picture word of their success spreading among the shipmasters gathered at Canton and to realize that thereafter, ships which left that port, with intention to return, may often have augmented their crews with Chinese.

It was the Chinese "handy-craft" men who had built the little North West America, the first European-style ship to be constructed on the northwestern shore of North America. And it was doubtless the same men who after arrival in Hawaii, built the first armed vessel belonging to a native chief.

The Iphigenia and North West America remained for the four

Early Relations between Hawaii and China

winter months in the islands. During this time the Iphigenia's captain did not stay aloof from local politics. The islands, at that period were ruled, not by one, but by several high chiefs, who were engaged in a complicated game of political rivalry. This rivalry ended a few years later when one of the chiefs, Kamehameha, was able to subdue the others and make himself ruler of the entire island group.

After foreign ships had started coming to Hawaii, with Cook, it had taken the competing chiefs no time at all to realize that the firearms they carried, and even the vessels themselves, would give any island leader who possessed them, an irresistible advantage over a rival who had only spears and double canoes. Kamehameha was probably the first to realize this and undoubtedly the most successful in his attempts to obtain them, the factor to which his ultimate conquest is probably due. In this case he succeeded in getting the first armed canoe from the foreigners.

When Kamehameha learned that the small North West America had been built by men aboard the ship he wanted first of all, to have two of these "handy-craft men" left behind to build such a ship for himself. Being refused this, he then entreated the captain to give him a small swivel gun and have it mounted on a double canoe. Firearms and ammunition were among the things with which the foreign ships purchased their supplies. So the carpenter was ordered to form a stage on one of the largest canoes to receive the gun.

"In the afternoon," Meares writes in his record, "the carpenter having finished the swivel, she was brought alongside the Iphigenia when the gun was mounted; but it was with great difficulty that the King could prevail on his people to keep their paddles in their hands while he discharged the piece."

There is nothing in Meares' record to indicate that any of the Chinese on his ships left them and remained on the islands. But during the four months the Iphigenia and North West America remained in Hawaiian waters they made a series of leisurely stops at each of the islands. Wherever they went they were welcomed by the chiefs and people. There was much visiting ashore, feasting and entertaining . . . And while Meares is discreet, there seems little doubt that Chinese blood was first introduced into the islands at this time.

[Miss Kuck notes:] References in the above article are quoted from "Voyages made in 1788 and 1789 from China to the Northwest Coast of America with an introductory narrative of a voyage performed in 1786 from Bengal in the ship Nootka," by John Meares. London 1790. A reprint of the Hawaiian portions is to be found among the Hawaiian Historical Society Reprints.

A CHINESE WOMAN IN HAWAII, 1837

The news article below relates how it was ascertained that there was a Chinese woman in Hawaii as early as 1837. Since then it has been possible to elucidate her story, including her name, even further. Correspondence with the Reverend Carl T. Smith,[12] genealogist and historian, who first mentioned this woman in his writings, brought information that she was listed as Maria Seise in the San Francisco Protestant Episcopal Church records. Her name is the consequence of her marriage to a Portuguese sailor in Macao called Seise who was later lost at sea. She had come to Hawaii, returned to China, and was finally in the household of a Gillespie family who went to California from China and built a handsome house with Chinese furnishings.

From further research it was learned that a Chinese woman was in the islands on board an English ship bound for California from Hong Kong just before 1848. Samuel S. Hill who was visiting Hawaii on a whaleship at the time, heard of her and describes the situation: "The circumstances caused at least curiosity enough to make the event very soon generally known; and of course it reached the ears of the few Chinese that were residing in the place. Among these, and at the head of his people, was a Mandarin, Slam Sing [Sam Sing] by name, who was keeping a little store and dealing in Chinese merchandise; and this worthy magistrate, impressed, as it appeared, with a sense of the obligation which the arrival of his countrywoman imposed upon him, applied to the King, stating that whereas by the laws of China no woman was allowed to leave her country, it was his duty to require that this woman should be given up to him, as the chief of her nation resident in the islands, in order that he might deal with her according to the laws of the Empire."[13]

Sam Sing ignored the fact that the laws of the Empire also applied to him—no national of China was to leave that country, man or woman. It is plausible that this woman and Maria Seise were one and the same, for Seise arrived in San Francisco from Hong Kong aboard the *Eagle* in February 1848.

Her story is one of the interesting aspects of Hawaiian Chinese history.*

The question of who was the first Chinese woman in Hawaii has been traced by the Hawaii State Archives to "Lady of Ayum" who arrived on the Yankee sailing vessel on August 19, 1855. Now, however, I have traced the arrival of the first Chinese woman to an earlier date—that of 1837.

My discovery happened quite by accident when the Rev. Carl Smith of the Chinese University of Hong Kong showed me a copy of an article he wrote, "The Gillespie Brothers—early links between Hong Kong and California." He has been gathering material on the early history of Hong Kong.

In the article, there is mention of a Chinese woman who was taken to Hawaii in 1837 by an American family from Macao because she was a faithful and trustworthy servant. She remained in the Sandwich Islands for six years.

In 1843, she returned to China and found employment in the household of Charles Gillespie, an American businessman in Hong Kong and Macao.

In 1848, she accompanied the Gillespie family on the ship the "Eagle" to California where Mr. Gillespie was successful in his law practice and business.

The Gillespies took an active part in organizing the Trinity [Protestant] Episcopal Church in San Francisco on July 22, 1849. On this date, Bishop Ingraham confirmed 18 persons at the first administration of his rite in California.

One of the 18 who joined the church with Mrs. Gillespie was her domestic servant, quite familiar by this time with the English language, who knelt with Mrs. Gillespie to receive the rite at the same time.

Prof. Smith's notes are from Bishop Ingraham's report in the Journal of the Protestant Episcopal Church and are quite complete but he is still unable to provide the name of this Chinese woman or the name of the American family who first took her to Hawaii in 1837.

Other questions remain unanswered—why did they come to Hawaii and did they leave any descendants here?

* Tin-Yuke Char, "First Chinese Woman Arrived in 1837," *Honolulu Advertiser*, 10 January 1970.

During the period of this Chinese woman's stay (1837–1843), Hawaii was under the reign of Kamehameha III and the governor of Oahu was Kekuanaoa.

The present stone church at Kawaiahao was being built. Royal School was open and in 1841 Punahou School was established.

There must have been excitement in this American household when France began to extend her colonization to the Pacific and British naval officers attempted to place the Sandwich Islands under their flag.

This Chinese woman's daily life in the early nineteenth century Hawaii might well have included tending a vegetable garden and the few Chinese plants she probably brought with her.

She must have heard of the Chinese actively involved in the new sugar industry. Adventuresome pioneers like Wong Tze Chun had already started a Chinese-style sugar mill on Lanai in 1802.[14] Hung Tai and Co. followed with a sugar mill at Wailuku[15] and Chun Afong was already busy recruiting labor for his Pepeekeo plantation.

Unfortunately, this woman did not stay to see the waves of immigration started in 1852 by the sugar planters to recruit contract laborers from China.

KING KALAKAUA'S VISIT TO CHINA, 1881

Visits between private Hawaiian and Chinese citizens increased as the nineteenth century progressed, but none was so important as the trip of the Hawaiian monarch, King Kalakaua. The King visited China in 1881 as part of his tour around the world. After a royal welcome in Japan, the King sailed to Shanghai. He went as far north as Tientsin and was entertained there on 1 April 1881 by Viceroy Li Hung-chang.[16] The lavishly printed menu did not include Li Hung-chang chop suey but featured bird's nest soup, shark's fins, quail *pâté,* and other delicacies. The Viceroy asked penetrating questions about the natives and foreigners in Hawaii.

William Armstrong who accompanied the King was special commissioner of immigration. This tour gave him exceptional opportunity to gather information, and he recorded his observations.*

We arrived at Shanghai at noon. No notice of the King's purpose

---

* William N. Armstrong, *Around the World with a King* (London: Heineman, 1909), pp. 88–89.

MENU.

DINNER GIVEN IN HONOUR OF
H. M. KING KALAKAUA
OF HAWAII
BY THE VICE ROY LI
AT TIENTSIN
ON THE 1ST OF APRIL, 1881.

Bird's nest soup.
Fish, stewed and fried.
Shark's fins
Meat balls.
Mutton Cutlets.
Fried Pork.
Quail paté.
Cold Chicken
Ham and mushroom Pudding
Roast Turkey
Boiled Ham.
Roast Mutton.
Chocolate sponge cake.
Jelly, white & red.
Plum pudding &c.
Ladies finger cakes.

燕炸魚巴羊炸白凉車燒蛤燒火五大牛
菜魚翅地排紫鴿拌厘火火羊腿色這提刑
魚燴魚翅地排紫布鴿拌路火火羊腿蛋這子餅
燴肉骨盖布雞肉雞腿肉糕厘甸布

Menu of Dinner given in honour of King Kalakaua,
by Li Hung Chang.

to visit China had been officially given; if it had it would have created consternation in the Yamen at Pekin. No royal salutes were fired as we entered the Woosung River; we were now among a people indifferent and perhaps unfriendly to us. We dropped suddenly from the pinnacle of royal hospitality [i.e., their reception in Japan] to its base, and the royal standard lay dejectedly in its canvas bag. The American Consul-General, however, called on the King, who had taken lodgings in the "Astor House." He unwisely urged him to visit Pekin and be the first of foreign kings to enter the Forbidden City.

No diplomatic corps resides in Shanghai, but the *taotai* or mayor of the place was notified by the American Consul of the arrival of the King. The following day he appeared in a sedan chair, with a large retinue preceding and following him; while runners, with the beating of gongs and loud cries, notified the spectators to make the way clear. We observed at once the fine physiques, clear eyes, and intelligent faces of the men of the higher classes, but there was the inscrutable physiognomy which Europeans cannot penetrate. He said that he desired to honour the King of a foreign country, and asked if the King would condescend to dine with him. The invitation was accepted, but the dinner was postponed until after our return from Tientsin.

The manager of the China Merchants Steamship Company, which owned a fleet of thirty-six large steamers and looked for trade in the Pacific, had already sent several vessels to the Hawaiian group.[17] In order to make favour with the King he placed at his Majesty's disposal a large steamer, the *Pautah,* for the trip to Tientsin. . . . The manager was a fine American Negro who had shown much ability when employed by the American Legation in Pekin; he was not only well educated, but spoke several languages, including Chinese; his father was a Negro preacher in Washington, D.C. He had married a handsome English girl in Shanghai, who was an artist; but his marriage to a white person had much incensed the Americans living in Shanghai, though it was cordially approved by the English, Germans, and French residents. He caused some cabins of the *Pautah* to be refurnished and made provision for a sumptuous table. Though the steamer was on the regular line of travel between Shanghai and Tientsin, he refused to permit any persons to take passage in her, reserving this great vessel for the exclusive use of the King and suite; she became, therefore, for this trip, the private yacht of the royal party.

The cost was great, but the shrewd Chinese no doubt expected favours in their future trade with Hawaii.

On the morning of our landing in Shanghai, an American lad who lived in the Astor House showed great curiosity to see a "live king." He dressed himself neatly and waited near the door of the King's chamber. An American living in the city, who knew the lad, warned him against getting within the King's reach, for he said, "He is the King of the Cannibal Islands, and is uncommonly fond of roasted little boys." The little fellow disappeared instantly, but returned in a few moments covered with mud. The gentleman who had warned him asked his reason for rolling in the dirt. He replied, "The King would not eat a dirty boy."

We smiled at our luck in becoming the sole occupants of a fine steamer for the next ten days. We embarked without salutes or ceremonies of any kind. The captain was a Yankee skipper, with three American officers, while the crew were well-trained Chinese.

The numerous stewards stood about the saloon, with no duty but to wait upon the King's party; the table of an Atlantic liner was not better supplied. Around the sides of the main saloon were fastened racks filled with muskets and cutlasses, and amidships were several cannon, for there is danger, although remote, of piratical attacks on the Yellow Sea. It was possible that a Chinese Captain Kidd might bear down upon us, and if he captured us, the King and suite might be directed in forcible pidgin-English to "walk the plank." The King did not like the warlike look of the steamer, and asked the skipper whether he would fight or run if pirates should make an attack. The answer was characteristic: "Fight, by gum! Mr. King. I'd like to get a show at those yaller dogs!"

At the close of the day the steamer reached the mouth of the Peiho River. Extended fortifications stretched along the left bank, while on the right were the low batteries which crippled the British naval forces in 1860, upon which occasion the American commodore, Tatnall, allowed his boat's crew to man the British guns, and declared the future international policy of America and England: "Blood is thicker than water!"

Crossing the bar, we steamed up the river to Tientsin. The royal standard was hoisted and was recognised by the Consular Corps. The docks were soon covered with people, who stood silent and stolid. The King's arrival was announced to the *taotai,* who, with a large retinue, paid a formal visit to the King, who received him in the "compound" or premises of the steamship company. The *taotai* said that the Viceroy, General Li Hung Chang, had ordered a search to be made for suitable apartments for his Majesty, but they could not be readily secured. He asked if the King's country was a part of America, and if he had come around Cape Horn. He retired with much ceremony. After he left, a mandarin, Li Sun, the secretary of the Viceroy, called. He spoke English, informing us that he had been graduated at Hamilton College, Clinton, N.Y., many years ago, and that he had a son who was a student at Yale. He had known relatives of the King's Chamberlain, who lived in the town where the college was situated. We told him that we preferred to remain on the steamer, where we had excellent accommodations. He dined with us. While a member of the Consular Corps engaged the King's attention, the Secretary asked me if the King intended to visit Pekin. I told him that the King wished to meet General Li Hung Chang and would visit Pekin if it was practicable. Li Sun replied that the Viceroy would appreciate the visit, but a trip to Pekin would require much preliminary study; many communications would have to be exchanged, and the Yamen would carefully consider the matter; he thought it would be at least five weeks before it could be definitely settled. He declined, however, to represent the views of the Imperial Government. After he left I told the King that it was quite clear to me that he was not wanted at Pekin; in the eyes of the Dowager Empress and her consort he was only a *fanqui* ("foreign devil"). . . . Besides, as he had no army or navy behind him, he might be seized, put in a bamboo cage, and paraded through China. The King finally abandoned his intention of going to Pekin.

Mandarin Li Sun returned with a message from the Viceroy that he would send his own sedan chairs to the steamer in the morning, and they would bring the King and suite to the Yamen, which was the Viceroy's palace.

During the day several members of the Consular Corps called on the King, and we visited a part of the city; a number of Chinese merchants called and tendered banquets to his Majesty.

The Viceroy's sedan chairs arrived in the morning, with Secretary Li Sun, and we, in uniform, entered them; each was borne by four men. The bamboo carrying-poles bent as if they would break under the heavy weights of the King and the Chamberlain; the wiry and lean coolie bearers were soon in a profuse perspiration. The route lay through several miles of narrow streets, whose walls were so close to each other that the extended hands of one seated in a chair could almost touch both sides at the same time. The people, at the sound of the Viceroy's gong and the cry of the Governor's guard, packed themselves close to the walls, and gazed silently and stolidly into the dark face of the King.

At the gates of the Yamen a troop of soldiers awkwardly presented arms, and an explosion of three large fire-crackers—the regular salute—was made. Alighting in the court-yard, we advanced a few steps to meet the Viceroy, who stood alone, in a brilliant dress, while behind him was a retinue of his officials. He shook hands with himself cordially, according to Chinese custom, and then, in deference to the immemorial pump-handle welcome of the Europeans, shook hands with the King and with the suite. He led the way, between lines of bowing officials, through several large rooms, to a reception-chamber, where we sat around a large circular table. The room was ornamented with beautiful vases; and on the walls were silk curtains upon which were inscribed moral precepts. . . .

The Viceroy at once began to ask questions: "How many islands are there in your kingdom?"—"How old are you?"—"Do you have a Parliament?"—"How many people are there in your kingdom?" By his side stood his pipe-bearers. The bowl rested on the floor, and a servant holding a live coal knelt at the bowl, watching the Viceroy's face; the other bearer stood by the side of the Viceroy, who at intervals, without moving his head, raised and opened his hand, into which the vigilant bearer instantly placed the stem of the pipe, and the kneeling servant applied the fire. He took several whiffs of smoke, opened his hand, and the bearer removed the pipe-stem, while the lighter recharged the bowl with fresh tobacco. The Viceroy, who had information about the Hawaiian kingdom which Li Sun had given him, continued:

"You have many Chinese in your country, and you treat them well."—"Are you the son of your predecessor?"

"No," said the King, "I come from another old dynasty."

"What did you do when you were a boy?" asked the Viceroy.

The King hesitated for a moment, reflected, and replied at a venture:

"I went into the army when I was sixteen years of age."

This provoked instantly the ever-vexing question, "How large is your army?"

"I have few regular troops," replied his Majesty; "I rely on volunteers."

"Are the gentlemen in your suite Hawaiians?" continued the catechiser.

"Both are Hawaiians," replied the King.

"I see," said the Viceroy, "that he (pointing to Colonel Judd) is dark; but he (pointing to me) is white. Why are they different? Do you have white natives among your subjects?"

"The parents of both were Americans," was the reply.

"You have missionaries; do you like them?" was the next question.

"Yes they are good people," said the King.

His Majesty was rather confused with the rapidity of the questions. Secretary Li Sun was the interpreter.

The Viceroy rose and led the King to another room, where there was a table loaded with sweetmeats. Champagne was served. The Viceroy said he would return the King's visit the next day, and then walked with him to the court-yard and stood near the sedan chair while the King entered it. He remained there bowing until we had reached the gates and another salute of three explosions had been given. Mandarin Li Sun arrived soon after, and his conversation gave us much interesting information about the Chinese, the life of the Viceroy, and the international relations of China with the Great Powers. . . .

The next morning our temporary yacht, the *Pautah,* was decorated with flags, and the Viceroy's barge brought him down the river at ten o'clock. After some ceremonies on deck he entered the saloon with the King, and after tea was served he renewed his cross-examination. The suite aided the King, and the Viceroy would frequently turn to them and spear them with sharp queries. The King remarked that the Emperor of Japan had shown him great hospitality. The Viceroy replied that the Japanese could not be depended upon. He said he regretted he had no palace to which he could invite the King, but would give him a banquet the next evening in the compound of the steamship company. He then rose and walked slowly to the gangway with his Majesty; they appeared to be of the same height.

During the next day crowds of people pressed to the edge of the dock, peering into the doors and windows of our steamer. Some of them were motionless for hours, for they saw in the Viceroy's guest not only a "foreign devil," but a black foreign devil. The children were brought to the dock in their fathers' arms that they too might see the awe-inspiring sight.

Late in the day we walked across the street to the compound. The Viceroy had already arrived in his brilliant dress, and we appeared in full uniform. The Viceroy received the King at the door and led him to the reception-room, where the prominent men of the city, both Chinese and foreigners, were presented to the Viceroy and King. Tea was served, and we entered the dining-room. The Viceroy placed the King on his right hand, and myself on his left, and next to me his son, a young man who was studying the English language and spoke it with hesitation. When this young gentleman discovered that I was an American, he asked me many questions about the relation of the States to the Federal government, for he could not understand the dual system; he thought it confusing and dangerous. The dishes and food were entirely Chinese, but they were served at tables, and forks were furnished to the foreigners. The fine ware had been brought from the Viceroy's residence. The room was decorated with silk curtains and embroideries, upon which were worked moral texts from the Chinese classics, quite like the pious aphorisms which appeared on the walls of New England homes in early days, but which are removed as prosperity increases, because they are annoying and impracticable.

The democratic life of the Chinese was seen in the freedom allowed to the crowd to enter the compound and look at the guests through the window while they ate. The people stood on one another's shoulders and backs; some of them raised themselves with bamboo sticks, so that the windows were filled to their upper frame-work with stolid faces pressing against the glass. The Viceroy occasionally asked questions, but Li Sun was seated at a distance from him and could not interpret with ease. He asked me questions through his son: "Why is not your office of Minister filled by a native?"—"Are the natives incapable?"—"Do you fear the United States?"—"How much good have the missionaries done?"—"Do you know General Grant?—he is a great man. . . ."

HAWAIIAN STUDENTS IN CHINA

The 1881 Hawaiian legislature accepted the proposal of King Kalakaua to provide education in foreign countries for selected

Hawaiian youths. This progressive policy was inspired by what King Kalakaua saw on his journey around the world. The following students were sent abroad: James and Isaac Hakuole to Japan; James Kiawehaku to China; St. Chad Piianaia, John Lovell, and Makalua to England; Robert Boyd and Robert Wilcox to Italy. David Keawehaku was sent to China in 1882.[18]

During the period 1881 to 1884, Booth and Kamauoha died in Italy and England, respectively; Kapaa returned from China; and Prince Kawananakoa and Thomas Cummins were sent to San Mateo, California.[19] Despite some disappointments, the Hawaiian legislature continued the program, setting aside a generous biennial budget of $30,000 in 1887 and 1888 to send other promising Hawaiian lads to various part of the world to insure well-informed leaders for the future.[20]

Kapaa was sent to China in 1883. The Reverend Andrew Happer, a missionary in China and father of Mrs. Frank Damon (Mary), was asked to be Kapaa's instructor and guardian. Kapaa was introduced into China with a letter from Walter Murray Gibson, foreign minister of the Hawaiian Kingdom.*

Honolulu, March 7th, 1883

F. Bulkeley-Johnson, Esq.
H. H. M.'s Consul General
Hong Kong

Sir:

From information furnished me by our Consul General at Tokio, I learn that the official dispatch which should have accompanied Mr. Kapaa, has miscarried. I therefore hasten to inform you that Mr. Kapaa's visit to China is made in pursuance of a resolution of the Legislature, providing for the education of Hawaiian youths. His Majesty the King desired that one of these should proceed to China and there study the Chinese language and customs. I therefore invoke your good offices on behalf of young Kapaa, who has been selected for this career, and shall be obliged by your placing him where he can learn the dialects (Cantonese and Hakka) chiefly spoken by the

---

* Archives of Hawaii, Hawaiian Consuls—Hong Kong, Singapore and Shanghai, 1893–1900.

Chinese who are here, and the written language, acquiring at the same time familiarity with Chinese manners and ideas. I am of course anxious that while pursuing this course of study Mr. Kapaa should not lose such European culture as he has acquired. . . . Draw on me for disbursements . . . for Mr. Kapaa, considerations of economy cannot be neglected. . . .

                                        Walter M. Gibson
                                        Minister of Foreign Affairs

III. Contract Labor System and Immigration Problems

CHINESE IN SUGAR, 1802–1852

The impact of Western culture was much greater on the isolated Polynesian islands of Hawaii than it had been on China. Throughout the nineteenth century, the effect of Christian missions, foreign trade, commercial agriculture, and labor immigration disturbed every aspect of traditional Hawaiian society. The greatest impact was made by sugar, the first truly valuable commercial crop grown in the islands.

Sugarcane was growing plentifully in Hawaii at the time of European discovery. From its home in India, it had found its way to the South Pacific islands. Succeeding migrations of Polynesian peoples had carried it to faraway Hawaii.[1] But its commercial importance had to wait for the entrepreneurial skills of the Europeans and the Chinese.

There were an estimated seventy-one Chinese persons[2] among the total foreign population of 1,962 as counted by the Hawaii census of 1850. Several were already independently running simple sugar mills. They had come to Hawaii on their own initiative. These people had sailed on exploration and trading vessels and had settled in Hawaii between the time of discovery (1778) and the arrival of the first Chinese contract laborers (1852).

In 1802, a Chinese on a ship trading in sandalwood was said to have brought with him a vertical mill and boilers. His name, given as Wong Tze-chun, has not been verifiable in Chinese or other records. He reportedly set up his apparatus on the small island of Lanai, ground off a small crop, and made sugar. It was not a satisfactory production, and he took himself and his mill back to China the next year.[3]

A sugar mill was started by Hungtai Co. in Wailuku, on the island of Maui, in 1828. It was a partnership of two men, Ahung and Atai.[4]

Contract Labor System

In 1835, William French brought from China a number of Chinese with a mill and apparatus for the manufacture of sugar. He took them to Waimea, Kauai, where he had contracted with Governor Kaikioewa to grind cane supplied by the Governor.[5]

Another indication of Chinese involvement in the development of sugar was the report of 1851 on sugar cultivation acreage in Hilo: Ahsing Plantation at Makahanaloa, 400 acres; Ah Kina Plantation at Puueo, 90 acres; and Amoi Plantation at Ponoohawaii [Punohawai], 55 acres.[6]

Thus, the Chinese were pioneers of and played an important role in the commercial production of sugar in Hawaii. As one observer commented, "Whalers and other vessels touching at the islands had occasionally left some Chinese behind them; and it was soon discovered that not only were these men better laborers, generally, than the natives, but that they were so superior in industry and steadier, that they could be employed with the greatest advantage as overseers of estates."[7]

The early history of sugar is given in an early edition of Thrum's *Hawaiian Annual,* an important reference guide to Hawaii.*

Sugar cane . . . was noted by Cook in his visit to these Islands, as being "of large size and of good quality." The natives, however, made no use of it beyond that of food, and it was not until the settlement of foreigners that any attempt was made to utilize the vast fields of wild cane that natives say grew in every valley and plain. . . .

There are many localities laying claims to the first mill, and as many claiming the credit for the establishment of this industry, which has long since been the leading one, that it has been no easy task to define its legitimate founder. . . . In a paper read by the late L. L. Torbert before the Royal Hawaiian Agricultural Society in January, 1852 (Transactions of the Royal Hawaiian Agricultural Society, Vol. I) . . . he states that "the earliest sugar manufacture was in 1802, by a Chinaman, on the Island of Lanai, who came here in one of the vessels trading for sandalwood, bringing with him a stone mill and boilers, and after grinding off one small crop and making it into sugar, went back the next year with his apparatus. . . ."

* Thomas G. Thrum, "Notes on the History of the Sugar Industry of the Hawaii Islands," *Hawaiian Annual,* 1875, pp. 34–42.

Sugar and molasses were produced before the establishment of a mill.

Don Paulo Marin recorded in his journal of making sugar in Honolulu in February, 1819; but no other allusion is made thereto.

Sugar was made in Honolulu about 1823 by Lavinia, an Italian, who had the cane pounded or mashed on huge wooden trays (poi boards) by natives with stone-beaters, collecting the juice and boiling it in a small copper kettle. About this same time Antone Catalina is also claimed by some to have been the founder of the industry by making excellent syrup at Waikapu [a district of Wailuku town], Maui—the site of the present Waikapu mill—and Hungtai . . . is said to have established the first mills at Wailuku. . . .

We must give credit to Messrs. Ladd & Co. for the *bona fide* establishment of sugar manufacture, who in 1835 secured a grant of land at Koloa, Kauai, from the Government, for silk and sugar culture. This seems to have been the first systematic sugar plantation. . . .

Notwithstanding the difficulties under which this plantation . . . was working, it gave impetus to others in various parts of the Islands, for in 1838 there were in operation, and about to be erected, twenty mills by animal power and two by water power.

Previous to 1841, probably 1839, Governor Kuakini of Hawaii had a few fields of cane planted at North Kohala, about 75 or 100 acres in extent, with the expectation of a contract with some foreigner for grinding. [This type of cooperative project is illustrated in Appendix A.]

In 1841 thatched buildings were put up in Iole, Kohala, by the Governor, in pursuance with Aiko,[8] a Chinaman, who had previously followed the sea in some capacity under Capt. Brewer. . . .[9]
Aiko himself followed immediately and put up his mill—upright wooden rollers, 18 inches in diameter, by two and one-half feet high, bound with iron,—and an overshot water wheel for motive power. The planting was done by contract with natives in the old style, i.e. with an *oo,* digging off the grass and making the least bit of a hole possible for the seed. Labor was cheap and paid for in goods. Brown cotton at $1.00 per *pio* ("3 yards") and blue cotton and prints at $1.50 for the same quantity. . . .

The products of the mill were laboriously carted over the hills to Mahukona where they were shipped for Honolulu. The carts were very heavy and the wheels were cross sections of *koa* logs. The wear and tear therefore of oxen and carts over the rocky road were very great. Nevertheless the proprietor was successful in making money and would have remained, but the heir of Governor Kuakini so increased the rents of lands and other charges that he threw the whole thing up in disgust and left for Hilo, where he carried on a plantation with success for many years, and where he now resides.

Before leaving, however, he sold out his plantation to an invalid Chinaman. The latter deceased soon after and the establishment came back upon Aiko's hands and he returned, ground the last crop, and definitely closed up the business in 1849 or 1850.

Up to 1843, Hawaii sugars did not enjoy a favorable reputation abroad, partly from the low grades. . . .

During the season of 1851, the first centrifugal machine was put in operation at the East Maui Plantation.

Scarcity of labor was seriously felt on nearly all the plantations, but more especially on those of Kauai and Maui, and an effort was made to meet the difficulty by the importation of coolie labor from China, in 1852, to work under contract for five years. This for a time gave relief, but did not come up to expectations. . . . Labor was a vexed question in 1851, and it has continued to be so ever since.

Up to 1857 we notice the struggle of this industry to be one of hardships and disappointments. . . .

At this time, the number of plantations had dwindled down to five, consisting of the Koloa and Lihue on Kauai, which were run by water (Lihue having steam as an auxiliary), East Maui and Brewer plantations on Maui, worked by mule power and one on Hawaii near Hilo, by Chinese (Aiko), run by water power.

These were followed during 1857 by two new ones in or near Hilo, one by Samsing & Co., and the other by Utai & Co., Chinese merchants of Honolulu. . . .[10] (See Appendix B for the inventory of a sugar establishment with similar operations.)

ECONOMIC BASIS FOR CONTRACT LABOR

During the first half of the nineteenth century, the market increased for produce grown in Hawaii. Whaling vessels spent much time in island waters and took on heavy supplies of fresh provisions. The California gold rush heightened the demands for sweet and Irish potatoes, corn, wheat, coffee, squash, turnips and other salted vegetables.[11] Sugar and molasses were exported from 1837. Demands for labor increased and neither native labor nor voluntary immigration could solve the phenomenal needs.

The Chinese emigrant trade[12] as practiced along the Pearl River estuary was notoriously bad because of unscrupulous Chinese procurers and Western agents. The ocean passage was characterized by overloading and underfeeding, resulting in deaths, riots, disease. Destinations such as the gold mines of South Africa, the guano fields on the Chincha Islands off Peru, and the plantations of Cuba meant harsh treatment and conditions.[13]

The Chinese migrants to Hawaii fared better than their compatriots shipped to other areas of the world.[14] Concern for the methods of recruiting and transport was expressed by the Hawaiian government and citizens.

Katherine Coman's article describes the conditions that led to use of contract labor in Hawaii.*

The experience of the Americans who undertook to civilize the Hawaiian Islands is peculiar in that they enjoyed seventy-five years of immunity from outside interference. The measures determined upon for the development of the country were their own. There was no colonial office to over-rule the local policy. Every candid observer, however, must concede that there was nothing arbitrary in the methods of the missionaries, the white men who were in the long run most influential in directing the course of legislation in the Sandwich Islands. . . . Within the cycle of a hundred years a primitive agricultural community has been transformed into a highly specialized industrial system in which every capacity of land and people is subsidized for the promotion of a single product [sugar]. . . .

Sugar cane grew luxuriantly on the islands, and a low grade sugar had been manufactured as early as 1823, the cane being crushed between wooden rollers and the juice boiled down in open kettles; but the cultivation of the cane on plantation scale was not undertaken until 1835 [Ladd and Co.]. In this year a mill was erected at Koloa on Kauai, and the industry was fairly inaugurated. By 1838 twenty-two mills were in operation, the windward side of Hawaii and Maui proving to be as well adapted as Kauai to the culture of the cane. It was

* Katherine Coman, *History of Contract Labor in the Hawaiian Islands* (New York: Macmillan, 1903), pp. 485–496.

soon demonstrated that the islands afford almost ideal conditions for the growing of sugar—fertile soil, abundant rainfall, and a climate so equable that the cane can be brought to full maturity and the highest percentage of saccharine matter developed. These natural advantages guarantee the Hawaiian sugar planter to-day a yield three or four times as great as that of Cuba or Louisiana. Disadvantages quite as permanent and inevitable are the distance from the world markets and the scarcity of labor.

The scarcity of labor began to be recognized as a serious handicap to the industrial development of the islands as early as 1850. A law of that year recites: "Whereas, the native population is diminishing" and the "want of labor is severely felt by planters and other agriculturists, the price of provisions being thereby enhanced," and "whereas many natives have emigrated to California and there died in great misery, be it enacted that no native subject of the king may leave these islands without express permission given on proved necessity." The planters soon discovered that the cultivation of sugar on a profitable scale required a very considerable land area and an abundant supply of low grade labor. Every subsequent improvement in the industry, every new application of machinery, has emphasized this dual necessity. Steamplows, irrigation from pumping stations, hauling of the cane by rail, enhanced capacity of the mill—each effort to reduce cost of production involves an increased expenditure by way of fixed capital that is justified only by proportionate increase of the area to be cultivated. Moreover the vicissitudes of a sugar crop require that masses of labor be brought to bear without delay at the given time and place. Cane must be cut when it is ripe or the stalks grow dry and woody. Once cut, the cane must be got to the mill within three days or it sours and is unfit for use. Thousands of dollars may be lost by a delay of a few hours.

By 1850 it was becoming painfully evident that the native population would be quite inadequate to meet this labor demand. The Hawaiians were disinclined to the steady, monotonous labor required in the cane-fields; and, moreover, the race was dying out with startling rapidity. Captain Cook's estimate of the population of the islands in 1779 was 400,000. He was probably deceived by the crowds of people who came to the coasts to see the marvelous visitors, the fire-breathing gods. A more conservative estimate rates the population in the discovery epoch at 300,000. The missionaries in 1823 reckoned the population at 142,000. The first census, taken in 1832, enumerated 130,313. A second census taken four years later, returned but 108,579. A third census, taken in 1850, gave the native population 84,165 and the foreign 1962. The native race has continued to decline in numbers, the census of 1900 enumerating but 29,799 Hawaiians and 7857 part Hawaiians in a total population of 154,000.[15]

FIRST CONTRACT LABORERS ARRIVE, 1852

Captain John Cass, who brought in the first group of contract laborers from China on 3 January 1852, was referred to as "a man of much humanity and good sense."[16] He loaded about 200 men on his British bark *Thetis* and sailed from a south Fukien port, Amoy, on the long trip to Hawaii. "The passage was accomplished with a loss of but four or five men in 55 days." A second trip later in the same year made by Captain Cass increased the Chinese influx to a total of 293 for that year.

The contract of these Chinese laborers was "for five years at $3 per month, in addition to the passage money, food, clothing and house. An advance of $6 each had been made to them in China, to be refunded in small installments out of their wages, after their arrival. In addition to the laborers brought here under contract, there being room in the ship for about twenty more, it was occupied by that number of boys who were readily engaged by residents as house and other servants for five years at $2 a month, their passage advance being paid by their employers," reported the Bureau of Immigration which listed the arrivals for the *Thetis* on 3 January 1852 as 195 men, and 98 men on 2 August 1852.[17]

On his trips, Captain Cass also brought in some new plants— pomelo (edible citrus fruit larger than a grapefruit); wongpee (small, pulpy fruit with flat, green seeds and edible skin); longan (sweet, cherry-sized fruit with thin, hard, smooth skin; related to the lichee); mandarin orange; kumquat; lichee; and the fingered citron, which the Chinese called Buddha's hands.[18]

Before the coming of Chinese contract laborers, there was no special legislation directly applicable to Chinese nor were the laws that covered indentured servitude written especially for this labor system.

Applicable to Chinese as well as to other foreigners in Hawaii was the Alien Law of 1838 in which the government desired that foreigners marrying Hawaiians become naturalized citizens of Hawaii. The first

Chinese recorded as being naturalized was Apana Paké, Kina ("Apana, Chinese from China")[19] in October 1839.[20] Sometimes this wish of the government was interpreted to mean "Christianized." There is an amusing account of how a Chinese wishing to marry a Hawaiian damsel in Hilo was disappointed because he failed in learning Christian dogma.

"An Act for the Government of Master and Servants" passed on 21 June 1850, to protect native Hawaiians working as seamen on whalers gave legal basis for the contract labor system under which the labor markets were tapped first from China, then from Japan, Korea, Southeast Asia and the South Pacific, northern and southern Europe, and even from Russian Siberia. An estimated 46,000 Chinese laborers were to flow in from 1852 to 1898.[21] The Act of 1850 was patterned after the Seaman's Shipping Act of the United States and had some likeness to the apprenticeship laws of the United States.[22] It was applied to the contract labor system because agricultural labor under contract had similarities to the other forms of indentured servitude.

The Chinese migrants to the islands were soon considered a problem for Hawaii by reason of their numbers, the disproportionate male dominance, and their acumen in turning to gainful occupations other than plantation labor.[23] Successive legislation was enacted to limit them to agricultural pursuits upon completion of their contracts and to restrict the number of arrivals per ship.[24] Although some departed, others either renewed their contracts or worked without contracts as day laborers. Others left the plantations to work in rice plantations, vegetable farming, trade, or as domestics.

Regardless of legislation, restrictive or otherwise, the Chinese came to look upon Tan Heung Shan (Sandalwood Mountains) as a land of opportunity. They were not slow to learn new ways and to speak Hawaiian. The Reverend William Speer wrote in 1856, "One of the amusing sights I have seen on the islands has been 'Canton' men and 'Amoy' men resorting to the dialect of the Hawaiians as the only medium of ready communication with each other."[25]

The official view on the importation of contract labor into Hawaii was given by the Bureau of Immigration.*

The Royal Hawaiian Agricultural Society was founded August

* "First Chinese Coolies," *Report of the President of the Bureau of Immigration to the Legislative Assembly, 1886,* I: 4–6.

12th, 1850. . . . The introduction of Coolie labor from China to supply the places of the rapidly decreasing native population, is a question that is agitated among us, and should such a step become necessary, the aid of such an association in accomplishing this object would be of great benefit.

In the beginning of 1851, an attempt was made to procure some Coolies, but was for some reason a failure. The Royal Hawaiian Agricultural Society then took the affair into its own hands. . . .

[On January 3, 1852, Captain Cass] brought the first Coolies ever introduced into the country as laborers.

The experiment thus tried was one of considerable moment to the Islands, and had to encounter neither serious obstacles nor opposition. . . .

Until this time, there had been very few Chinese in the Kingdom, and those of the better class—mostly merchants and shop-keepers.

The arrival of these coolies was hailed with delight by all parties, and the Hon. W. L. Lee, President of the Agricultural Society, in his annual address said: "On the subject of labor, I am happy to say, there is less to fear than formerly. The enterprise set on foot by our Society for procuring laborers from China, has at last, met with success, and much credit is due to Captain Cass for the faithful manner in which he has carried out the experiment of introducing coolies. The Chinese brought here in the 'Thetis' have proved themselves quiet, able and willing men, and I have little doubt, judging from our short experience, that we shall find coolie labor to be far more certain, systematic and economical than that of the natives. . . . The cost of importing coolies is $50 per man, and it has been estimated by those that employ them, that their wages and support amount to a trifle under $7 per month. They are great eaters, but their food, chiefly composed of rice and a little meat, is of the cheapest kind, and to make them profitable, they should never be stinted in their allowance. To all those planters who can afford it, I would say, procure as many laborers as you can, and work them by themselves, as far as possible separate from the natives, and you will find that, if well managed, their example will have a stimulating effect upon the Hawaiian, who is naturally jealous of the coolie and ambitious to outdo him."

Elisha H. Allen [Minister of Finance] in his address to the same body remarks: "The introduction of coolie labor is as yet an experiment, but a very important one. It promises well and its success depends upon the judicious management and comfortable treatment they may receive. It is an entire change in language, manners, dress, modes of living and of doing; and your own good sense will teach you to forbear; and while it requires patience on your part, it can be no less trying to them, untaught as they are. . . . They are industrious, economical, careful, filling a space for which our people are not adapted. . . . They should not be left to the care of indiscreet agents. They will obey one master cheerfully—more they dislike; not differing in this particular from all the rest of the world."

The Polynesian Weekly, published an Aloha editorial on 10 January 1852 to welcome the newcomers and asked local residents to extend their sympathy and compassion:

The subject of cheap labor is one which has for a considerable period engaged the attention of planters here, as an indispensable requisite to successful competition with Manila and China, in the production of sugar and coffee. . . .

The experiment to be thus tried, is one of considerable moment to the islands, and we are glad to see it tested. . . . But their presence here imposes a weighty obligation upon strangers in a strange land, and should excite the sympathy and compassion of those who have it so much in their power to render their life miserable or comparatively happy. We sincerely hope that their introduction here may prove, not only serviceable to the islands, but also to themselves; and they have exchanged want and oppression, for a comfortable home, and the protection of a government and people actuated by Christian principles. . . .

LOCAL CHINESE PETITION FOR FREE IMMIGRATION, 1869

For the twelve years after the first Chinese contract laborers came in 1852, Chinese migrants arrived at the rate of about 34 per year to total 411 for this period.[26] Those who came had been brought in by independent planters or had come by their own means. Hawaii's economy was then in a period of flux. Both sugar and coffee faced problems of market and capital. The monarch, King Kamehameha IV, and advisers were interested in trying the importation of other Pacific islanders to bolster the diminishing Hawaiian race as well as to furnish the labor supply.

The ending of the American Civil War (1861–1865) affected the sugar market favorably. After a decision to seek further Chinese labor, Dr. William Hillebrand as Commissioner of Immigration, went to Hong Kong in 1865. With the help of the Reverend Wilhelm Lobscheid and the Chinese agency Wohang, Hillebrand carefully selected 521 Chinese, including 95 women and 13 children, to come under contract on two vessels, allowing for greater comfort on the passage.[27] The contract with the Wohang Co. is reproduced in Appendix C.

The morality of indentured servitude concerned many in Hawaii who were opposed to slavery and considered the principle of contract labor equally unacceptable. In 1869, there was a series of meetings in Honolulu to discuss the pros and cons of contract labor.

Chinese merchants already settled in Hawaii added their voices to those opposing the system. The following petition was read before one of the meetings.* Enough remarks had been made then as to the desirability of Chinese laborers to offset the remark about Chinese criminals. The Chinese had posed no grave problems as criminals, but there had been instances of vagrancy, rioting among themselves, gambling, and opium smoking.[28] From 1856 to 1880, various laws were introduced to control opium smoking. This vice had begun to infect the native Hawaiians too. An act of 1874 prohibited the importation of opium except for medicinal purposes on permission from the Hawaii Board of Health. Prior to that licensing had been tried.

The Chinese petitioners proposed that laborers be selected by Chinese agents from Hawaii who would understand the language and customs of their own people, that the laborers be given assistance for passage, and have freedom to sign contracts of their choice after arrival. This was considered impractical.

As sugar production increased and labor shortages became acute, Hawaii continued to turn to Chinese labor in spite of public sentiment against it. The desire was still voiced to import a "cognate," assimilable group, but the plantations in the 1870s turned to Chinese agents in Hawaii to try to bring in a better class of laborers. Chulan & Co. and Afong and Achuck,[29] both mentioned in the following petition, agreed to bring in 100 Chinese laborers each, contracted to the Hawaiian government. The former fulfilled its quota at $25 per head

* "Chinese Petition," *Pacific Commercial Advertiser,* Honolulu, 6 November 1869.

Contract Labor System

for men and $30 for women. Afong and Achuck were unable to meet their quota and returned $2,000. Probably Afong and Achuck wanted to concentrate on their own dialectal group in the Heungshan area of the Pearl River delta in south China and so get what they considered to be better selection and control. Also, there was competition among emigration brokers to meet the demands for agricultural labor in other plantation areas. Afong and Achuck did not want to include unsuitable men—the so-called *lup dai tsang* (bottom-of-the-basket oranges).

For the next two years, the government made further agreements with the above Chinese firms to bring in 1,400 more Chinese. The peak in Chinese immigration reached 25,497 between 1875 and 1887, as compiled by the Collector of Customs. See Appendix K for data on arrivals and departures of Chinese.

We, the undersigned, natives of China now resident in Honolulu, feeling with you the great need of labor in the Hawaiian Islands, desire to express the great need with those of you who are opposed to the coolie contract system. We heartily oppose the introduction of coolies here under that system. Some of the Chinese coolies are very bad men and criminals. We know our countrymen better than anyone else; and we believe that a much better class of men for plantation and other kinds of work can be procured from Chinese by some arrangement for the encouragement of free immigration and the payment of wages.

Young Sheong	Chulan & Brother
Afong & Achuck	Alee & Co.
Arsee & Achong	Ahana
Lam Yat	Onchong
Amau	Lo Nyok
Athony	Chung Cho
Awa	Ah Hon
Achong	Achung
Ahoo	Ah Kim
Lo Look	Aseung
Yat Chong	Chee Fui
Tong Kai	Ah Kong

Presented to the Citizens of Honolulu, in Public Meeting assembled at Kaumakapili Church.

FURTHER LEGISLATION ON CONTRACT LABOR

For practical purposes, a good labor contract was meant to be mutually advantageous. It had to attract migration and be profitable to the employer. For the plantations, it was a convenient system to recruit and import cheap labor. To protect the laborer there had to be a written guarantee as to wages, perquisites, length of contract, health and welfare arrangements. For the planter-employer, he had to rely on the written contract to give him a stable, dependable labor force for planting, cutting, milling in the whole plantation system. Appendix D exhibits a labor contract of 1870.

There was the greatest economic value in a human labor force. Expenditure to assist immigration of labor, from 1880 to 1886, was $930,000 from Hawaii's planters and $1,000,000 from government.[30] The contract was such that some return had to be made from the outlay of capital.

To the migrant, it was an opportunity to lift himself out of his village poverty; sometimes the alternate outlook was starvation. Overseas, there was a contract waiting for him which guaranteed employment and a "rice bowl."

As to the predominance of Hakkas among the earlier contract laborers,[31] one may conclude they came from areas near Hong Kong—farmers from Kowloon, New Territories, and the little towns along the Canton-Kowloon Railway built in 1907. They left towns like Shatin, Pukak, Lilong. Most were subsisting on small, meager farms. They had come to live in this coastal area only since the Ch'ien Lung period (1736–1795), after the lifting of the decree that had cleared the coast for 50 *li* inland during the campaigns to suppress Koxinga, the Chinese pirate.[32] Great was the suffering of the people during the forced evacuation. Following their return, the people had not yet recouped their losses enough to become deep-rooted so that they were easily lured by the money to be made overseas. Going abroad meant a chance to make money to send home to the family and hopefully to put aside enough to take home upon completion of the contract. If he chose to stay, it meant living in a land of opportunity as a free man, unless his contract stipulated repatriation. As long as he could continue to help feed his family, he did not feel he was cut off from them by living abroad. This was not the traumatic move of refugees who carried their ancestral tablets with them to start anew. Nor was this the practice to "split" the family (*"fun ga"*) when a branch would move elsewhere and declare itself no longer responsible to those at home.

As to lack of women migrants (one of the reasons given for further restrictive legislation against Chinese), one needs to understand conditions in Chinese villages. If the ablest woman of the family left, there would be no one to take care of those too old or too young to survive. Even today in the Hakka villages in the outlying, or New Territories, areas of Hong Kong, one finds mostly women, children, and old men living on the farm while the able men are abroad or living near their jobs in the cities.[33] Existence was subsistent, in spite of the picturesque scene of women wearing broad-brimmed hats pushing the plow through the heavy soil of rice paddy fields or carrying their loads on hilly paths. The reluctance to migrate with their men was based on survival economics.

Leaving the village as an emigrant to seek a better livelihood in a faraway land was not a joyful departure for the young man nor for his young wife. A Hakka folksong of that period, which I have translated, expresses well the poignancy of separation as the bride calls across the hills, *"Yit jook, yee jook"* ("One admonition, two admonition").

> I beg of you, after you depart, to come back soon,
> Our separation will be only a flash of time;
> I only wish that you would have good fortune,
> In three years you would be home again.
>
> Also, I beg of you that your heart won't change,
> That you keep your heart and mind on taking care
>   of your family;
> Each month or half a month send a letter home,
> In two or three years my wish is to welcome you home.

Another factor to increasing Hawaiian restrictions of Chinese in the late 1880s was that Hawaii had opened up relations with Japan after King Kalakaua's trip. The immigration convention of 1886 allowed Japanese nationals to emigrate to Hawaii. Their presence greatly overshadowed Chinese predominance in the labor market.[34]

The problem now became not the Chinese Question but a greater Oriental Problem.

The makeup of the population continued to vex Hawaii while labor supply problems continued. Many attempts were made by passing corrective legislation that had to be excepted whenever labor shortages became acute. On 28 August 1916 the United Chinese society, through its legal counsel, presented a petition (see Appendix I) before a Congressional hearing to permit the entrance of 28,000 Chinese laborers needed for rice cultivation of 7,090 acres of abandoned rice lands. As late as 1921, there were requests to allow the import of Chinese labor.[35] They were all turned down, of course, by Congress. (After Hawaii was annexed by the United States in 1898, the more severe American laws on Chinese immigration had replaced Hawaiian legislation.)

Official and public sentiment in Hawaii was in favor of a balanced racial mix. Some observers, however, labeled it a "divide and rule" policy of plantation employers. In 1921, there was support for importing additional Chinese labor to balance the greater influx of Japanese immigrants.

Throughout Hawaiian history, there had been a worldwide search for agricultural laborers. The search went to the South Pacific, Asia, Puerto Rico, and Europe. In 1879, J. C. Merritt & Co. of San Francisco offered 1,000 Black laborers, but public opinion was not favorable, and no action was taken. On 2 January 1901, a group of Tennessee Blacks arrived; most were sent to Maui but they did not prove satisfactory. Surplus Russian colonists were offered to Hawaii when Russian expansion plans in Manchuria met a setback in 1905 when Russia was defeated by Japan. On 22 October 1909, some 108 Russian men, 67 women, and 79 children arrived. More came in November to bring the total to 2,056 Russians admitted at a cost of $177,963.16.[36]

The story of Chinese immigration is part of the larger search for labor.*

Special precautions were taken by the passage of various laws between 1872 and 1892 for the protection of all contract laborers,

* H. F. MacNair, *The Chinese Abroad* (Shanghai: The Commercial Press, 1924), pp. 219–220.

Contract Labor System

Chinese and others, in the kingdom of Hawaii. In 1872 a law was passed requiring a contract to be acknowledged before an authorized government officer by both master and servant stating that the contract was clearly understood and a voluntary one. By a law of 1876, the length of a working day, if not already specified in the contract, was declared to be nine hours with additional pay for extra time. A sanitary standard for plantation camps was fixed by a law of 1880; this prescribed the type and repairing of houses, the amount of air space for adults and children, drainage, and sewage. In 1882, it was provided that there should be no extension of the term of labor as punishment for desertion. This was punished by fine and imprisonment only. Those who received ill usage by their masters might apply to the courts where, if the complaint was sustained, the employee was freed from his contract and the master fined. In 1884, a law declared that "every laborer serving under written contract shall be entitled to his full pay under the contract, according to the time he has worked, and no master shall deduct from the wages of any such laborer for lost time, more than the amount of money representing such lost time." Transfers of Chinese contracted employees from one employer to another was allowed after 1892, only with the consent of both laborer and employer. . . .

Opposition to the importation of Chinese laborers began in 1875 and culminated with the restriction and exclusion acts of 1885–1895. By 1888, there were 5,728 Chinese plantation laborers out of a total of 15,578 of all nationalities. A modification of the exclusion laws occurred in 1895 to permit employers to import Chinese laborers provided they would at the same time "introduce European and American agricultural laborers equal in number to one tenth of the Chinese permitted" them within a year after the date of the permit. By 1897, Chinese to the number of 7,364 had been brought in under this arrangement.

CHINESE STORIES FROM GROVE FARM PLANTATION

The following two stories* illustrate the two classes of laborers to Hawaii: free and contract. Kaipu of the first story, who had entered the country as a free laborer and came to work on the plantation

---

* William P. Alexander (as told to Bob Krauss), *Grove Farm Plantation* (Palo Alto: Pacific Books, 1956), pp. 130–131, 166–168; reprinted by permission of the author.

without a contract, was paid daily or monthly wages and given shelter. There were other Chinese in the same category who were attracted to the greener pastures of Hawaii from the gold fields of California or the road building of transcontinental railroads. Some others had fulfilled their contracts in Hawaii and chose to remain on the plantations without renewing contracts. In 1894 there were 165 Chinese men under contracts for all plantations and 2,444 Chinese "day" laborers.[37]

The other story tells of the contract men who came directly from China and signed contracts for three or five years. They passed quarantine at Honolulu, had clean bills of health, and were transported by interisland steamers to the island of Kauai for Grove Farm Plantation. In those days not all ships went to landings; they would stand offshore and let small boats take in men and goods. So, Grove Farm's new men would come splashing ashore.

Chinese laborers were generally housed together in "China Camps."[38] They had their own stores, tailor shops, Chinese Christian churches, fraternal society buildings, Chinese schools for their children, and Chinese cemeteries, either on or off plantation land.

George N. Wilcox[39] in the stories was then manager and also had a lease agreement on Grove Farm Plantation. He had a firm belief in its future and made it into a fine sugar plantation. The tunnel he wanted to build was to connect one section of his large water ditch to the other, through a ridge, to reach a natural source of water supply. Chinese were known to run water uphill in China by treadmill waterwheels. In Hawaii another one of their fantastic deeds was the building of a wagon road around the island of Oahu. This was completed in 1869, by thirteen men working three years under contract, when others thought it impossible, "for rains in winter swept away the work of summers and heavy swamps" on the windward side of the island gave unsteady footing for other attempts. The Chinese dug deep trenches in the swamps and filled them with rocks and gravel over which a firm road was built. The road was seventy-eight miles in length, sixteen to twenty-four feet wide with "new and commodious bridges to span streams."[40]

―――

The tunnel would save almost a week of digging, but the Hawaiians, even Pikau, refused to work in the darkness underground where the spirits of the dead might be lurking. George demanded, begged, cajoled. It was no use. Reluctantly, he put his men to work digging on the other side of the ridge.

Every day that break in his ditch exasperated George a little more. Then it began to worry him. If he couldn't get the tunnel through, the delay could put the whole project behind schedule. When the solution arrived, he did not recognize it. A young, short, chubby Chinese wearing a pigtail rode a mule into camp one day. He dismounted with surprising agility and crossed over to where George was checking the grade on a new section of ditch.

In very bad pidgin the bland little man said, "Come for make *puka* ["hole"]."

"Where you learn dig *puka?*" asked George.

"Californee, Long time me *keiki* ["boy"] come Frisco. Catchum *hana hana* ["work"] railroad. Beeeeeg mountain. Makum *puka* for track inside."

George looked skeptical. The man had told him that as a boy he had gone to California to dig railroad tunnels. "What's your name?"

"Kaipu," the man said.

"You haven't run away from Koloa Plantation, have you?"

The man shook his head firmly. George scratched his chin. The Chinese was the most unlikely looking construction worker he had ever seen, but George couldn't be choosey.

"All right, Kaipu. We'll give you a try."

"Fourteen dolla, please."

"Fourteen dollars! What for?"

"Make *puka!*" said Kaipu.

Pikau grinned at George. "He owes somebody fourteen dollars, Keoki. You pay him now and you'll never see him again."

"Make *puka!*" Kaipu insisted. "Fourteen dolla."

"It's a fair price," said George with a shrug. "Tomorrow I pay. You dig the *puka*."

They shook hands. The next morning at dawn, Kaipu showed up with another Chinese. They worked industriously all day. And the day after, in spite of Pikau's prediction. In two weeks the tunnel was finished. George kept the amiable little Chinese on as a part-time cook and field worker after the Widemanns moved away. The other Chinese remained also. . . .

Out of habit, he checked the bleak November [1870 +] sky for rain as the seven Chinese waded ashore. He wondered if they were as curious about him as he was about them. Almost all of his other workers were local Hawaiians who lived on the island, or itinerant laborers from Honolulu. Kaipu was the exception, and he seemed as Hawaiian as the rest. But with fields to open and additional acres to harvest, George desperately needed more men than he could hire at home. So he had contracted for seven of the Chinese who were flooding into the Islands from that strange land across the sea. These men were not Cantonese. They were bigger, rawboned, with a look of alert competence about them in spite of their ridiculous pigtails.

There were all sorts of theories about these Oriental laborers. Some planters claimed they were excellent workers. Some insisted they were worthless. George had heard that the Chinese coolie was docile, argumentative, adaptable, unadaptable, loyal, untrustworthy. These men, he decided, didn't appear to be any of these things. They just looked confused and a little frightened, the way he'd felt that first day at Punahou. [School established 1841 by missionaries for their children, now privately endowed institution, grades K-12.] The thought cheered him. Maybe he and the Chinese would get along after all. "Kaipu, tell them to get in the ox cart," George told the cook.

The little Cantonese barked an order, and the men climbed into the cart. A mill hand from Koloa Plantation watched in amazement. He laughed uproariously. "Since when are those coolies too good to walk?" he wanted to know.

"Never mind," George answered evenly. "I'll treat my men the way I please."

"You start coddling them, and you'll ruin it for everybody else!"

"Out of my way, Hiiiiiyaaa!"

"Don't say I didn't warn you!" the man shouted after them.

George smarted from the insult all the way across the plain to Kahalehaka Valley. There the men climbed out, looking curiously about the clearing under a mango tree where George had built a wooden house with a thatched roof for them beside the stream.

"Do they pick up your lingo pretty good, Kaipu?" George asked.

The small Chinese nodded. "Sabe ["know," from Portuguese *saber*] plenty!"

"Then you'll be in charge of these men from now on. Is that all right with you?"

"Kaipu boss man?"

Contract Labor System

"That's right, you're the boss. Will you tell them that?"

Kaipu launched into a harangue, pointing first to George, then to himself. The men listened, nodding. They watched George with new interest.

"Now tell them this. I've paid their passage from China plus an advance in wages and agents' fees that come to $154 per man. That's a total of $1,078 paid out in advance before I've got a lick of work out of any of them. They've signed for three years at twelve dollars a month, and I expect each man to earn his money."

Kaipu fired a volley of Chinese at the new men. They listened impassively.

"One more thing," George added, "maybe they've heard about whippings on plantations around here? Well, no man has ever been whipped on Grove Farm. And no man ever will be. That's a promise. No man is forced to work if he's honestly sick. But I expect every man to work as hard as I do. And if anybody has a complaint, bring it straight to me. Tell them that! Then have them start clearing the new field."

Satisfied, George drove back to the house. He had just finished supper that day when the whole troop of Chinese marched into the yard and came to a determined halt in front of the house. His heart sank. He hadn't expected trouble so soon.

"Kaipu, come here," he called as he walked out to the veranda.

One of the workers held a bowl of poi in his hand. He burst into a torrent of language that left George mystified. The men were obviously upset. But George couldn't make out why. Another Chinese snatched the bowl and spooned up some of the purple paste inside with his finger. He took a mouthful, and spat it out in disgust. The whole group began talking and gesticulating. Kaipu finally appeared at the door.

"Can you figure out what's wrong?" George asked. "It looks to me like they got hold of a bad batch of poi."

Kaipu shook his head. "Batch plenty good. Poi plenty bad. Chinamen want rice."

"But that's silly! Everybody I know eats poi."

"In China, no poi," said Kaipu firmly. "Rice!" The cook addressed a few words to the workers in their own tongue. They nodded vehemently. Then, one by one, they took a mouthful of poi and spat it out in violent dislike.

73

George scratched his head. "All right, tell them we'll find some rice tomorrow. And if they like, they can plant their own. How's that?"

Kaipu conveyed the message to the men. They brightened immediately. The Chinese on Grove Farm proved to be very good workers when they were treated with consideration. But from that day on George had a reputation for coddling his men.

PROTESTS AND COMPLAINTS, 1891–1897

The greatest boon to sugar was the Hawaiian Reciprocity Treaty in 1876 by which sugar could be exported to the United States duty free. The United States, in return, received permission to use Pearl Harbor as a naval station. The economy of the Hawaiian kingdom boomed. The need for Chinese labor was greater than ever in the next two decades. In spite of public sentiment against contract labor as such and against immigration of noncognate groups, the industry had no way but to continue indenturing the most amenable labor force then available to insure stable production.

From the Chinese point of view, the migrants were willing to hazard hardships that now were not unknown to them, for there had been enough returnees to tell the story. The Chinese had heard that some had renewed their contracts while others had successfully used the plantation as a stepping-stone to other occupations. Emigration brokers and shipping companies, often unsolicited and unauthorized, rushed in to bring shiploads of eager immigrants.[41] Laborers contracted themselves to plantations upon arrival. At one point, Chinese reached about 20 percent of the total population[42] (see Appendix J). Legislation in 1888 banned further Chinese labor immigration. Other Chinese—students, families, and domestics of merchants—were still eligible. The Foreign Office of the Hawaiian government established a Chinese Bureau (located in the Judiciary Building) to screen applications for entry.

With annexation in 1898, all laws of the United States, including the Chinese Exclusion Acts, became the law of the land. Chinese immigration to Hawaii faced greater restrictions.

Meanwhile, some Chinese laborers voiced their protests against injustices or mistreatments. The Chinese, unlike the Japanese in Hawaii, could not turn to their home government nor any official representative for help.[43] They, in their frustration, would quote that China was like "a pan of loose sand" (*yat poon sarn sa*). A Bureau

Contract Labor System

of Immigration had been formed in 1864 by the Hawaiian government to consist of the Minister of Interior and five other members of the Privy Council. Its records were interspersed with correspondence on protests and complaints. As vast an industry as Hawaii's sugar plantations could not but have instances of human fault and failure in employer-employee relations when the employer not only directed working conditions but was also responsible for the worker on a 24-hour basis, providing housing, food, medical care, and other perquisites. However, the brighter side of the coin was that the Hawaiian government made provisions for appeal within its courts and created the Bureau to scrutinize plantation practices, in addition to regulating immigration.

The following documents were selected to illustrate labor discontent and conflicts.* Luke Aseu (his name in full was Chang, Young Seu—Luke was his Christian name) went to China on a trip and gathered the laborers to help poor farmers migrate to Tan Heung Shan—the land of opportunity and plenty. He was a well-respected Christian worker among the Chinese in Hawaii. When misunderstandings arose, even Aseu received his share of protestations. There was no language nor cultural barrier, but Aseu had to take harsh criticisms from his fellow Chinese whom he helped to migrate to Hawaii. The terms of contract were spelled out (Appendix E) but misunderstandings still arose.

In the last document, names of the *lunas* ("overseers") who mistreated laborers have been deleted for this publication. An earlier case of cruelty was described in the *Polynesian Weekly*, 8 January 1853.

September 14, 1891—In the meantime reports reached me that there was serious trouble among these Chinese laborers in the Kohala District, and threats had been made against Mr. Aseu. On the 26th of August, I addressed a letter to Mr. Aseu asking him to state the origin of the trouble, what had taken place between him and the Chinese, and whether there was any prospect of its being amicably settled. Mr. Aseu replied in person Sept. 5th, having been obliged to leave Kohala and come to Honolulu with his family. He made a long statement to me in connection with the trouble, the origin of which was traced to the laborers objecting strongly to the deduction

* Archives of Hawaii, *Hawaii Board of Immigration Reports to Minister of Interior*, 1882–1898.

of one-fourth from their wages. So many conflicting reports were rife as to this trouble that I wrote to Chas. H. Pulaa, Deputy Sheriff, North Kohala, for information, who furnished a full report of the trouble. A thorough investigation was also made by E. G. Hitchcock, Sheriff of Hawaii by order of the Attorney-General. The laborers after this seemed to settle down somewhat.

Deputy Sheriff Pulaa's report is as follows:

Deputy Sheriff's Office,
North Kohala, Hawaii, September 14th, 1891.

His Excellency,

The President of the Bureau of Immigration,
Honolulu, Oahu.

SIR:

Your favor of the 8th inst., in regard to the trouble between my officers and the Chinese laborers came safely to hand. I have already submitted a report of this trouble to the Marshal's office, and as Your Excellency has requested to be informed in this regard, I beg herewith to make the following statement:

On the evening of the 23rd of August, between the hours of six and seven, a large number of Chinese arrived at L. Aseu's residence, and surrounded his premises and house. As soon as L. Aseu saw this, he asked some natives to assist him. Some twenty or more natives responded and also two policemen. They immediately made preparations to protect the place, which they did to the best of their ability, the Chinamen being there all the time. A little after twelve o'clock that same night, I arrived there and found the natives on guard. Some of the Chinese were asleep, others awake. It appeared as though they were taking turns in watching. I met Mr. Aseu that night, he was in a room with all his family and in a terrible fright. They had no lights. I asked him what caused the Chinese to come to him. He replied, "I don't know but surmise that it is on account of the money deducted from their wages every month." Then I said to him, if that was the case to wait until daylight and I would investigate the matter.

Next morning August 24th, between five and six o'clock, I commenced my investigation. The Chinamen in the meantime had possession of Aseu's house, the verandahs were crowded with them, the natives were outside in the grounds. I instructed my interpreter to ask the Chinamen to come off from the verandah, so that I could go up there, make my explanations and listen to their complaints. They consented to it. In the meantime other Chinese had arrived increasing the number to two hundred and more.

I asked the Chinese their reason for coming to Aseu's. They replied, "We came to Aseu to say that he did not inform us that $5 were to be deducted from our wages every month; what was told us was, that $1.25 was to be deducted for passage money, but now they also deduct $3.75, the balance being insufficient for our needs. Our wages are $15 per month. From this is deducted:

Passage	$1.25
One Fourth	3.75
Employer	.50
	$5.50

The balance from $15 is $9.50 out of which we have to pay for rice $7, tobacco, meat, etc., $2.50, leaving no money to buy clothing and other necessaries."

I immediately informed them that the $3.75 was deducted according to the law of the country, and when the amount of $75 was collected, this deduction would stop. This money was for themselves, provided they did not do anything out of the way, viz., run away, be disobedient or neglect to do their work. In case they desired to return to their own country this Government would hand them the money. In case they ran away, etc., the money will revert to the Government.

Another ground of complaint was, that L. Aseu and the Chinese lunas be arrested for deceiving them; another, that they don't want to work for the haoles but to go and work for Aseu, they don't know the haoles.

I explained to them all that was for their good, and

directed them to go to work for their employers, and further ordered them to leave Aseu's house and premises. Their answer was that they would not go until Aseu fed them with rice. This was a sort of joke of the Chinese on Aseu. I was at that time informed that a gang of Chinese from the Union Mill and Hawi were at the Hawaiian railroad station waiting to see L. Aseu, and they were going to kill him if he had gone by that train.

I again ordered them to leave Aseu's premises in the name of the Queen, four or five times, but they would not do so. I then gave orders to the policemen and the few natives that were about, to drive them away. The Chinese began to move, but how the disturbance that followed commenced, I could not make out. I do not know who started it. The Chinese were seen to pick up rocks and pelt them at the natives. They were running to and fro and the crowd was then mixed together. I mounted my horse and rode to the place requesting the Chinese and the natives to stop, but the Chinese would not mind me, and they commenced to chase and stone me. Seeing the trouble I was in, I let my revolver off four times in the air, and then they stopped chasing me. However they surrounded me, and I was expecting death every moment.

Two Chinese arrived who could speak Hawaiian, and they spared my life, as some of the Chinese were trying to get me off my horse. I called upon the two Chinese who spoke Hawaiian to stop with what they were doing. They would not, unless I consented to arrest Aseu and the Chinese lunas who had deceived them in China and Mahukona, the day they were employed. I gave my consent at once, my wish being that there should be peace and quietness, and that I might be released from them. They still had stones in their hands, and I knew if I tried to escape, the stones would be fired at me, so I took out a piece of an envelope and my pen, and asked them for the names of those parties they wanted arrested. They gave them to me and at once became quiet. I knew the Chinese had the control over us, and they tried their best to get hold of Aseu. My interpreter told me they also wanted to set

Aseu's house on fire. I instructed him to speak to them and tell them they must do nothing of the kind. Two Chinese were hurt on the leg during the fight, either hit by a pole or stone. Another Chinaman had a cut on his thumb, says he was hit by a bullet. Perhaps so, for there were other pistols fired besides mine during the time of the riot. They were fired from L. Aseu's so some one informed me. I heard the firing and at once sent word that it must be stopped. I examined the wound and think the man was hit with a stick.

They then all went to Kapaau, met other Chinese there, increasing their number to three hundred or more. Their employers were there, and every thing was under the direction of Geo. H. Williams, Deputy Sheriff of Hawaii. He gave orders for them to go to work, and that they would be assisted by the plantation owners. Another riot commenced, and orders were given to natives to arrest the Chinese, and 55 were locked up. They were prosecuted for battery on Government officers. A *nolle prosequi* was entered by Deputy Sheriff Williams and that was the end of it. From that time until August 29th, it was said, the Chinese were again ready to attack L. Aseu, they were to turn out with knives, etc. On hearing this, I went round the various plantations with my interpreter and other Chinese, and spoke to them quietly, and from that time they gave up their idea of going to Aseu's. From that time Aseu hid himself, and at last went to Honolulu. I am not very sure, but, that the Chinese will raise another riot.

The above is my full statement.

> I have the honor to be,
> Your obedient servant,
> CHAS. H. PULAA.

The Secretary reported to me that the plantations were not prompt in their returns of the reductions of the monthly wages of the men, and I instructed him to request them to comply with the law, and send in their statements as soon after the end of the month as possible. Though they were repeatedly written to, they refused to send any returns at all, informing me at the same time that they took off the amounts and retained them. At the latter end of September, four of these contract laborers, Chong Chuen, Leo Un, Wong Kim Shew and Ching Ye Meng, had Mr. L. Aseu arrested, and the first named laid the following charge against him: That L. Aseu on board the *Pactolus* when anchored off Mahukona, Island of Hawaii, on the 20th of July, A.D. 1891, did by certain false pretences, and with attempt to defraud, obtain the signature of one Ching Ye Meng to a certain instrument to wit: a labor contract. A similar charge was entered by the other three men. The case was heard before Mr. Justice Dole, on October 9th, 12th, and 14th. On the 16th, His Honor filed his decision which concluded with the following words: "On this question, there is not sufficient evidence to make it probable that a jury would find that the defendant had used false pretences in procuring the execution of the contracts. The defendant is discharged."

On November 5th, another laborer, Chong Chun, brought action against the Kohala Sugar Co., asking to have his labor contract cancelled or amended upon grounds set forth in a complaint. A demurrer was made to the complaint which Mr. Justice Dole overruled. An appeal was entered, and came before the court in banco on February 2nd, 1892. A decision was given on the 26th, of the same month, the court deciding as follows:

"In order to the binding effect of conditions and instructions to be imposed upon immigrants (from countries with which we have no treaty to the contrary) upon which they may be allowed to enter this Kingdom, the immigrants must have knowledge of them before they come to this Kingdom. Subdivision 4 of Section 1 of Chapter 67 of the laws of 1890, held to be unconstitutional."

This subdivision provides for the retention of one-fourth of the laborer's wages to be forwarded to and held by the Board, the deposit to cease when the sum had reached $75 to the credit of any one laborer. It also provides for the Board having the authority to pay the return passage of such person out of such sums so deposited.

December 31, 1897*—During the period 109 Chinese have been returned to China, 173 have deserted and 101 died. Of those returned to China a few had completed their deposit of $36.00. They should

---

* Archives of Hawaii, *Hawaiian Board of Immigration Report of Secretary,* 1879–1899, p. 8.

Contract Labor System

have worked twelve months more but according to the terms of their contracts if a Chinese laborer desires at any time to return to China, during the continuance of his agreement, he shall be released upon the conditions that he refund to his employer a certain portion of the costs of his passage. Several had to be returned on account of sickness, and their passages were either paid by the plantation or friends as their deposit was unsufficient. Of the 173 desertions, 80 were from the Spreckelsville Plantation, Maui. The Hawaiian Commercial & Sugar Co. have two Chinese contractors, Quong Fung and Sam Sing, who each employ large gangs of Chinese laborers. They obtained Foreign Office conditional permits at the end of 1895 as follows: Quong Fung 200, Sam Sing 120. Soon after these laborers arrived in the country, desertions commenced and as the period closes Quong Fung is credited with 46, Sam Sing with 34. There has also been quite a number of desertions from the Paauhau and Hakalau plantations.

Of the deaths all but two were from natural causes. One man was shot and killed at Lihue, Kauai, by a Luna during a riot, while another was practically throttled to death by a Luna at Hakalau, who is now serving a sentence on the reef.

Several plantations have reported a large number of desertions among Japanese laborers, who have gone to the coffee lands.

On April 21, 1897, I visited Lihue Plantation, Kauai, for the purpose of investigating the causes that led up to a riot there, and which resulted in the death of a Chinese contract laborer, and the arrest of fifteen others on a charge of rioting. Mr. Goo Kim, the Chinese Commercial Agent, had previously made a complaint that the Chinese laborers were not treated well at Lihue and requesting an investigation.

I spent two days at Lihue thoroughly enquiring into the matter, and on my return requested that the head luna, Mr. ———, be discharged at once and that Manager ——— be reprimanded and held to strict account for the better treatment of the laborers in the future. This was done and since then no further complaints have come from Lihue. Fifteen ringleaders in the riot were by order of the Court, returned to China. While on Kauai I also visited Hawaiian Sugar Co., Eleele and Koloa plantations.

Olowalu Plantation, Maui was visited on June 9th, 1897, where I investigated certain complaints made by the Chinese contract laborers there, in a letter to Mr. Goo Kim the Chinese Commercial Agent. It was not by any means the first time that complaints had come from Olowalu. The result of my investigation and report was such that no further complaints have come from Olowalu.

In July while at Hilo I visited Hilo Sugar Co., Onomea Sugar Co. and Waiakea Mill Co. Plantations, and I also made an inspection on Pioneer Mill Co. Plantation, Lahaina. Two trips were made to Ewa, one for conference with the Manager, the other to attend at the Court while a Portuguese laborer was tried for desertion.

Without any publicity, I have by correspondence investigated many troubles among the laborers (some of a very trivial nature) on different plantations, and in each case the result has been entirely satisfactory.

Attached to this report will be found two tables giving the number and nationality of all laborers on Hawaiian Sugar Plantations December 31st, 1896, and December 31st, 1897. [These are omitted here but a table of Chinese laborers on sugar plantations will be found in Appendix L.]

> Respectfully Submitted,
> Wray Taylor,
> Secretary Board of Immigration

CONDITIONS OF LABOR IN HAWAII, 1899

The following, although not quoted in entirety, represents the policy and thinking of the sugar employer group.* As stated, the planters were primarily interested in the economics of labor. They were not as concerned with the moral and social elevation of their work force which had been recruited from across the Pacific and even from over the Atlantic.

Free and Contract Labor

When contract laborers are needed from abroad, application is made to the Government for permission to import laborers of the

---

* Wray Taylor, "Labor in Hawaii," U. S., *Consular Reports* No. 620, 5 January 1900, Bureau of Foreign Commerce Department of State, Courtesy of Hawaiian Sugar Planters' Association Library.

Contract Labor System

desired nationality. If permission is granted, the order to recruit them is given to immigration companies, authorized by law, who employ recruiting agents in the localities whence the men are to be drawn. These companies are then responsible for the delivery of the required number of men to the final employer. . . .

Mail steamships, or those specially chartered, bring these immigrants in the steerage and deliver them to the quarantine offices in Honolulu. Here the health regulations require careful examination and fumigation of effects, and here also the laborers are apportioned to their several employers, signing their special contracts before an authorized Hawaiian official assisted by interpreters. . . .[44] [See Appendix F.]

Lodgings

The quarters furnished by the plantation are grouped together in camps, located with reference to convenience to work, and for the most part with regard to drainage and sanitary conditions.

The kind of building varies with the class of labor. European labor has for a family, or for two single men, two rooms in a four-room cottage. Chinese, being single men, are housed in barracks with from six to forty men in a room. . . .

These houses are rough frame buildings, shingle or iron roofed, with 6-foot-wide covered porches extending the whole length. All lately erected buildings are well raised from the ground. Most have walls 8 to 10 feet high from floor to roof plate. The height of ridge pole above this is from 4 to 6 feet. Beneath the roof there is no ceiling, and when divided into rooms, these are all open at the top, with a clear space above from end to end of the building. Cottages have partitions reaching the roof. All walls are whitewashed. Often, the space between the rafters above the roof plate is left open for ventilation.

These quarters furnish only a shelter and a place to rest. Nothing more is attempted. In barracks where many single men are collected, a platform 6 to 8 feet wide and raised 2 feet above the floor runs the length of the building, and each man has about 3 feet in width of space for himself to sleep on. The floor space is common property. Again, tiers of shelves 3 feet wide along the sides of the room, sometimes three or four tiers high, with some slight, low partitions give about 3 by 6 feet for a man. . . .

Food

The staple article of diet among the Orientals, here as elsewhere, is rice. Chinese add pork, or vegetables, and certain Chinese dried, salted, and otherwise preserved food, imported from their own country. . . . Ducks are in favor with them, and tea in quantity is a never-failing beverage.

Employment

Contract laborers are expected to do agricultural and mill work. The former comprises clearing land, cutting wood and brush, grubbing out roots, moving rocks and brush, teaming and plowing, care of horses, ditching, hoeing, irrigating, fertilizing, planting, stripping and cutting cane, loading and unloading cane cars, and any other necessary farming operations. In and about the mill they are occupied in feeding the cane carrier and furnaces, tending any of the mill machinery, handling sugar, loading cars, etc.

From the contract-labor class the carpenter, blacksmith, engineers, and sugar boilers select their assistants, and these, as they learn and become competent, obtain higher wages and often command from $30 to $35 per month. . . .

Actual Conditions

To take a general view of the real state of affairs one must consider that every labor camp is a busy hive. Work is going on, and work is paid for and is what the men come here for.

Now, what are the hardships? The main one is compulsory work under a master. Here the law compels. At home, need held the whip. They expected to work when they came; but the comparison with free men makes compulsion seem a hardship. Generally they are contented. The sewing machine is common in every camp. The tailoress plies her trade. The petty shopkeeper, with his room nearly filled with goods, drives his bargains with his countrymen. All day long the simple laundering is in progress. The mother works with her babe near at hand, while the older children are at school. The happy chatter of women's tongues does not evidence discontent. There is food enough and a place to eat and sleep and live in, equal in comfort to that they have left behind. Conveniences are multiplying. The laborer returns to his home in the evening, and every repression is relaxed. Sunday is a day for rest in most cases. The barber is in

Contract Labor System

demand. Clean clothes are donned, and the pipe and cigarette lend solace. No one would dream of hardship to look in their faces. . . .

But let some real or fancied grievance break the monotony, and the scene changes. A tin pan is beaten noisily to alarm and summon the camp. The motley crowd gathers, generally at night. The leaders harangue their followers, and the mob, most of them ignorant of the real cause, rush off to demand redress or punish the offender.

The grievance is generally an assault by the overseer upon some laborer, a fine considered unjust, a compulsion used to obtain unwilling work, or a privilege withdrawn. The grievance is to the individual, and the crowd make it their own. It is not generally felt very deeply, and in most cases a little tact smooths out everything, and the even flow of events is again attained.

The question may be asked, Why, if they are contented, do they desert? There are several reasons. Natural causes may render the work disagreeable and burdensome, as rain, cold, mud, and overgrowth of weeds. A severe overseer will render all discontented, and the boldest will desert. Accumulated debt is a prolific cause; pure laziness is another. The prospect of getting better wages and the allurement of being with friends entice many away from their contract master.

They came here not to settle and make homes, but in a few years as possible to accumulate sufficient to enable them to return to their native country with capital enough to live on in a manner superior to their own class at home. . . . It may be gathered that, as a rule, plantations furnish all that the law demands, but are not carried on primarily for the purpose of elevating the laborer to the standard of western civilization and morals any more than other corporations. . . .[45]

TWO STORIES FROM KOHALA

An English lad landed at Mahukona in 1896 and was employed at Kohala as field *luna* ("overseer"). Writing of men and events of old Kohala, he lightly touched upon plantation life.*

About 4:30 a.m. would see me out of bed and a little later, with a lantern, gumboots, pommel slicker and broad brimmed hat, on my

---

* Jack Hall, "Kohala's Gay Nineties or the Log of a *Luna*," reprint, in pamphlet form, of articles in *The Honolulu Advertiser,* June 1927, Hawaiian Sugar Planters' Association Library.

way to the camp to turn out my gang. . . . No Filipinos or Koreans in those days. All the laborers were shipped men, that is, they were under contracts, and the gangs were either Chinese or Japanese. Wages were twelve dollars and a half for men and eight dollars for women per month. After turning out the gang it was time for me to go to the stables for my horse, then to the field for the day's work. . . . The work was over at 4 p.m. unless it was *ukupau* ["piece labor, paid by job rather than time"], that is, at the commencement of the day the laborers were given to understand that when each man had finished a certain number of rows of cane he could go home. The Japanese seemed to appreciate this method and would work with vim but the Chinese appeared to prefer a regular steady pace and did not care to hurry and get through earlier. . . .

Dropping in the (Kohala) Club one afternoon, I found a stranger who asked me to join him in a Scotch and soda. He was a nice looking chap with the accent and appearance of a well-educated Englishman. He spoke Chinese fluently and it was a pleasure to listen when he began to speak of China, a country with which he seemed very well acquainted. This gentleman was "Opium Brown," I believe one of the most successful and daring runners of the drug at that time. I do not know if he made any more visits to Hawaii after that. . . .

"Kanaka or *wahine?* I almost got into trouble one day while engaged as *luna*. It was during the planting season and the gang in my charge was gathering the small lengths of cane to be used as seed and placing them in baskets and bags which were then loaded into wagons and conveyed to the landing field. It was a wet day and oilskins were in order. Among the gang, which was composed mostly of Japanese women, I noticed an individual I had not seen before. Rather tall, with broad shoulders, and of generous proportions in other ways, outer clothing consisting of an oilskin jacket and trousers, with a flapping straw hat tied under the chin, the mysterious stranger had me guessing. The manager's brother . . . assured me that it was masculine but, . . . I still had my doubts. Soon after this I noticed a few pieces of seed cane left on the ground and threw them along to where a few of the gang, including the party, were working. They were all bending and, unfortunately, one of the pieces of cane struck the stranger on a prominent portion of the anatomy and I soon discovered that the manager's brother had not given me the facts. It

was a Chinese woman named, as I found later when taking the names in my timebook, "Young Cow," not at all an appropriate cognomen [possibly Ah Yung Kau].

When the piece of cane landed, Young Cow stood upright and, not suspecting that I was the guilty party, picked on a Japanese *wahine* working a few yards behind her. The ensuing conversation between the two sounded like a jazz orchestra. I can remember something like this, *Peheoe* ["Why?"] you *kai tai* ["bastard," in Chinese], you *hana hana* ["work"] all same a little more *hana, maké* ["die"] you," this from Young Cow, to which the Nipponese lady, astonished at this attack, replied something like this, "Wasser matta you, blankety blank *baka tari* ["crazy" in Japanese slang from combining two ideographs, horse and deer—a "crazy" or impossible mating] you, *peheoe* you speak all same!" Had the deeply insulted Young Cow actually resorted to violence, of course, I should have interfered and explained that I was the unwitting offender but, as their warfare was only of words, I thought it unnecessary to confess.

IV. Economic and Social Development

CHINESE RESIDENTS BEFORE 1852

There were few Chinese living in the Hawaiian Islands before the arrival of contract laborers in 1852. About seventy-one persons from China were found living in the islands at various times between 1794 and 1852. There were merchants, shopkeepers, sugar masters, and a few domestics.

A Chinese bakery was seen in 1841 by a visiting Yale professor of science.[1] He wrote, "A Bakery has been established here by 'Sam and Mow,' bakers from Canton,[2] where bread, cakes and pies are manufactured in every variety and of excellent quality. Their advertisement:

> Good people all come and buy
> Of Sam and Mow good cake and pie,
> Bread hard or soft, for land or sea
> 'Celestial' made; come buy of we.

John Papa Ii (1800–1870) wrote of an earlier scene, "In the vicinity of the customs house at the beach was a house for the first Chinese ever seen here. There were two or three of them and they prepared food for the captains of the ships which took sandalwood to China. Because the faces of these people were unusual and their speech—which is not commonly heard—was strange, a great number of persons went to look at them."[3]

Even before the Great Mahele of 1848[4] (division of lands between king and chiefs) and the subsequent system of land tenure, some foreigners were owning and leasing land. In 1843, when the British occupied the Hawaiian Islands for a short period, those property owners were asked to register their land claims with a British com-

Economic and Social Development

mission. Copies of such claims are in the Archives of Hawaii. At that time, there were thirteen pieces of property claimed by Chinese, including holdings on various islands.

Three Chinese stores had been established in the busy port of Honolulu by 1845: Hungtai, Samsing Co., and Tyhune. Hungtai Store (major partners Chun Hung or Ahung and Atai) was in a building called the Pagoda,[5] probably built by American businessman William French, who in 1835 brought Chinese from China to operate a sugar mill at Waimea, Kauai. The store sold American and such China goods as porcelains, nankeens, silks (sarsnets and *senshaws*), velvet slippers, folding fans, grasscloth jackets, tea, China mattings and more.[6] At times, American businessmen used Hungtai Store for meetings. The store building was two-storied and the family of Chun Ahung lived upstairs. Some of the employees were cousins of Ahung who lived on the premises, too.

In 1845 Sam Sing Co. occupied a store under lease at King Street in what was formerly the White Swan Public House.[7] This company also had a retail store on Maui.

Tyhune Store sold liquor wholesale as well as other goods. The store was at Nuuanu and Hotel streets. Tyhoon negotiated a chattel mortgage for $16,060 in 1846, a large amount for those days, for some undetermined purpose.[8] He also had a store at Lahaina, Maui, under the management of his brother.

Hawaii Bureau of Conveyances' records show many business transactions involving Chinese at this time. For example, Ah Sing (Hu, Pok-Sing)[9] purchased the *ahupuaa* ("a land division marked from crest of valley fanning out to sea, inclusive of entire valley floor and offshore fish ponds"[10]) of 3,000 plus acres of Kahana Valley, on the island of Oahu, 13 May 1857, for $2,500. Kahana Valley is of historic significance in Hawaiian history and has been designated for preservation in its natural state as a state park.

A number of Chinese were brought to Hawaii in the first part of the nineteenth century as sugar masters because of their technical skills in sugar manufacture.[11] They became naturalized citizens and married Hawaiians. Some prominent families of Hawaii can trace their lineages to them. The Chinese sugarmen and businessmen were sentimentally attached to their families and to the Islands. The will of Aiina (Chee Inn as he signed in Chinese), who was in sugar but called himself a carpenter,[12] is a reflection of the sentiments of these men toward Hawaii.*

Piihonua, Hilo
June 9, 1846

I, Aiina, do hereby bequeath to you Kamokai and Mikaele my sons and to your assigns, my House Lot, including all land in House Lot subject however to the will of Kamehameha III and his heirs. All my own property I leave to you my sons. I wish you two to live on said place under the King of the Hawaiian Islands[13] as I have lived a Hawaiian Subject.

In witness hereof I hereby affix my name.

his
Chinese   x   Carpenter
mark

Witnesses:
Wm. P. Leleiohoku
L. K. Halai
Kui
J. W. Kaauwaepaa
Kanaina
L. M. Puuloa

CHINESE BALL FOR KING KAMEHAMEHA IV, 1856

In 1856 Chun Afong and other Chinese merchants gave a ball in honor of King Kamehameha IV. The Chinese hosts practiced quadrilles so they could join in the dancing. They persuaded four Caucasian men, dressed in Mandarin costumes, to assist with the hospitality. They were: Edward "Weong Chong" Hoffman, Barnum "Chong Fong" Field, Gustav "Ming Ching" Reiners, and C. C. "Weong Kong" Waterman.

The celestial evening turned out to be a social success, and the Chinese merchants enjoyed another event on 27 June 1861 at a *soirée dansante* given by British Consul General William L. Green for Lady Franklin, widow of Sir John Franklin, Arctic explorer. The *Pacific Commercial Advertiser* reported, "We noticed a striking and char-

---

* Foreign Office & Executive File, 1846, June 1–10 Aiina (Chinese carpenter), Will of (Archives of Hawaii).

Economic and Social Development

acteristic feature of our polyglot society, . . . namely, the presence of our leading Chinese merchants, than whom His Majesty does not possess more faithful and devoted subjects, as honored guests. Among the most distinguished and well known of these gentlemen were Messrs. Ahee, Chunghoon, Asing and Atak."[14]

But that first Chinese Ball of 1856 was unmatched for its gaiety and brilliance.*

November 13th, 1856, the Chinese merchants of Honolulu and Lahaina combined, gave a grand ball to their Majesties the King and Queen (Kamehameha IV and Emma) in honor of their recent marriage. It took place in the court house, and was pronounced the most splendid affair of the kind ever seen in Honolulu. It cost the Chinese the sum of $3,700. The names of the committee of arrangements were: Asing, Yung Sheong, C. P. Samsing, Utai and Ahee, Achu and Afong. The opening quadrille was thus made up: Her Majesty the Queen and Mr. Yung Sheong; the King and Mrs. Gregg; Princess Kaahumanu and Mons. Perin; Prince Kamehameha and Mrs. C. R. Bishop; Mr. Wyllie and Miss Hamlin; Captain Harvey, R. N., and Mrs. Anthon; Captain Gisolme, French navy, and Mrs. Henry Rhodes; Mr. Afong and Mrs. W. C. Parke; Mr. Ahee and Mrs. Cody; Mr. Gee Woo and Mrs. Aldrich.

Whenever the Chinese undertake anything of this sort there is nothing mean or stinted in the way of expenditure, and this first and best Chinese ball was gotten up in lavish style. The pastry and sweet-meats provided were something wonderful in variety and quantity. Two of the items for supper were six whole sheep roasted, and 150 chickens. The affair was the talk of the town for a month after.

RICE INDUSTRY, 1857–1929

Rice was a major agricultural crop in Hawaii that owed much to the efforts of the Chinese although its cultivation was not started by them. The Chinese soon became owners and employers as well as the principal source of labor for rice production. At the height of production in 1890 as much as 10,579,000 pounds of rice were exported. More than 5,000 Chinese were directly or indirectly engaged in the industry.[15] Severe competition from the cheap rice grown by the planters of California, Texas, and Louisiana, with their labor-saving

---

* "Chinese Ball," *The Hawaiian Annual,* 1931, pp. 36–37.

equipment, led to the doom of the Hawaiian industry. By 1929 there were only three Chinese rice mills remaining in Honolulu and three others on Kauai at Hanapepe, Hanalei, and Kapaa. Today, there are none.

Like other Chinese who migrated overseas, rice planters thought of themselves as *wah kiu,* or Chinese sojourners. They came to make money and then to return to their homeland with higher social and economic status. They did not come to stay permanently. This explains much of their early social and political behavior—the tendency to stay close together in segregated plantation camps and to form little Chinatowns. They left their families in the home country, thus creating a wide disproportion of adult males. They showed tolerance for temporary discomforts and discrimination and made little effort to participate in community affairs.

Professor John W. Coulter and his student Chee-Kwon Chun[16] have described vividly the working and living conditions on rice plantations.*

In 1858 Holstein, horticulturist for the Royal Hawaiian Agricultural Society, planted rice in a small plot in the Society's garden and raised a crop. . . .

In 1860 Holstein procured from South Carolina two pounds of seed of the variety of rice grown there, raised a crop successfully and distributed some of the harvested grain for seed for the new crop. In the autumn of 1861 a number of Hawaiians and foreigners were raising or preparing to plant the cereal.

In the summer of 1862 rice was harvested in scattered areas on Oahu. The paddy was packed in mat bags which natives took to Honolulu, slung across the backs of horses and mules. It was purchased by foreign brokers who exported it to San Francisco. . . .

The importation of Chinese as contract laborers for sugar cane plantations gave an impetus to the development of the rice industry. . . .

By 1876 there was still a considerable amount of former taro land available for rice farming. The great demand for rice land brought disused taro patches into requisition—especially because [of] water rights attached to them. Such a circumstance made it very difficult

* John W. Coulter and Chee Kwon Chun, *Chinese Rice Farmers in Hawaii,* University of Hawaii Research Bulletin no. 16 (March 1937), pp. 9–22, 35–51.

later on to mark exactly the boundaries between *kuleana*s (property right to a small, individual landholding, presumably to furnish the food supply for a Hawaiian family) and gave rise to legal troubles in courts.

As the demand for rice continued, it became profitable to bring into use land hitherto unused. The land most easily rendered fit for rice cultivation was swamp or marsh land of which there was a large amount in the islands. Most of such land was near sea level—undrained areas at the mouths of streams: lowlands, which could be reclaimed without great expense. Salt marshes at Mana, Kauai, were turned into rice fields. At Waialua on Oahu, about three hundred acres of swamp land were reclaimed for rice farming. Similarly at Punaluu and Kailua on Oahu, and in many other districts in the islands, lands hitherto unused became fields of waving grain.

The discovery and practicability of using artesian water for rice farming made possible the utilization of land for that industry which could not be irrigated profitably by any other method. In February 1883 there were some 30 artesian wells on Oahu. The drilling of artesian wells caused unbounded interest among the Chinese, who sought expansion of rice farming by every practicable means, but who foresaw its restriction when all the irrigable land was brought under cultivation. Lane McCandless, a very successful well driller, one of three brothers similarly employed, was popularly named by them *Sui Chiang Lane* or "Well-Water Lane". . . .[17]

The primary market for both husked rice and paddy raised in all parts of the Hawaiian islands was in Honolulu. The number of Chinese in the islands created a large home demand.

In 1880 the home market was made more secure by an increase in the duty on rice imported into Hawaii to 1 1/2 cents on paddy and 2 1/2 cents on hulled rice. It resulted in further checking the importation of foreign rice and giving an immense impetus to the home product.

Rice from Punaluu, Kaalaea, Laie and other parts of Oahu distant from Honolulu was shipped in early days on sail boats and later on steamboats. Rice harvests inaugurated a period of special activity for island ships. The shore near some plantations could not be touched by those boats because of reefs and shallow water. In such circumstances, the rice was taken off shore in row boats, from which it was transferred to the larger vessels. . . .

The foreign market for rice was enlarged by the increasing number of Chinese in California, and by the diminution of rice farming in the Southern States owing to the Civil War. In 1860 the number of Chinese in California was 34,933; in 1870 their number was 43,910; and in 1880, 75,132. . . .

The foreign market was further increased by a reciprocity treaty with the United States in 1876, by which sugar and other commodities including rice were admitted into the United States free of customs duties. The treaty by increasing the demand for laborers gave Chinese immigration to the islands a great impetus. . . .

Other factors which contributed to the success of rice farming in Hawaii were ready ways of financing the industry and the cooperative nature of the Chinese.

Much of the money to promote rice farming was advanced by companies who played the part of entrepreneurs, organizers, and financiers. Among them Chulan and Company played a preeminent role. Other companies and individuals, both Chinese and American, also helped.

Among American financiers the firm of J. A. Hopper and Son (called by the Chinese, "Happa"), was outstanding.

In the early '80's, Hopper and Son were the largest rice millers and dealers in Hawaii. At that time they milled and sold about 60,000 bags of rice a year. Their peak year was 1888, when they milled and sold 94,000 bags of rice. They had a steam rice mill in Honolulu—a three-story brick building, the largest mill in the islands—and large warehouses for storing the grain.[18]

Some small farmers financed their way from savings which they accumulated by thrift and farming ability; others were helped by friends and relatives; a considerable number borrowed money from local grocery stores. That type of borrowing was common and was the chief means whereby capital was available to support small planters. Such loans ordinarily were not secured by a lien on the crop or even a note, but were made merely on the basis of confidence and trustworthiness. . . .

At planting and harvesting times, when a considerable number of extra laborers were needed, laborers for plantations on Oahu were generally recruited in Honolulu, and for plantations and farms on other islands at a labor market on each island; for example, at Lihue on Kauai, and at Hilo on Hawaii. However, even from those islands plantation managers came to Honolulu to get laborers.

During the height of the industry the wage level on big plantations was about twelve dollars a month and bed and board. However, there was no system generally followed of paying at the end of the week or month or at the end of a series of months, except for temporary extra labor taken on at the peak of the season. Permanent workers demanded small sums from time to time for spending money or to mail back to relatives in China. Their monthly wages, less the small deductions, accumulated in charge of the managers year in and year out until for some reason they decided to quit their jobs or were about to return to China. Just before each Chinese New Year a statement of his account was made out for a laborer.

Many Chinese farmers went back to China after accumulating two hundred or three hundred dollars. However, it was not unusual to find a laborer homeward bound with $1,000. Some, after a stay in their native land, returned to Hawaii, earned more money and again went home. Others took trips to China every two or three years, going back five or six times before their final return to their homeland.

The Chinese farm laborers in general did not look upon their part in the rice industry in Hawaii as something permanent. They wanted to earn as much money as they could as quickly as possible and return to their native land, either to invest or to spend it. . . .

TABLE III[19]

Rice Farming Districts on Oahu, 1892

	Acres		Acres
Aiea and Kalauao	76	Mokuleia and vicinity	738
Halawa	117	Palama	200
Hauula	25	Palolo	102
Heeia and Kaneohe	200	Punaluu and vicinity	300
Honouliuli, etc.	147	Waialae	32
Kaalaea and Kahaluu	300	Waialua	180
Kahuku	50	Waiau, Manana and Waiawa	262
Kailua and Waimanalo	400	Waikane and vicinity	200
Kalihi and Moanalua	150	Waikele and Waipio	333
Kewalo and vicinity	75	Waikiki	542
Laie	45	Waimalu	135
		Other places	50
			4,659

TABLE IV
Rice Farming Districts on Kauai, 1892*

	Acres		Acres
Anahola and vicinity	150	Kapaa	45
Hanalei and Waioli	750	Kilauea and vicinity	55
Hanamaulu	60	Lawai	70
Hanapepe	145	Lihue	50
Huleia	170	Wailua	200
Kalihi-kai	70	Waimea	80
Kalihi-wai	50	Waipa and Wainiha	160
			2,055

* Mana, a large rice-producing area, was not included here.—Ed.

TABLE V
Rice Farming Districts on Maui, 1892

	Acres
Honokowai	25
Keanae and Wailua	75
Waihee to Waikapu	150
	250

TABLE VI
Rice Farming Districts on Hawaii, 1892

	Acres
Waimanu	85
Waipio	200
Pololu	72
	357

Total—7,321

After Hawaii was annexed by the United States the circumstances which made rice farming profitable changed. The supply of cheap Chinese labor was cut off, the market in Hawaii for Hawaiian rice was greatly curtailed, and that in San Francisco was filled from elsewhere. . . .

Economic and Social Development

In the pioneer days of rice farming and until after the industry reached its height, as already intimated, nearly all the immigrant Chinese were bachelors. A few of them were married men who had left their wives and children at home. . . . [Some] husbands sent for their wives and families. They arrived in Honolulu by steamer and, if the destination was on another island, they got there by an interisland boat. Nearly two-thirds of the rice farmers were on Oahu and the journey from Honolulu to the rice plantations or farms on that island was generally made overland.

Most of the immigrant wives had bound feet, so walking was out of the question. The most practicable means of reaching the rice districts was on horseback, though these ladies from the Far East had never been seated on such animals. A dirt road to the top of the Pali was traversed in a wagon coach and the horseback ride began at the bottom. The trail down the cliff was too steep to negotiate on a [coach or] horse and the women had to get down some other way. It was customary for the women to wear two or three pairs of trousers and make the descent assisted by kindly Hawaiian women delegated to such responsibility by the husbands of the new arrivals. . . . At the foot of the cliff waited the horses on which the women were to ride, led by Hawaiians or by Chinese laborers.

Young bachelor laborers on rice plantations and farms obtained Chinese wives in three ways. Some went home and brought brides back with them. Many were married *in absentia* to girls in China whom they had never seen, and then the newly wedded wives came out to join their husbands. Such marriages were arranged by friends of the brides and grooms. . . .

The presence of women and children in rice farming areas created a more wholesome atmosphere than before. There appeared more stability, since normal family life was an incentive to permanent settlement. . . .

Women spent part of their time sewing working clothes for their husbands and other laborers. Such apparel was very simply constructed, in part from fertilizer sacks, rice sacks, or flour bags obtained in Honolulu. Some women earned small sums of money by becoming men's and women's dressmakers.

The celebration of New Year's, Chinese Decoration Day, and other social and religious events in the rice farming colonies was enhanced by the presence of women and children. When a rice planter called on his friend's family at New Year's, he was sure to give in little red paper packages presents of money to the children. If the children did not appear he left the gifts for them with their mother. Boys ably assisted in exploding firecrackers as the occasion demanded.

When the problem of educating children appeared, a literate laborer was hired by a group of parents as schoolmaster for part or full time. Generally he was the man who wrote the letters to relatives and friends of the laborers in China, and who helped the rice planters when contracts had to be signed or other documents drawn up. Instruction was given exclusively in Chinese. When village clubs or societies were formed they arranged for the education of the Chinese children. . . .

Many rice farmers rented their paddy fields from native holders of *kuleana*s and had frequent intercourse with them regarding payments and leases.

Rice farmers had many contacts with Hawaiians in connection with getting regular supplies of fish. Fishing was a common occupation of the natives and they sold or bartered large parts of their catches to the immigrants. They were frequently seen with sacks of fish on pack horses going from the shore up the valleys where they disposed of their loads to the Chinese.

Some Chinese who spoke different dialects found the Hawaiian language the most practicable means of communication between themselves. . . .

Between Hawaiian landlords and Chinese tenants relations were specially cordial. . . .

During harvesting seasons—days of many working hours—there were five meals a day. However, those included two light refreshments served in the fields, one in mid-morning and the other in mid-afternoon. During both planting and harvesting seasons there developed the practice of having big dinners with liquor to drink on Wednesdays and Fridays. . . .

Chinese in each rice district formed a community and social life centered in a small assemblage of houses, including the "village" store. People in some rice farming districts were neighbors and friends in China before coming to the Hawaiian islands. Some plantation managers employed as far as they could men from the same village in China. Social solidarity was enhanced by isolation. Life in a Chinese rice district in Hawaii was in many ways similar to life in China.

Economic and Social Development

The center of village life was the store, a one or two-story frame building with five or six rooms. Adjoining the store there was generally an inn or hotel where travellers and visitors stayed. Also there were generally a few Chinese farm homes from which the lessees of farms went out to work them. . . .

Especially on Sundays was the store a social center. On that "day off," a day of rest adopted by the Chinese in Hawaii from the Occidental calendar, people came dressed in their Sunday clothes, purchased candy or sweetmeats, opened their packages in the store, and shared the delicacies with friends. There was an atmosphere of gayety, and, among younger men, something of hilarity.

A room at the back of the store was used almost exclusively for playing cards. On Sundays and in the evenings several games of *Tin Gau* [Chinese dominoes] were generally going on at the same time. Other card games commonly played were *Sup Dung Hu* and *Dou Sup Chai*. Throughout all of Sunday and sometimes throughout an entire night one could hear the clicking and hustling of cards. Usually several non-players stood or sat about to watch those participating in the games. Late in the evening or on the following morning a laborer might be heard saying, "Mr. So-and-so won so much, but I had no luck and lost all the time," or vice versa.

Near the village store there was generally a house devoted entirely to gambling, and many plantation laborers lost their earnings in that way. Rice planters did not have to go to the gambling house to play the very popular lottery, *Chee Fa*. They bought "chances" from solicitors who visited the rice fields from day to day, and which were turned over to the clerk in charge of the gambling house. When the tickets were drawn the solicitor took the winnings to the lucky laborers in the fields. Large companies made daily drawings on tickets purchased by workmen's wages.

The week's work on a rice plantation ended about the middle of Saturday afternoon. As soon as work was over many rice planters on Oahu, within riding distance of Honolulu, got on horses and rode to town to see Chinese shows, provided by actors from China. Others spent Saturday evening lounging in the plantation mess hall listening to a din of musical talent by the plantation orchestra. Gongs, drums, cymbals, flutes, and Chinese violins, instruments common in China, furnished entertainment. . . .

A few literate Chinese spent some of their leisure hours reading ancient Chinese literature, legends and novels; some read aloud for fellow workers in a singsong monologue. . . .

A considerable number of the Chinese spent their time off smoking opium. They kept little opium lamps lighted near their beds and lay stretched out, filling their long pipes and lighting them at regular intervals. When friends called they also enjoyed the drug and smoked far into the night. Many Chinese laborers squandered their wages on the drug, and not a few incurred heavy debts to obtain money to indulge in the vicious habit. Addicts demanded their wages weekly and did not keep the money long. . . .

One [person] was recognized as the headman of the village. He was generally the storekeeper or the manager or financier of a plantation, and usually known also for connections with wealthy and influential people in Honolulu. He was arbiter in disputes between Chinese in the rice colony. An injured party reported his alleged grievances to the headman, who took immediate steps to get in touch with the offender and to bring the persons involved together to settle the affair with honor and justice to both. Usually the honor of the parties involved was appealed to and they were made to see the folly of quarreling, especially in a strange country where they were working hard for a livelihood. Often friends of the participants in a dispute remonstrated with those involved and urged them to prevent trouble and help keep peace in the community.

On a judgment from the headman a small compensation was not infrequently made by an offender to the plaintiff, depending on the merit of the case. Minor disputes over water rights were settled by the headman, perhaps with the help of another arbitrator. Important conflicts over water rights, however, went through legal battles in public courts in Honolulu. . . .

In large rice farming areas where there were a considerable number of wealthy planters, a Chinese club or society was formed and a commodious club house was built. Those who could afford it contributed sums of money towards the construction of the club house and others contributed labor during their time off from work in the fields.

The society was governed by a small group of officers or leaders who performed duties some of which were similar to those of village headmen in that the adjudication of local affairs was under their supervision. The club also protected its members from injustices by

Economic and Social Development

Caucasians and Hawaiians and sometimes sought judgments and recompense on their behalf from the courts.

Matters pertaining to the interest and welfare of the community at large were relegated to supervision and action at regular meetings of the organization. Such societies undertook the responsibility of looking after aged and indigent poor, and aided their members in illness or other misfortune. Sometimes, through their agency, funds were raised to send old and ailing Chinese back to China. Chinese charitable societies were formed in all parts of the Hawaiian islands where Chinese lived, and they were well known for their attention to cases of distress and grief among the immigrants to the new country. . . .

BUBONIC PLAGUE AND THE CHINATOWN FIRE, 1900

On 12 December 1899, a death in Chinatown was diagnosed to have been caused by the bubonic plague. The Board of Health chose fire as the most thorough and expeditious method to control the plague. A sanitary fire got out of control when a change of wind carried blazing embers to the dry timbers of closely packed buildings.

Thus, in the Great Chinatown Fire of 20 January 1900, thirty-eight acres were heavily damaged, and 4,000 inhabitants were rendered homeless. To government authorities, it was a fire that became uncontrollable because of the sudden change of wind. The inhabitants of the area, who were principally Chinese, Japanese, and Hawaiian, were not convinced that this was an accident. The use of guards and volunteers from outside Chinatown to cordon off the burning area added resentment. Even today, when one talks with members of the older generation whose families lost their belongings and went through quarantine and fumigation, one learns that it was an emotionally scarring experience for people who found it difficult to hold the authorities blameless.[20]

The human aspects of the fire were described in an article entitled "A Great and Sore Disaster" in the *Friend,* February 1900, p. 3.

> By the unexpected conflagration of Chinatown, nearly 4,500 persons were driven hastily into the street from their burning dwellings. It was a distressful and panic-stricken mass of humanity. This feature of the great disaster far exceeded every other. . . . To a great extent, these crowds were in a state of panic, as well as of anger at the whites,

who, as they believed, had deliberately burned them out. In their fright they had saved little of their belongings from flames which so rapidly swept down upon them. . . . Wives were often separated from their husbands and children from parents, and wailing in distress. . . . Several hundred citizens were at once armed with improvised clubs such as pick handles, to assist the military and police. Forming in lines along the streets, the frightened crowds were driven between the brandished clubs, but without a blow struck, to the large Kawaiahao Church yard, a distance of three-fifths of a mile.

The Board of Health applied the same rules and methods to all areas in fighting the plague. The *Friend* (February 1900), p. 4, reported the death of a Mrs. Boardman from plague. She was living in Manoa, one of the best residential sections of Honolulu. She was forty-six years old, a long-time resident, and an employee of Jordan's large dry goods store downtown. The *Friend* reported, "Mr. Boardman merits the deepest sympathy as deprived at once of wife and home. His house has been burned, with the whole of the furniture, and Mrs. B's rare collection of curios. This case illustrates the determined and, we trust, successful effort to abate the scourge which has invaded our city."

Severe measures were taken to prevent the plague from spreading to neighbor islands. Dr. Clifford B. Wood gave an account of six deaths in February 1900 in Kahului on the island of Maui, "We burned the whole row of shanties and that ended Kahului's trouble." He also reported one case in Hilo, island of Hawaii, in Serrao's Store. "We salvaged the goods and burned the store and that settled that."[21]

The Archives of Hawaii has a volume full of court records of the Fire Claims Commission (see Appendix H). Oriental businessmen asked for more than $3,000,000. They were awarded about $1,500,000 because of the government's limited funds.[22]

Immediately after the fire, Chinese throughout the islands rallied to send over $20,000 to help distressed Honolulu residents. C. K. Chow (Chun Kam-Chow) on Kauai collected relief funds for which he received an Order of the Sixth Rank from Peking.[23] By this time, the Chinese government had become increasingly concerned for the Chinese abroad. After the annexation of Hawaii by the United States

Economic and Social Development

in 1898, China sent Yang Wei-pin, who arrived 12 October 1898, on the S. S. *Peking,* to be Chinese consul. He was said to have been instrumental in leading some of the Chinese to safety during the height of the fire.

A well-researched article written by a university student is worthwhile reading for Chinese and others who remember hearing bits and pieces of information about the holocaust.* Ms. Iwamoto concludes with a hopeful note that Honolulu suffered much and learned much from the plague and fire, and that these lessons were applied to create a new and better city. Yet today, seventy years later, Chinatown has so deteriorated that it faces another mass reconstruction and renewal program.[24]

The Black Death—that ancient scourge of mankind—seems only a faint echo from the past; a medieval horror, a banished specter that haunted an untaught and unwashed era. But not so: Within the memory of living men, Honolulu, the official capital of Paradise, blanched before the threat of bubonic plague. It was on December 12, 1899, that the disease was announced after a special Board of Health meeting called to discuss the death of the first plague victim, You Chong, a Chinese bookkeeper employed by Wing Wo Tai on Nuuanu Avenue. At nine o'clock the night before, Dr. G. H. Herbert of the Board of Medical Examiners had examined him upon the request of the attending physician, Dr. Sun Chin. The patient, who had a high temperature and a suspicious swelling in the groin, had been ill for three days. He died at five the next morning. An autopsy was performed by Dr. W. Hoffman, a government physician, in the presence of Dr. Herbert; Dr. F. R. Day, the port physician; Dr. Carmichael, the representative of the U. S. Marine Hospital Service; and Dr. Sun Chin. The diagnosis: bubonic plague.

At the special meeting the Board of Health authorized its president, Attorney-General Henry E. Cooper, to build a crematory on Quarantine Island and to cremate the bodies of all plague victims. He was also directed to quarantine all people living in houses where the plague had occurred. Because the disease had broken out in the Asiatic quarter, the Board ruled that no Chinese or Japanese could leave

* Lana Iwamoto, "The Plague and Fire of 1899–1900 in Honolulu," *Hawaiian Historical Review* (Honolulu: Hawaiian Historical Society, 1969), pp. 122–141; reprinted by kind permission of the author as is the map on p. 104.

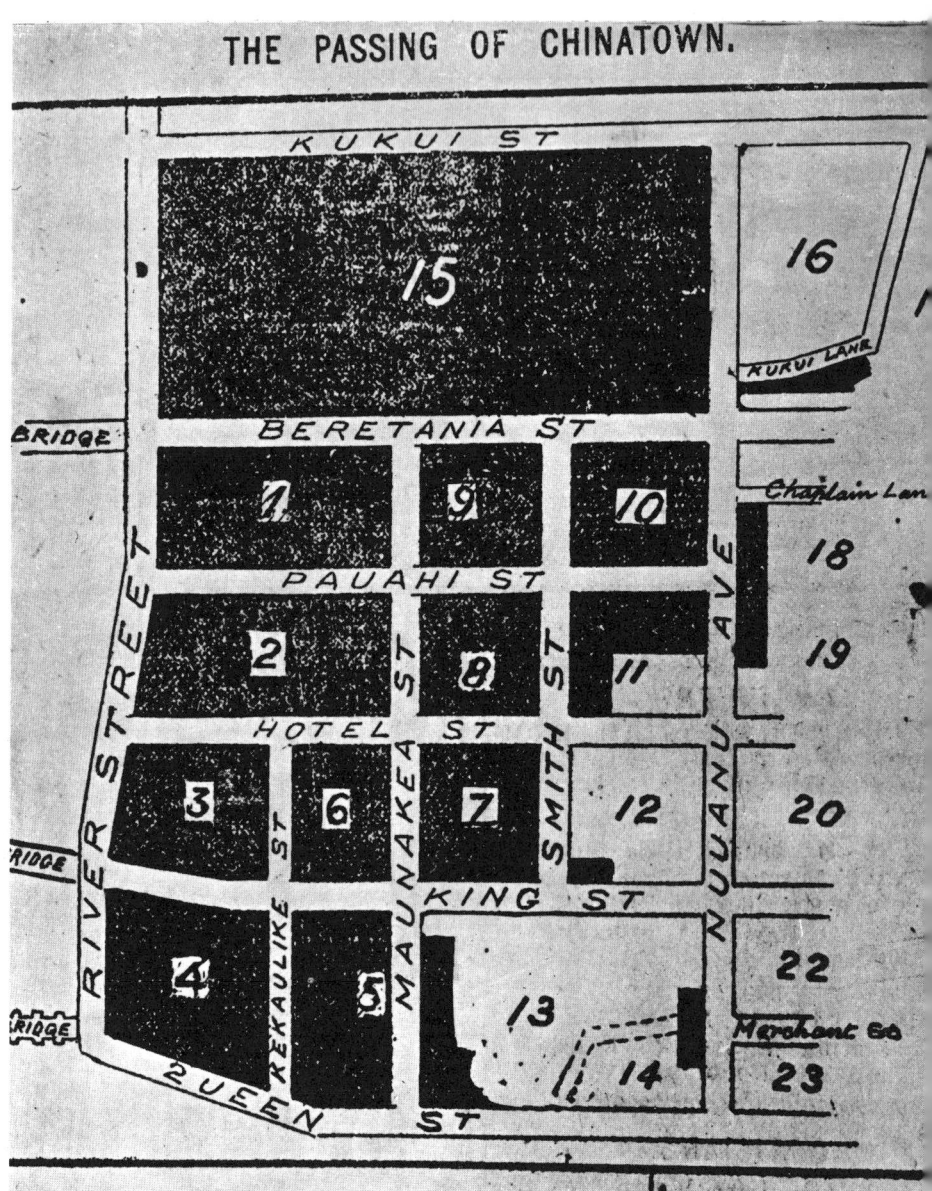

Extent of destruction caused by the great Chinatown fire of 20 January 1900. Map appeared originally in the *Pacific Commercial Advertiser*, 22 January 1900.

Honolulu for other ports. Those of other races could not travel until they had had a medical examination and got passes from the Board of Health. Government schools were closed by order of the Minister of Public Instruction. Cleaning and removal of garbage were also instituted, besides other work deemed necessary to stamp out the plague.

But the killer was already loose. On the same day two other cases, both in the same part of Chinatown, were reported. One victim was Makanaila, a South Sea islander, who died on Queen Street near Mililani. The Board of Health organized a house-to-house inspection on the afternoon of December 12, with volunteers in charge. The next day it laid a strict quarantine on the area bounded by Nuuanu Street, Kukui Street, Nuuanu Stream, and Queen Street—that portion of the city then as now called Chinatown. Military guards enforced isolation.

On December 13, the affected district was subdivided into 15 parts for inspection and sanitary work. On the 14th sanitary headquarters were set up at Kaumakapili Church [see map] inside the quarantined section. Cleansing and disinfecting of the entire district started; this included gathering and burning rubbish and garbage, digging new cesspools, and filling old ones. Dr. J. S. B. Pratt directed the inspectors.

Thus began an energetic and systematic effort to restrict the plague to Chinatown and more broadly, to Honolulu. To effect the latter, regulations bound seagoing vessels and their passengers. Island steamers due from outer ports were considered clean ships if they anchored offshore and held no communication with land. Vessels already in port were sent out and required to undergo seven days' quarantine before being allowed to leave for other islands. These vessels were to load and discharge cargo by lighter. Foreign vessels were not allowed to touch the wharves, but were kept from six to ten feet away, with all cables guarded by rat-proof guards. No goods of Japanese or Chinese origin could leave port [for outer islands] until they had been thoroughly fumigated. All shipping was done under Board of Health inspection. . . .

They studied Chinatown, a practically rectangular area including part of the main business section of the city. This area, with an overwhelmingly Asiatic population of 7,000, was bounded by River, Queen, Nuuanu, and Kukui Streets. The most important difference distinguishing Chinatown from the business section east of Nuuanu was that the Asiatics lived as well as did business in their sector. . . .

When the Sanitary Commission gave its report, there had already been nine plague cases since the outbreak on December 12. . . .

The first of many sanitary fires was started . . . December 31, by order of the Board of Health. With the fire department standing by, the torch was carefully applied to a row of wooden buildings on Nuuanu Avenue across from Block 10. The occupants of the buildings had been removed to a quarantine camp at Kakaako. Their belongings and the merchandise from the stores were taken by the Board to be disinfected and stored until the owners were out of quarantine. Evacuation, fire, the quarantine camp, and fumigation were to be the standard pattern for the sanitary control from then on. . . .

Upon the condemnation of a building, and upon order of the Board of Health to destroy it by fire, the Fire Department proceeded to do so. A total of 41 fires were set between December 31, 1899 and August 13, 1900, when the pesthouse and morgue at Kakaako were burned. The concentration of fires came in the first three months— 19 in January, 12 in February, and 7 in March. There was only one each in December, April and August. In every case the Fire Department stood by, and safety precautions were observed to the utmost. Thus all sanitary fires were controlled and destroyed only intended areas—except the great Chinatown fire of January 20, 1900.

The Board of Health had decided that the portion of Block 15, between Kaumakapili Church and Nuuanu Avenue and mauka of Beretania Street should be burned because the area had been the site of five deaths and one suspicious case within the past week. Because this was an especially large area, extra precautions were taken and plans made to preserve the church. Chief Hunt and the entire Fire Department personnel with four engines began the conflagration at 9:00 a.m. on Saturday, January 20. A fair northeast wind was blowing, so that Engine No. 1 was placed at the intersection of Maunakea and Beretania Streets as a precautionary measure should the wind rise. A two-story frame structure behind the church had been selected because it was intended that the fire should eat its way back toward Kukui Street.

Everything was fine for one hour. Then the wind began to rise and shift to the east, which caused blazing embers to be carried to the dry roofs of closely-packed buildings in the vicinity. In a short time many other buildings were aflame. Then embers lodged on the

Waikiki tower of Kaumakapili Church and set it afire. The firemen struggled desperately, but they could not force water to such a height. The blaze leaped to the other tower. From the twin church towers, sparks and embers were flung by the strong wind to rooftops around.

The spreading holocaust now became a raging, uncontrollable beast. Heat forced men beyond effective fighting range. Water pressure had gradually decreased; in a moment, the fire leaped out of control. The entire Beretania Street frontage was now a mass of flame. Sparks leaped across from Block 15 to Block 1, and the high wind fanned the flames so that they vaulted fifty and sixty feet to Block 2. Engine No. 1 on Maunakea Street was enveloped, and the Chemical Engine House in Block 2 burned. The Board of Health had earlier notified ships to leave the wharves for their own safety, and as the fire coursed through Block 2, vessels began moving out into the stream.

Now the conflagration jumped to Blocks 3 and 6. Citizens and guards rushed to warn any remaining residents, but they had already fled with whatever belongings they could snatch up and carry. Volunteers combined efforts to form bucket brigades to put out fires caused by flying embers. They failed to stay the blaze. But other volunteers helped by passing buckets to drench the firemen as they fought on.

Several dynamite charges were set off in the buildings along the corners of Kekaulike and King Streets. Useless: The strong winds carried the flames to the wharves. After 2:30 p.m., every block from Beretania to the harbor was ablaze. By 4:00 p.m., Blocks 3, 4, 5 and 6 were smouldering ruins. Fortunately, the *U. S. S. Iroquois* and the tug *Eleu* were near the wharves and directed streams of water toward the Honolulu Iron Works and structures in that vicinity. Two hundred employees of the iron works set up a bucket brigade from the wharves to the buildings. By these means the iron works and several warehouses along the waterfront were saved.

By 1:30 p.m. the fire began making its way from Beretania Street along Achi Lane toward Kukui Street. People feared that the mauka section of the city would be destroyed. Chinatown refugees rushed back to save belongings, but were driven back by fire and smoke; they formed a seething mob near the bridge and Kukui Street. Citizens and guards armed themselves with sticks, pick handles, bats, shovels, and similar weapons to beat back the desperate Chinatown residents. This counterforce centered at Kukui Street, but a long line of Honolulans stretched across King Street to prevent any refugees' escaping the quarantine district. A strong military guard reinforced this cordon. Nearly every business house closed its doors, and the employees lent their aid. . . .

At Nuuanu and King Streets a Japanese committee calmed the mob, and wherever it set its standards (a white flag with the red cross on it, and the Japanese flag), the people rallied. The Chinese consul and vice consul also circulated among the people and tried to pacify them, since at this time the Chinese believed that the Board of Health had purposely burnt their homes.

Thus, through the efforts of concerned citizens, guards, the fire department, and others, not a single life was lost in the Chinatown fire. However, 38 acres—almost all of Chinatown—was burned. The maps reproduced from the *Pacific Commercial Advertiser* for January 20 and 22 show the extent of the destruction.

This disastrous sanitary fire practically ended the existence of Chinatown, and 4,000 people, most Oriental, were rendered homeless, without food and with little to begin life anew. Even those in the quarantine camps suffered, because when their homes had been sacrificed in earlier sanitary fires, their belongings had been collected, fumigated, and stored in the cellars of Kaumakapili Church, which was destroyed with everything in it. The fire killed Chinese trade and restricted local business in general to very narrow limits.

The whole of the burnt Chinatown was enclosed with a high board fence in order to prevent plague germs from being carried by debris searchers and looters. Until May 17 no buildings could be erected on this land. It was tabooed ground, although King Street was opened through it after very thorough disinfecting.

So it was that the sanitary fire of January 20, which had been lighted to purify the area, did an unexpectedly complete job, cremating as it did nearly every building, with its rats and fleas. After the Chinatown fire, the number of plague cases dropped, but it is interesting to note that 31 later fires were ordered by the Board of Health. . . .

How did Hawaii's people respond to the presence of the plague and to the Board of Health's measures? Reactions were mixed: some were terrified, some were indifferent except as they were affected personally, and some showed social responsibility to the point of volunteering their services. Throughout the epidemic this latter group donated much time and effort to relief designed to supplement government activities.

Economic and Social Development

As merchants suffered and shipping lay idle at the wharves, several businessmen closed their offices and took charge at the detention camps, where thousands of refugees were quarantined. The extensive nature of the camps showed the vigor with which the Caucasian community fought the pestilence. Several people worked day and night, looking after the health guards and bringing people from plague-ridden houses to camps. Concerned citizens who did not work directly for or under the Board of Health did what they could to help. For example, the business firms complied with the Board's request concerning opening and closing hours. . . .

Citizens spontaneously offered supplies of all kinds; merchants liberally gave food, clothes, cash, and the use of vehicles to convey goods. On Sunday, the day after the fire, the women of Central Union Church organized relief work and committees and assisted the public authorities in the work of meeting the needs of destitute refugees. And a number of Nuuanu Valley ladies started a sewing bee to make women's and children's clothing for the homeless. They eventually produced 350 articles.

These were not the only ones who gave to the unfortunate. The Japanese had three societies working in their behalf (a fourth appeared at the time of discussion of fire claims). . . .

Nor were the Chinese abandoned; there was the Chinese Society (or the Chinese Relief Society).[25] A committee of ten was appointed to solicit money for the care of the poorer class of Chinese who had suffered in the fire and who were unable to get a new start because they lacked funds. This society also had some 1,000 wards—men, women and children who got supplies of rice twice a week. In addition, shelter was provided in the Kalihi Detention Camp for those without homes. The Society was able to raise approximately $8,000 in one week; this sum went into a special charity fund to provide food for victims of the fire who had been released from detention camps. . . .

Another group which provided important aid during the plague was the Hawaiian Relief Society, which ordinarily cared for indigent natives. However, from the early days of the epidemic, it looked after sufferers in quarantine. On the night of the Chinatown fire, it fed 50 people at Relief Camp 1 and furnished them clothing and blankets. This service continued until the following Thursday. . . .

As noted above, a chief effect of the black death was the uniting of

The Sandalwood Mountains

individual concerns, if only for a short period. Other important consequences were: (1) realization of the need for a good sewer system. Therefore, $345,253.24 were appropriated for its construction and extension. With sewers installed, there were no privy-vaults or cesspools in downtown Honolulu; (2) desire for a better and more efficient water supply; it had given out during the Chinatown fire, and many did not trust the purity of the water. These demanded a filtering of the supply from Nuuanu Valley. This was done, and a new pump installed on Beretania Street; (3) appointment of a city sanitary engineer to inspect buildings in process of construction and to pass on applications for permits to build; (4) construction of a garbage crematory (money was appropriated in 1900 for this object); (5) adoption in Chinatown of the sanitary regulations passed by the Board of Health. Chinatown had been razed by the fire; in rebuilding it, the mistakes of the past could be avoided. New buildings had to comply with Board of Health rules; (6) improvement of the downtown area through destruction of unsightly and unsanitary old buildings; (7) spread of Chinese and Japanese settlement to the outskirts of Honolulu, such as near Moiliili and McCully, because no new houses could be built in Chinatown until May 17, when the soil was pronounced clear of plague bacilli. The Orientals needed housing, and they could not wait; (8) emphasis on the need for alleyways in Chinatown to cut the blocks and thus make throughways; (9) most important, general awareness of sanitary conditions in Honolulu, with resulting improvement in plumbing, water supply, sewers, regular garbage pickup in all parts of the city, and not only in the School-Liliha area.

During those bitter months of 1899–1900 Honolulu had suffered much. But it had also learned much, and these lessons were applied to create a new and better city.

KULA CHINESE AND HOMESTEAD LEASES

Chinese living in Kula,[26] on the western slopes of Mount Haleakala on the island of Maui, had their economic survival threatened when the lands they were tilling under lease were threatened with public auction as homestead lots. "Kula San" (Kula "mountain") had attracted many of the Chinese workers who did not drift to the cities or return to China after the expiration of their plantation contracts in the 1880s and 1890s. The big attraction was the opportunity for

Economic and Social Development

independent farming on homestead land.²⁷ Also, those with wives and children welcomed the chance to get away from plantation camps. A great number moved from Kohala on the island of Hawaii so they could be their own bosses and bring up their families in a better environment. Many were Christians, and they supported two churches —St. John's Episcopal and Kula Chinese Congregational Church.²⁸

In 1912, the Chinese in Kula feared losing their lands because they were to be publicly auctioned as homestead leases open only to American citizens. Their hope was to be allowed the leases in the names of their children who had been born in Hawaii and who were entitled to American citizenship on the basis of *jus soli*. In this matter the Chinese in Kula did not turn to their own fraternal society nor to the United Chinese Society in Honolulu. They found effective help and influential support from their spiritual leader, Bishop Henry B. Restarick of the Episcopalian diocese, who appealed to Governor Walter F. Frear. The Governor was favorably impressed. He instructed Public Land Commissioner Charles S. Judd to take steps to have the lands occupied by the Chinese at Kula put up for lease so that the Chinese could obtain them through their children who were citizens and had been educated in the public schools. Assurance was given that Cornwall Ranch, the chief competitor for the lands, would apply only for those lots not occupied by the Chinese.

In the Archives of Hawaii are the letter from the Kula Chinese asking for the Bishop's help and his immediate response in the form of a letter to Governor Frear in 1912.*

Kula, Maui, Aug. 6th, 1912.

To the Rt. Rev. H. B. Restarick,
    Bishop of Honolulu.

Dear Sir,—We, the Kula, Maui Born children and our parents invite you to be present at a reception which is to be given at St. John's rectory, Kula, Maui, on August 11th 1912 at noon.

This reception is specially given to your honor, to show our gratitude and high appreciation of your great effort which caused the

* Governor's File: Frear, Terr. Depts., Public Land Commission, Aug.–Sept. 1911 (Archives of Hawaii).

Government to give us a place to live in which our possible livelihood can be obtained. Furthermore, you have given us an able teacher, Mr. Shim Yin Chin, who taught the community with moral and intellectual education through whom we have received untold benefits. We greatly desire that your honor and Rev. Mr. Kong Yin Tet together with Rev. W. S. Short of Wailuku, to come to us on the above mentioned date. We shall prepare ourselves to hear you. If you will be unable to come on the stated date, will you please set a date for us? Hoping you will make no refusal.

In regard to our present situation and on what ground we are standing with the rules of the Government, we do not understand. Will you kindly get a written regulation from the Public Land Commissioner so that we may have guidance to follow.

On the 29th of July Mr. Pia, [probably Pia Cockett, translator] Mr. Brown, and Mr. Aiken came to St. John's rectory in order to find out whether the lots were given to the proper applicants. And they found all correct, and they asked us if we wanted five years lease from the Government; we answered "Yes," (if possible 10 yrs. lease is better) they promised to send the lease to us when it is drawn up.

In the meantime we understood that the lots of land which were obtained by the under age Hawaiian born are all settled, but the remaining lots which were not called for will go through a public auction.

On July 29th Mr. Pia and Mr. Brown came to Mr. Chong En Young, who occupying Lot No. 14. They advised Mr. Chong to sign a document which will give consent for the lot to go to public auction, but Mr. Chong refused to sign his name on the ground that he has no right to assign government land. Then they said "no matter, you will sign or not, the lot is going to be at auction if we get the land you will lose your lot your house and your corn." On the next day Mr. Pia went Mr. Chin Sam Fat who was occupying Lot No. 7, for the same purpose. Mr. Chin also refused him.

We are greatly disturbed by their action. Will you kindly advise us as what to do. We shall be ever grateful to you.

Hawaiian Chinese residents of
Kula, Maui,
by Shim Yin Chin.

Honolulu, T. H., Aug. 7, 1912.

Economic and Social Development

My dear Governor Frear,—You will remember some months ago my going to you with the Rev. Kong Yin Tet in relation to the lands occupied for many years by the Chinese at Kula, Maui, and tilled by them for a long period. Also, that their children, now 15, 16 and 17 years of age, were born on the lands. You were kind enough to be interested in the matter, as was also Mr. Judd, then Land Commissioner.

It appears from the enclosed communication which I have received from the Chinese at Kula, that they are afraid that some attempt is being made to get their lands. Of course you are aware that the older Chinese there are unable to speak English, and are naturally timid and suspicious of the White people. I am quite unaware of the real motives behind this attempt to get them to sign their names to documents. I am quite sure it is within your power to ascertain what it really means, and to prevent any injustice being done to these worthy people.

You will remember that it was your policy to lease lands to the Chinese for such period as would enable their oldest Hawaiian-born sons to take the land as citizens, and they were greatly rejoiced when they learned that the Governor of the Territory had issued directions to this effect.

I am leaving Honolulu for ten days, and I shall be greatly obliged if, in the midst of this very busy period of yours, you will give audience to the Rev. Kong Yin Tet who was with me before when I called on you in regard to this matter, and let him explain the situation.

Anything you can do in this matter will be greatly appreciated by me, and I only hope that some day I shall be able to show my gratefulness for your kindness.

Faithfully yours,
[snd] Henry B. Restarick
Bishop of Honolulu.

OCCUPATIONAL AND EDUCATIONAL ADJUSTMENTS

For the Chinese in Hawaii, the 1930s were a time for review of their Hawaiian experience. This was in part due to stimulation from Professor Romanzo Adams and his fellow sociologists who were among the first to study race relations by exploring the backgrounds, experiences, and interactions of Hawaii's peoples.

A group of bilingual Chinese, educated in Hawaii and also with some education in China or local Chinese language schools, formed an Overseas Penman Club in 1929 and published occasional editions titled *The Chinese of Hawaii*. They were interested in recording the history of their American experience. Kum Pui Lai edited the 1936 edition and wrote the following definitive article.[29]* Lai carefully gathered demographic statistics and graphed them into pyramid studies of age and sex distributions as exhibited in Appendix M.

Success in cultural adjustments of the immigrant groups in Hawaii seems to vary with their length of residence, numerical size, and group solidarity. With the plantations as their first destination seven racial groups invaded Hawaii at different periods, the latest group, the Filipino for instance, taking the role in the plantations left by former groups, the Chinese, Japanese, Portuguese, Koreans, and others. This "graduation" from the rural plantations to the business houses and then to professional occupations in the cities of Honolulu and Hilo appears to be duplicated by each group after a period of labor in the sugar camps and pineapple fields.

The Chinese, with a longer average length of residence than any other group in Hawaii, have had greater opportunities to make progress in their occupational and educational adjustments. They migrated from South China to work on the sugar cane plantations of Hawaii. In 1882, there were 5,037 plantation Chinese, 49% of the total plantation employees or 28% of the Chinese population; in 1932 Chinese laborers numbered only 706, 1.4% of the total employees or 2.5% of the Chinese population. The total Chinese population was 18,254 for 1884 and 24,235 for 1932.

However, when the Chinese left the plantations they met slight competition in the retail business because the field was relatively unoccupied. In 1910 out of 13,742 Chinese males 10 years of age and over engaged in selected occupations there were 2,658 sugar farm laborers, 1,634 rice farmers, 1,067 retail dealers, and 1,059 servants. During the period around 1910 there occurred a start towards the selection of professional occupations by both sexes:—68 teachers, 51 bookkeepers, and 4 physicians.

* Kum Pui Lai, "Occupational and Educational Adjustments of the Chinese in Hawaii," *The Chinese of Hawaii* (Honolulu: Overseas Penman Club, 1936), 3: 1–4.

Economic and Social Development

Ten years later, out of 11,110 Chinese males 10 years of age and over engaged in selected occupations 1,735 were sugar farm laborers, 1,324 rice farmers, 1,018 retail dealers, and 886 servants. By that time both sexes had tried their skill in a wider field of professional occupations: 255 bookkeepers, 240 clerks, 143 teachers, and 18 photographers found enumeration in the occupation census.

The year 1930 presented a still wider selection of professional positions. Out of 9,779 Chinese 10 years old and over in selected occupations for the Territory 444 teachers, 32 technical engineers, 31 dentists, and 20 physicians and surgeons had been enumerated.

One does not need to wait for the 1940 U. S. Census on occupation statistics to follow the trend of the Chinese and other racial groups in a more varied distribution of their gainfully employed. A preliminary survey by the Overseas Penman Club in 1934, discovered that there were 37 dentists, 31 physicians and surgeons, and 5 attorneys at law among the Chinese in the Territory.

Other immigrant groups have followed the same occupational succession of the Chinese in their familiar movement from the plantations as laborers to "white-collar" jobs in the city. This movement sooner or later influences the establishment of educational institutions, i.e., language schools and cultural societies by the Chinese. The language schools, especially, take on certain roles and functions which change from time to time. From an occupational standpoint, the function of the Chinese language school would vary in response to the changing occupations of the second generation Chinese. When the first generation orientals toiled from dawn to dusk as common laborers or rice farmers the language schools did not attract them with any tangible economic rewards. For the retail dealers and domestic servants a knowledge of Hawaiian and broken English was necessary for business and social transactions, and whatever Chinese necessary for daily use the merchants had already acquired in the old country.

Thus in the fifties, sixties, and seventies the Chinese in Hawaii made no consistent attempt to establish language schools to teach Chinese to either adults or children. Besides, urbanization of the Chinese had only begun; scattered groups of Chinese on various plantations were at a disadvantage to pool their financial efforts or leadership together. In fact, in 1878 the early Christian mission schools with instruction in Chinese and English for the Chinese adults and children were maintained by annual grants from the Hawaiian Government. The Bethel

Chinese School under Dunscombe received $200 annually from 1878–1882. In 1882, the Chinese Children's English School with Adela M. Payson as principal and Tang Peng Sum as teacher of Chinese secured $404.50 for the education of 50 boys and two girls in the Chinese and English languages; the Bethel Chinese School received a six hundred dollar grant that year. The Chinese population in 1878 numbered 6,045; it jumped to 18,254 in 1884. At that period of occupational exploration the Chinese placed a premium on learning the English language and religion.

Evening schools for Chinese were conducted by the Seamen's Institute and by the Y.M.C.A., for the purpose of teaching English, and in 1872 a Chinese Sabbath School was started by the Y.M.C.A. in the Fort St. Church. The business of this Sabbath School was primarily to teach the 27 Chinese men enrolled to read and to speak the English language. In that year the population was estimated to be 1,938 (in Honolulu).

In June 1885, they subscribed $2,000 to build a new hall for the Chinese Y.M.C.A.; in 1897 the Chinese merchants of Honolulu contributed over $500 to aid the Chinese mission schools. From an economic standpoint they were not ready to establish large and exclusive Chinese language schools.

But nevertheless, travelling scholars and private tutors taught Chinese via the rote memory of the classics in the homes of their students.[30] Among the earlier teachers, peddling their intellectual wares from home to home, were Chang Siu Hon, Ching Yau Hong, Hee Jack Sun, Lee Kai Chuck, Wong Min Tim, and Young Kam Hoy.

Besides, young Chinese and Chinese-Hawaiian boys were frequently sent back to China to be orientalized. The well-to-do merchants of Hawaii had the means to send their children to their ancestral villages. The biographies of the Chinese makers of Hawaii in the Overseas Penman's volume published in 1929 recorded in many instances the orientalization of the Hawaii-born youths in the village schools.

The economic stabilization and subsequent residential dispersion of the Chinese to better areas put them and their children within educational advantage and in contact with the well-to-do classes of other races. As a result, there were an increase in school attendance and a decrease in the number of illiterates, thereby placing the Chinese in a favorable position to learn more about the American culture. In

Economic and Social Development

1910, 71.4% of the Chinese between 5 and 20 years of age attended the American schools. This rose to 72.9% in 1920, and 75.8% in 1930. Chinese girls are no longer detained at home by custom; 64.1% or 1,274 in 1910, 70.0% or 3,225 in 1920, and 75.2% or 4,730 in 1930 attending American schools show that the traditional belief in education for boys only has largely disappeared.

With the early education of a great majority of the youngsters and the disappearance of the older aliens by death and departure for China the rates for Chinese illiteracy (10 years and over) in the Territory of Hawaii reflected the following changes: 1910, 32.3%; 1920, 21.0%; and 1930, 15.7%. Chinese ten years old and over who were unable to speak English numbered 6,907 or 38.1% of the total Chinese population in 1920 and 4,528 or only 22.4% for 1930.

However, the exploration in a wider area of professional occupations by American-educated Chinese gives the language schools a new function. Whereas, the early Chinese conceived of the language institutions as a means to retard the too rapid acculturation of their youths and cultural estrangement from the first generation, they now place value on bilingualists. Salesmen, physicians, surgeons, photographers, dentists, and businessmen find the older Chinese their best racial customers. From a business standpoint a knowledge of Chinese is essential. The frequent advertisements in the Chinese newspapers by these dentists, physicians, etc., indicate the source of their income.

The movement of the Chinese from Chinatown to better residential districts such as Bingham Tract and Kaimuki presupposes that the Chinese have improved their economic status in Honolulu and therefore are in a more advantageous position to contribute to the huge expenses of the Chinese language schools. Therefore, the Chinese public and a few American friends were able to raise about $10,000 in 1932, $17,000 in 1933, $18,000 in 1934, and $21,000 in 1935 for the various semi-public Chinese schools in the Territory. According to the *Hawaii Chinese Annual,* Volume VII, the Chinese people in 1935 subscribed $21,685.25 to the various schools; the amounts were: (in Honolulu) Chung Shan, $10,599.31; Hoo Cho, $3,661.71; Mun Lun, $3,500.00; Dai Goong, $1,839.00; Fook Hing, $1,363.00; (in Kapaa) Wah Mun, $1,323.00; and (in Hilo) Wah Mun, $1,000.00.

Besides aiding in the maintenance of the Liberty Bank (opened for business, Feb. 18, 1922) in Honolulu, the Chinese also organized the American Security Bank which was incorporated March 1, 1935 and opened for business on April 20, 1935.[31] While the total Chinese savings accounts in the various banks, personal and real property, and other investments may fluctuate from year to year, there is no doubt that the Chinese have become economically more stable in the larger community.

The occupational trends, economic stabilization, residential movements, and educational organizations of the Chinese in Hawaii are modified by the age groupings of the population; and the Chinese language schools seem to have flourished together with the attainment of equilibrium in the sex ratio, which in turn produces age groups as expected in a theoretical normal distribution of population. The population pyramids [Appendix M] . . . illustrate the stabilization of the Chinese population in Hawaii. The percentages of the age groups are of the total Chinese population. Deviations from the norm for the Chinese have decreased from 74.77 in 1910 to 47.85 in 1920, and to 32.25 in 1930, signifying that the group is rapidly assuming stability.

The Chinese immigrants came over in two great waves: from 1876–1885, and 1890–1897. About 11,165 men arrived in these two periods, besides many from 1885 to 1890. Consequently, the highest deviation from the norm in 1910 would include the men in the age groups from 35–39 years and above. Thus in 1910 the men in the age group from 35–39 totaled 12.52% of the entire Chinese population, the highest of all the age groups. However, when stability was more or less reached in 1930, the highest age group included the Chinese men in the 55–59 group (only 4.68% of the total).

The fewness in the number of Chinese females in the upper age groups was seen readily in the earlier years, but in 1930 the age groups of the female from 25–29 and below were assuming stability rapidly.

This inevitable stabilization of the population means that the younger age groups would increase and thereby demand attention along educational lines if effective social control is desired.

In the private and public schools of the Territory of Hawaii the Chinese between the ages of six and nineteen numbered as follows:

Year	Private	Public	Total
1930	1,288	6,854	8,142
1931	1,399	6,726	8,125

[Continued]

Economic and Social Development

Year	Private	Public	Total
1932	1,392	6,678	8,070
1933	1,408	6,668	8,076
1934	1,677	6,609	8,286
1935	1,968	6,643	8,611

The ratio by year for the number of students who attended Chinese language schools to those registered in the American public and private schools of the Territory was as follows:

1930	.2951
1931	.3001
1932	.3071
1933	.3327
1934	.4070
1935	.4235

Having made satisfactory adjustments in the economic, educational, and residential phases of their contacts with the new environment the Chinese in Hawaii, on achieving a stable population with a more equal sex ratio, are now watching the younger generation establish social and political organizations for further assimilation of the new culture in Hawaii. Especially in politics, the Chinese have gained recognition as a minority group with 6,398 eligible to vote in 1930, 6,982 in 1932, and 7,546 in 1934. Registered voters of both sexes for the group were 4,402 in 1930, 5,356 in 1932, and 5,991 in 1934. At the 1934 election 33 of Chinese or of part Chinese ancestry were among the 256 candidates seeking public offices in the Territory.[32]

The younger Chinese are becoming more Americanized, but at the same time they have attempted to retain the best in Chinese culture. The first generation Chinese have done their part faithfully and judging from present trends the new generation youths have grasped their spirit and will hold the torch high for the oncoming generations.

CHANGING FAMILY RELATIONS

Social practices among Hawaii Chinese varied from family to family, clan to clan, dialectal group to dialectal group. There were many changes with changing times in Hawaii. A sociology paper written in 1937 by a student who preferred to remain anonymous depicts wedding customs, *mui-tsai* ("bondmaids"), plural marriages, funeral practices, and festival celebrations in an immigrant family of the 1930s.* An engagement gift of 100 pigs, as mentioned in the article, would seem to be out of proportion. The usual custom would be one or two roast pigs for a village wedding. It is fortunate that some of these transplanted customs have disappeared in a more favorable social climate. Every Chinese, however, looks forward to eating moon cakes, oranges, and other goodies for the Moon Festival just as he does to eating turkey for Thanksgiving.

The plural marriage in this selected reading was rather exceptional in that it did not disrupt family harmony. Usually there were family squabbles, and some cases were taken to court over estate priorities and fights. The local term for this type of legal dispute is *jang sai guy* ("fighting over worldly possessions").

Even the Christian church was faced with the problem of plural marriages. One Chinese Christian took a second wife—"a course fully sanctioned by Chinese usage and standards of morality." However, he belonged to a church with a morality different from Chinese usage. As he persisted in his course, the church had to take action and asked for his resignation.[33]

One of Hawaii's greatest sociological problems is the Americanization of its predominantly Oriental population. We of the second-generation Chinese are caught in a cultural whirlpool which gives us a peculiar Western-Oriental outlook on life.[34] In everyday dealings we think in American ways, being educated in American schools, but our life is largely motivated and built around a philosophy that is Oriental. Most matters of daily living have been secularized, but our spiritual life is centered around filial piety, which is a sacred principle of the greatest importance in the civilization of the East. To view this complex situation with understanding, one must consider the social forces at work in the life of an American of Oriental parentage.

Ours is a large family. Father had eight children; four boys from the first wife and four girls from the second wife. All of us children called the first wife "mother" regardless of whose children we really were. The second wife we call *"Jah"* which in Chinese means "second mother." This seemingly strange family situation can be explained by

* "A Chinese Family in Hawaii," *Social Process in Hawaii* 3:50–55; reprinted with permission of Romanzo Adams Social Research Laboratory, University of Hawaii.

Economic and Social Development

the age-old Oriental custom which allows a man to have more than one wife. Polygamy in the East is practiced by those who can afford it. A man takes a second wife for these various reasons: when his first wife fails to bear him children, when she fails to bear him a son, or when she is ill and incurable so that another woman is necessary to the household.

Father and Mother never saw each other before their marriage. Their respective families arranged the affair. After setting the date of the marriage, my father's family sent 1,000 cakes and a hundred pigs to my mother's family. (The greater the figure the wealthier and nobler is supposed to be the groom's status.) This gift was passed out among my mother's friends and was the means of announcing her engagement.

On her wedding day Mother rose early and dressed in her wedding garments, and then served tea to her mother for the last time as a daughter. Then she rode unaccompanied to her husband's village, six miles away, in the Chinese sedan chair. Being the first wife of the groom, she had the privilege of a formal ceremony which consisted merely in serving tea to her mother-in-law, and then in having tea with her husband.

After three days of festivity, mother returned to her former home with a lunch for her mother. At this time she formally bade goodbye to her mother and family, to start life anew in her husband's home. According to Chinese custom when a girl is married she automatically loses her position in her childhood home and becomes a member of her husband's family. Upon her arrival at her husband's home, she was formally greeted as a daughter in what Americans would call a "tea."

Life being hard in China, Father and Mother decided to come to Hawaii to live. Mother brought two slave girls who were both fourteen years of age. They worked for her until they were old enough to be married, at which time they were given their freedom so they could have homes of their own. Incidentally, they are still living in Honolulu. Their children call us "cousins" although we are not related in any way by blood or marriage. They are grateful to my mother for their happy life in Hawaii and though mother is now dead, they never fail to bring our family oranges and moon cakes on New Year's and during the Full Moon festival.

It is generally believed that in a typical Oriental family, the mother is secondary and unimportant, she being so submissive and meek. But this is not the case in our family. Mother was always the all-important mate of her husband. She was decidedly the ruling agent in the family, for father was too busy attending to his business (he was a merchant) and had little time to devote to the family.

Based as it is on a strict family system, an Oriental household is, economically speaking, carried on under communal principles. Our home is no exception. Our family is closely integrated, and we all work for the welfare of the home with that oft-quoted adage, "one for all and all for one," as the central motivating force.

Father was the economic head and all the things regarding financial matters were carried out under his direction. Mother and Jah took care of the details of running the house and bringing up the children, but it was father to whom they were ultimately responsible.

All earnings by the members of the family were turned over to father. My brothers' pay checks were given directly to father. Whenever anyone needed money, father was always willing to meet the demands provided they were not too extravagant.

From the time that we could help around in the house we were taught to be useful. We girls were taught to clean the house, help with the cooking, wash the dishes and in general to do all the household duties that a good daughter should know. Our brothers, on the other hand, were required to keep our yard well trimmed and well groomed. In addition they were given the task of caring for the chickens that were kept in our back yard.

Every morning we got up at six. It was cold and dark, but duty was duty and we did our chores without complaint. While I boiled the water and warmed the soup, my sisters would sweep and dust. The eldest daughter usually supervised our work. Our brothers, too, got up early to water the yard and feed the chickens.

It was not so much that our help was needed at home but that our parents believed that we should be properly trained for our roles in later life. It is an old Oriental tradition that sons and daughters must be properly brought up and parents should train their children to be useful.

My parents were especially anxious that the boys should be given every oportunity to live a wholesome, worthy life. They were offered the best in education and other worthwhile enterprises. Father seemed more interested in them than in his daughters. Indeed, it is an accepted fact that in the Orient boys are more highly considered than girls.

This is so because they can carry on and perpetuate the family name, thus easing the parent's constant worry of family extinction.

All of the boys were educated in private American schools and were taught to accept the American code of morals, e.g., respect towards the female sex, monogamy, etc. But it isn't easy to change custom. Living in a home of Eastern culture, it seemed inevitable that my brothers should carry on the traditions. Let me cite one example. The eldest son has two wives, and his home is an eternal battleground. He made the mistake of trying to combine two cultures. He took a Hawaiian-born Chinese girl to China as a happy bride. Eight months later he brought a China-born girl into the home as second wife and forced his first wife to accept the situation. The wives are always fighting over each other's children and each has taught her respective children to call her "mother." It is difficult to understand how any home could overcome destruction when children within the home claim one common father but different mothers.

Our family life, however, was very different. Mother fell ill and became a semi-invalid. Being weak and without the services of her slaves it became necessary for someone else to run the household. Father conferred with mother and gained permission to bring home a young girl, who had just come from China, as second wife.

Jah had no marriage ceremony, she merely came into the home and was made a part of the family because Mother accepted her. Mother taught her sons to call her second mother. She and Jah lived and loved each other like sisters. When Father died a number of years later, they continued to carry on the household affairs together.

Jah is my real mother. Yet I called her second mother, and gave all of my allegiance to the first wife. My sisters and I went to mother for advice and sympathy—not to Jah. Every morning it was Mother who received our first greeting. It was she who gave us permission to do what we asked. Should you ask us whom we loved more, mother or Jah, we would be at a loss to answer for we loved them both equally well.

Mother was not very harsh with us. To be sure, there were certain things we were taught not to do. If we disobeyed, we were punished. Smoking was absolutely prohibited among the girls although the boys were allowed to smoke or drink. One day my sister was caught playing with a cigarette. My mother pronounced her a disgrace to the honor of our family and punished her severely.

Mother was also very much opposed to interracial marriages. In fact, we were told that we must marry in our own "Punti" class. My sister fell in love with a Chinese boy whose parents came from "Hakka" stock. The Hakka class is considered by the Punti as inferior and Mother absolutely forbade the marriage. She sent my sister to ———— where she died a few months later from illness.

When I was ———— years old the entire family returned to China. Mother felt that she was soon to leave the earth and wished to die in her own country. We went back to the old village where Mother first went as a bride. How different was her attitude from that of ours today. While we shun death and cling to the hope that it is far away, she calmly prepared to receive death in dignity, knowing that her time to go was drawing near. Like a typical Chinese, she awaited her time with the fatalistic philosophy of the Orient.

I can never forget her funeral. The horrible chant of the native women made everything seem so gruesome. A beautiful house made of paper and bamboo, a sedan chair, money, human figures, and other useful things were made and taken to the burial grounds. We walked five miles to the place of burial, dressed in black, our faces covered with white sacks. As the coffin was lowered into the grave all of the bamboo and paper goods were burned as a part of the funeral ceremony. This was to insure her getting a good house, a sedan chair, servants, and plenty of money in the next world. After the funeral we rode home and were made to jump over a small fire which was supposed to cleanse us of all the devils which we acquired at the funeral.

Following Mother's death, Jah became the head of the household. I returned to Hawaii to continue my education.

Religion played an important part in the rituals of our family life. We had a separate room for the gods and goddesses with miniature shrines built for each. Every afternoon at three, the head of the household burned incense before the shrines. On the birthdays of certain goddesses we fasted and pledged ourselves to certain beliefs, e.g., if it were the birthday of the goddess of mercy, Kwan Yin, we prayed to her to help us to be merciful and to teach us to carry out her ideals in our world. From our earliest days we were taught the rituals and teachings of the gods by our parents, who always prayed and asked that we grow up imbued with the virtues of the deities.

Jah believes in spirits. She spends thousands of dollars trying to delve into the mystery of death. Every year she goes to a Chinese woman who enables her to speak to the dead. The woman prays, then goes into a trance. As she sits in a trance, the spirit enters her body and speaks through her. On one occasion Jah spoke to my father and asked him how he was. He answered that he was "fine" but had frequent colds because his body was in a damp ground. Jah had his grave dug and, to be sure, there was a lot of water below. She moved his remains to drier ground.

Through this spiritual medium she always asks Mother's advice regarding her perplexing problems. Invariably she follows Mother's words as she believes that now that Mother has entered the higher world, her knowledge is unlimited and her judgment correct.

Jah always celebrates the death of Father and Mother because she believes that their death on this earth signifies their birth in the next world. We always have a feast and shoot firecrackers to frighten the evil spirits away. However, when we children burn firecrackers, we think only of the fun of it and forget about the spirits.

The Chinese have many holidays but the most important ones are Chinese New Year, the Full Moon festival, and our individual birthdays. On Chinese New Year we rise early and pray to the goddesses. Then we serve tea to the various members of the family according to rank, e.g., Jah serves the goddesses; the eldest son serves the second son, and so on down the line. This is a day of great rejoicing and feasting and Chinese believe that the narcissus flower is a symbol of good luck and at this time every Chinese family has several pots blooming in the house.

Full moon is celebrated in respect to the moon goddess. This is why we have moon cakes and oranges. These foods are not supposed to be eaten but many people eat them. In fact, these originally holy days are now being secularized into days of festivity and merrymaking.

Serving tea is a very important function in the Chinese family. On our birthdays we serve tea to all of the family. For example, if it were my birthday I would serve tea to everyone in the order of their importance in the family. Whoever receives tea gives me money wrapped in red paper. However, if it were my mother's birthday, she does not serve us, but instead, each of us serves her.

However peculiar may have been the household situation, I can say with sincerity that the happiness I found and the culture I received in my home are equal, if not superior, to the culture that could be got under any other family culture. I can say with a deep sense of pride and gratification that the teachings and training of my parents were of the highest order. Although educated in the American manner, it is my firm belief that my life will be guided by the truths taught me by my parents, for their teachings were sound.

I am an American-Oriental product, but it is my hope that my parents have not taught in vain and that when the sweet-scented incense burns before the family shrine it will bear to my forebearers the message that I am fulfilling my task of carrying on my heritage of the East with honor and dignity.

CHINATOWN STORES IN THE 1930s

In 1884 the Chinese population in Honolulu reached 5,000, and 75 percent of them were concentrated in the twenty-five acres of downtown called Chinatown. By 1900, the Chinese population in Honolulu totaled 9,000 of which 40 percent lived in Chinatown. The 1960 census showed only 300 Chinese, or 5 percent of the Chinese in Honolulu, residing in Chinatown.[35]

In the 1930s Chinatown was a busy area. The Chinese merchandise store was still a key community center serving as a bank, a postal agency for sending letters and remittances to home villages, and as a hotel for stopover immigrants. Gathering there was a form of social outlet for persons from the same hometown. The immigrant who went back to China for a visit came in to bring village news. He may have stayed over a year in his home village—long enough to witness the birth of a child, preferably a son, and to start a second child before leaving to come back to Hawaii to begin another cycle of working hard and saving money. He would have much news for others at the store.*

There were similar stores, some of them branches of Honolulu firms, at sugar plantation camps and at other rural settlements.

The larger Honolulu Chinese merchandise stores in the thirties were Yuen Chong, Kwong Chong Lung, Wing Wo Tai, Wing Sing Wo, and Wing Hong Yuen. They are no longer in business. Chinatown today has a few smaller Chinese grocery stores to serve customers who enjoy Chinese cuisine. However, almost all of the more popular Chinese merchandise is carried in large supermarkets.

* Bung-Chong Lee, "The Chinese Store as a Social Institution," *Social Process in Hawaii*, 2:35–38; reprinted with permission of Romanzo Adams Social Research Laboratory, University of Hawaii.

Economic and Social Development

The Chinese stores had corresponding relations with export merchants (*kum shan jong*) in Hong Kong. Large export firms specialized in Hawaiian and American trade. For example, Kwong On Chan served emigrants from Tungkun county, Wong Chong Kee for Pao On county. Kwong Sam Kee for Wai Chow county, and Wui On Sheong for all three counties. These Hong Kong export stores took care of recruiting and financing emigrants to Hawaii and America, exporting Chinese merchandise there, and receiving remittances from overseas Chinese paying back loans and forwarding savings to families in the villages.[36] This system of overseas Chinese remittances promoted business for stores in Hawaii and their correspondents in Hong Kong, and it helped to perpetuate the strong ties that immigrants had to homeland families. The local Chinese Consulate reported that in 1930, $3,930,000 was remitted to China.[37]

The Chinese merchandise business and the rice industry in Hawaii have been closely interrelated during the greater part of their history. During the peak, the rice industry employed over 5,600 Chinese laborers, and it was largely operated and controlled by Chinese proprietors. The rice planters depended on the merchants for the supply of capital, merchandise, and equipment, while the stores looked largely to the rice plantation workers for the purchase of their goods. The store served also as a market for the produce of the planters. In 1896 there were in Honolulu 118 Chinese general merchandise establishments and 35 retail grocers, of which 72 were located in Chinatown and presumably catered chiefly to Chinese. Gradually, however, the rice industry has declined, the Chinese population have largely concentrated in Honolulu, a Hawaiian-born generation has supplanted the immigrants, and the Chinese stores have changed and slowly lost their once unique functions.

The foremost function of the Chinese stores was to serve as a bank. Chinese immigrants had been largely of the illiterate class. Very often letters were written and read for them by the storekeepers. A postal system was developed by the stores whereby large sums of money and bundles of letters were sent to agencies in Hongkong, relayed to inland cities and then distributed to the designated parties in the villages. On each envelope the amount to be remitted, the district, the village, the names of the sender and receiver were written. The immigrants were charged a small fee for every letter sent to China. In former years the fee was as low as 40 cents for sending a 10-dollar gold piece. This was the only way by which the immigrants could send their money and letters to the village. In the first place, there was no postal system between the villages. If money was sent through the banks to Hongkong, the villagers could not afford to take a trip to the city to receive it.

In many instances the stores served as depositories. The immigrants because of their inability to use English and their unfamiliarity with the American banking institution often deposited their earnings without interest with the storekeepers and frequently borrowed money from them. The storekeepers were persons who had status and commanded the respect of the immigrants.

The stores became social centers whenever a boat came to Honolulu from China. Hundreds of letters would be disposed of within a few hours after their arrival. The storekeepers did not deliver the letters but the immigrants came in for them. Each receiver contributed what general news there was in the letter for the information and discussion of the many immigrants. The letters brought joy as well as sorrow. They revived cherished memories from home. The life of the village was relived in Hawaii. The reputations of villagers were discussed and their morals were gossiped about.

The appearance at the store of an immigrant who had been home to China for a visit was as important as a personal letter. He also brought news and family tidings from the village to the immigrants in Honolulu. He could relate events with a personal touch and could give his views on village gossip. Sometimes he brought small bags of herbs, beans, yam flour, or sweets from the wives, parents, mothers-in-law, or godparents to the immigrants. The returned immigrant also helped to refresh memories of the village as shown by the following conversation heard in a store:

Immigrant: E—hee! (as he enters the store and sees the returned immigrant). So soon come back? You went how long?
R. Immigrant: I used up the few bits (money); I have to come back. Went home for 13 months.
Immigrant: Have son born?
R. Immigrant: Picked a daughter.
Immigrant: Also good. Have pregnancy when you come?
R. Immigrant: Don't know. Your family every one peaceful. Ah

Economic and Social Development

Wah (the immigrant's son) very nice. Studies at the village school. Your wife asked you send a little more home—not enough to spend.

Immigrant: I make not enough! For a time, no work. Village peaceful?

R. Immigrant: Very peaceful, but some small burglaries. Last month Ah Sai Pak lost a coop of seven chickens. Somebody said Ah ——— stole them. Don't know. Now in the village many young men have nothing to do. Very bad. They do whatever bad. Much gambling and eating opium.

The store was a club where the immigrant had status. His words found meaning; he could be understood and his conversation appreciated. He could talk at length and be listened to. He could boast of his catching the largest cricket on a certain hill and of seeing the largest snake in a certain rice field in China. He talked of his achievements; he shared his sentiments, his experiences, his memories with his fellow-villagers. Every little nook, hill, and lane, the temple, the goddesses, and the many village legends were reviewed in intimate detail. Through gossip in the stores, the village mores were re-enforced, and the immigrant's life was organized.

When the immigrant from the rural district went to Honolulu he sought out the store of his fellow villagers. He could have a meal or two, and could find lodging for the night without paying a fee to the storekeepers. This hospitality accounted for the absence of hotel life of the Chinese in Honolulu. The storekeepers were always hospitable to their fellow villagers. Newcomers or returned immigrants from China always found the stores a place where they could stay until they were accommodated elsewhere. The storekeepers also gave a hand in finding employment for them.

In most cases the employees of the stores were made up of fellow-villagers of relatives of the partners or owners. It was not uncommon to find that all of the personnel of the store were immigrants from the same village. Through their personnel the stores were often known as the stores of certain villagers. The Chinese, in searching for a countryman of a certain village, could always go to the particular store where there were fellow-villagers of the person sought.

Besides the economic and social functions, the Chinese stores served as meeting places for the oversea village clubs. Though the Chinese have organized district societies, benevolent societies, family tongs, guilds, unions, and a few village clubs with their society halls, many village clubs did not own any halls. The stores also acted as agencies for Chinese community subscriptions of various sorts. The stores rotated in taking charge of the memorial services of the Chinese cemeteries. They gave large shares to welfare work, helped to support the Chinese schools, and responded to subscription campaigns for local and homeland causes. In some cases the stores had served as headquarters for the Chinese political revolutionary movement.

The Chinese stores in Honolulu are gradually losing their economic and social functions in the community. As long as the Chinese community consisted chiefly of the first generation, the economic basis of the Chinese store was secure.

The Chinese took their three meals of Chinese foods daily and used many things which were imported, such as salted eggs, preserved ducks, and sausages. But the first-generation immigrants have either returned to China or are fast disappearing in Hawaii. In 1930 only 7,468 or 27.5 per cent of the total Chinese population in Hawaii were foreign-born. The second and third generations are losing taste for Chinese food and use American products more and more. They enjoy their toast, cereals, and milk, chocolate, or coffee in place of Chinese sausage or Chinese canned goods and rice in the morning. The consumption of Chinese goods tends to be less and less as the number of young Chinese in Honolulu increases, and the number of first generation decreases. Food products to the value of $353,688 were imported from China from July 1930 to June 1931. This is an average import value of only $12.97 per Chinese resident of Hawaii.

Chinatown during the Chinese New Year enjoys a period of business fervor when the old and young do their shopping of Chinese delicacies, but this prosperity is brief. Many of the traditional festivals have lost their flavor and the consumption of Chinese goods has suffered in proportion.

The decline of the rice industry has severed one of the principal market channels for Chinese goods. Surplus goods can no longer be dumped into the rice plantations. Today there are five ranking importers of Chinese goods in Honolulu, but a large part of their business is with non-Chinese. Seven smaller stores deal chiefly with the Chinese population and in another decade this number may be further reduced. More and more the Chinese merchants, of whom there were 160 in Honolulu in 1934, are catering to Americanized and Hawaiianized tastes.

Economic and Social Development

In addition, Chinese banks have developed where the Chinese can deposit their earnings and some even deposit with banks in Hongkong. Many buy insurance policies, bonds, stocks and other investments. The earnings of the Chinese are no longer deposited with the storekeepers. However, the postal system of sending letters and money still remains, for no responsible system has emerged in its place.

The Chinese store of today is only a shadow of the once unique institution. Its original economic support has largely disappeared and many of the stores have changed their character to meet the demands of a non-Chinese clientele. A very few of the stores remain where the old Chinese men still gather in the familiar atmosphere to relive memories of the past.

SOME OLD CHINESE CUSTOMS IN HAWAII

Chinese customs did not change or disappear overnight. However, they were modified by the different social environment of Hawaii.*

Chinese funerals are now usually arranged to be held on weekends so that relatives and friends may find it more convenient to attend. Before World War II it was customary for the family to stay all night for a funeral wake at the mortuary, but black-out restrictions helped to change this practice which was a great hardship and emotional strain.

Some old Chinese marriage customs, such as trousseaus and dowries, tea-pouring ceremonies, and nine-course dinner receptions, are still maintained by some of the younger generation, but probably more from pressure from their parents and well-meaning elders than because of their own wishes.

One comment made by more recent immigrants and visitors from China has been that overseas Chinese are more "old-fashioned" in keeping to social customs and practices which they remember from the "good old days" in the village.

In order to avoid arguments on "correct" marriage, funeral, or other social etiquette, a favorite defense is to say, "In my village (or in my part of the country) our practice is to do it this way."

It will shortly be a hundred years since the first arrival of the

* Marion Wong and Richard Wong,[38] "Some Forms of Chinese Customs in Hawaii" in *The Chinese of Hawaii* (Honolulu: Overseas Penman Club, 1936), pp. 18–21.

Chinese in Hawaii. It is true that they were of the peasant class, hired ostensibly to answer specifications for plantation labor, but they brought with them not only hands to turn the wheels of the infant sugar industry but the very essence of China.

Many of the factors that motivated them to observe social customs in China were present in this new land. Indeed the isolation that was first imposed upon them fostered fertile ground for survival of Chinese customs. The inaccessibility to rural camps was itself a potent factor that prevented any active interplay of Western influences. Except for the "haole" lunas and some native men and women, there were practically no foreign contacts. True, the lack of a family life proved a handicap to a full participation of many customs, but this was soon remedied when many Chinese procured wives from China.

They learned a little plantation English and some new techniques in work, but they remained in large part untinctured by local and home influences. The hardships of plantation life and limited outside contact were not enough to quench the little flame of social consciousness that burned in them. The plantation conditions of long hours, insanitary and comfortless homes, and severe penalties were harsh, but the Chinese were "harsher" in temperament.

When the Chinese ended their contract, they refused to continue as laborers, but instead reached out for an independent livelihood. Their initiative found an answer in small farming. Little plots of ground were cultivated, and soon many had accumulated sufficient capital to venture in merchandising. The effects of the resulting new influences brought about many changes in their ways of living. Moreover, the increasing sense of economic security made it possible to have families. Many confronted with the problem of securing wives were forced under the circumstances to accept native wives, and, in such matches, the native influence lessened the hold of Chinese customs.

A family system, swaying first this way and then that way, vacillating in its efforts to steady itself left Chinese customs in Hawaii in a state of indefiniteness. Here customs not too firmly entrenched fell into disuse and were even forgotten.

However, the Chinese are so thoroughly imbued with the customs that attend the three vital stages of the life cycle—birth, marriage, and death—that they are most reluctant in these instances to forsake them. All their holidays and festivals may not be heeded with the same zealous care, but without exception, these periods are observed

Economic and Social Development

with the most reverence. Here in Hawaii we find that the Chinese are clinging to them tenaciously in a quiet manner that almost escapes detection, so unobtrusive are its ways, for the customs of birth, marriage, and death have not the dramatic qualities that characterize New Year's or the Festival of the Moon.

Childbirth Customs

Chinese childbirth in Hawaii is still assured of being formalized. The child may be delivered by a midwife, for many still hold distrust for Western medicine. The midwife is remunerated with a small sum for her professional services and is presented with an additional sum of money (li shee). Pig's feet boiled in vinegar and ginger is an unfailing sign of a birth in the Chinese family. However, this is present not so much from a custom with superstitious import as from the nutritional value to the mother in bed; it is sometimes distributed to intimate friends. Gifts of money, personal wear, and jewelry are still given to the baby. The most important day for the child is at the end of a month when offering is made in the local temple for propitiation of the gods. Slices of roast pork garnished with pickled ginger, dyed eggs, and stuffed buns are delivered to all friends who have made presents. They in turn reciprocate with a gift of money wrapped in red paper. A sumptuous nine course dinner may culminate the day's celebration, or a modest family dinner may be held. Whatever the family circumstances, the Chinese are loathe to relinquish this custom.

Marriage Customs

The modern Chinese wedding is an expression of a partial acceptance of Western form. Although there are weddings that depart so far from Oriental traditions that they are totally foreign, the greater majority persist in retaining some Chinese features. To see a bride costumed in a white dress and marching up a Christian church aisle to the strains of Wagner's Wedding March and then to be inducted into matrimony in Chinese by a Chinese minister is a seeming incongruity. Emancipation from the family solidarity system that exists in China results in marriages founded on the Western conception of love, and Chinese couples no longer follow the desires of parents but of their hearts.

We find marriages performed either in the home or in the church. The church wedding assumes Western conventions almost in toto, and

The Sandalwood Mountains

it is after the wedding and at the reception that we find some semblance of surviving customs.

The marriage in the private home, alone, is a significant fact that couples have not been proselyted into full acceptance of Western form. The modern bride may choose the conventional Western bridal veil, dress, and an entourage of bridesmaids or a dress of Chinese cloth and cut. The arrival of the bride is heralded with a blast of firecrackers. The marriage is then performed according to the conventional Western wedding rituals. The custom of retiring and changing into a new dress to serve tea and candied fruits to friends and relatives still holds, and the friends may in return offer "li shee." A feast usually precedes the wedding ceremony to which friends and relatives are invited. Only the bride attends this, as the custom of forbidding the groom to appear is still valid. The custom of segregating women and men by tables is still practiced. On the third day of the wedding, the bride returns to her home accompanied by her newly acquired groom. She takes clothes, bed covers, teapots, and cups to her home. A feast awaits her, and this time the groom makes his appearance. The custom of hanging a pair of trousers over the doorway when the marriage of a daughter precedes that of an older brother still exists.[39] Modern couples no longer seek shelter under the family roof but strike out in pioneering fashion to start a new home. The custom of giving cakes and roast pork to relatives and friends at the engagement of couples is still evident. The kind and number is usually determined by the girl's family, and the greater the number of cakes the higher the girl is held in esteem. Many of the customs that required the prospective bride to rise at an early hour, to eat special food, and to bow to parents in ancestral halls have been discarded along with other outmoded practices.

Funeral Customs

A Chinese funeral with its full array of ceremonies is full of spiritual significance. Much of its form has been shorn of Chinese traditions when it was transported to American soil where so many Western funeral innovations obtrude themselves; however, we can perceive forms that still survive this modern invasion.

No longer are clothes and a casket bought beforehand for the old one who wants to be assured of a decent burial. Ablutions consisting of warm water flavored with the leaves of the Chinese tree [pomelo] are still performed. The deceased is removed to the undertaking parlor for modern embalming and all Chinese ceremonies are enacted there. The body is placed on view for three days and nights and attended by the family and friends who keep constant vigil.

On the day of the funeral, members of the family are each clothed in a plain white and unbleached robe with a cape to match, grass slippers, and a black gauze band over the left arm. The services of a male and a female priest are still solicited and they make it their duty to chant the past events of the dead one's life. A Chinese orchestra is usually hired. The funeral procession may also include images to scare evil spirits away, an orchestra, a tablet for the soul and insignia bearing the titles of the deceased. Spirit money may be scattered along the route to prevent the soul from being snatched away by evil spirits. At the grave, clothing and other accessories of the dead may be burned to transfer their necessities to the other world. After the funeral, cubes of Chinese brown sugar are distributed to those who have attended to offset the bitterness of the occasion. Gifts of money may also be given with the understanding that it be spent on the same day. A feast may be held after the funeral, in which a meal without any meat or fish is served. Periods of mourning . . . may be over in three months to 100 days, though rites for the dead may be performed at regular intervals throughout the year.

Ching Ming

Usually in the third month of the lunar calendar comes Tomb's Day [Chinese Memorial Day] when the Chinese visit the graves of their ancestors and present offerings. The worship is sometimes held a few days prior to or after the appointed date in the calendar to meet the convenience or necessity of living relations. An organization—a local firm—is in chatge of such an occasion. When the day arrives, the persons engaged in worship proceed to the hillside where the graves are located. Here candles and incense are placed and lighted before the tombs. Offerings of pork, vegetables, chicken, or fish may be made. Here the family beginning with the headman kneels and bows to the ground three times. Mock money may be burned, wine from a small cup poured over it, and firecrackers set off. The food offering is then removed and eaten then and there.

New Year Celebration

Doubtless the custom that foreigners will most likely associate with the Chinese is the celebration of New Year's. What Christmas is to the Christians, the Chinese find their equivalent in New Year's, for here is the focal point of the year's celebration. The celebration of Chinese New Year is divided into two groups—one which follows the lunar calendar and the other, the Gregorian calendar. The younger generation no longer participates or realizes fully the significance of Chinese New Year's other than its more obvious functions as: the shooting of firecrackers; eating water melon seeds; and receiving "li shee."

The festivities connected with New Year's are usually observed in five parts: The sacrifice to heaven and earth; the worship of the gods and idols belonging to the family; the worship of deceased ancestors; prostration before living parents and grandparents; making of New Year calls.

The sacrifice presented to heaven and earth, usually called "presentation of rice on New Year's" is the first thing done on that morning. Many families do not retire to rest on the last night of the old year. A table is spread with offerings to heaven and earth in the front part of the room. Offerings may consist of a bucket of boiled rice, five or ten bowls of different kinds of vegetables (no meats are allowed) ten cups of tea, ten cups of wine, two large red candles, and three sticks of common incense or one large stick of a fragrant kind. Near the center of the table is always placed a plate or bowl full of the loose skinned orange ("ket"—tangerine).

The head man of the family, all of the rest being present, now comes forward and kneels down in front of the table, and bows his head toward the ground three times, holding one or three sticks of lighted incense in his hands. On rising to his feet, he places the incense in the center on the table. In some families the one who kneels and bows, repeats, while on his knees, his thanks to heaven and earth for past protection and favors, and a prayer that his family may be protected from sickness during the year now begun, and that it may be successful in business. At the conclusion, firecrackers may be set off, and mock money which has been prepared for this occasion is burned.

The performance of another important ceremony now takes place.

Economic and Social Development

The junior members of the family must kneel before the grandfather or grandmother, uncles or aunts who are present. The adult male members of the family start forth to make New Year calls on their friends and relatives on this day. Adults when calling must invariably be treated with hot tea to drink, tobacco, and watermelon seeds, and candied fruits. A loose-skinned orange (tangerine) named "ket tse," meaning "lucky" is given and this is equivalent to wishing an auspicious year. It is customary for all stores to close during New Year's for at least one or two days.[40] Most families do not eat any meat on this day on account of their reverence for heaven and earth. The New Year's festivities last from the first to the fifteenth of the month.

Moon Festival

Another custom that has survived and perhaps will retain its popularity is the Festival of the Moon. A delightful custom of paying homage to the moon on the fifteenth of the eighth month, we find a more sympathetic attitude from the younger generation towards it. The romantic aura that surrounds this festival is more persuasive than the stiff formalities of other festivals. On this day, shops display cakes made in the fashion of a moon—round and frequently impressed with figures of gods, trees, or animals on the face. On this night an offering consisting of meat, fowls, rice, fruits or vegetables is made to the moon. Autumn is the season when fruits are at their most luscious stage and we find the plum, peach, grape, pear, and the pomelo form an important part of the offering. The taro is an essential part of the offering too, for legend tells us that at the creation of man, the taro was the first food found by man with the aid of the moon.

Festival of the Fifth Moon

A custom that occurs in the fifth day of the fifth month is called the Festival of the Dragon Boats. This custom is kept alive in Hawaii only by the most loyal of Chinese. For the younger generation, it means only a time for rice puddings, its original significance being lost. In China it is celebrated in a way befitting its name by the racing of dragon boats and the dumping of rice puddings into the river as offering to Kieh Yuen, a high minister of the Chou dynasty who, failing to convince the prince of his salubrious reforms and being dismissed, drowned himself in a river; his countrymen who loved him immediately boarded small boats and rowed the length and width of the river in hopes of finding his body. The only obvious clue of this occasion now is the sale of steamed rice puddings shaped in a pyramid form and the exchange of these puddings between intimate families.

Other Festivals

A more obscure custom is the festival which occurs on the seventh day of the seventh month. Participation is usually by women whose desire is to acquire proficiency in the domestic arts. That evening they burn candles and incense, present offerings of food, bow and in the usual ways pay respects to the male and female stars who are meeting each other at the "Silver River" or Milky Way (as the legend goes). A superstitution attached to this occasion (believed profoundly by many) is that water bottled this day may be preserved indefinitely, and used as medicine.

A more important custom in the seventh month is "Ghost Day" which is held on the fourteenth day. Its object is to furnish the dead with clothes and money. To accomplish this purpose, mock money and mock clothing are burned before an altar with lighted incense and candles. An indispensable part of the offering is the duck which may be broiled or fried in oil. Besides this there may be a watermelon, meats, fish or crabs. All these are arranged on the altar before which the customary worship of the dead is performed.

SUMMARY OF SOCIAL PROGRESS

Dr. Romanzo Adams (1869–1942), eminent pioneer sociologist at the University of Hawaii, summarized the early Chinese immigrant experience in Hawaii. He and his teaching associates were of greatest influence to the generations who graduated and are now in positions of community leadership and who are today gaining increasing prestige and honor. They were guided in bridging the gap between the China-born and younger generations and were given insight and awareness of the ever-present interaction of Hawaii's ethnic groups by the work of Dr. Adams and his colleagues.*

The meaning of a beginning is manifest only through a consideration of later developments. The situation of the Chinese in Hawaii is

* Romanzo Adams, "The Meaning of Chinese Experience in Hawaii," *The Chinese of Hawaii* (Honolulu: Overseas Penman Club, 1929), pp. 10–12.

still far from stabilized. Much progress in many ways has been accomplished, but still further and equally significant developments are in prospect.

While any attempt to interpret the experience and behavior of the Chinese in Hawaii must be regarded as tentative, it may be worth while to make the effort. We now have a larger body of experience, and of experience representing a more advanced stage of development, than was available when current conceptions came into existence. In considering the status and conduct of the Chinese of an earlier period it was more difficult to distinguish between the influence of transient factors and those of a more permanent character. Effects due to temporary and often unknown or uncomprehended conditions were attributed to something inherent in the nature of the Chinese people. This procedure made them seem queer to others. It prevented understanding. It exaggerated the significance of race by failing to give proper weight to circumstances. A reinterpretation made in the light of more recent developments serves, therefore, to emphasize the special circumstances under which they have lived and thus to make them more understandable to others on the basis of our common humanity.

There were a few Chinese in Hawaii more than a hundred years ago. Between 1853 and 1878 their numbers increased from [about a] hundred to over six thousand.

But the largest section came in the years 1878–83. Another important body came in 1893–97. Like most immigrants from all countries they were, as a rule, poor men and they accepted such economic opportunities as were open to them, mainly plantation labor. But most of them found more attractive opportunities in the course of five or ten years. By 1890 large numbers were found in rice growing and gardening, in the skilled trades, in small merchandise establishments and in numerous other city occupations. Their thrift, industry, shrewdness, dependability and enterprise made them strong competitors for the preferred opportunities.

It was not possible for them to win their improved economic status without provoking some opposition and unfriendly feeling and this was the more acute because of the quickness with which the change was made. The natives who were losing some of their jobs to the Chinese felt much resentment and the planters deprived of their services regarded them with disfavor. They did not "keep their place," and so there were many uncomplimentary things said and printed about them. It is interesting to note that after they had won their superior status the antagonistic feeling gradually subsided and a distinctly friendly attitude has developed.

At present about 75 or 80 percent of the Chinese live in Honolulu and Hilo and most of the others are in the leading towns or villages. Typically the Chinese man uses his first savings for business purposes, but now there are considerable numbers who own their homes also.

The conditions of immigration for the Chinese were such that very few brought wives. In 1884 about five percent of the Chinese men had Chinese wives in Hawaii. By 1900 only about ten percent were so provided and at so late a date as 1920 less than one third of the Chinese men had Chinese wives living in Hawaii.

This abnormal sex ratio had been an important factor in the social life of the Chinese in Hawaii. In the first place it explains the failure of the Chinese population to make a normal growth. There were 25,767 Chinese in Hawaii in 1900 and only 23,507 in 1920. Since 1920 there has been a small gain due to the fact that the sex ratio is becoming more nearly normal.

The fact that a few hundred Chinese men have married non-Chinese women is explained by reference to this same factor of the situation. The number of men so to marry is much smaller than popular opinion has it.

We know that in 1920 there were nearly seven thousand people classed as Asiatic Hawaiian and it is commonly supposed that nearly all of these are of mixed Chinese stock. Probably about 5500 were in reality such, but when one reflects that there were a few intermarriages nearly a hundred years ago and others about fifty years ago it is evident that the 5500 persons of mixed ancestry do not represent a very large amount of direct intermarriage. One Chinese man who married a Hawaiian woman eighty years ago may have a hundred descendants today. Most of the children of part Chinese blood born in recent years are the children of part Chinese, not of pure Chinese on either side.

A superficial consideration of the fact that in Hawaii we have several thousand people of part Chinese ancestry has led to the belief that the Chinese do not have a strong preference for Chinese wives, that, in a somewhat indifferent sort of way, they marry freely with people of other racial stocks. The present writer believes that the

Economic and Social Development

Marital Condition of the Chinese Men of Hawaii for Three Dates

	1900	1910	1920
Males over 21 years old	18,595	13,695	11,223
Single, widowed and divorced	13,449	8,021	5,763
Married:			
A. Wives in China	3,362	3,539	2,134
B. Wives in Hawaii			
1. Chinese	1,409	1,535	2,576
2. Hawaiian	300	390	430
3. Part-Hawaiian	50	150	220
4. Other races	25	60	100

contrary is true and offers the following considerations in support of his belief:

According to the ancient ethical standards of China—standards which have been observed in practice for many centuries—unfilial conduct is the greatest sin of which a man may be guilty; and, of all kinds of unfilial conduct, the worst is to fail to leave descendants to continue the family line. In China boys commonly marry when about 16 years of age to make sure of no failure. For a normal man to remain unmarried for life is almost unthinkable. If one gives due weight to this background of custom and ethical standard it is easy to believe that the only reason for their remaining single in Hawaii was their inability to secure wives of the sort they preferred, i.e., Chinese wives. If such preference had not been very strong they would have married non-Chinese women in much larger numbers.

The relatively large numbers who chose to return temporarily to China in order to marry is further evidence to the same point. Thousands of Hawaiian Chinese have maintained their wives in China because they could not legally bring them to Hawaii. When one sets the few hundred who married non-Chinese women over against the thousands who remained unmarried and the other thousands who married and maintained wives and families in China a strong preference is evident. More recently the sex ratio of adults has become more nearly normal through the maturing of the Hawaiian born and, as a result, the ratio of marriage with non-Chinese has decreased.

Perhaps another interesting trait of the Chinese in Hawaii is explained in part by this abnormal sex ratio. With romantic love playing a smaller part and parental management a large part in the making of marriage arrangements than is common in America, a favorable economic position has been a factor of preference in marriage. Parents of daughters have not favored young men of no property or position. Practically, a young Chinese man of Hawaii must win his status—must have property, a good job, a profession, or a business before he can get a wife,—a Chinese wife. Chinese girls, since they are scarce, are at a premium. One result is that while in China the groom, typically, is younger than the bride, in Honolulu he is older,—older by a greater average number of years than is the case for any other group. This necessity of winning their spurs before they can marry must be an important factor in the explanation of the energy and persistence of the young men in their effort to win advancement in business and the professions.

The favorable attitude of the Chinese toward education is well known. For many centuries the people of China have exalted the scholar. While most of those who came to Hawaii had not enjoyed great educational advantages themselves, they were familiar with the Chinese tradition and were disposed to give their children the best possible advantages. Very rarely would a truant officer be needed if all parents were as much interested in education as are the Chinese.

School attendance is compulsory in Hawaii up to 14 years of age, but optional thereafter. The ratio of attendance for the older children is, therefore, a measure of disposition,—of a desire for education. In 1920, 69.1 percent of the children of Chinese ancestry 16–17 years of age were in school as compared with 36.8 percent for all others of the same age.

The relatively large numbers in the University of Hawaii and in the Normal School and also the numbers in colleges, universities, and professional schools on the mainland could be cited if other evidence were necessary.

Perhaps the most interesting developments now in process among the Chinese of Hawaii are those that result from the fact that in recent years there has come to be a relatively large number of middle aged men and women of the second generation, while the school children are more and more of the third generation. In a brief article it will be impossible to present any adequate account of the significance of this new situation. Suffice it to say that American business methods are gaining. American style houses and furnishings are used more. Home life becomes more like that which is traditional in America and children are developing the distinctive American attitudes.

There was a time when only a few of the second generation had reached adult age. Educated in American schools, they had come to prefer the ways of America to those of their immigrant parents. They did not fit into the social life of the parental group and they had little opportunity for social contacts with Caucasians after they graduated from high school or college. They were too few and too young to build up a satisfactory social life on the American plan for themselves. Their position has been a source of misunderstanding. They seemed to desire unrestricted social relations with Caucasians, but what they really did want was a satisfactory social life on the American plan with people of similar education and refinement and most of such persons, for the time being happened to be Caucasians. But time is clarifying the situation. With the increasing numbers of middle aged men and women of the second generation they are creating a satisfying social life for themselves. There is, consequently, a growing indifference to the matter of social recognition by Caucasians and, for this very reason, such recognition comes in larger measure.

Non-Chinese have made a mistake in attaching too much importance to school boy beliefs and attitudes. It was perfectly natural under the circumstances for the school boys to have an exaggerated appreciation of certain aspects of things American and, correspondingly, to undervalue things Chinese. Apparently this tendency is being corrected as the young people approach middle age. Among the Hawaiian born there is developing a new appreciation of the character and achievement of the immigrants and of the ancient culture they represent. They possess a new sense of dignity as the representatives of a great race.

If one may regard these recent tendencies as representing the more permanent forces, it is possible to foresee a long period of increasing prestige and honor for the Chinese in Hawaii. When the immigrant generation shall have passed away their posterity will erect to them memorials in lasting granite. In literature their achievements will be celebrated and their virtues will be recounted for the instruction of youth.

This is a favorable forecast from the standpoint of American citizenship. In general, those immigrants to America who have brought a sincere love for their native land and a high respect for the cultural achievements of their ancestors and who have taught these things to their children have contributed most to America. If immigrants are so little social minded that they are willing to forget their native land the outlook is not favorable to America. But if they entertain just sentiments of appreciation for the land of their origin their grandchildren, with similar disposition, will manifest their loyalty to what is best in America.

V. Chinese Organizations in Hawaii

CHINESE TONGS AND SOCIETIES

Many Chinese societies use the word *tong* in their names. There are many uses of this same word *tong* in the Chinese language. This has caused confusion and misinterpretation to those not familiar with Chinese language and culture. As a basic word, *tong* can mean a hall, a mansion, a courtroom, a public hall, or large residence. Used in combination with other words, it has such different uses as: *lai tong,* formal hall; *lai bai tong,* place of worship; *miu tong,* temple or shrine; *gau tong,* church; *hawk tong,* school; *chee tong,* ancestral hall. The word *tong* could be used to make up the name of a shop, e.g., Chee Wo Tong, the herb store on Maunakea Street in Chinatown, Honolulu. It could be used with the name of any Chinese social organization, such as Chee Kung Tong, or a cemetery association, such as Man Fook Tong.

Tong wars, in which rival organizations fought for control over illicit activities, as in New York City or San Francisco before the 1930s, did not occur in Hawaii.[1] Fortunately, Hawaii Chinese do not bear this stigma, for they have managed to solve their problems without resorting to violence or secret assassinations.

Instead of *tong,* a great number of Chinese societies use *wui goon* as their designation. For example, the United Chinese Society, or Chinese Benevolent Association, is known as Chung Wah Wui Goon. Ket On Wui Goon is the name of a fraternal Hoong Moon (as pronounced locally) society while Leong Doo Wui Goon is made up of members from the Leong Doo sub-district. Before World War II, there was a Kwangtung Wui Goon in Peking which was built by benefactors of Cantonese origin to serve as an inn or lodging house for scholars coming from Kwangtung to prepare for the Imperial examinations, and for traders from the southern province coming north to transact business. Other provinces also established in Peking similar provincial hostels to take care of their own travelers.

In Hawaii the United Chinese Society was organized in 1884 to represent the entire Chinese community. In San Francisco a similar community organization is the Chinese Consolidated Benevolent Association, better known as the Chinese Six Companies.

In traditional China, the secret society (*bee mut say wui*) was the principal instrument for expression of grievances against Imperial authority. Aggrieved people would form a society of outlaws or join an existing one. They sought concealment in secrecy and preyed upon the countryside. These were "social bandits" or "Robin Hoods"—robbing the rich and helping the poor. The successful ones overthrew the ruling dynasty and established a new order under the Mandate of Heaven. Naturally, the ruling government banned secret organizations and treated them as rebels and traitors. The Triad or Hoong Moon fraternal society is an example of a secret society persecuted by the ruling authorities. The members were banded together as a sworn brotherhood.

In Hawaii, the immigrant Chinese formed many clubs, associations, and societies. They formed a *hui*[2] to pool resources for business ventures, clubs to gather together those persons originating from the same villages or the same districts, and transplanted organization patterns from China to Hawaii. It seems almost as if a fellowship were organized whenever a few Chinese came together in this new land. In the villages in China, there were not as many organizations. Banding together was a product of being away from home, and the multiplicity of organizations is evident in all overseas Chinese communities.

There were certain characteristics common to all the early societies in Hawaii: (1) the emphasis on owning a clubhouse; (2) the shared goals of building fellowship, providing social and recreational outlets, helping each other in a strange land, assisting the unemployed and the sick, burying the dead with respect; (3) women not forming societies of their own but having limited participation in the general activities of the all-male clubs; (4) membership generally lifetime, hence the distorted figures in the membership rolls of these societies (Actually the active members are few. There are usually no annual dues. When funds are needed, the financially able members are solicited for donations which are acknowledged by lists in Chinese

Chinese Organizations

newspapers or lists posted in society halls); and (5) withdrawal from wider community activities to one of social and cultural isolation.[3]

Differing from this tendency toward isolation was the attitude of the Hawaii Chinese Civic Association. The leadership of the Hawaii Chinese Civic Association was in the hands of college graduates who had returned from the mainland United States. As Hawaii-born Chinese, they were American citizens but had faced discrimination on the mainland. They met with immigration detention and examination when they sailed into San Francisco. They faced unnecessary delay at the Canadian border when they tried to cross over to visit Vancouver, Windsor, or Niagara Falls—Canada often refused to recognize citizenship identification cards issued by the U.S. Department of Labor to American citizens of Chinese ancestry from Hawaii. These students met landlords and landladies near their college campuses who would not rent to them. They could not get haircuts from more conveniently located "100 percent American barbers" of European extraction. They were often refused elevator service and told to use service elevators. They were in a quandary when traveling to the South and saw restrooms marked "white" and "colored." These "returnee" graduates also met discrimination in entering local professions and occupations.

Members of the Chinese Civic Association took political action and entered politics. They protested against Hawaii's "English-standard" schools as undemocratic and discriminatory. These schools were set up as a result of complaints from haole parents about the poor speech habits of other pupils. Therefore, beginning in 1920, public schools were segregated according to pupils' proficiency in English. By 1955, "English-standard" schools were abolished.

Today the Chinese Civic Association confines itself to two annual functions—a Fourth of July picnic and a Mandarin Ball in November. There are far fewer complaints of unequal treatment and American-born Chinese are blended into the broad spectrum of Hawaii's peoples. They are now involved in politics as Democrats or Republicans. They become members in the PTA, Boy Scouts, Rotary, Masons, Lions, and other nonethnic organizations.

Chock Lun, a news publisher, prepared a comprehensive inventory of organizations formed by Chinese in Hawaii for the 1936 issue of the *Chinese of Hawaii*.* It is of value to show the variety and multi-

---

* Chock Lun, "Chinese Organizations in Hawaii" in *The Chinese of Hawaii* (Honolulu: Overseas Penman Club, 1936), pp. 22–35.

plicity of Chinese organizations and for comparison with organizations of other immigrant groups. Because of its length, the article has been cut and edited.

The survey lists a hundred Chinese clubs and societies active during the heyday of Chinese organizations in the thirties. As one local-born middle-aged, bilingual Chinese businessman remarked, "I join over forty clubs, both Chinese and cosmopolitan; it is good for business." Today he would have the choice of some seventy organizations from a list prepared annually by the United Chinese Society in Honolulu.

Although there were four and a half times as many American citizens of Chinese ancestry as the alien Chinese in Hawaii, as of June 30, 1935, the organizations for the latter group outnumbered those for the former group.

Many of the old generation organizations have their own clubhouses while many are planning to build them. Most of the first generation organizations were formed with the object of assisting their members in time of need. The younger set however, do not think them necessary.

Membership of the organizations, formed by the old people, now also includes the descendants of the promoters or original members. Some of the young people have been even elected to the presidency of these organizations.

Let us now describe, first, the old generation organizations, then, those that have been formed by the young.

The United Chinese Society, which has its headquarters adjacent to the Honolulu Chinese Chamber of Commerce, should be considered the representative Chinese organization in the territory.[4] Although every Chinese adult is eligible to membership, there are only 500 members, according to the records.

The society was established in 1882. . . . After the fire of 1886 which destroyed the original society building, the present headquarters at 42 N. King St. was built in 1887. . . .[5]

The society works in conjunction with the Chinese Chamber in undertakings for the Chinese community in Hawaii and for China, such as raising flood relief funds. . . .

The Chinese Chamber of Commerce of Honolulu was originally called the Chinese Merchants' Association when it was organized on August 4, 1912. . . .

Chinese Organizations

The headquarters of the association was at first located on the second floor of C. Q. Yee Hop Market. In 1914 it was moved to the premises on Maunakea St., opposite the present Roosevelt theater. . . . The new headquarters of the chamber [was constructed adjoining] the United Chinese Society at 42 N. King St. . . . The building, which cost $12,000, was dedicated on February 9, 1929, the New Year's Day of the lunar calendar.

Besides being a meeting place for the Chinese business people, the chamber has branched out in many activities. It has been the headquarters of the Chinese group for the United Welfare Campaign conducted annually in Honolulu. Several times it has raised flood and famine relief funds for China, notably in 1930 when it raised $42,800 gold and forwarded $146,000 Chinese money to the flood relief fund.

When old and indigent Chinese wish to return to China, the chamber recommends to the Dollar and Canadian Pacific steamship companies for a reduction of 25 percent of steerage fares thus saving $16.25 for each of those old people. The number of old men returning to China annually for the past several years averaged 70. . . .

[*Regional Societies*]

The Yin Fo [People in Harmony] Society, or Nyin Fo Fui Kon, is an organization for the people speaking the Hakka dialect. It is estimated that out of the 27,000 Chinese in the islands, there are 7,000 speaking the Hakka dialect. The old generation of the Hakka people did not come from just one district, but from 16 districts of Kwangtung province. . . .

The first Yin Fo Society is said to have been organized about 75 years ago in San Francisco when there was a Tong war. The war was settled by the Hakka people and the peacemakers therefore formed the Yin Fo Society. . . .

At present there are about 1,000 members. The society has bought a clubhouse on Maunakea St., opposite the Roosevelt theater. After the new clubhouse is dedicated, the name of the society will be changed to Soong Jin [Tsung Tsin] Society. . . .

For wide representation, next comes the See Yup Benevolent Society, . . . an organization for people of four districts in Kwangtung province, namely, Toyshan, Sunwui, Hoyping and Yenping.

It is estimated that there are 3,000 See Yup people in Hawaii, including, of course, the first generation and their descendants. . . .

The Sandalwood Mountains

The society was organized in 1897. . . . The society clubhouse is at 456 N. King St., near Webb lane. The property cost about $30,000. . . .

The Yi Yee Tong is another organization for the See Yup people. . . . It was organized in 1901 for physical training of the members, while the See Yup Society is for charitable and benevolent purposes.

The original headquarters was at the corner of N. King and Aala Sts. In 1903 it was moved to the present location, 116 N. Hotel St. . . .

The Kong Chau Society, for the people of Sunwui district, Kwangtung province, was established in 1907. As Sunwui is one of the "four districts," collectively known as the See Yup, it is the only Chinese society in Hawaii that represents the people of any one district.

Its headquarters was originally situated on Beretania St., near River. In 1922 a new clubhouse was built in Webb Lane, in the rear of the See Yup Society building, near Palama Junction. . . .

There are many organizations for the people of Chungshan district, because the bulk of the Chinese population in Hawaii are natives, or descendants of natives, of that district. It was formerly the Heungshan district until 1925 when the name was changed to Chungshan, in honor of Dr. Sun Yat-sen, known also as Sun Chung-shan, who was a native of that district. . . .

The district is divided into 10 Doos and in each Doo there are upwards of 20 villages. The Doos are Wong Leong Doo, Gook Doo, Kung Seong Doo, See Doo, Dai Doo, Duck Doo, Leong Doo, Yun Doo, Lung Doo, and Larm Doo.

There is no society in Hawaii that represents the residents of the entire Chungshan district, but the people, however, are represented by the societies of the various Doos. [In 1950 a Chungshan Tung Heung Hui was formed.]

We have in Honolulu societies for Lung Doo, See Dai Doo, Leong Doo, Duck Doo, Kung Seong Doo, and Wong Leong Doo. . . .

The Lung Doo Benevolent Society, or Lung Doo Chung Sin Tong, Aala St., between Beretania and Kukui Sts., was organized about 47 years ago. It has about 2,000 members. Besides the society building, the society also has buildings and houses for rent, making it one of the "wealthy" Chinese organizations.

One of the objects of the society is to exhume the bones of the dead members from the local cemeteries every five years and transship them to China for burial. The society also maintains rooms for members who are sick or destitute. . . .

Like all other societies, its objects are to do charity work, to hold reunions and to settle disputes among the members. It has no political affiliation. . . .

As there were about 2,000 Leong Doo people in Hawaii in 1915, the Leong Doo Society (or Leong Jun Society) was formed and a charter secured from the territorial treasurer for the incorporation of the society.

In 1922 . . . a society building was erected on Vineyard St., and dedicated on New Year's Day, 1923. . . .

The Duck Doo Society, or Duck Doo Kee Loo was founded in 1906. The society's headquarters is at Kauluwela Lane, near Vineyard St. It also has some buildings for rent. . . .

Prior to the Honolulu Chinatown fire in 1900, Wong Leong Doo Kee Loo was formed. The society headquarters was then located at River and Hotel Sts. After the 1900 fire, the society clubhouse was moved to N. King St., in the present location of the Kong Chau Society. . . .

The Kung Seong Doo Society is the newest among the Doo societies. It was founded in February, 1930. . . .

The Oo Sack Kee Loo, for the people of Oo Sack village, Gook Doo, was organized in 1897. The society owns its clubhouse at Kamakila lane, off Kukui St. . . .

The On Tong Villagers' Club was organized in November, 1926. Beginning August, 1928, the club has a rented headquarters at 283 N. Kukui St. A new clubhouse was built at 522 N. Vineyard St. and was dedicated October 20, 1935. . . .

The Lungtauwan Villagers' Club was formed in February, 1926. It has about 200 members. . . . Lungtauwan, like Ontong, is a village in Lung Doo. . . .

The Wai Bok Say is a club for the people of Cha Yuen village of See Doo, and was organized in 1927. . . .

Siu Yun Quon Chark Say was organized in 1921, by and for the people of Siu Yun village, in See Doo. It has about 60 members but no clubhouse. . . .

This concludes the description of the local Chinese "regional" organizations so far as the active ones are concerned. Two other villagers' clubs, which are not active and which have not been mentioned, are the Buck Toy Villagers' Club and Yung Wo Tong. The former is for the people of Buck Toy village in Leong Doo and the latter, for Yung Mark villagers in Gook Doo.

[*Clan Organizations*]

There are several organizations for the various clans.

Lung Kong Society is an organization for four clans, Lau, Quon, Chong and Chu. Members of the society are called brothers, due to the fact that Lau Bee, Quon Wun-Chong, Chong Fee and Chu Wun were four sworn brothers during the period of the Three Kingdoms, beginning 220 A.D.

The society was promoted in July, 1919, and was formally organized in 1922. The society headquarters is at 1448 Liliha St. There are about 1,000 members. . . .

Lum Sai Ho Tong is an organization for the Lum clan. It was founded in 1889. Original headquarters was on Smith St., opposite the Sun Yin Wo. . . .

Wong Kong Ha Tong is for the people of the Wong (Huang, in Mandarin) clan. It was organized in 1902. The original clubhouse was on King St. In 1906 the society built its own headquarters on Vineyard St. There are about 1,000 members. . . .

The Mau Association was formed about five years ago, the members of the association being of the Mau clan of Sun Chin village, lower Kung Seong Doo, Chungshan district, Kwangtung province. . . .

The On Kai Say is an organization for the Ching clan of On Ding village of Dai Doo. It was organized five years ago. . . .

The Chun clan people in Honolulu organized the Chun Wing Chin Tong this year. . . .

[*Trade Guilds*]

We have many organizations for the various trades or occupations. Such organizations may be called guilds or trade associations.

The United Chinese Labor Association was originally known as the Chinese Labor Party. It was organized in August, 1917 by some Kuomintang members.

Its rented headquarters is on the second floor at Smith and Pauahi Sts. It is far from being a labor union, because there is no labor leader and it does not represent the laborers. It ought to be called a laborers' club.

Chinese Organizations

In 1935 . . . the association established a library and an employment agency. The two functions are still being maintained. Funds for their upkeep and maintenance are being provided by the Chinese community. . . .

The Seong Gah Hong or the carpenters' guild, was formed about 32 years ago. Its original headquarters was on River St. near Vineyard. In 1915, the guild was reorganized and the clubhouse removed to Hall St. In 1928, a new clubhouse was erected on Liliha St., near Hiram lane. . . .

Wing Lok Ngue Hong or the fish dealers' guild, perhaps is the most active among the guilds. It was formed in 1903 with the original headquarters on Maunakea near King St.

In 1920 a new clubhouse was erected on Kukui St. At the beginning there were only about 40 members, but now the membership has been increased to about 150. It also has property for rent. . . .

The Chinese Butchers' Association or the Ngow Yuk Hong was formed in 1928. Its original headquarters was on the second floor at the corner of Hotel and Maunakea Sts. . . .

The Hoy On Tong the headquarters of which is at the corner of Beretania and Maunakea Sts., may be called the Chinese Seamen's Institute, for it is an organization for the Chinese people working on steamships. It was founded on February 2, 1903.

It is a mutual benefit organization. The original enrollment was 90. The membership dwindled to about 50 at present. There is no known activity except the annual election. . . .

The Quon On Kwock, Smith St., near Beretania, is an organization for Chinese people working as cooks or waiters in hotels or restaurants. Most of the members, however, have changed their occupations since their affiliation with the society. It was organized on August 1, 1901. The annual election is held August 1, the anniversary date for the organization. . . .

The Gut Hing Kung So is an organization for the Chinese musicians and actors. It was founded on May 20, 1922. Its clubhouse is on Hall St. near Kukui. . . .

Tan Sing Dramatic Club is also an organization for the Chinese musicians and actors. Most of the members, however, are of the young element. . . .

The Jing Sing Musicians' Club was formed during the mid-autumn festival of 1934. . . .

Besides the foregoing active guilds, the local Chinese previously had organized the Wah Hing Tong, or laundrymen's guild, the Bark Yee Hong, or the dressmakers' guild, the Gum Yee Hong, or the tailors' guild, and the Luen Hing Club, or the waiters' guild, but all of them have ceased functioning, due to the lack of interest of the members....

[*Literary and Educational Societies*]

Next, we have several literary organizations.

The Chinese-English Debating Society was organized in 1893 by Luke Chan, the late Ho Fon and others.

Mr. Ho was then a reporter for the Lung Kee Bo, a Chinese language newspaper in Honolulu, working for the cause of Dr. Sun Yat-sen's revolution. He advocated the organization of such a club whereby the young people of those days (about 43 years ago) could further their studies in the Chinese and English languages.

The society's first clubhouse at the corner of King and Kekaulike Sts. was destroyed by the great Chinatown fire. The society then bought a piece of property on Vineyard St. which has been leased to some other people. The members have become the well known group among the older generation, a majority of them being outstanding business men.

There are no other known activities besides the election and dinner held annually on Washington's Birthday at the Sun Yin Wo. . . .

The Moo Hawk Club is the organization that conducts the Mun Lun Chinese school, which was promoted by its members. . . .

In 1910 . . . [the] president of the club . . . advocated the establishment of a Chinese school, and the Mun Lun school was founded in the following year, 1911.

The officers of the club have been and are the officers of the Mun Lun school. . . .

The Hoo Cho Society was founded in 1923 by a group of young Chinese who have been educated in China. In 1925 the society established and has been conducting for nine years the Hoo Cho Chinese school. In the latter part of 1935 the school was turned to the Chinese community at large. . . .

The Min Chung Literary Society was organized in 1935, the promoters being the faculty members of the Mun Lun school. . . .

The Hawaii Chinese Artists Association was founded in January,

1935. Since its establishment, the oil paintings of the members have been exhibited several times. . . .

The Hawaii Chinese Aero Club is a new organization, formed this year by local aviation students. . . .

The Chinese University Club was organized in 1919. . . . The members are graduates of colleges or universities in the United States, including Hawaii. . . .

The Chinese University Women's Club was organized five years ago. . . .

The Chinese Students' Alliance of Hawaii was founded in 1906. . . . There are . . . units, or branches, in the various English schools.

Besides the foregoing clubs there are many in the English schools, and the Chinese school alumni associations.

At the University of Hawaii there are the Peng Hui, the Yang Chung Hui, the Te Chih Sheh . . . and the Tu Chiang Sheh. . . . At the St. Louis College there is the Clia Club (Clia stands for Chinese Literary Improvement Association).

While we are on the subject of literary organizations, we might mention the clubs formed by the Chinese speaking element but which do not function any longer.

The Jup Mun Say was the oldest among the Chinese literary clubs. It was founded in 1891, or 45 years ago. . . . The organization lasted only for two years.

The Young People's Literary Club was organized in 1910, by Sun Fo, son of the late Dr. Sun Yat-sen, . . . and others. It existed for about a year.

In 1912 the Young People's Oratorical Association (YPOA) was organized by a group of students. . . .

In 1918 the Chinese Literary Association was formed. It became inactive in 1928. This club, perhaps, was the only Chinese literary club that had been incorporated under the territorial laws. Its headquarters was at the rear of the Chungshan school, Kukui St.

The Chinese Educational Association was organized in 1928 by the teachers of the various Chinese schools in Honolulu. . . .

[*Political Parties (China Oriented)*]

The Kuomintang was established in Honolulu in 1894 by the late Dr. Sun Yat-sen, although it was known then as the Hing Chung Hui, or the China Reviving Society. Dr. Sun was then 29 years old. It was the first revolutionary organization he established.

In 1905, or 11 years later, Dr. Sun established the Tung Ming Hui in Tokyo, Japan. In 1907 he sent Loo Sun to Hawaii to preach the revolutionary gospel. Mr. Loo established *The Liberty News* in 1908. . . .[6]

In March, 1910, Dr. Sun came to Hawaii for the fifth time and founded the Tung Ming Hui. . . .

After the establishment of the Chinese Republic in 1912, and the inauguration of Dr. Sun as president of the republic, the Tung Ming Hui was given a new name, the Kuomintang. . . .[7]

Historically, the Kuomintang had been a political opponent of the Chinese Reform Society, or the Constitutionalist Party, as compared to the Republican and Democratic parties in America.

The Chinese Reform Society was originally the Bo Kwock Hui, or the National Protective Association, the promoters of which included the late Kang Yu-wei and Liang Chi-chao. They and their followers initiated the Chinese reform movement in 1898.

The reform movement was a political revolution without bloodshed. It failed. At that time, the empress dowager had the absolute administrative power, while the emperor was just a titular head. The reform movement was to depose the empress dowager and restore the real power to the emperor, Kuang Hsu.

An attempt was made to convert the absolute monarchy of the Manchu (Ching) dynasty into a constitutional monarchy. This irritated the empress dowager, whose followers caught and killed six of the Kang-Liang disciples.

The reform movement having failed, Kang and Liang fled from China, for they were wanted by the empress dowager. The emperor, Kwang Sui [Kuang Hsu] was imprisoned, having been accused of conspiring in the so-called reform movement.

Liang Chi-Chiao first fled to Japan, promoting the organization of the Bo Kwock Wui, or the National Protective Association, in order to save the emperor, Kwang Sui [Kuang Hsu], and to drive out the cohorts of the empress dowager. Subsequently, the name of the association was changed to Bo Wong Wui, or Emperor Protective Association. They believed that the emperor must first be saved and protected before the nation could be saved.

In March, 1900, Liang secretly came to Honolulu from Japan. It was just after the great fire of Chinatown in Honolulu. The Chinese here were so heartbroken that they were anxious to convert a weak China into a strong China. Liang got hold of the opportunity and organized the Bo Wong Wui in Honolulu.

W. W. Ahana and the late Chung Mook-Heen (father of Senator William Heen) were among those supporting Liang in organizing the Bo Wong Wui here. The first meeting was held on the second floor of Wing Wo Tai. The clubhouse was later moved to the corner of King and Nuuanu Sts., now occupied by a furniture store.

A vacant lot at the corner of Kukui St. and College Walk was donated to the association by W. W. Ahana, and a new clubhouse was erected.

As oration was inadequate as a means for propagandizing, Liang promoted the publishing of a newspaper. The first issue of the *Sun Chung Kwock Bo,* or the *New China News,* was published in the latter part of March, 1900.[8] This paper is still in existence.

The Bo Wong Wui, as a name, existed until 1908 when Emperor Kuang Hsu died and the name was changed to the Imperial Constitutionalist, or Dai Kwock Hin Jing, Party. When the Chinese republic was established in 1912, the name of the party was changed to the Chinese Constitutionist Party, or Chung Kwock Hin Jing Dong, but the English name of the party is Chinese Reform Society. . . .

The Chee Kung Tong could be termed as a Chinese political party. It was a secret Chinese organization during the Ching (Manchu) dynasty and exists in many parts of the world, particularly on the mainland United States. Such organizations are known generally as "Hoong Moon." The object of Hoong Moon societies was to "overthrow the Ching dynasty and to revive the Ming dynasty. . . ."

Hoong Moon societies in Hawaii were established about 80 years ago. The Chee Kung Tong is composed of the Bow Leong Say and the Wo On Society. The Bow Leong Say was formed in 1892, while the Wo On Society was organized in 1905. When the two societies were merged in 1913, the name was changed to Yee Hing Chung Wui and the latter changed to Chee Kung Tong in 1919.

The Chee Kung Tong has its headquarters at Aala lane, near Kukui St. It had about 5,000 members, but the number has declined to about 1,000, as many have passed away due to old age. Not very many members are under the age of 35. . . .

The Chee Kung Tong is an organization incorporated under the laws of the Territory of Hawaii. No election of officers had been held from 1923 to 1934, a total of 11 years, due to litigation between two factions within the society. Election was resumed in 1935. . . .

The Chee Kung Tong formerly conducted a newspaper. The last publication was the Hon Mun Bo, which went out of business five years ago.

Ket On Fui Kon, or Kwock On Society, Kukui St., is another of the local Hoong Moon societies. It was founded about 65 years ago. . . .

[*Civic Associations*]

Now, we shall describe the Hawaii Chinese Civic Association which, in some way, is an organization relating to American politics.

The association is an organization for the American citizens of Chinese ancestry, including those born here and those who had been naturalized. Aliens are not eligible to membership. . . .

Members of the association hold a picnic on the Fourth of July every year. They are active when there is a territorial election.

There were 1,600 members in 1934, but there are only 800 this year after a membership campaign.

Another noticeable organization of the younger generation is the Kau-Tom Post No. 11 of the American Legion, which was organized in 1927. . . .

On April 6, 1917, the United States participated in the World War. More than 1,000 local born Chinese were enlisted in the American army for service. Apau Kau, well known baseball pitcher, and George B. Tom were the two local Chinese among those killed in the battle front in Europe.

In March, 1919, or four months after the armistice of November 11, 1917, the American Legion was organized, the members consisting of those who had taken part in the war. The local Kau-Tom Post organization was organized in commemoration of Apau Kau and George B. Tom. . . .

In conjunction with the Kau-Tom Post, there is the Kau-Tom Unit No. 11 of the American Legion Auxiliary, which is in brief, known as the Kau-Tom Auxiliary.

It is an organization of the sisters or wives (or any other female family member), of the members of the Kau-Tom Post, and was established three years after the Post was formed. . . .

Chinese Organizations

Other Clubs

Kwong Yee Society, organized in 1899, has no activities other than the annual election. Members of the society, however, have organized a corporation called the Kwong Yick Real Estate Co., Ltd. to handle the property of the society. . . .

The Chinese YMCA, located on Beretania St., near the central fire station, was established in 1895.

The Chinese Mutual Benefit Association is a very new organization, established February 26, 1935. . . . As the name implies, it is a Chinese mutual benefit association. It will aid the sick and give help to the family of the deceased. . . .

The Chinese Commercial Club is an organization of the business and professional people of the second generation. It was formed in 1935. . . .

The Triple C Club was organized in 1922 by some young business men. The members were originally graduates of McKinley High School, but the present membership includes graduates and undergraduates of other high schools. It has a clubhouse in Waimanalo, Oahu. . . .

The Council Club is another organization of the young men. It was formed in March 1935 with about 250 members. . . .

Besides these, there are other clubs organized by the younger generation. Among them are the Chinese Catholic Club, Pagoda Club, Fat Sut Circle, Cathayan Associates, the A.C.A. and the Chinese Ladies' Aid Society.

The Chinese Women's Club [still very active in 1974] is an organization of the English speaking Chinese women in Honolulu, founded on 25 August 1928, at the suggestion of Dr. [Mei-jung] Ting, a Chinese woman physician of Tientsin, who visited Honolulu as China's delegate to the Pan Pacific Surgical Conference. . . .

The purposes of this club are to better social relationships and to promote civic improvements among the Chinese.

FRATERNAL SOCIETIES

Fraternal societies in Hawaii were of the Hoong Moon (Hung Men) type, Triad branch. The society here helped the cause of the Chinese Revolution of 1911 when Dr. Sun Yat-sen, in his many efforts to enlist the help of overseas Chinese, joined the Ket On Society of Hawaii in 1903.

The societies in Hawaii were, from the beginning, engaged in peaceful activities of mutual protection and mutual welfare. Their chief concerns were care of the elderly and disabled and burial of the dead. They did not develop into corrupt syndicates employing violence to settle internal disputes nor become involved in notorious *tong* wars which disrupted Chinatowns and Chinese settlements elsewhere. It speaks well for Hawaiian government that foreigners on her shores had recourse to her courts. Smaller disputes among the Chinese were settled by Triad moral codes.

The basic idea of the fraternity of a sworn brotherhood gave significance to Kwan Dai (Kuan Ti) who was a military hero in the period of The Three Kingdoms (200 A.D.–280 A.D.). He with Liu Pei and Chang Fei started the first fraternity in the "Peach Garden," legendary to Chinese folklore. Kwan Dai became patron saint and symbol of loyalty to Hoong societies. One may find this deity in statue or, more often, in picture form before an altar in such Chinese fraternal society halls in Hawaii. Kwan Dai was one of many deities of Chinese folk religion, and in secret societies was worshipped along with the "Five Founding Fathers" of Hoong Moon and the usual Heaven, Earth, and even door gods. These were in the secret Halls of Loyalty, usually the upper story ceremonial halls of two-storied fraternal society buildings, ruins of which may be seen in old or abandoned Chinese settlements in Hawaii.[9]

Although females could not be members of a sworn brotherhood, arrangements were made to take care of their spiritual needs by adding separate altars or niches in the building to house popular deities like Kuan Yin, Hau Wong, and Tin Hau.

Ground floors were used as school rooms for teaching the Chinese language, as game and recreational rooms, and as an assembly hall for festive occasions like the Chinese New Year celebration when the wider community participated—haoles, Hawaiians, and others. The Tong Wo Society in Kohala conducted bazaars with tents out on the lawn to sell home-cooked Chinese food and home-made handicrafts. Of course, the familiar pig oven was worked overtime to produce roast suckling pig, duck, chicken, and *char-siu* ("barbecued pork").

The local pronunciation for Hoong Moon has been used for trans-

Chinese Organizations

literation; however, the reading uses romanization, Hung Men, from standard speech or Kuo Yu.*

Secret societies have existed in China since ancient times but their activity and numbers increased markedly from the time when the Sung dynasty was invaded by barbarians from the North. Because of the secrecy which has surrounded them and because scholars have regarded them as unworthy of attention, little reliable information about these societies has come down to us. However, generally speaking, they are represented by two broad movements, the White Lotus and the Hung Society. The White Lotus Society has predominated in the North. It has been chiefly religious (though it has started and participated in many revolutions) and has a great number of branches loosely organized and related to one another. The Hung Society, on the other hand, has predominated in South, West, and Central China. It has been primarily political, though with a religious coloring, and has branched into several well-organized groups. The White Lotus and some of its offshoots have already been mentioned. In this section, we shall confine ourselves to the Hung Society.

The Hung Society (*Hung men*) may possibly have its origin in the White Lotus, though more probably it was organized in the middle of the seventeenth century by supporters of the Ming dynasty with the avowed purpose of overthrowing the Manchus and restoring Chinese rule. According to the society's own account, it was founded by a scholar named Yin Hung-sheng in 1631, whom its members consider to be their First Founding Father. In the declining years of the Ming, Yin rallied a number of prominent scholars about him in an effort to save the dynasty. His efforts were unsuccessful, however, and he died in 1645. A decade or so later, a group of monks in the Shao-lin Temple in Fukien secretly organized for revolution. In 1672 when the Manchu emperor called for volunteers to fight an invasion by a western tribe, they answered the call and expelled the invaders. But when it was finally discovered that they were actually rebels in search of an opportunity for an uprising, their temple was surrounded and burned. Five monks (later honored as the "Five Early Founding

---

* Wing-tsit Chan, "Secret Societies," in *Sources of Chinese Tradition*, Wm. Theodore de Bary et al., ed., (New York: Columbia University Press, 1963), pp. 649–651; reprinted with permission of Columbia University Press.

Fathers") escaped, hid under a bridge, and were saved by five brave men (the "Five Middle Founding Fathers"). These were later joined by five other monks (the "Five Later Founding Fathers"). After much fighting against the Manchus, they met Abbot Ten-thousand-Cloud Dragon (Wan Yün-lung) and Ch'en Chin-nan (the "Great Ancestor"), who started an independent uprising. Ch'en and the Five Early Founding Fathers plotted their revolution in the Red Flower Pavilion in present Hupei province. In the second period (1:00–3:00 A.M.) of the twelve-period day cycle on the twenty-fifth day of the seventh month in 1674 they and their followers formally took a vow to be fraternal brothers, overthrow the Manchus, and restore the Ming. The conspiracy spread to South China. By 1698 Ch'en had died but his successors continued the fight. Members of the society worshiped Heaven as father and earth as mother and for this reason the society is also called the Heaven and Earth Society (*T'ien-ti hui*).

It is doubtful if any of this account is reliable. Even the origin and meaning of the name Hung is in dispute, but the majority opinion holds that it refers to the reign Hung-wu of the founder of the Ming dynasty. At any rate the story of the burning of the Shao-lin Temple has become a colorful and exciting part of Chinese folklore dramatized in endless variations on the popular stage and in story telling, and the Bridge and the Pavilion have been adopted as sacred symbols in the society's ceremonies. The movement, starting in Fukien, spread later to Formosa, to East, South, and West China, and finally to the far Southwest and Northwest. The society participated in many revolts, notably those of 1774 and the Taiping Rebellion.

Like most secret societies, the *Hung men* has developed into many branches, such as the Double Sword Society, Dagger Society, and the Clear Water Society. Their history is vague and their relationships are uncertain. Two branches of the society, however, stand out prominently and are known at least in broad outline. One of these is the Triple Harmony Society (*San-ho hui,* referring perhaps to the harmony of Heaven, earth, and man; or to the three "rivers," also pronounced *ho,* where the rebels met). It is also called the Triad Society (*San-tien hui,* referring perhaps to the three dots on the left side of the Chinese character *hung*). The other branch is the Elders Society (*Ko-lao hui*). The Triad Society was strong in South China, especially among farmers and working people, as well as among the overseas Chinese. In the United States it has branched into or affiliated with the Chih Kung Tong ("Society to Bring About Justice"), which is now no longer secret but a purely charitable organization. In recent years the Triad Society took an active part in the Revolution of 1911 led by Sun Yat-sen, in the revolution against Yuan Shih-k'ai's attempt to become emperor in 1915, and in resisting the Japanese invasion in the Second World War.

The Elders Society, variously named in different parts of China, originated in Fukien somewhat later than the Triad Society. One theory is that in 1853 when the Triad Society was resisting the Manchus in South China, the Elders Society arose in Central and North China in sympathetic response. In any case it spread over most of the country but became particularly strong in Central, North, and West China. It is said to have been so powerful in the nineteenth century that even leading government generals such as Tseng Kuo-fan (1811–1872) and Tso Tsung-t'ang (1812–1885) were obliged to join it. In recent times it was the most extensive, well organized, and influential of China's secret societies.

The ideals of the Hung Society may be summed up as patriotism, chivalry, fraternity, and traditional morality. The spirit of patriotism of the society needs no comment, except to add that the society worships Emperor T'ai Tsung (r. 627–644), founder of the T'ang dynasty. Like other secret societies, it employs pass words, hand signs, signs by arrangement of tea cups, and so on, about which members are pledged to keep absolute secrecy or suffer death. Unlike other secret societies, however, the combined spirit of chivalry, fraternity, and patriotism makes the Hung Society unique. It regards as its model the famous fraternity of the Peach Garden, where Kuan Kung (d. 219, erroneously called in the West the God of War) and two other heroes vowed to be brothers and to defend the Han dynasty, and also the well-known 108 rebels vividly described in the novel *Shui-hu chuan* (*The Water Margin* or *All Men Are Brothers*).

THE THIRTY-SIX OATHS OF HOONG MOON SOCIETIES

Most of the active Hoong Moon fraternal societies in Hawaii keep a charter and are registered with the State Department of Regulatory Agencies (formerly the Territorial Treasurer). It is possible to review through government sources the legal and tax status of each society.

The Chee Kung Tong at 357 North Kukui Street, Honolulu in 1963 combined its *New Building Issue* of 1956 together with its *70th*

The Sandalwood Mountains

Anniversary Supplement of 1962 into one publication. It made public its by-laws and traditions. It is interesting to note:

1. There is no racial discrimination as to membership.
2. There is no sex restriction. (Here in Hawaii, however, there are no known instances of women becoming full-fledged members or officers.)
3. There are limitations as to age. A person below 16 is considered too young to participate. A person over 60 would join to make use of the old-age benefits—food and lodging for the needy and funeral benefits and shipping of remains to China.
4. There is no restriction on a member of one lodge joining another in the same town or territory.
5. After initiation and payment of initiation fees membership is for life.

A traditional part of Hoong Moon societies is the Thirty-Six Oaths which play a most important part in the fraternal ceremonies.[10] For example, at Lahaina, Maui, the Wo Hing fraternal society keeps a six-foot square banner with beautiful calligraphic writing of the oaths. On the four corners of the yellow silk piece are the four characters for "Overthrow the Manchus, Restore the Ming" (*fan* Ch'ing, *fook* Ming).

Of course, this precious relic of over sixty years had been carefully folded and stored away. It was taken out for the initiation of new members to impress on them their responsibilities as members of a brotherhood. It was also used in membership disputes. The senior officers would sit in front of the banner, listen to both parties' complaints, and make their judgment for a peaceful settlement without resort to court or violence, basing their decision on the moral codes of the oaths.[11]

The oaths from a Hoong Moon society in Hong Kong are similar to those in use by all such organizations.*

---

1. After having entered the Hung gates I must treat the parents and relatives of my sworn brothers as my own kin. I shall suffer death by five thunderbolts if I do not keep this oath.

* W. P. Morgan, *Triad Societies in Hong Kong* (Hong Kong: Government Press, 1960), pp. 157–158.

2. I shall assist my sworn brothers to bury their parents and brothers by offering financial or physical assistance. I shall be killed by five thunderbolts if I pretend to have no knowledge of their troubles.
3. When Hung brothers visit my house, I shall provide them with board and lodging. I shall be killed by myriads of knives if I treat them as strangers.
4. I will always acknowledge my Hung brothers when they identify themselves. If I ignore them I will be killed by myriads of swords.
5. I shall not disclose the secrets of the Hung family, not even to my parents, brothers, or wife. I shall never disclose the secrets for money. I will be killed by myriads of swords if I do so.
6. I shall never betray my sworn brothers. If, through a misunderstanding, I have caused the arrest of one of my brothers I must release him immediately. If I break this oath I will be killed by five thunderbolts.
7. I will offer financial assistance to sworn brothers who are in trouble in order that they may pay their passage fee, etc. If I break this oath I will be killed by five thunderbolts.
8. I must never cause harm or bring trouble to my sworn brothers or Incense Master. If I do so I will be killed by myriads of swords.
9. I must never commit any indecent assaults on the wives, sisters, or daughters, of my sworn brothers. I shall be killed by five thunderbolts if I break this oath.
10. I shall never embezzle cash or property from my sworn brothers. If I break this oath I will be killed by myriads of swords.
11. I will take good care of the wives or children of sworn brothers entrusted to my keeping. If I do not do so I will be killed by five thunderbolts.
12. If I have supplied false particulars about myself for the purpose of joining the Hung family I shall be killed by five thunderbolts.
13. If I should change my mind and deny my membership of the Hung family I will be killed by myriads of swords.
14. If I rob a sworn brother or assist an outsider to do so I will be killed by five thunderbolts.
15. If I should take advantage of a sworn brother or force unfair business deals upon him I will be killed by myriads of swords.
16. If I knowingly convert my sworn brothers' cash or property to my own use I shall be killed by five thunderbolts.
17. If I have wrongly taken a sworn brother's cash or property during

a robbery I must return them to him. If I do not I will be killed by five thunderbolts.
18. If I am arrested after committing an offense I must accept my punishment and not try to place the blame on my sworn brothers. If I do so I will be killed by five thunderbolts.
19. If any of my sworn brothers are killed, or arrested, or have departed to some other place, I will assist their wives and children who may be in need. If I pretend to have no knowledge of their difficulties I will be killed by five thunderbolts.
20. When any of my sworn brothers have been assaulted or blamed by others, I must come forward and help him if he is in the right or advise him to desist if he is wrong. If he has been repeatedly insulted by others I shall inform our other brothers and arrange to help him physically or financially. If I do not keep this oath I will be killed by five thunderbolts.
21. If it comes to my knowledge that the Government is seeking any of my sworn brothers who has come from other provinces or from overseas, I shall immediately inform him in order that he may make his escape. If I break this oath I will be killed by five thunderbolts.
22. I must not conspire with outsiders to cheat my sworn brothers at gambling. If I do so I will be killed by myriads of swords.
23. I shall not cause discord amongst my sworn brothers by spreading false reports about any of them. If I do so I will be killed by myriads of swords.
24. I shall not appoint myself as Incense Master without authority. After entering the Hung gates for three years the loyal and faithful ones may be promoted by the Incense Master with the support of his sworn brothers. I shall be killed by five thunderbolts if I make any unauthorized promotions myself.
25. If my natural brothers are involved in a dispute or law suit with my sworn brothers I must not help either party against the other but must attempt to have the matter settled amicably. If I break this oath I will be killed by five thunderbolts.
26. After entering the Hung gates I must forget any previous grudges I may have borne against my sworn brothers. If I do not do so I will be killed by five thunderbolts.
27. I must not trespass upon the territory occupied by my sworn brothers. I shall be killed by five thunderbolts if I pretend to have no knowledge of my brothers' rights in such matters.

Chinese Organizations

28. I must not covet or seek to share any property or cash obtained by my sworn brothers. If I have such ideas I will be killed.
29. I must not disclose any address where my sworn brothers keep their wealth nor must I conspire to make wrong use of such knowledge. If I do so I will be killed by myriads of swords.
30. I must not give support to outsiders if so doing is against the interests of any of my sworn brothers. If I do not keep this oath I will be killed by myriads of swords.
31. I must not take advantage of the Hung brotherhood in order to oppress or take violent or unreasonable advantage of others. I must be content and honest. If I break this oath I will be killed by five thunderbolts.
32. I shall be killed by five thunderbolts if I behave indecently towards the small children of my sworn brothers' families.
33. If any of my sworn brothers has committed a big offence I must not inform upon them to the Government for the purposes of obtaining a reward. I shall be killed by five thunderbolts if I break this oath.
34. I must not take to myself the wives and concubines of my sworn brothers nor commit adultery with them. If I do so I will be killed by myriads of swords.
35. I must never reveal Hung secrets or signs when speaking to outsiders. If I do so I will be killed by myriads of swords.
36. After entering the Hung gates I shall be loyal and faithful and shall endeavour to overthrow Ch'ing and restore Ming by co ordinating my efforts with those of my sworn brethren even though my brethren and I may not be in the same professions. Our common aim is to avenge our Five Ancestors.

INVENTORY OF FRATERNAL SOCIETIES, PAST AND PRESENT

At one time, at least twenty Hoong Moon societies were established in the Hawaiian Islands. They had clubhouses where elaborate secret rituals and ceremonies were held. Of these only three were located in Honolulu where other social organizations satisfied the need for fellowship. It was in the rural towns and plantation communities that these societies flourished because their clubhouses served as community centers for lonely laborers.

Professor Rose Hum Lee has made this observation on Chinatowns and their social organizations:

> The Chinese represent slightly less than one-tenth of one per cent of the total population of the United States. . . . About 7 cities in this country have large enough Chinese populations, 2,500 and more, to be recorded by the census as exhibiting a distinct social organization. . . . Once the population becomes predominantly native-born, the various associations weaken and their control over members' behavior is ineffective. . . . Associations met the needs of the foreign-born when they settled in a strange land, had few resources to meet life crises (sickness, death, burials, feuds, and so on), and acted as a meeting place (headquarters) for the membership. Until recently, few Chinese were eligible for Old Age Assistance, Social Security, or welfare aid of various forms, so that these associations served a needed function. . . . As the needs of the older segment outdistance the ability of the associations to provide sustained services, the association's influence also wanes. Most native-born see little need for such ties and prefer joining organizations of the larger society, or if there is a sizeable group of them they form their own organizations based on common interest rather than on territorial or clan origins.[12]

Unlike Elks and Masonic types of American fraternal groups, the Hoong Moon societies did not use one name to identify themselves. However, one can take an intelligent guess whether or not a club is a Hoong Moon society by their use of certain Chinese characters in club names: *hing* for "restoration," *kung* for "public good," *yee* for "righteousness," *wo* for "harmony," *on* for "peace," *chee* for "towards or to attain," *ying* for "heroic." In various combinations of two ideographs these usually make up the name of a Triad society. The most common combination used is *chee kung* which means "to attain the common good."

Here is an inventory of such fraternal societies in Hawaii, past and present, active and inactive, and their dates of organization wherever obtainable. A few names and dates need further verification; some buildings have been abandoned or demolished. Identification of location is mostly by tax keys to tax maps. The tax maps in the State Department of Taxation help to locate the clubhouse sites, to get the legal name and status of the society when disputes arise as to owner-

Chinese Organizations

ship or control of property. They identify whether the land is fee simple, on lease, or owned by a plantation. The title history verifies changes in ownership.

I. Island of Oahu
   Honolulu
   1. Ket On Society on 1125 Maunakea Street, tax key 1-7-03-52. First organized in Koolau in 1869 under the name of Tung Hing Society. Moved to Honolulu in 1899 and changed to present name of Ket On Society.
   2. Chee Kung Tong—new building under construction in Cultural Plaza, on Beretania and Maunakea streets. Tax key 1-7-05. First started as Bow Leong Sheh in 1892 and merged in 1919 with Wo On Society which was formed in 1905.

   Heeia
   3. Bow Yee Tong organized in 1903. Consolidated in 1933 with Chung Hing Society of Kaneohe. Old site given up for shopping center development. In exchange received in 1970 some 34,000 square feet of vacant land on Lilipuna Road, tax key 4-6-02-24.

   Waipahu
   4. Tsoong Yee Society located at 94-717 Waipahu Road. Main building constructed in 1909 collapsed from recent windstorm and now abandoned. Tax key 9-4-10-19.

II. Island of Kauai
   Kapaa
   6. Yan Wo Company on Kamoa Road. Building torn down for parking lot of Mokihana Lodge. Tax key 1-3-07-12.

   Hanapepe
   7. Chee Kung Fui Kon off Alahula Road. Tax key 1-9-12-29. Building abandoned and vandalized.

   Lawai
   8. Hop Hing Co. off Koloa Road and Lauoho Road near the Cannery. Clubhouse abandoned. Tax key 2-5-04-2.

Lihue-Kapaia
9. Hung On Sheh on Lihue Plantation land(?). Tax key 3-7-04-9. Off Laukini Road on Kuhio Highway. Building collapsed and abandoned.

Hanalei
10. Yee Hing Society on plantation land, tax key 5-4-03-5. Building torn down and demolished after appropriate Taoist ritual (1955?).

III. Island of Maui

Keanae
11. Lin Hing Society clubhouse built in 1908, tax key 1-1-03-40. Abandoned and vandalized.

Kula
12. Ket Hing (Kwock Hing) Society. Tax key 2-2-03-36. Organized in 1900; present clubhouse built in 1907. Of the founding membership list of 71, about 25 percent were bachelors.

Lahaina
13. Wo Hing Society. Located on Front Street. Tax key 4-5-01-17, 45, 51. Organized in 1909 with C. Ah You (Chung Kon You) as founding president.

Wailuku
14. Tow Yee Kwock Society, tax key 3-4-13-55. Organized in 1906. Dissolved and sold property to Maui Savings and Loan Association in 1964.
15. Chee Kung Tong (Gee Kung Tong), tax key 3-4-13-40. Clubhouse located at 2145 Vineyard Street. Organized in 1904. Clubhouse condemned, abandoned, vandalized, barricaded.

Kipahulu
16. Chee Kung Tong. Organized in 1908 before the Keanae clubhouse was built. Possibly tax key 1-6-09, subject to verification. Further research is needed.

IV. Island of Hawaii

Hilo
17. Ling Hing Society. Organized in 1899. Destroyed by tidal wave 1960. In a temporary location at Pele Lane.

Chinese Organizations

Hamakua

    18. Chee Yuen (Chee Ying) Association. Organized in 1907, on Government Main Road. Tax key 4-5-09-11. Clubhouse is abandoned. University of Hawaii, Hilo Campus, conducted historical research here in 1970 as part of a field survey of historical sites.

Kohala

    19. Tong Wo Society, tax key 5-3-08-20. On main highway, Halawa. Founded in 1886. Custodians Ah Fook Ching, James Chai, and Florence Shim. University of Hawaii, Hilo Campus, anthropology classes under Prof. William Bonk conducted surveys in 1970. Results to be reported to State Department of Land and Natural Resources.

Kailua, Kona

    20. Gee Hing Chinese Co. On Kuakini Highway, near Mokuaikaua Church. Tax key 7-5-04-13. Clubhouse constructed in 1901 and destroyed by fire in 1971.

Naalehu, Ka'u

    21. Chinese Society Church (Bow Sin Tong). On Mamalahoa Highway across from Naalehu School. Tax key 9-5-08-12. Cemetery in back is on land granted in 1874 by King Kalakaua for cemetery use.

CHINESE CEMETERIES

"The Chinese, more than some other groups, have a reverence for the cemeteries and the ceremonies conducted there, honoring the dead members of their families. This is true of Hawaii even among those of Chinese ancestry who, in other ways, have discarded the customs of their forefathers. . . . Location of the cemetery is on sloping ground and has great natural beauty, two essentials of a place to honor one's deceased family, according to Chinese tradition."[13]

In isolated plantation camps and rural agricultural communities, the Hoong Moon fraternal association was usually the community organization available to carry out burial and cemetery care. The lonely laborer joined the fraternal club to assure that he would be given a respectable burial, that his bones could be disinterred later and be shipped back to his home village, and, if he had chosen a permanent burial site owned or managed by the fraternal society, he could

The Sandalwood Mountains

depend on the annual *bai-san* ceremony in April conducted by his brotherhood.

The fraternal society's cemetery could be next to its clubhouse or at some other location. The cemetery might be operated by a separate cemetery association on its own land or on plantation or government land. The following is a list of identifiable Chinese cemeteries. Tax keys are used to identify the exact location and make possible title history searches. Those under the auspices of Hoong Moon fraternal associations are identified as "fraternal."

I. Island of Oahu
   Honolulu
   1. Hook Chu Cemetery Association
      Located at 2219 Pauoa Road, tax key 2-2-12-108. For the use of early Chinese immigrants of Hookien-Chuchow (Fukien-Chaochow) dialect. They were a seafaring people speaking the southern Fukien dialect but occupying the northeastern region of Kwangtung province with Swatow as the seaport. As mentioned in note 13 to chapter 1, Akaka (Lee Shak) of this dialectal group is buried here.
   2. Manoa Chinese Cemetery (Lin Yee Chung)
      Located on East Manoa and Pahanu Street, tax key 2-9-43-1, B1, 2 and 4. The earliest burial was reported to be that of Lau Juck who died in the 1800s. He is given the title of Manoa Gung, the Great Ancestor at Manoa. Annual Ching Ming ceremonies are traditionally conducted on April 5 at 11 a.m. Thereafter, every weekend of that month is busy with family groups and clan associations gathering to "sweep the graves" and pay respects to the departed members.
   3. Pauoa Chinese Cemeteries on Auwaiolimu Street with areas under four associations:
      A. Yee King Tong, established in 1885, tax key 2-2-14-16.
      B. Man Hing Tong (fraternal), established in 1885 for the benefit of members of Ket On Fraternal Society. Tax key 2-2-14-2 under Ket On Fui Kon Association.

Chinese Organizations

      C. Tong Sin Tong, also established in 1885 for the Sam Yup dialectal group. Tax key 2-2-14-7.

      D. Pauoa Chinese Christian Cemetery, organized in 1919 by the Chinese Christian Cemetery Association of Hawaii, tax key 2-2-14-3.

   4. Makiki Chinese Christian Cemetery
Located at the corner of Pensacola and Wilder Avenue, tax key 2-4-31-1. Managed by the Chinese Christian Cemetery Association.

   5. Ocean View Chinese Cemetery
Located at Hunakai and Waialae Avenues, tax key 3-3-12-1 and 29 under Ocean View Cemetery, Ltd. Most of the land is leased to Royal Theaters, Ltd. for the Waialae Drive-In Theater. A small section, tax key 3-3-12-26, is set aside for the trustees of Jack Sin Tong for the burial of their members (Wong Leong Doo sub-district).

Heeia-Kaneohe

   6. The old Chinese cemetery was located at Lilipuna Road. A land developer needed the area for his subdivision and worked out an arrangement to transfer all remains to a special section for perpetual care at Hawaiian Memorial Park, Kaneohe, in exchange for the land. Annual Ching Ming ceremonies in April are now conducted in this section.

Waialua

   7. Tai Sing Society (fraternal)
The Chinese cemetery for the old residents of Waialua is listed under Tai Sing Society, the Hoong Moon fraternal lodge which is no longer active. The cemetery is located by Kamehameha Highway across Weed Junction at Waialua Beach Road. Tax key 6-6-18-25. Two elderly widows with the help of their families conduct the annual Ching Ming ceremonies in April.

Wahiawa

   8. Wahiawa Chinese Cemetery
Located at 130 California Avenue next to Kaala School, on Castle and Cooke, Inc. land set aside for cemetery use by Japanese, Chinese, Korean, and other

The Sandalwood Mountains

Dole Co. employees, tax key 7-3-07-3. A news item in *The Honolulu Advertiser* (6 November 1972) reported that Mililani Memorial Park will begin reinterment of remains from this old Wahiawa Cemetery which has no provisions for perpetual care.

II. Island of Kauai

The Chinese cemetery associations on Kauai are usually called Bark Fook Tong (Hundred Blessings Society). Some of the identifiable locations are:

Kapaa

    9. Apopo Road, tax key 4-5-15-14, under the name of Bark Fook Tong Society.

Kekaha

    10. On state land, between Waimea and Kekaha, next to Japanese Cemetery, tax key 1-2-06-4.

Hanapepe

    11. On county land, next to Veteran's Cemetery, tax key 1-8-08-18 under Chinese, Filipino, and Portuguese Cemetery.

Lawai

    12. On Hop Hing Society land (fraternal), tax key 2-5-04-2. The Office of Sanitation, State Department of Health reports: "The jungle has taken over this old abandoned cemetery. Almost inaccessible due to heavy vegetation."

Lihue, Kapaia

    13. On Lihue Plantation land, Waialua Falls Road, tax key 3-8-03 portion 1.

Hanalei

    14. On old Homestead Road, tax key 5-4-03-5. Under name of Hanalei Cemetery Association for all racial groups.

III. Island of Maui

Kula

    15. Fook On Tong, tax key 2-2-05-39. The Kula group is updating its register of the 150 or more graves.

Wailua

    16. Disinterment and removal of remains in 38 stone

crocks from Wailua Valley Cemetery to Waiehu (Wailuku) Cemetery in 1947. Some say the stone crocks contain remains removed from a Hana sugar plantation cemetery.

Hana
17. Old Chinese Cemetery located back of Hana High School under the name of Roland H.C. Chang, tax key 1-4-04-2.

Waiehu
18. Kwong Fook Tong (Waiehu Chinese Cemetery Association), tax key 3-2-13-4. The horseshoe- or omega-shaped mound used as ceremonial altar at Ching Ming season is dated 1888.

Paia
19. 1883 Hawaiian deed to Heong San Chong Sau Co. later changed to Paia Chinese Cemetery Association, tax key 2-6-04-2.

Lahaina
A. Puehuehu Cemetery, tax key 4-6-13-11 on Aholo Road off Honoapiilani Highway. State-owned.
B. Puupiha Cemetery, tax key 4-5-04-12. Chinese perform Ching Ming ceremonies here. State-owned.
C. Old State Cemetery on public beach area near Kaanapali golf course. Seven Chinese graves remain off Kainau Road. Tax key 4-5-21-07.

IV. Island of Hawaii
Hilo
21. Hilo Chinese Cemetery Association (Soong Yee Wui) Located on Ululani Street, tax key 2-3-18-23, 31, and 62.

Hamakua
22. Paauilo Chinese Cemetery
Located on plantation roadway off Hawaii Belt Road, adjacent to Latter Day Saints Church. Not verified. Tax key 4-3-05-8.
23. Chee Yuen Association (fraternal)
Located on government main road to Honokaa. Tax key 4-5-09-9 and 4-5-09-11, two sections.

Kohala
24. Tong Wo Society (fraternal)
On government main road, tax key 5-3-08-20.
25. Lock Shin Tong Society
On government main road, tax key 5-3-08-17.
26. Dun Wo Tong (Kona Chinese Cemetery Association—fraternal)
On Kuakini Highway, tax key 7-8-05-50.

Naalehu, Ka'u
27. Bow Sin Tong (fraternal)
On Mamalahoa Highway, tax key 9-5-08-12.

TONG WO SOCIETY IN KOHALA

The Tong Wo Kung Si (Tong Wo Society) still exists in Kohala. This society uses the term *kung si* as its organizational designation. Vertical plaques by the entrance give 1866 as the year in which this "Together in Harmony" fraternal society was founded. Because of the legal requirement to register as an association to be granted a license in Singapore, Hong Kong, and other British colonies, the Chinese sometimes used *kung si* in place of *wui goon*. *Kung si* was used in these British territories for commercial companies or corporations. To satisfy government requirements, the Chinese used *kung si* to avoid attracting government inspection of its activities, especially when its membership was involved in extortion or other criminal activities.

Interest in Tong Wo Kung Si was aroused by residents of the island of Hawaii who were concerned about historic sites. Prof. William J. Bonk with his graduate assistant, Clyde Wong, and the anthropology class at the University of Hawaii, Hilo campus, made extensive studies of the buildings and contents and researched the society's historical background.

Some help on this project was given by the Hawaii Chinese History Center, a newly formed historical society. Some members joined in field trips to Kohala. The society cooperated in the ceremony to rededicate the society building in 1971.*

HALAWA, Hawaii—Until World War II, Hawaii's Chinese people were linked to their traditional culture by the numerous [Hoong Moon]

* Hal Glatzer, "An Old Society Gets a New Life," *Sunday Star-Bulletin and Advertiser,* 31 October 1971.

Societies which served the communities' social needs [as] here in North Kohala.

Once there were more than 60 clubhouses in the Islands. About 30 are still active, most of them in Honolulu. In Hilo, the Ling Hing Society now meets in a small, unpretentious building on Pele Lane. Elsewhere on the Big Island, the old clubhouses are in disrepair.

But people of Chinese descent who still live in Halawa have undertaken to partly restore the buildings and grounds of the Tong Wo Society.

Tong Wo (together in harmony) was one of many so-called "secret" societies of heads of households, that had their origins in the 16th century. Then known as the "Triad" societies, they were first organized to overthrow the Manchus and restore the Mings to power. Members identified each other by making special gestures, manipulating chopsticks, and using "passwords."

The Societies flourished in China and continue to be active in Chinese merchant communities such as Hong Kong, Singapore, Vancouver, San Francisco, and New York. Political maneuvering was carried on throughout the Manchu Dynasty. Sun Yat-sen cooperated with them in the early 20th century to finance his revolution. They say here that he visited the Societies in Hawaii at the time while on a fund-raising tour.

Tong Wo is typical of the rural Societies which developed in the plantation camps of the first- and second-wave Chinese immigrants. It was probably founded in Halawa by the first bachelor laborers and later expanded by the family men who arrived with their wives in the 1870's. . . .

The hall at the Halawa temple is ornate, but not elaborate in its construction. A balcony surrounds the building on the second floor. Scrollwork links the beams and posts, and plaques engraved and painted with proverbs and phrases surround many doorways and windows. Older residents remember a tall flagpole in the front yard and a kitchen in back. Both are gone now.

Behind the main structure is a large room, with holes in its roof, where the men once played fan-tan and other games. . . . A loft accessible only by a rope ladder was said to have been used by some of the bachelors for opium-smoking. During weekday afternoons, the Society operated . . . a language school in one of the rooms. Only the desks remain.

In back of this building are the remains of the pensioners' quarters. Elderly men who were unable to maintain a house alone lived in these rooms on the Society's grounds. . . .[14]

Funeral services were held there afterward. In keeping with the custom of having burials only on a hillside, the slopes of Halawa Valley are dotted with antique headstones. Many are now entirely obscured by weeds, and weathered by rain.

Nearby fruit and nut trees provided some of the food for meals and large parties. Some residents who were children around 1920 estimated the Tong Wo fed as many as 400 people on special occasions such as the Chinese New Year.

In 1966, a race-car mechanic named Jimmy Chai moved back to Kohala after 40 years on the Mainland. He remembered the Society's activities and undertook to clear the weeds from the gravesites and the front yard. He was helped by Ah Fook Ching, the last surviving member of the Society. Together, they also repaired the roof of the main building.

In the summer of 1970, a Hilo College anthropology class headed by Dr. William Bonk helped work on the main building. They took photographs and mapped out the kitchen and outbuilding sites with funds from the University and the State Department of Land and Natural Resources. One student also tape-recorded the reminiscences of elderly local Chinese.

Bonk has since proposed that the State or the University restore the site, for its cultural value and for use in Kohala archeological research.

This year the project attracted the attention of the newly created Hawaii Chinese History Center. The center is interested in tracing genealogies of families with roots in rural areas of the State like Kohala.

Mrs. Irma Tam Soong, executive director of the center, said many Honolulu families have "lost interest" in preserving the Society buildings around the Islands. . . .

One of the most talkative among the older people is Mrs. Chong Tai-Lai. Now 86, she is the widow of the last caretaker of the Society. They were married on the site before World War I. She has been a farmer and a butcher, she now lives in Volcano.

"My father and mother came here the year before I was born,"

Chinese Organizations

she said in Hakka. "I was born and grew up in the Halawa Plantation camp. There were big parties then. The Hakka and the Punti men would gamble together. . . . The old ones smoked opium because they had no cigarettes."

Women were not permitted in the temple then. They had their own shrine and altars in another part of the complex. All of the religious functions were carried out by a priest, assisted by the members themselves.

The main altar in the temple is dedicated to Kwan Dai, the God of [War and patron saint of fraternal loyalty]. In a smaller room is an altar dedicated to Kwan Yin, Goddess of Mercy. In another niche the deified ancestors of the Society are honored. By the doors and windows, small shrines and altars serve the Gods of the Doorways and Windows.

Coordinating a rededication proceedings ceremony held on Wednesday, Douglas Chong of Honolulu, grandson of a Taoist priestess, helped direct the placement of incense, flowers and food offerings around the building.

Lee Han, a Taoist priest from Honolulu, came to Halawa to perform the ceremony. He was accompanied by Chun Ah Wing, a musician who played the *tita* (an oboe-like bugle) while Lee Han clanged and beat on a small drum, a cymbal and a gong.

At 2 p.m. Lee Han donned an embroidered red robe and ceremonial crown and began the invocation. Chong explained that the priest was inviting the gods to come and celebrate at the Temple. Food was provided for them to eat. "Money" was burned.

Specially purchased clothing, shoes and crowns were consecrated on the altar and burned. . . .

Cups of tea were then spilled before the altar. Lee Han dipped into a basin of pomelo leaves and water and sprinkled the water around the room, the altar and the offerings to cleanse and purify them. Smoke from hundreds of small sticks, and large columns of yellow incense filled the hall. Red candles, inscribed with characters, burned with a flickering light.

The *tita* was loud and reedy. The chanting was sometimes muffled by Lee Han's movements in front of the altar. When it was over, the two men went downstairs and set up a similar table of offerings in front of the main stairs. Chong explained that the spirits of the dead, who inhabit the grounds and the graves, were being asked to come to eat the food and join the celebration.

When Lee Han finished, Ah Fook Ching lit a long string of firecrackers, which marked the end of the ceremony, the first such event here in more than 40 years.

VI. Religious Faiths and Practices

CHINESE RELIGION AND CHINESE TEMPLES

One of the major adjustments that the Chinese coming to Hawaii had to make was to a society based on Christian faiths and practices. By 1840 the Hawaiian Kingdom included in its constitution that Hawaii was officially a Christian nation.[1] As already mentioned, some of the Chinese who immigrated to Hawaii were already Christians, and many more were converted after they had settled here. But an important segment chose to follow traditional Chinese religious practices in what was essentially an unfavorable atmosphere.

Traditional Chinese religion is actually a blend of three different religious philosophies and practices—Confucianism (not really a religion but a system of teachings), Taoism, and Buddhism. Each of these traditions had its place and function. Each had its own mode of belief and worship which were at times combined into a system of beliefs. It has been said that "when a man is in a position of authority he is a Confucianist, because that doctrine supports the status quo. Out of power or office, a man becomes a Taoist, because Taoism deprecates both the worldly authority and individual responsibility. As death approaches, a man turns to Buddhism, because that faith offers hope of salvation."[2]

The common man, however, is polytheistic in his beliefs and practices. He embraces folk beliefs of supernatural beings, magic, charms, astrology, fortune divinations, and deified warriors, heroes, and sages taken from legends and fables.[3] In Hawaii, it has been difficult to label which Chinese temples and shrines are Buddhist and which are Taoist. Both Buddhist and Taoist deities are commingled in the same temple.

A Confucian temple in China has always been conspicuous by the absence in it of statues and images. The bare interior of the temple may have only a plaque on the altar bearing the sage's name. There has been no Confucian temple in Hawaii, but a Confucian Society was formed in the 1900s. It combined its activities with those of the Mun Lun Chinese School where Confucius' birthday was celebrated annually.

Chinese had been in Hawaii for over a century when, in 1953, a formal Buddhist society was organized. At that time, the Hawaii Chinese Buddhist Society sponsored Buddhist priests from Hong Kong in opening their Tan Wah Temple at 1614 Nuuanu Avenue. Another Buddhist group in Honolulu formed the Chinese Buddhist Association in 1955 and built a temple at 42 Kawananakoa Place.

The immigrants necessarily modified their religious customs and practices in the new cultural atmosphere. The old customs were followed with less regularity. In following their religious traditions, the Chinese in Hawaii went to the temples of their choice two or three times a year to offer thanks for divine protection and good fortune, or at times of a family crisis such as sickness.[4]

Simple, private ceremonies at home were held on occasional festival days. This form of open worship was called *dong tin bai* ("offering prayers before Heaven"), usually on a porch or in the garden. Religious training in such families centered on ethical teachings—*tso hou yan, tso sin shee, mok tso kwai sum shee* ("being a good person, doing good deeds, refraining from doing things which hurt your conscience").

Chinese who practiced this syncretic religion did not fit into the mold of Hawaiian society. Non-Christian children who had to fill out forms on their religion, nationality, and Christian names were sometimes confused as to what was the appropriate answer. (It was not until 1967 that the State Legislature abolished the old requirement that children born in Hawaii be given a "Christian name, suitable to their sex.")

The following selection is a discussion of the temples and religious practices of the Hawaii Chinese as it was in 1937.* The research team working with the author of the paper was made up of observers who were students at the University of Hawaii and who spoke Chinese to their parents at home well enough to understand the religious feelings of an earlier generation. Since that time, the number of temples, which

---

* Sau Chun Wong, "Chinese Temples in Honolulu," *Social Process in Hawaii*, 3 (1937):27–35; reprinted with permission of the Romanzo Adams Social Research Laboratory, University of Hawaii.

Religious Faiths and Practices

were concentrated in Honolulu, has dwindled. Urban redevelopment and street-widening projects have caused some temples to be moved elsewhere. Others were closed down from lack of patronage. Also, there was no adequate replacement for the departure or death of the old temple keepers. For example, How Wong Temple on School Street moved its deities to Lum Sai Ho Tong on River Street; Quan Dai (Kwan Ti) Temple on Vineyard Street and Sing Wong Temple on Kukui Street closed down. The two or three remaining temples, situated in better locations, attract tourists who are on Chinatown and temple tours as well as the patronage of the Chinese who still worship there. This is so at the Kwan Yin Temple on Vineyard Street, which is of beautiful architectural design.

The religion of the Chinese combines the beliefs of Buddhism, Taoism, and Confucianism. The objects of worship are the forces of nature, ancestors, ancient heroes, and patron deities. Religion, as observed by the uneducated masses, is handed down from generation to generation chiefly through ceremonial practices and tradition and differs greatly from the philosophies and moral systems propounded by the sages.

The Chinese temple in Honolulu, like many other immigrant institutions, arose in response to the need for security and confidence in a strange land. Almost every Chinese mutual aid society had its special altar room for worship of the familiar deities of the homeland, and special temples with sacred idols and priests from China appeared more than fifty years ago. This paper will attempt to describe six of the temples now existing.

The Temples.—1. The oldest and most frequented of the various Chinese temples in Honolulu is the "Goon Yum"[5] (Kwan Yin) Temple or the Goddess of Mercy temple on Vineyard Street. Established first in the early eighties and later rebuilt several times, it is now situated near the river and stands as a guardian over it. Only a narrow gate with three large characters painted on it informs the visitor of the temple's existence. It is a two-story structure, the lower portion of which is used to house the caretaker and the priest. On the upper floor, reached by an outside stairway are the four shrines clustered about the central figure of Kwan Yin. Bedecked with paper flowers on either side, with gilded detailed carvings framed about her, and gorgeous embroidered fans on either side, Kwan Yin resposes calm and serene in the center of lesser gods and goddesses. The heaven table is directly in front of her and is laden with copper kettles of sand, drum and gong, incense, candles, "chi-chi" [*chim* or "fortune stick"] cylinders,[6] and offerings.

As legend tells us, Kwan Yin was the youngest and most beautiful daughter of an ancient king of China. As she grew older she observed the many trials and tribulations that humanity had to endure. In spite of the loud protests of her father, the king, she vowed that she would never marry. In order to escape the punishments threatened by her father, she renounced the world and became a nun. The gods took pity upon her and made her the Goddess of Mercy. Worshippers pray to her for long life, for many sons and children, for fortune, and for strength. Four holidays are celebrated in her name: February 19, her bithday; September 19, her baptismal day; November 19, her ascension to heaven; and June 19, her death. It is believed that Kwan Yin can transform herself into any imaginable form. People call her the woman with a million eyes and hands. Usually her disguises are used to help those in distress.

The shrine situated on the right of Kwan Yin's is the shrine of the Seven Sisters. There are seven figures seated in the shrine, one of which, as legend discloses, returns to her mortal husband on the seventh day of the seventh month, and remains for seventeen days during which time she washes chopsticks and bowls for every day in the year. Girls especially who desire to be skilled in embroidery work come to worship her.

Other shrines in the same temple are the Wah Tow or Doctor's shrine, famed for helpfulness to the sick and diseased, the Quan Dai or war god, worshipped for life and strength, and the shrine of the "king of gods, king and ruler of earth and heaven." Still another in the corner of the room is the shrine of Choy Sun, the god of fortune, worshipped particularly by merchants, housewives, and sons.

Each figure is brightly decorated, and small oil lamps are kept burning before them constantly. Soot-covered lanterns hang humbly down, and strands of crepe paper flowers waver in the heavy air. Worshippers kneel on the badly worn mats and cushions before all the separate shrines, but it is evident that most prayers are made before the image of Kwan Yin.

The caretaker is a middle-aged, wizened-looking man and is usually clad in a pair of soiled woolen trousers, a grimy cap, and Chinese shirt and slippers. Several assistants help with the preparation of images and the care of the shrines.

The temple is supported by donations from the Chinese public and by the sale of ceremonial papers, candles, and incense. The caretaker and his staff receive their wages from fees given by the worshippers. Other sources of income are few.

2. Another important temple is the How Wong Temple on Fort Street opposite the Y.M.B.A. [Young Men's Buddhist Association]. The founder even as a child was considered to be a living god as she healed people with her miraculous power and the potions which she concocted. In all her life, a span of some eighty years, she had never partaken of any solid food. Her diet consisted only of fruit juices, citron water, small lemons, and carambolas. When she left China to come to Hawaii, she brought with her the How Wong god after whom the temple was named. Later, after the temple was built, she had the Bak Sak or White Mountain Temple in China send the other gods. All the money for the temple was earned by this priestess, and today the temple is one of the few that are self-supporting. The present caretaker is unmistakably proud of her mother who, she claims, prayed with such concentration that even the entrance of bandits did not break her trance. She is credited with predicting the Chinatown fire in 1900, even disclosing the number of days of the fire. This increased her popularity tremendously.

There are five different shrines in this temple. Several of them are similar to those of the Kwan Yin Temple. The center shrine is reserved for the How Wong, or the fisherman's god. Legend discloses that once, when a fisherman was fishing out at sea, a white rock kept coming up to him. Sensing some unseen power at work, the fisherman picked up the stone and said that he would take it ashore and erect a shrine for it if it would give him more power and more fish. The shrine, originally for fishermen, has gradually expanded in use, until today people of any profession or trade may petition the god for good fortune, protection, business success, and safety in travel to China. On either side of the god are seated his two assistants still and solemn in their dignity.

To the left of How Wong is hung a piece of white cloth with small black characters of the thirty-six gods, "Jung Sun." The worshippers must not forget this small shrine, as it represents all of the gods. He must be careful not to invoke the anger of any god through negligence.

Directly in front of the How Wong shrine is a high table with two large copper incense burners, a pair of kidney-shaped wooden blocks and a cylindrical box with [*chim*] sticks, and oil burners which are kept burning constantly. The copper burners were presents from a rich Chinese merchant and philanthropist.

To the right of the fishermen shrine is the abode of the Zeus of the Chinese gods, "Yuk Wong Dai Dei," the king and ruler of heaven and earth, while to his right is the doctor's god with a round pill in his outstretched hand. The shrine to Kwan Dei, the war god, has smaller incense burners but no oil burners or "chi-chi" [*chim*] or blocks.

To the left of the fisherman's shrine is the maternity shrine, consisting of three figures. The central figure is of course the mother god with a baby in her arms; on her left is the father who presents the child, and on her right is the nurse who holds a pair of scales to weigh the baby. This shrine is naturally endowed for expectant mothers who pray for a good son, good luck, and happiness.

Each of the side walls has a shrine. "Hin Tan," the tiger keeper and trainer with tigers by his sides, has control of thunder and lightning. On the other side wall is the life-sized figure of "Choy Sun" the god of fortune. He is arrayed in his mourning clothes, as his mother had died, and is leaning on a frilled paper stick which he uses as a cane. He is bowed in grief, and the stick helps him to hold his head bowed, as holding his head up, which signifies happiness, is unfilial. In his left hand, he carries a fan which is supposed to fan away evil. A collection of fans reclines behind him. His ceremonial day is January 26 according to the lunar calendar.

The present caretaker of this How Wong Temple is Hawaii born and has a fair education in Chinese and a little in English. Her knowledge in ceremonial procedures was received from her mother.

The temple is supported by donations from the public and through the sale of offerings of candle, punk, and ceremonial papers. A worshipper pays twenty-five cents for a sheaf of ceremonial papers with two candles, a sheaf of incense, and punk, so the profit is very little. As she has to keep the oil lamps burning day and night she is glad when some one donates a bottle or two of oil.

This temple is popular with mothers who bring their month old babies to the temple to thank the gods for their safe delivery and to celebrate their birthdays which makes them one year old. The mother brings with her some form of meat, usually a succulent roast pig, wine, tea, incense, sweet bread, and rice. The caretaker helps her pray after the mother pays her a fee wrapped in red paper.

3. A very picturesque temple is the How Wong Temple on School Street, beyond Liliha Street. It is surrounded by small residential cottages and is itself a rented cottage made over for temple purposes. It is quite colorful with its bright red fence, cement incinerators, and shrines. As one enters the gates, he notices a remodeled garage enclosing a large shrine immediately on his left. No idols can be seen, but two large rocks stand imposingly with red paper arrayed about them and incense and candles burning before them. These gods guard the premises of the temple.

The temple is a one-room affair with the gods facing the door and a pair of guardian gods near the door. In the center is the How Wong or fishermen's shrine. Two additional shrines, for Wah Tow, or the god of doctors, and Choy Sun, or the god of fortune, are also worshipped at this temple. The offerings of worshippers are placed on the table in front of the center shrine. These offerings include sweetmeats, to sweeten the god's palate, rice for food, wine and tea for drink, and ceremonial paper as money for the gods. Although ancient in atmosphere, the temple carries a few modern touches as electric lights, electric clock, telephone, doorbell, and a license for operation artistically framed. Even the young caretaker, clothed in American style, is modern and radical in some of his ideas, derived from a western education.

The caretaker states that he came from China to Hawaii, attended the St. Louis College until the seventh grade, then had to return to China. At that time he had no belief in any religion and used to disfigure the idols and the temples. Then suddenly, one day, the spirit entered his body. He could not study, eat, or sleep for seven days and nights. He acquired the power of healing the sick, and his conquests over disease and death were famous. Many came to him for healing. Even the insane and epileptic benefited from his power. He came back to Hawaii with no intention of continuing his healing practice, but his relatives and friends insisted, so he did whatever he could. He became a priest and took charge of the temple. He secured another job but was unable to keep it. Some misfortune always stalked him whenever he was away from the temple. He states that he remained in good health only when he was healing people.

This caretaker laments that because of ignorance, people in China and in the islands are superstitious over small matters. Take the subject of hair washing. Chinese people insist that there are only certain ordained days when they can wash their hair, so they look it up in the "tung see," a horoscope-like book. The caretaker shakes his head and laughs. "What difference does it make when you wash your hair. When it's dirty, you know it is, so wash it when necessary, not upon the advice of a book!" He says that as long as the "heart is good," there is no use in offering a huge roast pig to the gods, as the gods do not care. A little incense is as big a thought as roast pig. Only ignorant people do such unnecessary acts. He laughingly says, "If fate determines your life, why do so much unnecessary worship to curb its whims?"

4. The Quan Dai or War God's Temple is situated in a dark, musty room over a row of grocery stores on Vineyard Street near the river. An old man, about seventy years old, a retired vegetable vendor, is the present caretaker. He bought it from the former owner, and although he did not know much about the procedure, "the gods taught him." In a week's time he learned practically "the whole business." The Quan Dai shrine is black from the fumes of the candles and is shaded in the background by many high tables laden with copper kettles filled with sand and ashes. Quan Dai is worshipped for life and strength.

5. A slightly different temple is located on River Street near the Japanese produce markets. In the center of the upstairs rooms is the shrine of Leong Ma, the goddess of safety, who was a beautiful woman, as one can see from the clear-cut features of the idol. She has bound feet and holds a mirror in her hand. She is surrounded by lesser goddesses, and many have mirrors in their hands which help to light their paths. This temple was built by the "Lum" clan and supported by it. Scattered about the walls of the room are pictures of famous Lums and photographs of Lum gatherings. The caretaker, a toothless gentleman clad in an undershirt and a pair of trousers, is also a Lum. He has a small room adjoining the big room and one can spy a tiny sink, dishes, and an iron bed within. This temple is not often frequented by worshippers but is chiefly used for clan meetings and gatherings.

6. Another temple is the Sing Wong Temple located on Kukui Street. The temple proper occupies one side and the proprietor's home the other, where ceremonial papers and offerings are sold and where the proprietor sits and gossips with frequent cronies. This temple was founded at Hanapepe, Kauai, by the present caretaker, who is educated in Chinese history and language. The temple houses "guardian gods" who keep watch over the temple, and "Choy Sun" or god of fortune. The center shrine holds the "Eight Great Spirits" while on the right are the King of gods, and the "Fut Mu," the teacher of Kwan Yin. The caretaker is also a spiritual medium and a chanter at funerals, both these occupations being better sources of income than the temple. The temple is not supported by public donations but is supported through sale of ceremonial offerings.

Procedure of Worship.—The ceremonials in all of the temples tend to be chiefly of a magical character designed to coerce the gods and spirits to grant the expressed desires of the worshippers. Among the recurrent values sought are: sons, happiness for departed spirits, family happiness, long life, wealth and health, and security against accident and misfortune.

A worshipper usually brings with him on special holidays, and celebrations, a basket of food composed of some form of animal flesh, as pork, chicken, or fish (or if he is rich, all of the above), wine, tea, and three bowls of cooked rice, and a vegetable dish, as tofu [soybean curd] or "jai" ["monks' food"]. As he enters, he hits a panel and a drum several times to arouse the gods to listen to his supplication and also to chase away the evil spirits that are lurking near. The priest may assist if the worshipper desires. He endeavors to get all the information he can as to the desires of the worshipper. Then he chants in a sing-song manner, all the while kneeling in front of the shrine on the mat or cushion. (If information is sought as to the future of sons and daughters, their names and birthdays are written on a piece of paper.) He picks up the pair of kidney-shaped blocks and answers to questions are secured by the throw of the blocks. If both fall with the curved side up, it is a good sign; if one is flat and the other curved, it is also good, but if both fall on the flat side, the future is not propitious and one should take care. The priest may also secure answers to questions through the [fortune sticks or the "chim."]

This is the procedure followed by a young Chinese who has had an American education, has all the external marks of a westerner, and who is praying for some member of her family who is suffering from a headache. She buys incense from the caretaker, lights it and distributes it among the gods. The caretaker helps her light candles and takes up the tea leaves, after which both kneel down before the shrine and ask the gods for help. Then the caretaker takes up the "chim" and shakes them up and down until one drops out, chanting while he is doing this. He then looks up the predictions for the number in his case book. Gathering up the ceremonial papers he burns them and then dusts the incense-ash into the tea leaves and wraps both in red paper. He rings the gong and beats the drum. The girl departs after paying and giving thanks with the thought that after drinking the tea the headache will disappear. If it does not, she will come again to pray.

Caretakers.—Every caretaker seems to think of his task as ordained by the gods. As one caretaker said, "I didn't like religion at first; I used to draw mustaches on the gods and mark the temples. But suddenly, I was "gong" (the spirit entered my soul) and I became a priest. The gods wanted me to be a priest, so I had to become one or I would be unlucky and have many accidents." This fatalistic viewpoint is rather common.

Pride of position prevents the caretakers from seeking other more remunerative tasks. As one caretaker says, "I tried to look for a job, but after securing one for a while, I would get sick and couldn't go back to work; so I have to stay in the temple." Another caretaker who has been a vegetable vendor says, "I couldn't make much money selling vegetables. Too much competition. When I heard of this chance to take care of the temple, I took it so that when I get old, I can still make a little money without too much effort."

The caretakers and priests, of course, must make a living, and that is one of the chief concerns of some. All lament that too many people come with their own ceremonial papers instead of buying them from the temples, and also do their own praying instead of paying the priest a fee to do it for them. But as the temple is supposedly public, the priests can do nothing.

Each caretaker assumes that his temple is the one truly ordained by the gods and that other temples and priests are fakes. There is not much cooperation among them and no guild to protect and raise their interests.

Worshippers.—The worshippers at the temples are chiefly first generation women who most strongly adhere to the traditional religious values and observe the ancient ceremonies, both at home and at the temples. They pin their faith on one or more experiences which have coincided with the priests' predictions.

Most worshippers visit the temples on holidays,[7] as neglect would invite misfortune. Some more devout, however, visit on any good day of the lunar calendar. Some, thrifty or miserly, bring their own offerings and chant their prayers instead of buying them from the temple or securing the priest's services; others do not visit the temples at all, as they say they can pray to the gods just as effectively at home. The gods, they add, are everywhere.

Some believe in going only to one temple as their faith has strength and security in that certain temple, not because of the sect, but because of the priest who might have a greater influence on the person than would the other priests, and who might have predicted some truth or facts which strengthened the person's faith.

Ceremonies.—Altogether there are thirteen definite times for worship. The first and fifteenth of every month are also considered as worship days. Other important days of worship and the items of food usually offered are listed below:
1. New Year's Day—vegetables.
2. Second day of New Year—meat and vegetables.
3. Twelfth day of New Year—pork, chicken, and fish.
4. Tsing Ming—anything.
5. Fifth day of fifth month—pork and sweets.
6. Fourteenth day of seventh month—anything.
7. Fifteenth day of eighth month—pork and mooncakes.
8. Winter of the eleventh month—pork and sweets.
9. Last day of old year—fish, chicken, and pork.
10–13. Birthdays and death days of fathers and ancestors.

Changing Functions.—Religious devotion to spirits and natural objects has controlled the life and activities of the Chinese people to a great extent. It was the center about which their life revolved as they believed that the spirits controlled and motivated their activities; in other words, no differentiation was made between fate and the will of the spirits. Ancestor worship was adhered to closely as an example for future generations to follow in respect to the departing generation. Ancestor worship considered the family.

Now, since the advent of Christianity, modern science, and public education, the older type of Chinese worship has ceased to control the life of a large part of the second and third generations of the Chinese community of Honolulu. The first generation go to the temples on feast days, a few consistently, while the younger generations seldom do. The same practices, however, tend to persist, with the exception that ancestor worship has been neglected in the temples but not in the homes. Once a year at about Easter time, "Tsing Ming" is held at the ancestral graves and this is a time when even babies are taken [along].

KOHALA SUGAR HIRES CHRISTIAN WORKER FOR CHINESE, 1878

While the plantations have been criticized for the economic exploitation of immigrant laborers, credit should be given to Kohala Plantation for hiring a Christian religious worker for its Chinese Christian laborers. Many of the workers on the plantation had already become Christians, some coming from Christian families in China.

Father Elias Bond (1813–1896) was an early missionary to Kohala, Hawaii, who helped to start Kohala Plantation. He had a good rapport with his workers.[8] One thing he had insisted upon was that laborers at the Kohala Sugar Company be able to bring their families with them from China.

The Chinese evangelist, Kong Tet-Yin (Kontetyn) was hired in 1878 (not to be confused with Kong Yin-Tet, pastor of St. Peter's Church in Honolulu from 1897 to 1928). Evangelist Kong Tet-Yin was trained by the Basel (Lutheran) Mission in Kwangtung. He joined the Anglican Church in Australia to serve as an evangelist among the Chinese attracted by gold in Sun Gum Shan ("New Gold Mountain"). He came to Hawaii with a letter of recommendation from his Australian Bishop.[9]

Ethel Moseley Damon (1883–1965) who wrote the book from which the reading is taken was granddaughter of Samuel Chenery Damon and niece to Frank Damon.*

During the decade of the sixties Chinese began to be seen more numerously, brought in as plantation laborers. On the heart of the

* Ethel M. Damon, *Father Bond of Kohala* (Honolulu: The Friend, 1927), pp. 210–259.

Religious Faiths and Practices

Kohala pastor the need of these newcomers lay as heavy as that of his own people, for they were all God's children, and had no right, he felt, to be bound by "this diabolical coolie law and the shameful doings under the master and servant law." As early as 1868 he wrote to Boston from the annual meeting of the Hawaiian Board in Honolulu:

> It was a new feature in our meeting to see a pure Chinese with us as a Delegate from the church in Lahaina. He is a young man, not much beyond 30, able to speak twelve Chinese dialects, a good singer and player on the melodeon, perfectly at home in what interests our Hawaiian Zion and speaking on any topic brought before us with intelligence and unaffected Christian attachment to our work. You will hear more of this man through others and of his engagement to devote a year as an evangelist to his fellow countrymen scattered throughout the Islands [Samuel P. Aheong]. . . .

On December 23rd, 1876 there arrived for the Kohala plantation thirty Christian Chinese, four with their wives, and two children. The following year the little Oriental colony had increased to forty-five, the second company of Christian Chinese arriving in January. How eagerly Father Bond welcomed them to his fold and how he rejoiced in the greater freedom of action furnished by plantation dividends, may be seen in a letter of October 17, 1877:

> I sent in August for a minister to preach to our English speaking population. . . . Now I write to see if we can obtain from the coast a Chinese Evangelist for these growing numbers of Chinese among us with no possible medium through which we may speak to them of Jesus. . . .

And soon the long anticipated arrival and labors of Kong Tet Yin were announced:

> March, 1878. . . . My errand to Honolulu was to get a Chinese Colporteur and Evangelist. It was an unexpected opening, the man with highest testimonials from China and Australia.
> The Master favored my errand. I secured the man, and

> secured from the Kohala Sugar Company the means for paying his salary. Thanks to God for all.
>
> April, 1879. . . . Our Chinese work is gradually getting into shape. I am much pleased with the Evangelist, though I sorely feel the difficulty involved in our inability to communicate freely, he having no knowledge of the English. He is a good speaker and manifestly a man of character.
>
> We have just arranged for an independent Chinese service on the Sabbath, excepting on Communion and Monthly Concert Sabbaths when they will meet with us. This arrangement will probably draw in more of the pagan element among our Chinese population.
>
> My idea was to have them meet with us only on Communion Sabbaths, but they wished to meet also on Monthly Concerts, and probably, till they attain to a somewhat enlarged measure of the habit and grace of giving for religious purposes, it will do them no harm to meet with our native congregation on such Sabbaths.

Thus, all went well, if slowly, with the little "Chinese Zion" in Kohala. February of 1883 saw a plot of ground given by the plantation and set off for a church building for the Chinese, the first in the Islands. In May of the same year a visit was recorded from "Father Damon," who shared to the full Mr. Bond's interest in the Chinese and was one of the first to organize Christian work among them in Honolulu.

On July 29th of this same year the Chinese church body of Kohala was formally organized. On the first of August "the Damons" arrived and on the fifth the new church was dedicated. With Father Damon was his son Frank who seconded every missionary interest of the good fathers, and who returned to the Canton mission the following year for his bride, Mary Happer. And in November of that year, 1884, both bride and groom visited Kohala in eager conference on the beginning of the Chinese work there. To the fair young bride, a stranger in a strange land and far from her father's house, the cordial welcome at Iole meant riches indeed. . . .

EARLY CHRISTIAN ARRIVALS, 1878

One of the most adaptive groups of immigrant Chinese laborers were the Hakka Christians recruited from Pao On and other districts

Religious Faiths and Practices

northwest of Hong Kong. They had been under the influence and instruction of Basel German missionaries of the Basel Lutheran mission who continued a deep interest in their converts.[10] An early group of these Christian Chinese men, women, and children arrived in Hawaii in January 1878 on the *Auguste*.

In teaching the men and women to read the Bible and sing hymns, the Basel missionaries taught the people to read and write Hakka *shuk wa* (Hakka colloquial) in Roman characters. This was of immense help in learning the Bible more quickly than from the difficult Chinese characters. Not only did these people bring their own form of religious practice, but they also brought the bread-making methods learned from German missionaries. When employed as cooks and domestics, they taught this to their Congregational mistresses.

Editor Samuel C. Damon of *The Friend* added his own comments on the Chinese Christians recruited by Hawaiian plantations to a letter he received from the Reverend Lechler of the Basel mission.*

We have received an interesting letter from the Rev. R. Lechler, German missionary at Hong Kong. Nearly one hundred Christian Chinese men, women, and children came per the *Auguste,* which arrived here about the first of January 1878. These Christian Chinese had been under the influence and instruction of the German missionaries, who continue to feel and express a deep interest in their converts, who have come to reside and labor on the Hawaiian Islands:

Hong Kong, 22d April, 1878

Rev. S. C. Damon—Your favor of the 6th February was duly received with a number of letters from my friends there. We were not a little comforted to hear that it had pleased God, to bring the *Auguste* and all her passengers safely to Honolulu. I desire to thank you most cordially for your kind letter, and for all the kindness you and others have shown to our people. We rejoiced to hear that the wedding between Joseph Ten-syan and Lai Tet-Sin has come off so nicely. I hope she will be a good mother to the two children of Joseph. Or are they continuing in the school with that kind lady in whose charge he gave them when he left for China. I am also obliged for the copy of

---

* Rudolf Lechler, "Letters from China," *The Friend,* July 1878, p. 58.

the FRIEND you kindly sent me. I have sent it and previous numbers on to Europe, as people at home are greatly interested in the fate of the Chinese Christians, who emigrate to the Sandwich Islands. I shall always be greatly obliged for any printed communication referring to what is being done for the Chinese in your quarters.

There has been some agitation here against emigration to Honolulu, on the plea that letters had been received from there by Chinese complaining of hard labor, and of being forced to make a contract. I gave six of my letters, in which no complaint had been mentioned, to the *China Mail*, and the editor printed them to show that the Christians did not complain of anything. Two steamers had been stopped on account of this agitation, and great loss been inflicted on the parties concerned. The other letters containing the above mentioned complaints were received subsequently. I have written a Chinese letter to my people in Roman characters, and besides I got my teachers to write, one a letter on money matters, and the other who is Catechist a letter on doctrine and general subjects concerning them. I also send them a copy of a poem which describes the famine now devastating the North of China so fearfully. . . .

Yours sincerely,
R. Lechler

The foregoing letter affords the pleasing evidence of the abiding interest which this faithful missionary cherishes towards his people. We feel confident the Chinese laborers by the *Auguste* were by far the most promising and hopeful company ever landed upon these islands. So far as we have learned respecting their conduct in Honolulu, Kohala and the Hilo district, they have fully sustained their good reputation.

We regret exceedingly that any injurious report should ever have gone back to China; but it only shows the importance of those who act in this business conducting it with fairness and honesty. It is a point to which we would call the attention of the Board of Immigration. It is our firm belief that if the Board will send a proper Commissioner to China, and confer with the German missionaries, as well as the authorities, much good might be accomplished.

Religious Faiths and Practices

Furthermore, we are confident China is the proper country from which laborers are to be obtained for these Islands. Has not the time arrived for a Chinese Consul to be sent to Honolulu? Chinese Consuls have recently been sent to San Francisco and other cities in the United States.

BASEL MISSION WORK

In a follow-up letter to the one above, the Reverend Rudolf Lechler explained the activities of his Basel mission and indicated his continued interest in the welfare of his flock overseas.*

Rev. S. C. Damon, Honolulu:

Two letters from you, dated 5th October and 25th November, are before me. The first came by the sailing ship *Amy Turner,* and the second by the steamer *Perusia.* Many thanks for your kind communications, and no less for the papers you sent me, which give me always great pleasure to read. There is at present a sailing ship here, the *Crusader,* which is bound for Honolulu, and a Hawaiian woman, the widow of a Chinaman of the name of Ahyong [Mrs. Samuel P. Aheong] who seems to have been engaged in evangelistic work, expects to return to her native land with three boys of hers. A certain Dr. Kitteridge wrote to me about this woman, and said that he would send the money for her passage if he knew how much was wanted. She now tells me that the Hawaiian Consul here has promised to provide a passage for her and her boys. The man who returned to China in the *Amy Turner* brought a good many letters and also some money from different parties for their relations here. I was also much surprised and pleased to receive a handsome subscription from my old friends the Chinese Christians of the Sandwich Islands to the amount of $137.50. I value this token of grateful acknowledgment very highly, and it shows how unfair the slander is which now and again is uttered against the Chinese in newspapers. It was only under date the 17th October that the *China Mail* copied a letter from a Foochow paper, where it was said that large sums of money were annually collected in England and America for mission work in China, but is it wisely or properly expended, and have the united Protestant missions in all China one single sincere and thorough convert to Christianity except-

---

* "Letter from China," *The Friend,* March 1879, p. 26.

ing those whose services are regularly paid for by the mission? A high authority in mission work in China has frankly stated he is afraid not, and it is notorious that all the servants in foreign employ, female as well as male, who have been educated at the expense of a mission, are most vicious in all their habits; and as to their morality and virtue, the least said on this subject the better. It so happened that on the 3rd of December there was the annual day of intercession for foreign missions, and the English Bishop invited me to give an address on mission work. I brought my subscription list from Hawaii, and referred to the above unkind expressions, and asked the auditory to compare and judge for themselves. I also translated some of the letters and gave them to the editor of the *China Mail,* who made extracts and admitted that these facts practically disposed of such aspersions as were made in the above-mentioned letter. However, the principal drift of his leader was to the effect that the Chinese seemed to be well off on the Sandwich Islands, and it was a pity that the Governor had stopped two vessels from taking emigrants there. . . .

> Yours, in Christian friendship,
> very sincerely,
> R. Lechler

CHRISTIAN HAWAIIAN FAMILY STRANDED IN CHINA, 1879

The Hawaiian widow referred to in the letters reproduced above and below was Mrs. Aheong, not Mrs. Ahyong or Mrs. Acheong. Her husband, Samuel P. Aheong, surname Siu and given name Phong, probably came to Hawaii with an early group of contract laborers. He found an opportunity to learn English and religion in the Makawao home of the Reverend Jonathan Green. At the end of his five-year contract, he moved to Lahaina, married a Hawaiian woman, became a shopkeeper but remained active in church work. Aheong became the Hawaiian Board's first Chinese colporteur in 1870. He later took his family with him to China to do missionary work.

In the Hawaiian Mission Children's Society Library is a file on Chinese Missions in Hawaii. It contains two letters from Aheong in China, handwritten in beautiful script and in understandable English. The first, on 25 July 1870, reports on his arrival in Hong Kong after a 58-day voyage from Honolulu: "I found some friends here, they invite me to stop with them a few days until I get steamer to go to Swatow my home." The second, written 10 August 1871, reports,

Religious Faiths and Practices

"Since I got home, my health getting poor, taking medicine allmost the times . . . we do not forget the Islands all the times, and expecting to go back there soon. . . ."

Aheong died in China, and his widow applied at the Hawaiian Consulate in Hong Kong for help to get back to Hawaii, as reported in the correspondence of the Consul.* After her death here she was buried at Makiki Cemetery. Her gravestone reads: "Naukana Hikiau, 1847–1891, widow of Rev. S. P. Aheong."

There were other cases when the Hawaiian Consul in Hong Kong came to the rescue and repatriated Hawaiian wives who were stranded in Chinese villages.[11]

To William Keswick, Hawaiian Consul in Hongkong:

April 1, 1879

Sir:

I have . . . communication of date January 14th last past, informing "that you had rec'd an application from Mrs. Acheong, a widow, a native of Honolulu, to assist her in returning to her own country as she had no means here (Hongkong) to enable her to do so and in consequence you had procured a passage for herself and three children by bark "Crusader." Also enclosing an account current with vouchers showing expenses incurred of two hundred ($200) dollars at 4/ exchange equal to 250 sterling, and desiring that the amount be remitted to Messrs. Matheson and Co. No. 3 Lombard Street, London. For your kind and prompt assistance to Mrs. Acheong and her three children, I thank you. By next mail steamer for the East (14 inst.) the amount of your disbursement ($200) will be remitted at your request.

. . . Jno M. Kapena
Ministry of Interior

TOURS TO CALL ON CHINESE IN PLANTATION CAMPS, 1882

The best accounts of the conditions of the Chinese colonies and labor camps spread over the islands were written by Frank Damon.

* Hawaiian Consuls to Hongkong, Singapore and Shanghai, 1873–1900, Vol. 10 (Archives of Hawaii).

On his tours as superintendent of the Chinese mission, he saw and reported about the people and their work on rice and sugar plantations. The Chinese opened their minds and hearts to this haole who tried to communicate to them in Chinese and who had no interest in sugar. Aside from some sentimentalities in Damon's accounts, they are good firsthand observations about the Chinese of that time. It was a period of high production and heavy immigration.[12] Chinese labor was used not only on sugar but also on rice plantations owned and managed by the Chinese themselves.

Frank Damon's tours took him to widely dispersed settlements of Chinese on several islands. Among his calls was one to Ka'u, Hawaii, where there was a Chinese Christian colony made up of Chinese laborers who had come on the *Septima,* accompanied by Tsang Kwai, who had worked as colporteur under the Reverend Happer in Canton. Kwai's wife was a Christian with a good education, and his sister had been to a boarding school for girls run by the German missionaries. Peter C. Jones of Ka'u plantation made generous provision for Tsang Kwai and family to act as the pastor at Ka'u. The Board of the Hawaiian Evangelical Association contributed $100 per annum to his support, as reported in the *Friend,* April 1881.

Frank Damon strongly supported the idea of including wives and children in labor immigration, opposing "the transportation of so many working machines" into Hawaii.[13] He saw thousands of men in early manhood or in the prime of life herded together in sugar and rice plantation camps. The restraints of family and social traditions were removed, and full scope was given for the play of those influences that tended to degrade and lower the standard of life. He looked upon opium, gambling, and secret societies as obstacles to missionary efforts. His accounts of visits to Chinese laborers are valuable social documents.*

The Island of Oahu

Being aware of the kind and cordial interest which a number of Christian friends—both here and elsewhere—take in missionary work

---

* Frank Damon, "Tours Among the Chinese," *The Friend,* April, 1882, pp. 36–37; July, 1882, pp. 70–76; November, 1882, pp. 116–118. (Long passages have been broken into paragraphs to aid the reader.)

Religious Faiths and Practices

among the Chinese on our Islands, I have thought that a few words in reference to a recent evangelistic tour which I was privileged to make among them might not be out of place in this issue of our "Chinese Supplement". . . .

I was accompanied by my faithful friend, helper and teacher, Ho Ah Pui, who is at present employed by the Y.M.C.A.[14] of Honolulu as colporteur for the island of Oahu. He was educated in the Presbyterian Mission Training School in Canton, conducted by the Rev. Dr. Happer, and there labored for some time among his countrymen. After this he was employed in the service of the Chinese Mission in California for a number of years. For the past two years he has been stationed on the island of Kauai, where he has been a conscientious and efficient worker. . . .

Ewa

Our first day's ride took us as far as Ewa. . . . Anyone laboring for the Chinese need never be at a loss for employment for a more omnipresent people it would be difficult to conceive of. Though there are but twelve or fourteen thousand of this race scattered over our Islands, no very great number, still when you come to consider that they are nearly all strong, healthy working men, in the prime of life, possessed of all the "push" and energy and tireless industry, for which these people are famous you can form some idea of how even this number must make themselves felt in this kingdom. All are at work, in motion, on the road, in the field. You meet them at every turn. From the first moment of our leaving Honolulu till our return it seemed as if we were kept constantly occupied.

A few miles out from town the rice plantations begin, and form a fringe bordering the shore for a long distance. This is the season for planting the rice, and the men are busy in the marshy fields from early morning till evening. The wide expanses lying at the foot of the valley are just now beginning to be covered with the tender shoots of the rice, which in a few weeks will grow into a swaying luxuriant mass of verdure. It requires a steady head and considerable balancing to run along the narrow foot paths separating the fields, for every available inch of ground seems to be utilized, and no superfluous room is left for the pedestrian. But a little practice enables one to get over this difficulty. Off in the distance we would see a group of men bending to their work and it was not long before we were off our horses and hastening towards them, with our gift of books or papers or tracts. At first we were eyed with considerable surprise, and were often-times, I imagine, regarded as some dread messengers of justice, armed with a warrant or something equally unpleasant. But as soon as they perceived that our errand was one of peace, we were always cordially welcomed, and our papers most kindly received. . . .

At one place near the harbor of Pearl River [Pearl Harbor] we were most hospitably received at the house of a well-to-do Chinaman married to a half-caste woman. She has with her husband visited China, and speaks Chinese. Of course, here, as well as everywhere else, we were invited to take tea, a custom which I soon found was universal among the Chinese. No matter how poor the house might be, or how brief our visit, how humble its occupants, or occupied with business, the attention was never omitted, and proffered with a kindness and courtesy, which was often striking, considering the surroundings.

Beyond this point was a large rice plantation with mill, where we left a plentiful supply of reading matter. These little cultivated valleys, often present a very picturesque appearance. . . .

At another plantation which we visited we found that the former colporteur for this Island was most pleasantly remembered, and the men were glad to receive our books and cordially pressed us to spend the night with them, but we felt it to be necessary to get further on that day. At the store at Waiewa we received a hearty welcome from the Chinese storekeeper who has been many years on the islands and who promised to make us as comfortable as might be in his power for the night, a promise which he abundantly redeemed.

But for the Chinese, Ewa would be indeed a desolate place. The natives seem to have disappeared from the face of the land. But the former nationality have entered in most emphatically to possess the land and their rice fields stretch in every direction. The large native Church stands sad and solitary on the hill, a mute and eloquent reminder of other days. In the hollow beneath are the old Mission premises where the oleanders bloom in rank and luxuriant beauty. I could not but recall, in contrast with the present, a description of Ewa written by E.O. Hall and published in the *Hawaiian Spectator* in 1839, where he speaks of the populous settlement of Ewa and draws a pleasing picture of the natives assembling at early dawn "in great numbers to spend their accustomed hour in the worship of Jehovah."

We started out soon after our arrival, hoping, if possible, to secure something of an audience among the laborers on one of the rice plantations. We found quite a company assembling for their supper and though we did our best to interest them and offered to wait till they were ready to hear our message, they did not seem desirous that we should hold a service among them. So leaving some tracts with them, we trudged home in the rain just a little down-hearted at our lack of outward success. . . .

Back at the store again, we found a little company who asked us to talk to them of the "Doctrine of Jesus," so that we passed a pleasant evening after all, telling to a motley but very courteous assembly the simple, grand truths of the Gospel. Our host's wife, a woman with "small feet" sat in an adjoining room, and listened with the others.

On a Rice Plantation

Up bright and early the next day, with a charming morning to welcome us, our host very kindly fastened a little leaflet, containing an invitation to the church in Honolulu, with a text of Scripture, to his wall in a conspicuous place, so that all who visited the place might see it. This we have had done at all the Chinese stores, lying on our route.

Just as we were leaving, one of the boys from the Chinese school in Honolulu, a bright eyed young fellow, rode up to us. He was spending the vacation here and, as he knew the vicinity well, proved an excellent guide to a number of houses which we had yet to visit at Ewa. We found one or two families and a number of children. It would certainly be a great benefit to the mission if in time we could have a boarding school in Honolulu, where these children from the out-districts could be gathered. . . .[15]

We continued along the shore, purposing to reach Waianae on the following day. We were occupied as on the first day out, in visiting one rice plantation after another. Happening to come at noon to a large Chinese house at Waiole, we found the men taking their "nooning" and had an excellent opportunity of holding a service with some twenty or more of them, concluding with a prayer. At a number of points we saw evidences of the heathen beliefs of the Chinese. In one of the fields a little shrine with candles was arranged. Towards evening we reached Honouliuli, where the whole valley is leased to rice planters. Intimating our desire to hold a service, we were most kindly received by the manager, who did everything in his power to assist us, sending out word for the men to come in the evening. A company of fifty or sixty men assembled in the main room of one of the houses. We had brought with us from Honolulu cloth rolls, on which the Lord's Prayer, Verses from 3d of John, beginning "God so loved the world," the hymn, "Come to Jesus" and other appropriate selections were written in large Chinese characters. These fastened on the wall gave something of a chapel-like appearance to the different rooms in which we held our gatherings. On this evening as at all our services, the colporteur preached in Chinese, after which I said a few words in English interpreted by him, in reference to the object of our visit, and the desire Christian friends felt to advance the mission work among the Chinese, and the purpose of the Hawaiian Board to carry it forward. . . .

This was one of the largest rice plantations we visited. Sometimes two or three men only, have a few fields which they cultivate for themselves, and we often came upon houses where there were eight or ten men working their own land. But the larger plantations are owned by merchants in Honolulu, who have a manager acting for them. The houses are destitute of all but the barest necessities of life, except those of some of the more wealthy planters. The wood-work is unpainted. The beds are arranged around the rooms like berths in a ship. Sometimes these are quite prettily ornamented with a border above the netting of Chinese silk, on which graceful sprays of flowers are painted and Chinese characters written. In the center of the room is a large table where the meals are taken in common. They never need lack for rice, and of this most excellent article of diet they seem never to weary. In many of the houses we saw large pictures of their favorite God, with joss-sticks sometimes standing before it. As this was shortly after their "New Year," the vermilion colored visiting cards received at that season, were arranged in rows on the walls. Over all the doors and windows were pasted slips of the same brilliant paper, on which a variety of propitious wishes, for the occupants of the house and their visitors were written. Many of these were in reference to becoming rich, enjoying length of days, etc. One was, I thought, a very pleasant one to have over any door, *"Out-going, Incoming, Peace!"* But on the rice and sugar plantations I was saddened

Religious Faiths and Practices

by the sight of so many men, without women and children. It seemed unnatural, inhuman, this herding together in 'quarters' of scores of laborers, as if they were so many animals. We speak of Chinese immigration to these islands. It is properly speaking no immigration, it is simply the transplanting of so many working machines to our fields and valleys. These same men would be better, more desirable laborers, if they had their wives and little ones with them. And how much of an impetus would be given to the missionary work, if there were here little children, who would help us in getting at the *father's heart!*

Waianae

After a long, hot ride around Barbers Point, it is very pleasant to catch sight of the little settlement of Waianae, with its pretty Church, its Sugar Plantation, and white cottages nestling among the coconut trees near the ocean, with a blue misty valley in the background. A large number of Chinamen[16] are employed on the plantation and we found them ready to come out to our meetings. The native minister stationed here is a faithful and good man and was of great service to us. As we arrived here on Saturday, we held a service in the evening and one on the following day at noon. The little Church was filled with Chinese and Natives. At both meetings, the choir of the Church sang several hymns and as we had one or two of these written in their language the Chinese had an opportunity of forming some idea of Christian hymns and music. I think this was the first time a Christian service had been held among the Chinese at Waianae. One of the men welcomed us most cordially. He has lately been at the hospital in Honolulu, where we had become acquainted with him. He is, I trust a Christian or one certainly "coming into the light." Formerly he attended Mr. Gibson's school in California, where he received religious instruction. I trust he may yet be enrolled among our church-members. It was most pleasant to have the cordial help and cooperation of the Hawaiian Christians here. They have been holding a series of revival meetings which some of the Chinese have attended.

Waialua

There are not more than a hundred Chinamen in all the Waialua district. I should think some thirty or forty of them are on the Sugar Plantation, and the rest are traders or workers on the rice plantation.

Both evenings we spent at Waialua, we held services. The first night [was] at the store in the village, where only a few were present as we had arrived so late that we had not had time to visit more. The following day we spent in going from one house to another and in visiting the men at the mill and in the fields. The keeper of the principal Chinese store proposed that we should hold an evening service at his store near the plantation. The little "Coffee Room" was filled to overflowing with Chinese and on the verandah, which was ornamented in our honor with Chinese lanterns; there were both Chinese and Natives. Some of them came from a considerable distance, rather to my surprise, for after working hard all day, this was a good deal to ask of them. . . .

The Island of Kauai

There are very few nooks and corners in our Islands where the Chinese have not found their way. And most of all, they seem to have entrenched themselves on the charming Island of Kauai, and accordingly this part of our mission field called loudly for an early visit. . . . I visited Kauai in company with the colporteur, Ho Ah Pui who was formerly stationed on this Island. The eighty miles or so of restless ocean lying between Oahu and Kauai have lost for travelers much of their old terror in these days of steam. How many of us have doleful memories of the agonies of this transit in years that are past, when our only method of conveyance was the uncomfortable and wearisome schooner! . . .

Lihue and Neighborhood

Lihue is a thriving busy place. The neighboring uplands are covered with verdant fields, which form a beautiful picture. One of the most pleasing features in the landscape is the white spire of the Protestant Church, rising from the waving cane fields. Our first service was held in the Chinese "Quarters," just above the mill. I was forewarned that they were rather a "hard set" but I have found very few Chinamen as yet who would not respond to a friendly smile and a kindly word. Nor did these disappoint me in this regard. . . .

That evening the colporteur spoke to them in reference to the "Ten Commandments" and then my turn came. I had been busy for some little time before leaving Honolulu in committing to memory a

Religious Faiths and Practices

short discourse in Chinese, the fruits of my few months study. This consisted of some friendly words stating the object of my mission, the desire of the Hawaiian Board to see this good work extended among the Chinese exhortations to believe in the true God, etc. etc. With this I had flattered myself that I would make rather a brilliant debut in this most difficult of languages. I had practiced the *tones* most conscientiously, and had startled the neighborhood by my daring explosions of sound and now I was face to face with my first critical audience. It was not a very grand auditory, only a company of hard-working, rough-looking "field-hands." Some were mounted on boxes, or tables, others leaned out of the loft of the room which formed a sort of gallery. Here and there were a few struggling candles, which lighted up their yellow-brown faces with fitful flashes of light. Certainly there was nothing you might say to try even a very modest speaker. The first few sentences with all their peculiar twists and turns and tremendous demands upon a Caucasian throat and lungs were gotten through with well enough and then came a *pause*. How to go forward or even backward I did not know I had lost the thread and felt myself hopelessly involved in the intricate mazes of this linguistic labyrinth. My *tones* so zealously shouted in the first seemed to forsake me and all the forces of this ancient Titan of speech appeared to be in arms against the barbarian stripling who would essay to enter the forbidden realm. It was certainly a most uncomfortable position. The wisest course I found was to retire from the field for a time. And how did this "hard set" behave? With a gentleness of courtesy and a thoughtfulness and kindliness which touched me more than I can now put into words. No sneer or smile but a friendly cordial reception of the "will for the deed." They assured me that *maan-maan,* bye and bye it would be all right and that I should be talking to them without difficulty in their own language. This was balm to my troubled spirit and I went home much comforted and determined to try again. Intercourse with the "lower ranks" teaches me that courtesy of manners and delicacy of feeling are not monopolized by the so-called upper circles.

One day was spent in visiting the rice-growers who have their home in a valley not far from Lihue. Then we found a few more Chinese down by the seashore, and in the stores at Nawiliwili. At one of the houses we visited, we found a "Gospel of Mark," which its possessor told us he had purchased of a friend in Honolulu. How wonderfully this precious Bible of ours, in whole or in part, finds its way into the hands and homes, and we will hope the hearts of men! In the afternoon we stopped at several houses where the Chinese employed on one of the sugar plantations make their home. At one of these settlements we found the men just coming home from their day's work. I was especially pleased with the arrangement of their houses. Instead of having one main building, where they are herded promiscuously together, there were separate little cabins, with accommodations for two or three and there was an air of comfort which was in pleasing contrast to some of the abodes I visited on this Island. The men seemed to be a happy and contented lot and were delighted to see the colporteur who had often visited them before. We left books and tracts with them.

[*Hanamaulu*]

I was pleased to see that a number came to our meeting later on at Hanamaulu some distance away. Here we found quite a company of Chinamen. As we came into the main room of their house I was led to feel that to some at least we were not very welcome guests. There had arrived before us, one of those gambling "tramps," who earn an an infamous livelihood by going around from plantation to plantation, leading the laborers to waste their hard earned wages on gambling. This vice seems to have a tremendous power over the Chinese. It is especially prevalent on the sugar plantations—where the men are left to do pretty much as they list after they have left the field and mill. On the rice plantations the Chinese seem to be far better off in many ways than the laborers of the same nationality on sugar plantations. The former are conducted by Chinamen who naturally understand their countrymen far better than their white employers can. The houses are as a rule much larger and better ventilated. Some little attention seems also, to be paid to the morals of the men. Opium smoking is entirely prohibited, and gambling is allowed as an *especial privilege,* for three days only at New Years time! We had the pleasure at Hanamaulu of breaking up an evening's sport. The men themselves seemed kind and received us pleasantly—while the disappointed "Gambler," left us the field. The "speech," so disastrously terminated the previous evening was again attempted and this time with better results and afterwards there was no trouble about its delivery. It was a great

Religious Faiths and Practices

pleasure to see how this humble effort to get to the people through their own language was appreciated by them. It established a friendly bond immediately. . . .

Kapaa and Kealia

At the landing place near Hanamaulu we received a cordial welcome from some rice-growers, with whom we remained to lunch. We found a prominent Chinese merchant of Honolulu waiting for the weekly steamer. Although this man has not as yet united himself with the Church, still his influence is strongly on the side of Christianity and he has been and is of much assistance to us. We reached *Kapaa* towards evening and had but little time to call the people out to the evening meeting, still a company of thirty or so were present. As there is no large room in the Chinese houses here, and as the native Church is at a considerable distance from the mill, we held our service in the "Coffee Room," attached to the principal store of the little settlement. It would be a great advantage on the plantations if the owners could see their way to put up some plain but commodious room for the use of their laborers where they could meet after the day's work was over. There are on some of the plantations, reading rooms for the white employees. Why would it not be wise to try a Chinese "Reading Room." There are plenty of Chinese newspapers which could be procured from San Francisco, Hong Kong, or Shanghai, besides a variety of excellent religious reading matter. One or two magazines, with illustrations, are now published in China, which would be of interest to this people. If some such effort as this should be made, toward elevating and enlightening the thousands of Chinese laborers employed on our large plantations, it could not fail to be productive of good results. . . . Such an appointment as this could be made for religious services, when no Church was available. As it is at present, the missionary very often finds it difficult to procure any sort of a room in which to hold a service.

An afternoon was spent most pleasantly riding over the uplands and lowlands lying about the plantation of *Kealia,* calling the people to the evening meeting. There were various settlements of Chinese in the vicinity where we left goodly supplies of reading matter. Now and then we had the pleasure of giving a little surprise. I can fancy the astonishment of a laborer returning to get his coat which he had left by the side of the field as he had been busy with his work to find rolled up in it a copy of the Ten Commandments or Creed or Lord's Prayer deposited there by some unknown hand. We will hope that after his astonishment is over he will profit by his discovery, as he goes homeward.

At Kealia we were most hospitably entertained by a Chinaman at his house where we passed the night most comfortably. Nothing could have exceeded his courtesy, and the only thing I had to find fault with, was the disagreeable picture of Kwan-Ti, the God of War, beneath which we took our meals. It gave me an excellent opportunity, however, to discourse upon the evils of idolatry. I imagine however, it was his wife "the mean one of the inner apartment" who kept the light before it "trimmed and burning." Quite a company of men gathered in the evening, and we endeavored to speak to them as well as we could of the great truths of the Gospel. . . .

Easter Sunday at Kilauea

The previous evening we had made a tour of the Chinese "quarters," which form one division of this plantation settlement, made up of so many different nationalities. We found curious little crowds who gathered round the "white man" who had thus unexpectedly come among them and who had no interest in "Sugar." The Chinese seem to find it difficult to understand how any one can be going round the country without having some "business" end in view. We held our "Easter Service" in the little native School-house, near the main road. By this time the nice new Church building, which was then in process of erection, is probably completed. For all the little community, this comfortable and commodious Church edifice will be a great convenience, and we may hope blessing. The worthy native Minister Mahoe, formerly Missionary in Micronesia, and now pastor to the Hawaiians and South Sea Islanders living here, was unfortunately for us, absent at Anahola, a neighboring valley, attending a communion service there. But some of the native Christians most kindly and ably assisted us with the singing and seemed to enter most heartily into the spirit of our undertaking. The little School house was neatly filled with Chinese, who paid respectful attention to all we had to say—and received our words with thanks.—It was a singular little company, the natives themselves, separated only a generation or so from heathenism and these still heathen men from the land of China. . . .

Religious Faiths and Practices

Hanalei Valley and Its Inhabitants

As we started out on our way to Hanalei, we met a young Chinese colporteur Dat Ming now employed on this Island for evangelistic work, returning from the valley, where he had been holding a service on the previous day. It was most pleasant to see him after an interval of some months and he was overjoyed to meet us again. This is his first field of labor and it is one which presents difficulties which might well daunt an older and more experienced worker. . . . Only those who have directly engaged in missionary work among the Chinese can understand how hard it is to reach them and their own countrymen feel this peculiarly. Here we have different clans, with sectional prejudices; a diversity of dialects, a peculiar jealously and suspicion, the evils of secret Societies, &c., &c.; all these difficulties the Christian worker has to meet in addition to the natural unwillingness of the human heart to receive the pure truths of Christianity. . . .

I can scarcely imagine a more charming morning's excursion than that from Kilauea to Hanalei. You have fine wooded uplands on all sides, with stately mountains in the distance while on your right lies the glorious blue Pacific. There is perhaps on our Islands nothing more exquisitely beautiful than the little valley of Kaliwai which lies along the way. It is so complete and perfect in itself a verdant rift in the mountain's side, surrounded by mossy cliffs and tree-covered heights from which silver streams leap down to the river, which winds its way down to the sea, thundering on the shore like some mighty guardian of this secluded and yet favored child of nature. But in this quiet nook we find busy workers from China who seem to evince more than usual a desire to learn of the "Doctrine of Jesus."

At one of the Chinese stores, we received a cordial welcome from the keeper formerly in our Honolulu Sabbath School. This School has been doing good work for years. Many scores of men have come under the range of its influence. They always go where they may retain an "aloha" for the School and for the teachers who have there so kindly aided them. We may not see great and immediate results of our efforts but we may be sure . . . they are not in vain.

I wonder so few travellers come to *Hanalei*. Had this lovely valley with its winding willow-fringed river and grand old mountains, been placed in the heart of ancient Greece or modern England rather than in the midst of an almost unknown ocean, it would have been the favorite theme of poets and the delight of painters. I would rather own it, than any one of the great picture galeries of the old world! In one sense I have a share in it, for here my particular friends the Chinese seem fairly to have entered in to possess the land. With the exception of a small portion devoted to sugar the bottom lands of the valley have been turned into one waving field of rice. We spent two busy days riding hither and thither, through the length and breadth of the valley, leaving our little books and speaking a friendly word to these active workers. Some had crept far up into the recesses of the side valley and to reach them we forded rushing mountain streams and passed through beautiful groves of tropical trees and luxuriant ferns. Along the shore of the bay is a row of Chinese houses and the old Mission premises, now sadly overgrown and deserted, are surrounded by rice fields. There are rice growers further on some miles in adjoining valleys but as our time was limited we were obliged to give our books to a friendly Chinaman, going in that direction. We held an evening service at the large rice plantation of Chulan & Co., where we were hospitably entertained for the night. A number of men came in from neighboring houses, and there were those who gave good attention, while there were others who showed that they cared for "none of these things." The following evening we held another service at Princeville at the sugar plantation. The manager was most kind and helpful and had his carpenter arrange a room for us so that with its seats and lanterns it presented an excellent appearance. Beside the Chinese quite a large number of native laborers gathered to look on. Some of the Chinamen on this plantation have been here many years. It is a singular fact that the more recent arrived men seem to give better satisfaction. . . .

Koloa and the Southern Side of the Island

We now retraced our steps to Lihue and then went on to Koloa. Just as we approached this place, we met a company of prisoners who were at work upon the road. A number of these were Chinese, and we exchanged a few friendly words with them. Some days afterwards on returning, I was pleased to see how cordially they greeted us. There are not very many Chinamen in this vicinity. Still, however, at the evening service in the Koloa Church, a company of forty or so were in attendance. It was pleasant to have with us also the veteran Missionary, Rev. Dr. Smith, who takes such a warm and active interest in the work among the Chinese. A number of the Chinese came quite a distance from their homes in a neighboring valley, showing that they had a friendly feeling. From Koloa our way lay along the South side of the Island as far as Waimea.[17]

All along the way were scattered Chinese houses so that we had frequent stops to make. At Eleele we held an evening service with the Chinese working on the plantation. Then followed the beautiful Hanapepe valley, where there are a large number of Chinese rice growers. A busy Saturday was spent in the Waimea valley, fording the river, which rushes over great boulders. This is one of the most beautifully tropical spots on the Islands. The Chinese have found their way quite up to the head of the winding valley and after visiting one house it always seemed as if there was just one more beyond. In the evening we visited the Kekaha plantation[18] and gathered a few together for a service at the Chinese store. On the following Sabbath a service was held at Waimea at which a few Chinese were present. Before this we attended an interesting native service conducted by the Rev. Mr. Rowell. This concluded our missionary tour of the Island.

. . . I regret especially to see what a strong hold the Chinese secret society, the "Triad Organization" has on Kauai; it is a great hindrance to Christian work. When will our Government take energetically in hand the task of investigating and suppressing this baneful association?

               F. W. Damon,
                   Superintendent of the Chinese Mission

During the past summer [1882] in company with the Chinese colporteur, Ho Ah Pui, I have been privileged to make a most interesting tour on the Islands of Hawaii and Maui. . . . As on the islands of Kauai and Oahu, so on these two islands, there was no lack of occupation, for we found Chinese laborers and settlers scattered through all their various districts, even the most remote.

Pahala

Taking steamer from Honolulu early in July last, we first visited the Southern or Ka'u district of Hawaii. . . .

The [Reciprocity] "Treaty" has given a great impulse to the sugar interests in the Ka'u district, and large mills at Pahala, Hilea, Honuapo, and Nalehu, with their attendant plantations give occupation to a very considerable number of laborers, the majority of which are Chinese. At Pahala, we found a band of Christian Chinamen, who are now laboring on this plantation. They with a few others working on neighboring plantations make up a company of thirty-two Christian Chinamen in the district. There are besides six Christian women, with nine little children, nearly all of these are from the "Basel Mission" in Southern China. One of their number acts as leader, or deacon . . . and conducts . . . services. . . .

It was a pleasant sight, early Sunday morning to watch them wending their way up to the pretty little foreign church on the hillside which has kindly been put at their disposal. They were all most neatly attired and brought their testaments and hymn books, which had come with them over the sea from China. I looked out over the company of earnest, reverential faces. . . . They still sing the hymns, taught them by their German missionaries, set to the music of the familiar chorals of the German and Swiss churches. Later in the day we met these Christian people, in the "Deacon's" room, where they meet every evening for prayers. . . .

Hilo

From Ka'u our way lay past the famous volcano of Kilauea (which even in its quietest mood, is strangely impressive, and when roused into great activity, as it has been of late, becomes indescribably grand,) and so onward, through the beautiful tropical forests which line the way to the lovely little town of Hilo, nestling among the palms, by its blue and peaceful bay. . . .

One of the most hopeful points on the Islands for missionary effort among the Chinese, is to be found at Hilo and in the surrounding country. At present there is no Chinese colporteur laboring here. It is the intention, however, of the Hawaiian Board to send a man for the coming year, if possible. There are twelve or thirteen Christian Chinese men and women and several children, working in or near Hilo, and many of the shop-keepers and well-to-do Chinese are most kindly disposed. Some of the leading young people of Hilo are descendants of early Chinese settlers who inter-married with the natives. The present judge,[19] residing here, is the son of an old Chinese resident. His house is one of the most beautiful in this pretty town. Several

Religious Faiths and Practices

bright young families, where the Chinese element is strongly represented are coming up here and the children take a foremost rank in the schools. Of course these persons of whom I now speak have had the benefits of Christian education and civilization. . . . The Foreign Church, of which the Rev. Mr. Baker, is now pastor, feels an earnest interest in the evangelization of the Chinese. The Chinese Christians meet for worship with their American and English brethren in this church, having united with it by letter or profession. A flourishing Sabbath School, under the superintendance of Mr. Terry, with the help of the young people of the church, is doing much good among the people. Mr. Lee Loi, who is now the Government Road Supervisor in the Hilo District, has also actively interested himself in this undertaking. It is most earnestly to be hoped that before long the way may open to the organizing of a Chinese Church here.

Kohala

This is one of the most important districts on the islands and is evidently destined to be one of the principal points for missionary work among the Chinese. There are already a considerable number of converts to Christianity here from among this people, about *one hundred* in all, men and women, besides which there is a fine company of children, who are being trained up to worship the true God. These Christian people have come to us from different missions in Southern China, Demerara [British Guiana], and California,[20] and a number, have learned to love the "Doctrine of Jesus" on these Islands.

Most of them are working on the plantations or as servants in families, and others are owners of stores or cultivating land for themselves. On the Kohala Sugar Plantation there is a large company of both Christian men and women. For a number of years the owners of this plantation have supported a preacher [Kong Tet-Yin] who has lived among his people, and is much beloved by them. He has been absent for some months in China, but we hope soon once more to welcome him back to his post. We trust the day is not far distant when our Christian Chinese brethren in Kohala, will have their church edifice and organization as their countrymen in Honolulu now have. The Rev. Mr. Bond, has taken much interest in the work among them, and many have united with his church.

On the Sabbath, which we spent at Kohala a large company of Chinese gathered at the native church, composed of the Christians and their friends, to welcome us. There were a number of natives also present. It was most delightful to see the heartiness and cordiality of our Chinese friends, some of whom had walked a number of miles over country roads to meet us. They were most anxious to see their preacher once more. During his absence our old friend and valued Christian helper Sit Moon, has rendered valuable assistance in keeping the little flock together. His health is still poor, and he is now cultivating a little piece of land at Makapala in this same district, hoping that the out-of-door life will benefit him. He has preached regularly to the Chinese Christians living in his neighborhood. Sabbath services are also held among the people working on the plantation. Mr. Dyer, with the help of a few kind friends, conducts a Sabbath School, for the benefit of the Chinese.

Paia

This station on the Island of Maui, is a few miles distant from Wailuku. Within a few years quite a settlement has sprung up here, especially of Chinese and it promises in time to grow into a place of some importance. It is the terminus of the railroad from Kahului, the steamboat landing. It is a central point for trade for the large plantations of this district. Owing to the active efforts of the Rev. James Alexander, an interesting work has been initiated here among the Chinese, in connection with efforts in behalf of the Hawaiians.

A most suitable and commodious church has recently been erected here, which is used by both nationalities, the natives in the morning and the Chinese in the afternoon. At a time when we hear so much about race prejudice and jealousy, it is pleasant to see such harmony existing here between these two races who have found in the religion of Christ, a bond of union. The church within and without, is most tasteful, and would serve well as a model for other country churches, which we trust may yet be built. Generous contributions from various sources, Hawaiian, Chinese and Foreign, have paid nearly all the expenses incurred in building. . . . The church was recently dedicated, and on this occasion fifteen Chinese were received into membership—some from the Makawao church (Rev. Mr. Rouse, pastor) and others presented their letters from their respective missions in China.

We were permitted to meet the Chinese Christians on two successive Sabbaths, and found much pleasure and satisfaction in so doing.

Religious Faiths and Practices

A number of them came from the great sugar plantation at Spreckelsville, where amidst the hundreds of their fellow-laborers they have stood true to their profession. One of them especially, a brother from the American Baptist mission in Canton, has been most zealous and has exerted a most happy influence. . . . For months past, in stormy as well as fair weather, the Sabbath meetings have been kept up at Paia, being held in the house of a Christian Chinese friend residing there, until the church was completed.

The "Hawaiian Board" has decided to send a young man by the name of Tshi Sak En, to act as the spiritual guide and leader of this little company, and as colporteur for the Island of Maui. He has been through the necessary course of study at the training school of the Basel Mission at Lilong,[21] and has in Honolulu been receiving further instructions in English, and seems to be in other respects well fitted for the post. . . . The Chinese Christians have, at their own expense, erected a neat little parsonage, on land most generously given by Mr. Alexander, which will be used by the colporteur and at the same time serve as a resting place, for those coming from a distance to attend the service on the Sabbath. . . . I found it given as the unanimous verdict of those who employed the Christian Chinese as laborers, that they were faithful and industrious, and showed their religion in their daily life. . . .

In the Field

I have dwelt more particularly upon the visits paid to the Christian Chinese as I felt desirous that the friends of the mission, who are more familiar with the work in Honolulu, should become acquainted likewise with the country stations. But interesting and stimulating as these visits were, our work lay mainly among the heathen, who are numbered by hundreds and even by thousands on these two Islands. As I have hinted above, our way lay from Ka'u through the Hilo and Hamakua districts, past Waimea, the home of that "sweet psalmist" and noble missionary, Rev. Mr. Lyons, to Kohala. . . . One especial feature of the work here, was the visit to the great plantation owned by Mr. Spreckels, where there are from six to seven hundred Chinamen, living at different camps.

                        Frank W. Damon
                        Superintendent of the Chinese Mission.

The Sandalwood Mountains

FRANK AND MARY DAMON'S WORK AMONG THE CHINESE

Frank Damon met and married Mary Happer in China. They were the greatest friends of the Chinese immigrants in Hawaii, both Christian and non-Christian. Both spoke fluent Chinese.[22] Both worked diligently and with success to improve the lot of the Chinese. In later years, Mary Damon became better known among the Chinese than many Chinese. She made home visits and was cordially welcomed by Chinese families. She was the haole friend who helped the immigrant mothers with their young tots at the free kindergarten in the Palama section of Honolulu. Many of these mothers, now *Popo*s ("grandmothers") and *Tai-tai*s ("great-grandmothers") remember with gratitude Damon *See-nai* ("the teacher's wife") and her help when most needed.

The following is from a talk given by Theodore Richards, educator, about Frank Damon.*

It was Frank Damon who first projected Aala Park—though he must not be held responsible for some of its abuses.

One of the institutions which causes as much pride and gratification as any other is the Free Kindergarten Association. Some woman ought to have had the honor of founding that—and right nobly have the women carried it on. But it was Frank Damon who, coming from Minneapolis in 1882, brought with him the enthusiasm and some of the materials for the first kindergarten. And it was characteristic of him that he did this when hardly recovered from a serious illness.

We owe to him the first Christian Boarding School for Oriental boys—established at his home in Chaplain Lane. He was a founder of churches—and many of our best prepared youth today came from families of these churches. These Christian centers all over these Islands had much to do with changes in China. Do you not see that it was in the south of China that the real ferment began that resulted in a Republic?—and it was from the vicinity of Canton that men kept going from these Islands full of the fine democracy that always grows out of Christian brotherhood. . . .

* Ethel Damon, *Samuel Chenery Damon* (Honolulu: Hawaiian Mission Children's Society, 1966), pp. 121–125.

Religious Faiths and Practices

No sketch of Frank Damon's life could approach completeness without a glimpse into the life of his ideal partner, Mary Happer Damon, daughter of Dr. and Mrs. Happer, medical missionaries in Canton. With deep blue eyes and the sweetest smile, she was a lovely bride.

More than once she told me: "In Canton, fifty years ago and more, my sisters and I had never heard these Hawaiian Islands called by any other name than Tan Heong Shan, or Sandalwood-Fragrant-Mountains. Certainly it never occurred to me even as a young woman that I should come here to spend the rest of my life!

"We had always lived in Canton. My sisters and I often went among the Chinese women to hold Bible classes. One day a young woman stayed after class to ask if we would help a poor woman who was in trouble. Of course we said we would do what we could.

"One evening after dark there came a knock at our gate. There stood a tall gaunt woman in blue coolie trousers and coat, with dark hair and brown skin deeply sunburned. She was timid, and uttered not a word, just watched us with her great dark eyes.

"My father joined us. When we spoke English the woman's face brightened, but no word was spoken. My father had known of returning Chinese who brought wives from various Pacific ports. He named over towns or countries he knew: 'Singapore—Manila—Papeete—Suva,' he pronounced slowly—all strange to us. On and on: 'Nukuhiva—Honolulu. . . .' At last the strange woman opened her mouth, but no sound issued from it. Then she gasped—leaned forward—whispered in echo, 'Ho-no——.' Apparently she could get no further. Then her eyes shone, and she whispered slowly, 'Ho-no-lu-lu!'

"Never can I forget the joy that dawned in her dark face. It was like watching the release of an imprisoned soul. Her eyes gleamed through a mist of tears.

" 'She must be a Hawaiian from Tan Heong Shan,' said my father, 'and she looks half starved.' Someone brought a bowl of hot coffee. Before it even reached her she began to sniff it like a wild thing. When it was put into her hands, she held it reverently—smelling it—a wordless joy shining in her eyes.

"We urged her to drink, but she seemed lost to any other motion—as if the utter joy of holding the warm bowl in her hands and whiffing it were an act of worship at a shrine from which she had been long absent. We watched her in her maze of joy, and wondered if such clumsy things as words had edged enough to penetrate her state of ecstasy.

"We brought her bread and butter. I thought she would never eat or drink. When she did finally eat, it was slowly—in the tiniest bits and sips.

"We were sure that she must have understood some English, and so it proved. My father hoped to find some way of sending her back to the Sandalwood Islands. Since it would not do to let her be far away, she stayed right with us in our home. I made clothes for her. Little by little we girls coaxed her to talk. Her name was something like Puiki. She had married a Chinaman in Hilo on the Big Island and had come to China with him—at the time, she motioned, when ladies were wearing hoop skirts. And we had a good laugh when she asked us why our skirts were so thin and weak.

"In her husband's village she had worked hard in the rice fields with all the others of the household. In time her husband died. Then her son died. Her Chinese daughter-in-law—as head of the household—was not over kind to her. The lonely Hawaiian widow slept on the ground and lived on what she could find—roots perhaps and stunted peanuts. Her only friend, an earlier Chinese wife of her husband, was now widowed like herself, and alike an outcast. The two grew very close to each other, sleeping huddled together and living largely on what they could glean in the fields.

"Yet even in such case the sense of family responsibility was strong. Not long after Puiki reached our house in Canton her Chinese brother-in-law came to take her back to the village again. But he was a reasonable man. Father explained that we were not holding her against her will, that we were only waiting for a conveyance to send her back to her people in Tan Heong Shan, and that if he would trust us, he would have one less mouth to feed in his own household.

"Little by little Puiki recalled an English word as she heard us use it, but of Chinese she knew very little even in the dialect of her husband's village. We American girls in Canton had the greatest difficulty trying to pronounce for her the few Hawaiian names we could find. In all these fifty years here in Tan Heong Shan I have never learned much more Hawaiian than the few names we learned from Puiki so long ago. Father sent her safely home and we never expected to hear of her again. Tan Heong Shan was so far, far away from our mission home in Canton.

"One day a young American came to visit my father and study the Mission work in Canton. His name was Frank Damon, and he was on his way home from Europe to Tan Heong Shan where his father was chaplain to seamen in Honolulu. What echoes that name brought back to us all! We could hear Puiki crooning it to herself as if to recall a song long lost. Of course Father told Mr. Damon about her. The young gentleman was so serious and so busy that we girls saw very little of him during his three day visit at our house, and if he had spoken to us, we would have been far too shy to reply at any length.

"When he was in Honolulu again he went to see all the Chinese mission stations in the Islands. At Hilo he asked for Puiki who was overjoyed to talk with him about Canton and the Happer girls. Suddenly she opened a little bundle of treasures and produced a picture of me! Just how the young man persuaded her to part with it I never heard. But many a time Father and Mother Damon told me of the little picture of Miss Mary Happer which Frank brought back from—of all places—Hilo! And little did I ever think, when Puiki begged that picture of me in Canton, that it would one day fall into a young man's hands, and never would I have parted with it, had I even dreamed such a trick of fate!

"So that is how I came to see Tan Heong Shan too. Frank's father and mother traveled with him to attend our wedding in Canton. Our church was just across a narrow street and long before the hour it was so crowded with people that I had to be carried over in a sedan chair, although I had of course planned to walk over. Hundreds of curious folk pressed in to see that strange thing a bride robed in mourning white, when she should be wearing red for joy! Indeed I did feel like mourning. It was hard to leave China. My Chinese friends, the Bible women, wept with me. And I have never been back in all these years.

"With Father and Mother Damon we made our first, and last, journey to Peking. Then we came back to Honolulu together, by way of San Francisco. Puiki was still living near Hilo when Frank and I went on one of our first mission tours among the Chinese in Hawaii. Arrived in Hilo, we went on horseback, carrying our books and few extra clothes in kerosene tins.

"Frank took my picture back to Puiki and many a laugh we had together recalling Canton and our notions of the Tan Heong Shan so far away. In 1885 I think that was. I never saw Puiki again. But I could never forget her. . . ."

VII. Family Histories, Lineage, and Genealogy

FAMILY ORGANIZATION

Study of genealogies and field research about the people of Hong Kong have increased during the years when mainland China became inaccessible.[1] Out of such research have come descriptive and interpretative materials about social practices and organizations of rural Hong Kong society today which help to reveal the nineteenth century background of Chinese who left homes in the Hong Kong-Macao-Canton triangle. The rural villages in the New Territories of Hong Kong still maintain traditional practices and the family structure of ancient China.[2] There have been changes, of course, but nothing like the rapid metamorphosis of Hawaii's Chinese from their ancestral ways to the lifestyle of American nuclear families. It is necessary to go to studies such as the one of Hugh Baker on clan organization in the New Territories for an understanding of the patterns before they were changed in Hawaii.*

The New Territories have been settled by the Chinese for nearly 1,000 years. Since initial settlement a continuous flow of people has been moving into the area. . . .

Many of the villages have been settled exclusively by groups of people bearing a single surname. These groups are known to anthropologists as lineages, and more popularly as 'clans'. . . .

Firstly, what is a clan? It is a group of individuals who are descended from one ancestor in either the male or female line. As in Europe so in China it is the male line which carries on the surname (females change their surname on marriage) so that this group of

* Hugh Baker, "Clan Organizations and its Role in Village Affairs," *Royal Asiatic Society, Hong Kong Branch, Weekend Symposium,* May 1964, pp. 4–7.

males all must bear the same surname as the original man who founded the line. We will call him the founding ancestor. The number of descendants of the founding ancestor will of course vary from group to group, depending on many factors, such as the number of generations which have elapsed since the founding ancestor, and the reproduction rate of the descendants. Attached closely to this male stem are the women who have married into the group, and attached more temporarily are the girls and young women who have not yet been married off. So the clan may be defined as all the living male descendants of a certain man together with their wives and unmarried daughters. The clan, or a portion of a clan, may form a residential community.

Who is the founding ancestor of such a community?[3] In every case it is the man who first moved to the village where the clan now resides. As we can tell from local historical records, many of the clans founded their villages in the New Territories several centuries ago. How then can we be certain that all the men now living in that village are descendants of the original founder? There are several ways of confirming this. Firstly, a large number of people have their complete 'family' (clan) tree committed to memory, and can recite the names of all their male lineal ancestors back to the founding ancestor. (It sounds rather like those passages in the Bible where we read '. . . and A begat B, and B begat C, and C begat D . . . and so on.') The simplest way of confirming descent, however, is by reference to the clan genealogies, which are usually meticulously kept historical records of the progress of the clan, amended and brought up to date every two or three generations. Nowadays there are many villages which have lost these records,[4] but some can still produce them, and still take pride in this visible evidence of their antiquity and development. . . .

The founding ancestor arrives at a spot, builds himself a house, and sets to work opening up some land for agriculture. He may have moved away from his native village because of a quarrel with his clan members there, or because of some political disturbance such as a revolt or a change of dynasty. He may have come from only a few miles away or from another province altogether. As time goes by, his descendants multiply and other houses spring up around his; if the land is fertile and plentiful more fields are opened up, and a certain measure of prosperity begins to creep in. This, however, is a mixed blessing, for the group is a worthwhile target for bandits, or perhaps

Family Histories

Government troops, or some other powerful clan already well established in the area. Some form of defense must be found. A wall is built around the village with perhaps a moat as well.

The founding ancestor dies, and suddenly the one link which holds all his descendants together has been broken—that is to say, the branches of the tree of descent are joined only at the stem, which is the founding ancestor. How can that stem be kept alive to hold the branches together? The answer is found in the traditional system of ancestor worship. If all the descendants club together to erect a hall to the memory of the founding ancestor, and place in it a tablet bearing his name, and in which one of his souls resides (the Chinese have several) then that ancestral hall and the worship of that tablet become focal points for the unity of all the descendants. The hall is built, and endowed with some land donated by the descendants, the produce from which can be used to pay for the ceremonies or worship of the founding ancestor. . . .

As the clan gets bigger it tends to split up into smaller groupings, each having as its focal point a certain descendant of the founding ancestor. Thus, if he had three sons, the clan may subdivide into three branches, each branch comprising the descendants of one of the sons. All still owe allegiance to the founding ancestor, but the members of the branch springing from his second son would not worship the first son's tablet. Again, each branch is likely to build a hall for the worship of his own founder's tablet if it has sufficient resources. These branches may subdivide again and again as the years go by—there is theoretically no limit. What is being achieved by this subdivision? In fact it amounts to a recognition of the unwieldiness of the clan as its members grow. Just as a national government must establish a hierarchy of area governments in order to make the administrative machinery work more easily throughout the land, so in the clan-village it is easier to have a system of hierarchial branches nestling one within the other and each controlled by its council of elders. This we may call a political reason for division. There are also economic and religious reasons. On the economic side, it happens that one section of the clan may become richer than another. If it remains undivided from the clan as a whole, it has an almost undeniable liability to spend more money than the other poorer members on general clan welfare. . . . On the religious side there is a general belief that the farther away an ancestor recedes from you in generation, the less benefit you are likely to receive from him. After all, I am much more likely to receive greater blessings from my dead father, who has only myself and my three brothers to look after, than from my grandfather who, besides myself and my brothers, also has my father's brothers' descendants to look after. With this reasoning, it follows that the establishment of a branch of the clan means that the descendants of that branch are then paying more attention in worship to those from whom they may expect to receive more benefits.

Still, the most important of these groups of kin is of course the clan itself, to which all other branches and sub-branches owe allegiance. What does the clan achieve? It is, as we have seen, at once Church and State, with the Clan Elder holding the positions of both Archbishop and constitutional Monarch so to speak. He is assisted and guided by his council of elders, and may well be swayed also by influential members of the community who are not old enough to be elders. The clan conducted the religious ceremonies of worship to the founding ancestor, with the Clan Elder taking lead. It assumed legal powers over its members and could punish and fine them in the past; and it still acts as mediator in disputes. It assumed responsibility for defence of the community, and could ally itself with other clans to do so. An important factor in its alliances with other clans was marriage. It is forbidden for anyone to marry a mate of the same surname,[5] whether there is any known relationship or not; and consequently, all marriages undertaken by clan members were in a sense 'diplomatic marriages'. It is obvious that it is not possible for someone to marry into the same village and marriage, therefore, linked villages. The clan also undertook local public works, such as building dams and paths. It made itself responsible for the education of its members by providing schools. This was one of the important functions in the past which it still performs in many places. It assumed responsibility also for each of its individual members in conflict with outside influences, and its backing was so important to the individual that it was a strong incentive to him to obey its rules in order to retain its support. Also the clan took care of the poor and the aged where possible.[6]

In present-day conditions in the New Territories, many of the functions of the clan have been superseded. Government is comparatively strong in the area, and there is no longer the feuding which disturbed the district in the past. But the clan village is still an important aspect of the scene. In many villages the clan is as active

Family Histories

religiously as it used to be. It still promotes education, assumes responsibility for many public works, performs acts of charity, and employs its own village watchmen to protect the villagers against thieves. Most important of all it has managed to look after itself with the British Government through the system of Village Representatives. These men are now performing almost all of the secular duties of the Clan Elder; and while it is not a new thing for the Clan Elder's authority to be subject to the influence of powerful members of his community—such as those who were officials in the old days—it is only under this system of Village Representatives that the basis of their authority has finally been called into question.

CHINESE GENEALOGIES

In the United States, there is increasing interest in Chinese genealogy as a complement to field observations and oral testimony in making anthropological studies.[7] Genealogical records have value in documenting mass migrations and family patterns. Recent wars and changing values have released many genealogies for use in research centers. Formerly, families in China regarded them as confidential and guarded them as family treasures.

A few families in Hawaii were fortunate in discovering genealogies (*chia pu*), brought over by their fathers or grandfathers. Immigrant forefathers in Hawaii had followed old traditions and kept their family records up to date. Even when separated by thousands of miles from ancestral homes, the birth of a son was reported and duly recorded in family registers kept in the ancestral halls. It was then duplicated in the genealogy or in an abbreviated record book kept in Hawaii. Some families, without such records but aware of their intrinsic values, are gathering data about their ancestral villages and the founding fathers of Hawaiian sub-branches. Part-Hawaiian families with strong traditions of recitative family histories have also been seeking recorded evidences of their Chinese ancestry.[8]

Besides registering the male lineages, some Chinese genealogies included literary gems composed by clan members, condolence sentiments about prominent members, Imperial awards and official ranks, and other records of achievements like the passing of Imperial examinations.[9]

Thomas W. Chinn presented a paper on Chinese genealogical methods at the World Conference on Records and Genealogical

The Sandalwood Mountains

Seminar held in Salt Lake City, Utah, on 5–8 August 1969.* Mr. Chinn was a founder and past president of the Chinese Historical Society of America which is active in many areas of research, field studies, preservation, and publications.

Nearly all Chinese families had a genealogical record, or "Generation Book." This gave the origin of the family, its collateral lines, names, age, registry of marriages, births, deaths, and generally, a business history of the male line. The book was called the *Chia Pu,* or "Family Table Book." Every thirty to fifty years it was brought up to date and a new copy made.

A board of editors was called upon to edit and preserve the *Chia Pu.* This board elects one of its members chairman, who must be: of old age; of the oldest living generation; and of good character. His term of office was for life. Also on the board must be, by virtue of birth, the oldest son of the direct descendant of the family or clan. This board was maintained by assessments collected from all members of the family.

When the time came to update the *Chia Pu,* the chairman gave appropriate notice. Each branch or subassociation then sent a representative to the appointed place and assisted in the editing of the new material. Groups or branches removed to another part of the empire were permitted to form a new association of their own, or join the same family association in their new abode.

Besides the principal duty of preserving the history and genealogy of the family, were imposed these additional duties: to worship and do reverence (in a Lodge of Sorrow) to their ancestors within the place of meeting; to judge and settle family disputes before it reached the magistrate or public court of justice; to preside at marriages and funeral ceremonies of its members; to establish scholarships for superior students, and finally, to aid and assist orphans, the poor, and the distressed. [These latter precepts were largely exemplified in the "new world"—in America—when the early pioneers arrived from China. With the gradual arrival of women, and the beginnings of families, a sort of *Chia Pu* was attempted amongst the families in America. How-

---

* Thomas W. Chinn, "Genealogical Methods and Sources for the Chinese Immigrant to the U.S.," *Chinese Historical Society of America Bulletin,* November 1969, Vol. IV, no. 9.

ever, the "genuine" book remained in China and relatives or associates at home continued this activity for those overseas members who kept in touch. For years (about up to the time the Communists took over mainland China following World War II), money was sent to relatives in China. Generally a part of the amount was for the "Lodge of Sorrow"—in memory of their ancestors]. . . .

When a child is born the parents select a personal name, and this name is registered. But should it afterwards be found that another person in the family association of the same generation as the child has already registered the name, then another name must be found, and the new name registered; it being the rule that no two or more persons of the same family and generation shall have the same given, or personal name.

Chinese immigrants and their descendants followed the traditional Chinese genealogical rules during the entire period such families in this country observed the custom. It would be safe to say that only a very few Chinese in America continue this custom today. . . .

Arriving in California, old ties soon asserted themselves, and groups by family name quickly formed for several reasons: mutual protection; group ventures; and eventually, employment opportunities.

The early treatment of the Chinese on the West Coast, and particularly in California shaped the course of their reaction for more than a century. Few persons were willing to talk about themselves, or about their family. This made any genealogy inquiry difficult, as it dealt with personal history and this was something that became a particularly secret matter. . . .

The problem of a minority group struggling to survive, their reluctance to inter-marry and most important of all, the "inquisition" of immigration authorities, led them to shun exposure to press or public. . . .[10]

When China emerged as a republic in 1912, many paths in the name of expediency were taken to modernize the decayed, backward and custom-ridden empire.

In America, the descendants of the early pioneers from China also stirred themselves and began to re-assess their future. Many returned to China, and brought back their western education and technical knowledge to assist in the shaping of a more modern China. Others, whose roots were planted deeply in American soil, remained here. In so doing, each new generation took a farther step away from the culture of the motherland. Many forgot the language, customs and teachings of the old country, and became thoroughly American in thought and deed. Their only link remaining was in their physical appearance.

The post-World War II period of the past quarter-century has seen for them a complete revision of discriminatory laws and with it a surge that has carried them even farther away from their motherland. With it came complete indifference by the large majority of descendants to the retention of any Chinese customs; although they seem to enjoy the holidays.

Genealogy became even farther removed from their thoughts because of the broken ties forced by the Communistic occupation of the Chinese mainland. The threads of genealogy could not be woven back to antiquity because the large majority of Chinese in America originated from China proper—not Taiwan.

Special notation should be made of the family associations flourishing in most large Chinatowns. In San Francisco, family associations have existed for over a century. It provided the means for persons, no matter how remotely related, to join together for the common weal. As noted previously, it provides a social outlet, some protection and job opportunities. But in addition, it is genealogy in practice. Through the family association, members who can trace their ancestors to the same original family, are actually living genealogic associations providing material benefits to members of their family tree. The records they keep are, in a sense, genealogic records.

But under present world conditions, genealogy as practiced in China is not a custom largely practiced here—except, as noted, by the family associations.[11] Its possible future revival would be closely tied up in the future of genealogy in an unrestricted mainland China and the free access of material to persons interested in perpetuating its practice in America. . . .

BIOGRAPHY OF THE REVEREND WOO YEE-BEW

Biographical sketches and autobiographies enhance family genealogies. They help to identify the family tree and add interest to the purely traditional generation books kept by the Chinese.

Dr. David Woo is one of the few second generation Chinese to write a biography of his father, the Rev. Woo Yee-Bew (1864–1930), the first Chinese clergyman of the Episcopal Church in Hawaii. It is

Family Histories

noteworthy that the Rev. Woo's father, Woo Set-Am, was a respected scholar and a Mandarin official, at one time serving as magistrate in the neighboring province of Fukien. This biographic sketch may well be incorporated into the Woo family genealogy.*

On the occasion of the Centennial celebration of the establishment of the Protestant Episcopal church in Hawaii, we pause to acknowledge that many peoples of all races have been influenced through it, one way or another. Many highlights and events of these early days, if not recorded, will soon be forgotten.

There is a chapter in the history of the church, concerning the Chinese congregations and their contributions to the cause of Christianity in Hawaii which has never been told.

This is a story of the first Chinese minister of the Episcopal church in Hawaii—a biography of the Rev. Woo Yee-Bew.

Mr. Woo was born in Fat San, near Canton, China in 1864. His father was the Honorable Woo Set-Am, Magistrate in Fukien, residing for a time at Hok San, in the Kwangtung province. He was an appointee of the Imperial Manchu Dynasty, after having duly travelled to the capital of Peking and there successfully taken and passed his examinations for official degrees. This made him a scholar and a mandarin, an official of the Emperor.

At about this time, Christianity first came to China when the Lutheran church was established in South China. The learned Elder Woo was intrigued by this new philosophy of life, studied its teachings, and became one of the first converts. He resigned his official position and preached the new gospel of Christ throughout the countryside.

In true pioneer fashion, he went about his mission, accompanied by his disciples who carried the conventional bamboo pole over their shoulders, slung with baskets from each end. In one basket were books and Bibles, and in the other, medicines and herbs. Thus, he administered to the spiritual as well as to the physical needs of his fellow countrymen. How like the Savior, but in a different age and in a different country. Until today, this beloved gentleman-turned-preacher is still revered and remembered, for his portrait still hangs in the village hall at Fat San, where he carried on his life work.

* David Woo, "The Reverend Woo Yee-Bew," *Hawaiian Church Chronicle* September, 1963, pp. 6–8; October, 1963, pp. 7–8.

The Woo genealogy contains sixty generations of recorded history, among whom were many scholars of literary repute, a fact the clan could be justly proud of.

With such a background young Woo Yee-Bew was baptized in the only Lutheran church there and in the course of time, was sent to study at the Lutheran Mission School in Canton. There, he diligently pursued the study of the Chinese classics as well as courses in German and religion.

In 1880, when only 16 years of age, he travelled to Hong Kong and matriculated at St. Stephen's college for the study of Theology. He graduated with the first class of twelve. It was there that he was confirmed by Bishop Burden, Bishop of Victoria.

Three years later, he left in 1883 for San Francisco where he was to be sponsored by a friend and colleague of his father, a German priest, to do graduate work in Theology. Alas, after a long and arduous trip, the ship arrived at California only to be quarantined off shore for three months. Small-pox had broken out on board ship! Disappointment followed, for when Woo Yee-Bew was finally allowed to land, he learned that this kind priest who was to be his benefactor, had died in the interval. Young Woo was stranded and lost in a strange country.

Luckily, there was a distant cousin, the Rev. W. C. Young, who was in charge of the Chinese mission on Clay Street in San Francisco, under Bishop Kip. Mr. Woo sought him out and was given a position as teacher of Chinese in the night school.

In December 8, 1883, Mr. Woo decided to come to Hawaii and arrived in Honolulu. He met and lived with Mr. Goo Kim and they were partners in a small business venture. It was through Mr. Goo that he was introduced to Mr. Frank Damon, as Mr. Goo was a warden of the Chinese Congregational church. A happy reciprocal arrangement resulted in which Mr. Damon taught Mr. Woo English, while Mr. Woo in turn taught Mr. Damon Chinese.

The two would often go out to preach together, for they were converting the Chinese community in Honolulu. Thus, in the early history of the formation of the Fort Street Chinese Congregational church, Mr. Woo also played a vital part.

During this early sojourn in Honolulu, bachelor Woo lived with Mr. Chang Young Siu (L. Ah Seu), and Mr. Coo Tet Tsin [Goo Akina] for six years. These were two enterprising gentlemen who became partners in opening a camp for Chinese plantation laborers in Kohala, Hawaii. They were also instrumental in developing a rice industry in Polulu, Hawaii. Eminent sons of the latter were Senator Ernest Akina, Representative Arthur A. Akina, and Chairman Clem A. Akina of the County of Hawaii.

Kohala then had a thriving Chinese community, made up of plantation laborers, farmers and others engaged in trades. There were even two rival Benevolent societies within view of each other across the Kapaau Gulch. . . . Each would vie with the other, especially during Festival time, to see which one could burn the longest or loudest chain of firecrackers, or whose gongs sounded the loudest.

A nucleus of Chinese Christians among the plantation laborers began to meet at the home of L. Ah Seu, with Mrs. Ah Seu conducting the meetings. In due time, his former roommates sent for Mr. Woo to come over, and he arrived in Kohala to conduct services of the church.

Mr. Woo Yee-Bew was granted an authority by Bishop Alfred Willis in February 26, 1884 as Reader, having been presented by the Rev. Herbert F. E. Whalley, missionary Priest of Kohala. The Rev. Mr. Whalley had arrived from England in 1882 to take charge of the district of North Kohala.

On Dec. 2, 1887, he was appointed Evangelist to the Chinese community. Mr. Woo worked with his fellow countrymen, preaching the gospel to them in their native tongue and converting them to Christianity, so that in time, the St. Paul's Chinese mission in Makapala, Kohala was established.

Things being stable, Mr. Woo decided to settle down. He met and married Miss Sarah Yap who had originally arrived in Honolulu during the reign of King Kalakaua. It took them fifty-five long and rough days for the trip from China on a sail boat. She was four years old then and remembered that her mother was so seasick that she developed bed sores from lying down in the bunk the whole trip and had to be carried ashore on arrival. They were Christians and the family attended the Fort Street Chinese church and recalled being in the congregation on the occasion of its grand dedication. They opened a tailor shop in Honolulu within the Chinese community.

Mrs. Woo worked beside her husband and assisted him with the work of the church and even learned to play the organ to provide music for the services.

Meanwhile, increased interest in Christianity was shown in Honolulu among the Chinese community at this time. Many families from the St. Paul's mission in Kohala had moved to Honolulu to live. On the recommendation of the Rev. H. H. Gowan, the Rev. Mr. Woo was persuaded to come to Honolulu in 1888. His first son, John, was only one month old at the time. Mr. Woo worked with Mr. Gowan and taught him the Chinese language also. Services were held then in the yard behind Mr. Chang Yen Bau's store. Later, they used the Hawaiian Church on the grounds of St. Andrew's Cathedral. This subsequently became St. Peter's church in Honolulu.

On Aug. 6, 1891, Mr. Woo was granted a license and authority to perform the office of Reader and Evangelist in the chapel of Saint Peter, within the Precincts of our Cathedral Church of Saint Andrew, Honolulu.

It was through his efforts in preaching the Holy Scriptures in the Chinese language and working among his own countrymen that enough converts were gathered to establish the St. Peter's Church in Honolulu.

On March 13, 1892, the Rev. Mr. Woo was ordained Deacon in the Cathedral Church of St. Andrew, Honolulu, by Bishop Alfred Willis, under the Church of England. Mr. Woo incidentally taught Bishop Willis enough of the Chinese language to enable him to administer the Holy Communion to the Chinese congregation on his official visits.

A letter from a grocery owner on Maui requested a teacher and preacher. Bishop Willis sent Mr. Shim Yin Jin, who came from China and later became a priest at Kula, Maui, the father of the Rev. Canon Wai On Shim, retired Rector of St. Elizabeth's Church and now helping with services at St. Andrew's Cathedral.

For the next five years the Rev. Mr. Woo served at St. Peter's Church, where among Chinese Christians he was considered a pioneer leader in the Christian movement. At about this time Mr. Chang Young Siu's sister, Mrs. Wong Kong, came from China with her son, Mr. Kong Yin Tet. He later entered the ministry and succeeded the Rev. Mr. Woo at St. Peter's Church in November 1896.

St. Paul's Church, Kohala, had been left without a priest and Mr. Zen Len Fui and Mr. Chang Young Siu had acted as Lay Readers. Mr. Woo's former congregation had requested his return, so he accepted the challenge. The Chinese community had grown

Family Histories

larger in the meantime and people were quite prosperous then. In fact, today when most of the prominent Chinese citizens in Honolulu are asked "where did they come from—" invariably they answer, "from Kohala."

The Rev. Mr. Woo's son, John, was nine years of age then and ready for school, so arrangements were made by the Rev. Mr. Fritz of Iolani School to enter him there. Bishop Willis accompanied him to Honolulu on one of his official visitations and safely deposited him in the school. Among his classmates was a young man named Y. Sang Mark, who years later became rector of St. Peter's Church.

When the transition from the Anglican Church to the American Church took place in 1902, new patents were granted all the clergymen. On January 6, 1902, the Rev. Mr. Woo was granted a license of authority to perform the office of a missionary in the Church of St. Paul, Makapala, Kohala, Hawaii, and was given a new parchment as Deacon under the new jurisdiction. He was ordained priest on Sunday, November 23, 1902, by Bishop Henry B. Restarick, in St. Andrew's Cathedral, under the Protestant Episcopal Church in the United States of America. In commemoration of his Consecration, the Bishop presented him with a copy of the Holy Bible, which he treasured.

The Rev. Mr. Woo remained at St. Paul's until 1915. He now had a family of 10 [*sic*—actually 13] so for schooling reasons moved to Honolulu. Throughout this period he served most happily with the Rev. James Walker (now retired) and Miss Anne M. Prescott of "Makapala-by-the-Sea" fame. Anecdotes of life during those days and of his family incidents could be gleaned from this book of pearls.

He then assisted with services at St. Peter's, which he helped to establish in 1888. At about the time of his return to Honolulu St. Elizabeth's Church was administering to a good-sized Chinese congregation in Palama. The Rev. Mr. Merrill requested his services as Assistant Priest, so that he might preach in Chinese to the predominantly Chinese congregation. He served at St. Elizabeth's under Canon Kieb in the same capacity for 22 years. At the Convocation of the District in 1929 the Rev. Mr. Woo was one of the oldest clergy men in time of service present for the event.

In 1920 because of increasing ill health he visited his native China to visit the tomb of his father, duly inscribed with the names of his

progeny, which was the Chinese custom. The Church now had four
Chinese clergymen in Hawaii—the Rev. Messrs.: Woo Yee Bew,
Shim Yin Jin, Kong Yin Tet and Mark Y. Sang, in order of seniority.

In 1930 he again returned to China to visit his children who were
grown and scattered in several places in the Far East. The oldest son,
now Dr. John Y. Woo, was in Nanking, where he established his own
hospital. David was studying medicine at St. John's University,
Shanghai. Dr. Paul S. Woo was practicing dentistry in Hong Kong.
A daughter, Mrs. Hannah Io, was a nurse in Singapore. Mrs. W.
W. Lau (Mary) had succumbed in the influenza epidemic in
Shanghai in 1918.

Left back home with mother were Philip, Jacob, Victoria, Ethel,
Francis, Ivan, Cyril and Thomas.

Unfortunately the winter season proved too severe for him and he
contracted pneumonia and died. He was buried in the Pokfulum
cemetery in Hong Kong. Surviving him was his wife Sarah Yap Woo
and her 13 children. Today his children are contributing their share
to the welfare of their own communities. They carry on his teachings
and philosophy of life in Christ so that in a small measure, Hawaii
is richer for his having come here.

Thus lived a real pioneer missionary in the Christian movement
among the Chinese in Hawaii, one who left his native land as a young
man to come to Hawaii to live, to preach the Gospel, and to convert
his people to Christ. He served as the first Chinese clergy man of the
Episcopal Church in Hawaii and was instrumental in establishing two
of its churches and indirectly, to assist in the formation of another—
all of which are prospering today.

A memorial service was held at St. Elizabeth's Church, at which
time a brass plaque was dedicated to his memory. Miss Hilda Van
Deerlin and Mrs. Merrill, Catechists, were in the congregation. His
wife played the organ for this final service. It was fitting that his
vestments, some of them beautifully embroidered in China, were sent
to a mission in Africa, to be used by other pioneer missionaries in
the work of Christ in lands also far removed from that of their native
home.

THE CHUN AFONG STORY

The story of Chun Afong (1825–1906), the first Chinese "millionaire" in Hawaii, makes a fascinating study of a man who migrated

Family Histories

as a merchant and definitely not as "a coolie who suffered blows from the overseer in the cane field" as he was described in Jack London's fiction.[12]

On Chun Afong's retirement and return to China in 1890, the Honorable J. A. Cummins, minister of foreign affairs of the Hawaiian Monarchy, wrote a personal letter of introduction to J. J. Keswick, acting consul general in Hong Kong for Hawaii.*

Honolulu, October 16, 1890.

Sir:

This will be handed to you by Mr. C. Afong, a Chinese merchant and planter for many years resident in this Kingdom where he owns large interests and stands in the highest consideration and repute.

I shall feel obliged if you will afford him any assistance in your power, and supply him with any information or guidance he may seek at your hands, and forward his views so far as may be in accord with your instructions.

I have the honor to be, Sir,

                Your most obedient servant,
                (sgd) J. A. CUMMINS,
                Minister of Foreign Affairs.

Hon J. J. Keswick,
H.H.M.'s Acting Consul General, Hongkong.

Tracing the descendants of Chun Afong was a pleasurable task that resulted in two news stories.†

The story of the Chun Afong family goes beyond "Thirteen Daughters," the delightful musical written by Honolulu playwright

* Archives of Hawaii, *Hawaiian Consuls—Hong Kong, Singapore, and Shanghai,* Vol. 10, 1873–1900.
† Tin-Yuke Char, "New Chapter in Afong Family Story?" *Honolulu Advertiser,* 14 June 1970, and "His Great-Grandfather is an Isle Legend," ibid., 11 July 1971.

237

The Sandalwood Mountains

Eaton Magoon. The descendants of Chun Afong and his wife, the former Julia Hope Fayerweather, include actually only twelve daughters and four sons, the eldest of whom was Toney Afong.

We came across the story of Toney Afong and his life quite by accident when we were in Hong Kong recently. Some friends who know about our deep interest in family genealogies mentioned the name Malulani C. Afong (who, we later discovered, is Toney's grandson).

The name was more than familiar. In glancing through my Yenching University (Peking) alumni of America newsletter in 1968, I came across the news item that Malulani C. Afong, class of 1948 and "descendant of a royal Hawaiian princess," had migrated to San Francisco to start a restaurant. He was accompanied by his wife Edna and children Grace, Joseph and William.

At Yenching he was known by his Chinese name, Chen Hsi-Hsiang. But I was intrigued by his other name. I wrote to him in August, 1968, for an appointment to call on him as a fellow alumnus. The letter was returned by the San Francisco post office stamped "moved, address unknown."

We have since learned that Malulani C. Afong has shortened his name to Max Chun Afong. In his San Francisco home hangs the portrait of his great-grandfather whom he refers to as "Chun Afong the Great."

The Hawaii side of the Chun Afong family history is well-covered by Clarice Taylor's series of 69 articles (October 7, 1953 to December 15, 1953) in the story of the Afong Family (Tales of Hawaii, *Honolulu Star-Bulletin*).

From her stories, we discovered why Chen Hsi-Hsiang used the name Malulani. It had been carried in the family for seven generations from the Beckley ancestry of Mrs. Chun Afong, born Julia Hope Kamakia Paaikamokalani o Kinau Beckley Fayerweather.

Her mother was Mary Beckley, sister of William Frederick Malulani Beckley, and daughter of Captain George C. Beckley, a Yankee who married High Chieftess Ahia, a hanai daughter of Queen Kaahumanu, and natural daughter of Huha Kaha (King Kamehameha's Warrior) and his wife Mohaloa-a-Malulani.

Toney, one of her four grandsons and Malulani C. Afong's grandfather, was born Anthony Keawemaihili in 1859 and was educated at Iolani and at Trinity College, Hartford, Conn. His Chinese name

Family Histories

was Chun Chik-Yee. He helped with his father's prosperous business until 1890 when he accompanied his father to China.

We learned that Chun Afong decided to retire in China and sold his interest in Pepeekeo Sugar Plantation for $600,000 and provided for his family in Hawaii.

He built his retirement home in his ancestral village and surrounded the house with coconut trees and other foliage he brought from Hawaii.

He continued to live the life of a merchant prince. He bought a hotel in Macao which accepted only European guests, razed the building and put up a mansion. He died in 1906 at the age of 81.

Son Toney returned to China at the age of 31 and immediately joined the mainstream of Chinese life. He looked after his father's business and became a comprador of Douglas, Lapraix and Co. in Hong Kong.

Here was a handsome young man of Chinese, Caucasian and Hawaiian heritage, proficient in both English and Chinese, a successful businessman and very sociable. He became involved in politics and met Dr. Sun Yat Sen, then a medical student at the University of Hong Kong, who was plotting the revolution to overthrow the Manchu dynasty. He joined in the revolutionary activities.

Like all Chinese who had money, Toney wanted to add a political office to his fame. It was rumored that he contributed $270,000 (Chinese currency) to General Chen Chiung-Ming's war chest and was rewarded with the office of Governor of Kwangtung province. However, he lost that job a short time later when General Chen was driven out of Canton.

Toney then lived in retirement in his Macao refuge, returning to Hawaii only once to visit his aging mother in 1904. His life in Macao was typically that of a retired Chinese court official.

In 1933, Mrs. Irma Tam Soong, then a student in Peking at Yenching University, spent a summer in South China and was a house guest at a neighboring Lau mansion. She called on Toney Afong and recalls him as having the fine physique and facial characteristics of a Hawaiian warrior. She remembers Toney as a Chinese gentleman, serene in old age, collecting jade and objets d'art.

Of Toney's sons, the first was Wing Sen who rose to political office as commandant of the provincial arsenal. He loved horseback riding and roamed about the countryside taking pot shots at game as well as at people. He died at the early age of 32.

Wing Sen left five children. The oldest son was not a success in business and died three years ago. The second son is Hsi Hsiang (Malulani). [Of Wing-sen's] three daughters, one remains in mainland China, while the other two are in the United States.

Toney's second son Wing Kei succeeded his father as comprador in Hong Kong. He left one son, Hsi Tan, who is a broker in Hong Kong.

Toney's only daughter is Wing Luen (Irene). Her marriage to T. Y. Lau was the social event of the year in Macao. T. Y. Lau, an engineer educated in America, was the son of Lau Yuk-lin, former Chinese ambassador to Great Britain. Both families maintained mansions on the Bund, in the wealthy section of Macao. Although their homes were only two doors away from each other, the dowry carried by traditional bearers circled several blocks. The whole street was lighted with beautifully decorated pailou (arches) erected for the occasion.

On their honeymoon to Peking, they visited Yenching University. I remember meeting them through his sister, my schoolmate. Irene and T. Y. Lau had four children, all of whom are living in mainland China.

Now a widow, Irene lives in Peking with her eldest son who is a journalist connected with the New China (Hsin Hua) News Agency, Premier Chou En-Lai's official organ.

This covers the China-side descendants of Chun Afong, merchant prince from Hawaii. As our informant summarizes: "No family holds its wealth for over three generations." (Yun Mu Sam Doi Fu). The Afong family today in China has not held on to the wealth and position of its colorful ancestor nor yet attained any success of its own. Perhaps Malulani C. Afong, great-grandson of Chun Afong, starting a Chinese restaurant in San Francisco, may succeed and build a new family fortune.

His Great-Grandfather is an Isle Legend

A little over a year ago, the Honolulu Advertiser published an article by me about the descendants in China of Hawaii's first Chinese millionaire, Chun Afong, and his Hawaiian-Caucasian wife, Julia Hope Fayerweather.

Family Histories

In that article I mentioned the name Malulani Chun Afong, great-grandson and only male Afong descendant in America, and of my unsuccessful attempt to meet with him in 1968 in San Francisco to where I had traced him.

We finally were brought together by a mutual friend in San Francisco in April. Malulani Chun Afong had been interested in this meeting since he received a clipping of The Advertiser article.

He was cordial and anxious to help me chart the Afong male lineage following the Chinese system of genealogy:

I. Great-grandfather Chun Afong (1825–1906), pioneer Chinese merchant prince and owner of Pepeekeo Sugar Plantation on the Island of Hawaii, married Julia Hope Fayerweather, who was brought up with King Lunalilo, having the same governess.

II. Grandfather Anthony Keawemaihili Afong (1859–1936), better known in China as Chun Chik-yu, one-time governor of Kwangtung Province, married Julien Chang in China.

III. Father Chun Wing-Sen (1887–1919), also known as Chun Wing-Sen Afong, who once served as commandant of the Canton Arsenal, married Lee Shee in China.

IV. Himself, Malulani (Max) C. Afong (born in 1918), also known as Chen Hsi-Hsiang, former principal of the YMCA Middle School in Hongkong, married Edna Liang in China.

V. Sons Joseph Malulani Afong, age 17, and William Mahinolani Afong, age 13.

Thus, the male line of five generations of the Afong family.

Malulani has made himself the family historian. He showed us a photo taken in 1964 when the late Marmion Magoon, grandson of Chun Afong and son of Emmaline Afong, visited his China-side relatives and had his picture taken with Malulani's mother and other family members.

Malulani talked about his family genealogy, that his ancestors in the Ming Dynasty in the 15th century had migrated from the province of Fukien southward into Kwangtung. Great-grandfather Chun Afong was the only male heir in his generation, and for seven generations previously, there was only one male heir to carry the family line.

This probably explains why Chun Afong wanted a large family and had four sons and twelve daughters in Hawaii.

Malulani hopes some day to spend some time here to further research his family history and to update the genealogy of the five generations of the Hawaii-China descendants of the Afong family.

During our visit, Malulani proudly showed an oil portrait of his great ancestor Chun Afong, painted by a Dutch artist named Hubart Vos. According to Malulani, Vos was commissioned to paint the portrait in 1898 and spent a year in Macao and Hongkong.

There was also a portrait of Malulani's grandfather dated 1919 when Tony Afong celebrated his 60th birthday.

In the ancestral village 10 miles across Macao, Tony was known by his boyhood name Tong. The villagers called him Fan-Kwae Tong (Haole Tong) because of his handsome Caucasian-Hawaiian-Chinese features.

Tony spoke fluent Chinese because he was sent back to China from age 3 to 11 to learn the ancestral language and culture.

He also studied at Trinity College in Hartford, Conn., and later at Yale University where he joined the earliest mission of Chinese students sent to America. One of his fellow students was Tong Shao-Yi, noted premier in the Chinese government and father of Col. T. S. Y. Tong-Lao, former Chinese Consul General in Honolulu.

Malulani turned to Jack London's book, "House of Pride," to the tale of Chun Ah Chun, which is actually the story of Chun Afong although the story is not all historically correct.

According to Malulani, however, the episode about the European hotel in Macao was substantially correct. Chun Afong, on his return from Hawaii, stopped over in the Portuguese colony of Macao before crossing to his native village in Heungshan district. Accustomed to Western accommodations, he chose the best hotel, but was turned down because the hotel catered only to Europeans.

Chun Afong bought the hotel which he razed and built his mansion on the site. This Macao residence on the Bund at 101 Praya Grande is still a tourist showplace. He landscaped his property with coconut trees and foliage he brought from Hawaii.

Chun Afong started a small power plant to furnish electricity to his villagers.

Malulani's father, Wing Sen, was born in Macao in 1887 and was sent to America to Hartford High School where he was assistant editor in 1906 and editor the following year of the school paper, the Hartford Chronicle. Malulani has a scrapbook of his father's articles.

Wing Sen continued his studies at Yale where he excelled in track and field. He liked to dress well and was voted the best dressed and

Family Histories

"sportiest" by his graduating classmates of 1912. He later attended Columbia Law School before returning to China where he was commandant of the Canton Arsenal. He died at 32 in a horseback accident.

Instead of going on to Yale like his father and grandfather, Malulani went to Yenching University in Peking as a pre-medical student. It took him eight years to graduate because of war interruptions.[13]

These experiences changed Malulani's outlook on life. He turned from medicine to philosophy and when the war ended in 1945, returned to Peking to continue his studies, graduating in 1948.

He taught in the middle schools in Hongkong and spent two years in British North Borneo in school administration work.

With mainland China under Communist control since 1949, he saw no future there for his three children, Grace Maheloa, Joseph Malulani and William Mahinolani.

He came to the United States by showing an American passport issued to his father in 1903 which he fortunately had kept. As further proof of his heritage, he had his father's Yale yearbook and sought an elderly friend of his father's to testify on his behalf.

The family left Hongkong in 1965 by ship. They had a few hours' stopover in Honolulu and that was their first glimpse of their ancestors' home.

They continued to San Francisco where Malulani intended to enter graduate school to qualify for teaching at college level, but the pressing need was to support his family immediately.

He bought a small coffee shop, a successful venture, and sold it. He now operates Bucky's Restaurant on Sutter Street.

My articles in the *Honolulu Advertiser,* reached Malulani (Max) C. Afong, his great grandson and a direct male descendant who now lives in the United States. Malulani, in San Francisco, is interested in compiling a thorough updated genealogy of the Afong family. Max Afong made a correction to the news story, saying that "Tony" was the way this name should be spelled.

NINETY-ONE-YEAR-OLD RICE PLANTER

In 1951, Harold W. Ching, presently Kauai correspondent for the *Honolulu Star-Bulletin,* wrote the story of his ninety-one-year-old father, Kin Moi Ching.* Gung-gung ("Grandpa") Ching died in 1955 at the age of ninety-five.

It is interesting that at Mana on Kauai there was once swamp land where ducks and mud-hens were plentiful. This is the area in which the Chinese once had rice plantations. Ecologists now wish its return to its natural state as a bird sanctuary.

You, too, would have kind thoughts of the good old days if your memories, like those of Mr. Kin Moi Ching, reached back more than seventy years in a land and among a people that have been kind and friendly. And if you, too, had lived through such an experience, you would have gained a solid faith in the future of this land.

Mr. Ching, now ninety-one years old, living in retirement in Wailua Homesteads, Kauai, first came to Hawaii in 1879 at the age of nineteen.

Just before the first faint glimmering of dawn came peeping into Hanapepe Valley, the big, fat river mullet used to come floating to the surface, gaping their mouths at the shore to "drink the dew" dripping from the grassy bank. They could be scooped up a bushel at a time, but in those days people had no use for more than they could eat, and mullet is best eaten fresh.

Old familiar scenes in Honolulu are few and far between for Mr. Ching. The old landmarks have been swallowed up by the progress of more than seventy years since he arrived, an immigrant boy from China, aboard the little Chinese steamer Wo Chung.[14]

Speaking from experience, Mr. Ching advised faith in the future of this land. Look at what has grown out of the scattered clumps of grass houses and a few handful of frame structures that made up the Honolulu he first laid eyes on.

Those were the happy days of King Kalakaua, the kindly monarch whose untimely death shortly thereafter was deeply mourned by the Chinese, who had migrated to the Islands largely due to word of the pleasant conditions in Hawaii under an unusually friendly and helpful ruler.

Because of troubled conditions in China—even as now—the Ching boys were encouraged to go forth into the world to seek their fortunes,

* Harold W. Ching "Kamaaina," *Paradise of the Pacific,* July 1951, pp. 36–37, 51.

Family Histories

and what was more attractive than the kindly, peaceful Sandalwood Islands? Four brothers and a married sister came to Hawaii; one met with a fatal accident and three others returned to China. Kin Moi Ching alone remained—and he has never regretted having chosen the Islands as his home for the rest of his life, although the Honolulu he first saw did not appear attractive for anything except possibly a store or a saloon business.

Hence he paused less than two weeks in Honolulu—only long enough to borrow a five dollar gold piece from a cousin with a small furniture business on Nuuanu Avenue, center of the little Chinese settlement, to send back home word of his safe arrival, and also long enough to get some advice that proved the best he had ever received.

Then he and an older brother, following that sound advice, continued to Kauai to look over the prospects at Hanapepe.

Today—after seeing seventy-one and a half years, five sons and six daughters, forty-six grandchildren and twenty-three great grandchildren in Hawaii—Mr. Ching can look back and say that, except for the first few days of uncertainty, he would not want it changed if he could live over again the days since he was rowed in from the interisland vessel and deposited ashore at Nawiliwili.

Only for the first couple of days did he feel any doubt. Things did not seem too promising when he first arrived at Hanapepe after the long walk through a strange land from Nawiliwili. He walked, he explained, because they obtained only three horses and one carried their luggage, the second carried his older brother and the third was made available to an older man traveling the same route. Age was respected in those days.

Except for a year of producing starch at Huleia and a brief period at Waimea, Mr. Ching settled down to [the] rice producing business at Hanapepe until 1919, when he moved to Wailua Homesteads where the family started growing cane and he gradually stepped back into retirement.

Over the years his trips to Honolulu grew infrequent as time took its toll of the close friends and relatives he had at the capital, and there was less need for long business trips on foot to various parts of Kauai.

Mr. Ching's kindest memories are of conditions and people at Hanapepe, home to him during the forty most active years of his life. It was to the valley that in 1891 he brought his bride, a recent arrival from China, after their marriage in Honolulu, and there it was that he raised his family.

He started growing rice on leased land on the west bank of the Hanapepe just above the old bridge—the only bridge, it was then, a wooden structure which the floods washed out several times before the then elaborate concrete and steel span was built. Later he moved farther upriver and, because it was not very profitable to ship rice out to be milled, he built a small mill some time about 1907 to process the rice for himself and a few friends and neighbors. It was a simple plant consisting of a water-wheel turning a heavy wooden axle that operated two heavy stone pounders.

While visiting in Wailua one day, he was told a set of discarded stone pounders was his for the taking. He had it brought to Hanapepe where, with the aid of a mechanically-minded friend, some hard work and a period of experimenting, he put into operation a makeshift mill adequate for his needs.

How much did it cost? In cash, not a cent, he said; but those were days when one gave much and obtained much without a cent changing hands. Except for leather belting and lubricating oil, he does not remember much about cash expenditures for the mill.

Those were days when homes never had locks and when a neighbor, finding nobody at home, would pay his debts by leaving a handful of silver dollars wrapped in a taro leaf on the doorstep. Those were days when for hapa-ha (two-bits) you got enough fish to feed the whole rice field crew for a whole day. Men worked hard, from before dawn to after nightfall, and the crew during the busy season ate breakfast, early lunch, late lunch, dinner and a late supper.

There were the days when someone's turkeys had gone wild, and a flock took up roost in the nearby trees, where a bird could be hauled down at night to supply food for another day. A small plot set aside for a garden produced all you could eat, and the banana plants, taro and fruit trees needed little tending for there were no fruit flies and few other parasitic insects.

You could easily gather a basket of mud-hen's eggs in a short time at the Mana swamps, where large flocks of wild ducks were to be seen. The ducks and mud-hens, the swamps and the large area of rice fields all disappeared later when the region was drained to develop the present cane fields.

Looking back over his lifetime, Mr. Ching commented, "My grand-

Family Histories

father lived until eighty-six, and my father also died at the age of eighty-six. If I had stayed in China, I would never have lived to this age."[15]

FROM SLAVE GIRL TO RESPECTED GRANDMOTHER

Elizabeth Wong writes another type of family history.* Fifty-four-year-old Mother Teng believed herself "sure lucky come Hawaii." Her story could have been told by other descendants of peasant families: starvation in the village; sale as a bond-servant (slave girl or *mui-tsai*) to afford a decent burial for a deceased father; life in Hawaii as a *mui-tsai;* an arranged marriage with an older man; and, in this case, a happy ending.

In Hawaii, the slave-girl was a domestic who lived in and was often treated as a member of the family. The shortage of women created a demand for her early marriage by eager bachelors in the community. At one time, a family of means in China would possess a number of domestic bond-servants. The girls were, as a rule, purchased from their parents, who were forced to sell them because of poverty. They were sold at a very young age, some as young as three years old but generally at seven, eight, or ten years. The prices ranged from ten to a hundred dollars. When married, the owner would recoup the cost of their upbringing from the wedding presents arranged through a marriage broker. Early Chinese immigrants of better circumstances brought *mui-tsai* with them to Hawaii. Some came posing as daughters or domestics of immigrants and were later consigned to their new employers as *mui-tsai* either by pre-arrangement or by sale after their arrival.

Hawaiian neighbors had to intercede in many cases of mistreatment of servant girls because their Chinese friends were afraid of getting involved. In one case, Mary Damon, in her home calls for Christian mission work, rescued two girls and placed them in Kawaiahao Girls Seminary.

(I am using a fictitious name for the lady who has given me her life account. She has used broken English and Chinese. I shall translate her Chinese accordingly and shall try not to change her style.)

* Elizabeth Wong, "Leaves from the Life History of a Chinese Immigrant," *Social Process in Hawaii* 2 (1936): 39–42.

"Lucky come Hawaii? Sure, lucky, come Hawaii," said Mrs. Teng, pushing back her black hair with her hands which showed signs of hard labor. "Before I come to Hawaii I suffer much. Only two kinds of people in China, the too poor and the too rich. I never can forget my days in China," said she, her mouth falling into a smile revealing a pretty good set of teeth. She is proportionally built for her five feet four.

"In a small crowded village, a few miles from Hongkong, fifty-four years ago I was born. There were four in our family, my mother, my father, my sister and me. We lived in a two room house. One was our sleeping room and the other served as parlor, kitchen and dining room. We were not rich enough to keep pigs or fowls, otherwise, our small house would have been more than overcrowded.

"How can we live on six baskets of rice which were paid twice a year for my father's duty as a night watchman? Sometimes the peasants have a poor crop then we go hungry. During the day my father would do other small jobs for the peasants or carpenters. My mother worked hard too for she went every day to the forest to gather wood for our stove. . . .

"Sometimes we went hungry for days. My mother and me would go over the harvested rice fields of the peasants to pick the grains they dropped. Once in a while my mother would go near a big pile of grain and take a handful. She would then sit on them until the working men went home. As soon as they go we ran home. She clean and cook the rice for us two. We had only salt and water to eat with the rice. Today when I hear my children grumble about the food I wish they could experience what I went through and what the children in China are doing to relieve their hunger.

"Father was suffering from dysentery so my mother went out to look for herbs. My father told me to take the baby out to play and not to come back until late. Being always afraid of him I gladly took the baby out. We were three houses away watching a man kill a chicken. Pretty soon a man came to call me to go home for my father is dead. I ran with my brother on my back and stopped at the door of our house. I took one look at my father dangling from the ceiling and started to run to where I don't know. . . .

"Poor people are buried in mats but mother bought a coffin for my father. She had asked the carpenter to give her a few weeks to pay for the coffin and the man agreed. My mother called me to her and put me on her lap.

"Do you want me to remarry or will you be a good girl and go to stay with a certain lady," she said. I told her that I do not want her to remarry but I will go with the lady so that she will have money to pay for my father's coffin. If she did marry again I would have a hard time looking for her when I came big. I leaned my head against her breast and if I knew that was the last time I would be so near to her I would have let my brother cry alone.

"I heard my mother tell this go-between lady that she wants me put in the hands of a lady or man who would come to Hawaii because she has heard Hawaii is a land of good fortune. All the other people who went to Hawaii sent money home every time. ("My mother has never told me that I was being sold as a slave until I came to Hawaii my mistress called me names.")

"My mother took off my mourning robes, dressed me in a colored dress with a red string on my hair. I went with this lady to the big house of Mr. Chin, two miles from our village. He was to look me over and I seem to be his choice for he took out ninety dollars to give to my mother. Every year in my age was worth ten dollars. I wished I were older than nine so that my mother could get more money.

"Before the actual parting I was happy and glad to go because I knew I was helping mother. When my mother and me went out of the house I took one look behind and did not want to go. I cried and begged and asked to stay at home. For once I had the sympathy of the neighbors. They cried and told me that I must be a good girl and go so that my mother can get the money to pay the coffin. I quickly wiped my eyes and went with my mother. When we got to this place we went to give our offerings to the temple god. It was eleven o'clock when we came to the gate of Mr. Chin's house. We stayed outside until it was twelve. It is said that it is bad luck to enter a master's house when the time is odd, it must be even time. Again the parting was hard. I ran after my mother but my master held me. He gave me a silver spoon, a jade bowl, sweets, and cakes—all that I always longed for. I was glad to stay forever. Next time when my mother came I did not care to go with her. I was so poor for a long time that those sweet and pretty things took a great hold on me.

"A lady in that house told me that Hawaii had big, fat, very sweet sugar cane—it was better than honey. I crazy for cane that I just waited for the day to come to Hawaii. She also told me that there was hardly anything to do but after I came I found out that this was not true.

"In 1891 my master and me sailed on the "Billy Jack" to go to my new mistress in Hawaii. We slept on canvas cots and had cheap meat and cabbage for every meal. We could not land in Honolulu because there was a small pox on board ship. We went directly to San Francisco and stayed there for two months. I never saw the shape of the land for I was below the ship. When we came back to Hawaii I was locked in the immigration office for three weeks. How happy I was when my boss came to me. I went to meet my mistress who was never pleasant to me.

"The first thing I asked my master was a piece of sugar cane. He said that there is none around the place where we live. How sad I was for I expected cane to be all around.

"Mr. Chin was the owner of a large carpenter shop on Nuuanu street. He had many workers. They cooked our meals and they ate in the shop. I always took the meals home for the family. We lived behind the shop. I had to wash clothes, clean the house and the basin. I also waited on the table and when the family was served then I took my bowl to my master for food. I always ate separately from the family table. Whenever I go back for a second helping my mistress would glare at me. Being afraid I used to press the rice in my bowl so that I had my fill and avoided her glance. Although she called me a "slave girl," a good for nothing girl, and beat me unmercifully I was happy to be in Hawaii. At least I had food in my stomach and ate with a silver spoon.

"Being a "China Jack" I was tempted by the good taste of the first cookie my mistress gave me. I saw her hang the can on the kitchen wall. As soon as she left the house I helped myself to a cookie and a cup of tea. In my little party she caught me. She took the ruler and beat my fingers to and fro, to and fro. They were all black and blue and she kept on until the ruler broke.

"One day after I had swept the house, washed the clothes I went out to play with the neighborhood children who wanted to have some fun with the "China Jack." I was having a good time when my mistress yelled "slave girl" at me. I went into the house expecting and prepared for the outcome. Afraid that the children outside would hear she stuffed my mouth with a dirty rag and beat me with a bamboo rod. I struggled but of no use. After her anger or jealousy was satisfied she made me clean the house again.

"Before I was real dumb. I was afraid to go to school on account of my mistress not giving me money to buy tablets and pencils. I didn't know how to explain to the teacher that my mistress would not give me money for books. I used to hide from the teacher. My mistress said that a "China Jack" like me need not go to school. I sorry I no go before.

"I used to go to a shoe maker's and take needles from him for my mistress refused to let me use her needles. Behind her back I learned how to sew. When I was sixteen she went to China for four months. I made sure I learned how to sew dresses for myself. Every ten cents that I earned for sewing button holes for the neighboring tailor I saved to buy materials. When my mistress returned from China she wanted me to sew for her. I wasn't very eager because she, herself, wanted to stop me from learning.

"The following year the plague invaded Honolulu. Chinatown was burned down.[16] All I can remember is that we went to live at Kalihi then to Vineyard. We had little to do.

"I believe the turning point of my life came when I was eighteen. One morning I overheard my master scold my mistress for wanting to marry me off to a man not of my same group. He said that long ago my mother made him promise that I be married to someone of my own group—Pun Dee [Punti]. He said that it is only fair to present the recent case [suitor] to me. I hurried away from the door and waited to be called any minute. I went before them. My master who was always nice to me said that my mother would be happy to know that I am married and on my own. He said that merchant, a Mr. Teng, from Wailuku, Maui, is looking for a bride. He is well-to-do but is forty years old. You are only eighteen. I leave the matter up to you. If he told me that the man was sixty I would have gladly said "yes." Here was my chance to escape from the harsh words of my mistress. Better than suffer some more I accepted. How he looks like I did not know but with that thought of freedom in mind I slept peacefully for the first time.

"As a fee for my master's successful matchmaking my future husband sent him one hundred fifty dollars, a roast pig, five hundred cakes, a half dozen bottles of wine, and a half dozen chickens. All day

I was buying things to take up to my new home. A lady took me down to the boat and when I landed at Kahului I was met by my brother-in-law who took me home to my husband. I became Mrs. Teng. My husband was almost bald but he was very nice to me.

"Right after my marriage I asked my husband to write back to my village in search of my mother. Lucky he asked my former boss for help. I told him of my hard times and how I came to Hawaii. He sent my mother fifty dollars along with that first letter. I was very happy that I cried when I received my mother's letter telling me that my brother is eleven and is watching cows. I wrote home and sent her money to send my brother to school. I only longed to see my mother again. I think I would fall in her ams and cry for days but I never had that chance. She died a year after my husband's death in 1921.

"The young people of today are very much changed. I cannot understand my daughter-in-law who never trusts me with her son. I am his grandmother. She is so afraid that I might put germs on him. When I have a slight cold I cannot go near him. How can I put germs on him? If he is healthy he gets no germs. The small children in China don't have enough to eat and no clothing and yet they don't die. The children in Hawaii have all the good food and clothing so why should they get sick."

With a wistful smile she went on commenting about her mistress. She said that no matter how rich you are or how much better you are than the other person never look down upon him because some day you may be in that person's position. "Today, my mistress lives in a one room house on Vineyard street. Her husband, three sons, and two daughters are dead leaving a son-in-law who told her to get out of his home. Now she know what poor means. She gladly calls me her "daughter" and even if she was mean to me I let that be forgotten. When I see her in town I give her a dollar or two. If she was nice to me maybe I would have been a little more glad to help her.

"My children call me a "jew" because I do not spend for clothes or other unnecessary luxuries. It is not that; I shudder at the thought of being poor. I was poor for a long while, that much suffering is enough for me. I can not spend here and there because someday I want to buy a new refrigerator, pay for doctor's bills, and pay for any emergency. I must save so that I may have money on hand.

"I am proud of my children. They are very good children and have helped me lots. I am looking forward to the day when I will have my

Family Histories

sons, daughters, and in-laws, and grandchildren with me. At present they are scattered on Maui, Kauai, and Oahu. I lucky come Hawaii."

AUTOBIOGRAPHY OF CHUNG KUN-AI

An informative autobiography by an immigrant Chinese in Hawaii was that of Chung Kun-Ai, *My Seventy-Nine Years in Hawaii, 1879–1958*. *Honolulu Star-Bulletin* writer Clarice Taylor (24 May 1961) reviewed this book in the light of its being a valuable contribution to Hawaiian multi-ethnic history. She wrote, "That book is important because of its simplicity—and is a mine of information." It points out the great need for simple biographies among the ethnic groups.

She continued, "We need factual stories of Japanese, Portuguese, Filipino, and Puerto Ricans. The stories should be simple and unembroidered. To stimulate the writing of such stories, we need many historical societies. Each ethnic group has a social organization . . . each ethnic group . . . should encourage a member to write a biography of some one person whose life in the Islands has been typical of all."

Two contemporaries of Mr. Ai wrote autobiographical sketches—Chun Quon, better known as C. Q. Yee Hop, in 1947, and Chong Sum-Wing, better known as C. S. Wing, in 1944. Both are in Chinese and have been privately published.

In Hawaii, there were two types of Chinese immigrants: (1) the agricultural laborers who came under contract or as free immigrants to sugar, rice, coffee, or pineapple plantations and (2) the immigrants coming in as merchants, students, ministers, and diplomats of the exempt classes under the immigration laws and their wives and children. Both found equal opportunity to climb the economic and social ladder.

In Hawaii, immigrants soon became "sojourners no more"—no longer transient strangers who spent many years of their lifetime in a foreign country without being assimilated into its social and political structure. They became, like Mr. Ai, "worthy Americans," living in the mainstream of community life and working in the pursuit of happiness—*on kue lok yip* ("living in peace and working in happiness").

The selection from his autobiography here contains excerpts about two phases of Mr. Ai's life: (1) his boyhood in a Chinese village,

1865–1879 and (2) life in Hawaii, 1879–1958.* The highlights of his life in Hawaii were his arrival and student years at Iolani School (1879–1881), his two carefree years in Kona, on the island of Hawaii (1881–1883), learning business and strengthening his innate honesty and trustworthiness while working for James I. Dowsett, and his founding of City Mill as a lumber business and rice mill (1883–1958).[17] City Mill continues in Hawaii as a lumber and building supplies dealer today.

My China Boyhood (1865–1879)

My name is Chung Kun-Ai. Chung is the surname and Kun-Ai the given name. Kun means "service" and Ai, "rain." I have been told that on the day I was born, it rained heavily, so grandfather named me Ai after the heavy rain. Perhaps in the back of his mind he associated rain-water with life, and that without rain-water, life on this earth would perish. Later I substituted for the Chinese character Ai meaning "rain" another Chinese word "Ai" meaning "the eaves of a house," so that my given name came to mean "The Chung who serves with houses," or in short, "Chung the home-builder." Don't you agree that "Chung the home-builder" is a very appropriate name for a person engaged in the lumber and home-building business?

Chung is an old and honored surname, tracing back in genealogies to one Chung Chien, an officer of state in the kingdom of Ch'u, who lived about 500 B.C. I do not know how my particular branch of the Chung family migrated from Central China south to the Province of Kwangtung, but by the 17th century my ancestors were in the District of Sun-wui, not too far from the town of Macau. In the middle of that century, six generations before I was born, my ancestors migrated again, this time twenty-five miles eastward into the village of Sai-San in the Chungshan District. Perhaps they had hoped to obtain a better living off the soil in the new land. They did not prosper from their farming. I have been told that my great grandparents were very poor, so poor that on one Chinese New Year's they did not have even one bowl of rice in the house. That was when my granduncle was eight

* Chung Kun-Ai *My Seventy-Nine Years in Hawaii (1879–1958)*, (Hong Kong: Cosmorama Pictorial Publisher, 1960), pp. 1–29, 36–42. Reprinted, with changes, by kind permission of Chung (also known as Ai) family.

years old, and my grandfather five. These too were the trying years when great grandmother had to beg for clothes-starch from our neighbors to stop their hunger. As soon as he was old enough, granduncle went out to peddle candy. Later he went to Canton, a city of merchants. He gradually prospered as a tea-merchant, exporting tea from Canton to England and other countries. Unfortunately for him, the Sino-British War of 1840–1842 ruined his export business, and he lost $285,000 [more likely $28,500, Chinese currency]. Other changes came fast. After suffering a huge loss, granduncle retired to our village to pass the twilight of his years. There he remained, leaving the tending of his business affairs to a younger kinsman. . . .

My grandfather had also gone into business. He had a store in Macau, but he too preferred to direct his business operations from our native village. His steward came regularly to the village to make his report and to turn over the money. As it was only a four-hour walk each way, it was not too difficult a journey for him to make.

Grandfather and granduncle owned much rich land, some located at a distance from our village. The land was cultivated by tenant farmers on a share basis, perhaps fifty percent to the farmer and fifty percent to the landowner. . . . Granduncle and grandfather wanted our family to continue to prosper, and they also desired to perpetuate the names of our ancestors. They finally decided to build an ancestral hall that would be substantial and enduring. As they looked upon such a hall as a family undertaking, they assumed the financial responsibility themselves. The structure that was built was one-story in height and occupied a floor area of about two Chinese mou's or one-third of an English acre of land. The square-shaped building was about 120 feet on each side, and had a large hall running down the middle, with a wing to each side. Over the main hall was built a watchtower, from which the night-watchman sang out the watches of the night. When the hall was being built, I remember seeing grandfather painting the wooden timbers with arsenic, to discourage termites from attacking those members. Termites are termites and they are as destructive in China as they are in Hawaii. Grandfather saw to it that the wooden timbers were adequately protected before they went into the structure.

Of course I was too young then to appreciate the craftsmanship that went into this building, but many years later, after I had had experience with home building here in Hawaii and saw our ancestral hall again, I realized that the man who had been in charge of building it must have been a master craftsman. . . .

The dedication service took place early in the morning, at the hour pronounced auspicious by our soothsayers. Visitors from neighboring villages came to admire the new building, especially the large kitchen with its own well, all within the building. They brought congratulatory messages in couplets on scrolls of silks and beautiful wood. It was indeed a very festive occasion. . . .

My grandfather had never gone to school, but he had taught himself to read and write. In his ignorance of what formal schooling was, he assumed that anybody could teach in the new school, and, as it turned out, the teachers that were hired to teach us youngsters were untrained. They made us memorize our assignments and trace our copy books. Ours was a whole day session in school, and from early morning till late afternoon we shouted our "Three Word Classic"[18] at the top of our voices until we could recite the whole book without a mistake. Unfortunately, we did not understand the meaning of one sentence that we read. The only break in that schedule came when we had our writing lessons. We would then trace in our copy books specimens of calligraphy accepted as standard. Yes, it was all "reading the book without asking for any explanation of the meaning." But, as we criticize the teaching method used in our village school, let us not lose sight of this very important factor: we youngsters of Sai-san Village had a school, in our own village. . . .

Life in a Chinese village was very interesting and attractive to us youngsters, especially our lunar New Year celebrations. That was the one occasion during the whole year that the villagers took off a whole two weeks to enjoy themselves. For weeks before the New Year's, preparations had been going on. The wine vats had been filled with rice and other ingredients and set aside to allow the grain to ferment. Every year our family stored away enough jugs of yellow rice wine to replenish those consumed. The longer the yellow rice wine was aged, the more potent and smooth it became. The bouquet also became more stimulating and inviting. Glutinous rice had to be ground into rice-flour for New Year pastries. The house had to be cleaned and the kitchen god had to be escorted to heaven a week before New Year's. Everyone had to have new and colorful gowns and other garments, and these had to be sewed and embroidered by hand. Members of the family who had left the village to earn a living else-

Family Histories

where also tried their best to make this annual pilgrimage back to the ancestral home, in time to participate in the family gathering on New Year's Eve. Each family closed the old year with as sumptuous a feast as it could afford. The dining and wining went on till midnight, when firecrackers were kept burning and the proper obeisance paid to all the gods that ruled the Chinese universe. . . .

We youngsters could do nothing wrong during this season, for New Year's was the only time during the whole year when it was inauspicious for anyone to scold or nag. Now that I think about it, henpecked husbands in those days must have found this season very relaxing and refreshing. And so we did as we well pleased and none dared defy the gods by chastising us when we were naughty. If only the whole year could be one New Year's!

Our elders also provided other forms of entertainment. They would band together and parade through the villages with their dragons or lions, prancing and dancing as firecrackers were thrown at their feet. Shopkeepers and the wealthy in the village would show their appreciation and also wish themselves greater wealth by tying a gift of money in red paper with a sprig green of vegetable leaf, just high enough above the gate to call for special effort by the dancers to collect their "fee." The Chinese words for green vegetables ("sung choi") and those for growing riches ("sung choi") are homonymous, and what Chinese does not want to grow richer? Within the past few years, Honolulu's Chinatown has revived the dragon, lion, and unicorn dancing of their grandparents, and at Chinese New Year's, it is now possible to see them dance in Chinatown, to what others would call the infernal din of firecrackers and gongs. Yet the scene is vivid, and gay, and brings back to those of the older generations the memory of similar celebrations in their now distant village homes.

Another favorite pastime in the villages was the composing of couplets of poetry and the scribbling of longer poems, and then having other participants guess at the meaning of the lines. "Dah dung mee"—guessing the meaning conveyed by lines of poetry is still enjoyed by Chinese everywhere, even here in Hawaii today, for during the past few years, such verses have appeared in the Chinese language newspapers challenging solution. To me, as I look back over the years, the surprising thing was that so many who participated in these poetical competitions were ordinary tillers of the soil who have not had formal schooling of any kind. In the China of that period, when schooling was denied those who did not have the money nor the facilities for formal education, it was indeed a gracious Heaven that saw to it that her people retained their literary culture through oral tradition, where a hardworking father still had time in the evening or during the long winter recess to pass down by word of mouth something of the great wealth of poetic background, as well as of poetic technique. This oral tradition was a great source of spiritual satisfaction to the villagers, and enabled them to enjoy their festivities the more when spiced with stories from their great literary storehouse.

In making the statement above, I spoke from personal experience. The front porch of our home was paved with granite, and we used to gather there in the evenings after supper to listen to our elders. Someone would start off with a story from the Three Kingdoms period, perhaps one of the many stories of K'ung Ming, the sagest tactician in that period of Chinese history, of how he outwitted the enemy when the enemy surprised him without military protection in a walled city. . . . And the story-teller, whenever the action became exciting, would burst into lines of poetry that said so much in so few words, often chanting the words in sing-song fashion that appealed to us. And that night, before we could fall asleep, we must repeat those lines of poetry until they too became a part of our being. We had become heirs to our great literary tradition.

Wandering minstrels and story-tellers also shared in handing down this tradition. . . .

The years of my grandfather were the years when China reeled under the impact of foreign aggressiveness. . . . Those were also the years which saw the incipience of emigration from South China to foreign lands, especially to Malaya and America. . . .

How did these poor villagers from South China raise the money to make these long and perilous journeys, you may well ask? They all had the most difficult time to make both ends meet out of tilling the soil in their native villages. Whence came the wherewithal to finance the trip? Of course, thinking only about those who came to Hawaii, we know that the plantation companies supplied money to their Chinese recruiting agents who went into the villages of the Kwangtung seacoast to sign up contract laborers for the plantations. The first of these contract laborers arrived in Honolulu in 1852. Other groups followed. All these migrants had their passage paid for by the plantations, so that financing a sea journey was no problem for them. In the colorful colloquial language of that day, those who signed on as contract laborers were labelled as villagers who had sold themselves as "pigs." The smaller group that came on their own either had parents who had the money, or borrowed money from others at home or abroad, to be repaid out of their earnings. At least, that was what these migrants promised to do when they borrowed money—to return the money with interest. Now I do not know how other money-lenders fared in their projects of this nature, but I do know that my grandfather went into such money-lending as a business venture, and I wish here to report on the outcome. Grandfather went into this project with his eyes wide open. One condition of his loan of $60 was that each borrower was to pay back $120 as soon as he was able to do so. In all, grandfather must have helped 70 young men from our village and nearby villages to migrate to North and South America and also Australia. So far as I know, not one of these seventy odd persons repaid one cent. Only one of the migrants returned to the village and called on grandfather; all the others settled down in the countries of their adoption and remained there, or returned to their native villages quietly. Oftentimes, the parents of these young men would come to grandfather to demand that grandfather return their sons to them, holding grandfather responsible because he had supplied them with the money to leave home. The only man who returned to our village was surnamed Chung, but was no blood relation of our family. Not long after his return, he came with two packages of cake and one of his daughters to call on grandfather and to inform grandfather that he had no money to repay the loan. He suggested that grandafther release him from the obligation. What else could grandfather do but agree to the proposal? Grandfather told me that he had to write off the whole money-lending project as a total loss. How true is the Chinese saying: "Never lend money, and never be a guarantor". . . .

While I was enjoying my boyhood in the village, my father had been in business in the Hawaiian Kingdom. The Hawaiian Kingdom was better known to the Chinese as the Sandalwood Islands in those days, even today, because the Hawaiian kings then shipped sandalwood to sell in South China, and brought back Canton silks and even paving stones. There was a Captain Meeks who sailed his ship with a cargo of sandalwood to China where the wood was used to make religious sticks. On his return trip he filled his ship with tea, mats, granite stones and anything else that was useful to man. He also filled the deck of his ship with livestock such as pigs, geese, chickens, and ducks which were put on board the day before sailing. The man who owned the pigs was a shrewd one. He gave the pigs all the feed they could eat so that they would weigh more and bring him more money. But Captain Meeks was just as shrewd and refused to weigh the pigs immediately. He would weigh the pigs the next day, because the pigs kept overnight on board would by then have lost about twenty pounds. He would then pay less for them. . . .

When father came back to the village after his absence of twelve years, . . . [he] spent a whole year at home in the village. He would frequently leave us to visit Canton city. Coming home one evening from one such visit, he announced that he had booked passage for mother, my younger sister, then only two months old, and myself almost fourteen, to return with him to Hawaii. He had undoubtedly convinced grandfather to allow us to go back with him. We were to leave the village the next day, but as it was *ching ming* [spring festival], we paid our last respects to our ancestors at their graves. Of course we were all excited that morning. I regretted very much not saying goodbye to grandmother and grandfather. Both grandparents were very fond of me as I was then the only grandson in the family. This incident makes me sad even this day whenever I think of it. The day had been bright and clear, but just as we left the village, a shower fell. It did not take us long to reach Canton. All the vessels from foreign lands sailed up the Pearl River in those days and dropped their anchors opposite Whangpoo, very near to Canton. We had to wait two weeks in Whangpoo for our ship. I did not mind the delay, for I found the Pearl River bank very interesting. . . .

After two or three days, I got over my seasickness and began to enjoy the voyage. The ocean in time calmed down also, and it remained smooth sailing for the rest of the voyage of forty or more days. I remember that we were in all about three hundred passengers on board. I was a growing lad, and the salty sea air whetted my appetite. Father believed in taking just two meals a day, but at noontime some of the other passengers took their noonday bite of bread boiled in water. My mouth watered. Fortunately those who were having lunch were kind enough to share their bread with me.

Well, a sea voyage in those days dragged on and on. Once in a great while, some excitement changed the monotonous routine. For instance, we sailed one day into a school of skipjacks. The sailors tied

Family Histories

pieces of white cloth to their hooks as bait and caught a few. Ordinarily we would not consider the skipjack a good eating fish, but on that occasion it proved a delightful and delicious variation in our diet. We enjoyed the skipjacks.

At last, land was sighted. We had reached our destination, Honolulu. I was glad that our long sea voyage was at last over.

Schooling and Carefree Years in Hawaii

When father brought me along with the family to Hawaii, he had no thought of sending me to school. Fortunately for me, father had among his friends, Young-On, or Aona,[19] as he was better known among his Hawaiian friends, a storekeeper at Honaunau in Kona, [island of] Hawaii. Aona knew the value of a good education and sent his children to good schools to be educated. When he learned from father that I was staying in Honolulu doing nothing, he strongly urged father to send me to Iolani School. . . . Therefore, he came back to Honolulu from Kailua in July to get me registered in Iolani College, popularly known as Bishop's School [1879].

In September I went by myself to register at Bishop's School. Bishop Willis interviewed me that afternoon. He asked me a question that I couldn't understand. I guessed that he must be asking me for my name. I said, "Ai," for in my ignorance of the language, I gave him my given name, "Ai" and not my surname "Chung." So I was registered in the school as Chung K. Ai, with "Ai" as my surname. Because of this initial mistake, I have continued to call myself C. K. Ai. Except for my youngest son who recently legally changed his surname to "Ai," all my other children use the correct family surname "Chung". . . .

Two weeks after school had opened that fall, Sun Tai-Cheong enrolled as a student, the fourth Chinese lad to enter. Sun Tai-Cheong is better known to the world as Dr. Sun Yat-Sen, emancipator of China's four hundred millions from the yoke of the Manchu Dynasty. . . .[20]

That first Chinese New Year's, every Chinese student except myself went home for the festival. As I had no home in Honolulu, I stayed behind in school. . . . When the next Chinese New Year's came around, the situation was quite different. I had by then become a very close friend of Sun Tai-Cheong. He invited me to spend the holiday with him at his brother's store. Brother Ah Mi had a store on Nuuanu Street where Leong Chew's once was. He was very courteous and had also invited several other friends to share in his celebration. We all had an exciting time. In those early days, Chinese New Year's was *konohi fat-choy* time (wishing you happiness and wealth) and everyone felt free to call, especially the Hawaiian policemen and regular customers, who dropped in for their tips wrapped in red paper, and for food and drink. Even the *haole* businessmen paid calls on their Chinese colleagues. . . .

Two Carefree Years in Kona (1881–1883)

When summer vacation came in 1881, mother wanted me home for a visit. I, therefore, booked passage and sailed on the *Likelike*. The *Likelike* took all of three days to sail from Honolulu to Keauhou. . . . My parents were very happy to see me, especially my mother from whom I had been separated for two long years. . . .

One day, not long after I had been with my parents, I was called upon by father to read and explain a letter from an American friend. The letter was in English, but the handwriting was so difficult to read that I could not make out the contents of the letter. Father was very peeved with me, told me that he had wasted money sending me to school for two years. . . . So, formal schooling stopped for me. I voluntarily became a taro and tobacco planter in Kona, later became father's assistant and travelled about the countryside trying to collect bad debts for father in Honoapo, Waiohinu, Pahala, Hilo, and Kohala. I thus whiled away two happy and carefree years in Kona. Then in 1883, father had a change of heart and allowed me to return to Honolulu to resume my schooling. I went instead into business.

My Early Years in Business (1883–1887)

I was staying then at the Sing Chong Company, father's purchasing agent in Honolulu. Sing Chong occupied a three-story building on the mauka side of Hotel Street between Nuuanu and Smith Streets. My old schoolmate Tong Phong also stayed there. He told me that he and Sun Tai-Cheong (Dr. Sun Yat-Sen) had already become convinced that the Christian way of life was the one they wished to follow, and that Tai-Cheong had already returned to China. When I told him in return that I too believed that Christianity was the true religion, he was very happy. Let me add here that Sun Tai-Cheong and Tong Phong were soon baptized in Hong Kong. Because of

Family Histories

strong objection on the part of my father (He told me to go out and earn a living), I was not baptized until 1896. . . .

Jobs, however, were not easy to find. . . . Finally I learned of a tailor shop . . . [and] under the most favorable of circumstances the new partnership of the Chung Yee Tailor Shop was set up. . . .

I wish I could boast that my first business venture—the Chung Yee Tailor Shop—turned out a success; but it was not. Towards the close of 1885, we had to dissolve our partnership because we ran into debt endorsing a note that we had to make good.

I Work for Mr. James I. Dowsett (1887–1898)

In January, 1887, father wrote me to call on James I. Dowsett on some business transaction. . . .

The next morning, March 31, Mr. Dowsett introduced me to his old clerk——and informed him that I was taking over as new clerk the following morning. April first, 1887 was the beginning of my service with Mr. Dowsett that lasted eleven years, two months, and ten days, until after his death. During those years, Mr. Dowsett had the utmost faith in me. [He] never questioned anything I did as his office clerk. . . .

Mr. Dowsett's business interests were many and varied. Foremost, perhaps, was his ranching business. He had a cattle ranch that extended from Moanalua to Aiea, and other [Oahu] ranches at Nanakuli, Maile, and Mikilua. He loved horses. He owned a 1800-pound stallion that was powerful and was worth $1,800. He also bought a donkey for Mikilua Ranch which cost him $1,200. . . . Later, Charles Judd transferred his Leileihua Ranch to Mr. Dowsett. This Leileihua Ranch was crown land, but later was purchased by the United States Army and made into Schofield Barracks. He also had a ranch on Maui, called Rose Ranch, sometimes the Ulupalakua Ranch. Captain Makee, who originally owned the Rose Ranch, had put it up for auction. Captain Makee's son, Charles Makee had married Mr. Dowsett's oldest daughter Phoebe, and it was for his son-in-law Charles Makee that Mr. Dowsett bought the Rose Ranch for $70,000. When I began working for Mr. Dowsett, Charles Makee was in charge of Rose Ranch. He used to ship all of his Ulupalakua products, such as butter, turkey, pigs, horses, everything marketable, to our Honolulu office to sell. . . .

James I. Dowsett had meant much to me in my life and I will

The Sandalwood Mountains

always think of him as my benefactor. . . . When the new City Mill building was dedicated in 1950 . . . [it was] named the "James I. Dowsett Building."

Marriage was a family affair with the Chinese. . . . Father had been most anxious for me to get married ever since I had become old enough, but somehow I kept postponing the matter. . . . I was not surprised, therefore, when father returned to Hawaii from attending grandfather's last sickness for two years, that he had betrothed me to a very suitable young lady of the Chang family who had been highly recommended by one of my cousins. I had no objections. Finally, in September, 1889, father and I sailed on the steamer *Oceanic* for Hong Kong. I have already mentioned my meeting with Dr. Sun Yat-Sen soon after my arrival there. I was married in our village and within four and a half months I was back in Honolulu alone, [my wife following later]. . . .

In 1893, she gave birth to Hung Lum, my eldest son; . . . she passed away in 1895.

In 1896, I married my second wife, a lady from the Siu family. . . . She passed away in August, 1951. She gave me the following children: Anna, Bessie, Clara, Dora, Henry, Samuel, David, Esther and Jane. All are living except Bessie and Jane. . . .

The Story of City Mill Company, Limited (1898–1957)

To my friends and business associates, C. K. Ai and City Mill are one and the same. What these friends of mine do not know is this: that City Mill was the brain-child of my business partner, Mr. Chun Mun-Kai, better known as C. M. Kai. It was he, who in 1899, suggested that we start a company to go into the lumber business together with rice milling. He knew of a piece of land at the corner of Queen and Kekaulike Streets that . . . could be leased for $100 a month. With W. W. Ahana as middle-man, we secured the lease to the land. We then worked up the prospectus for a lumber and rice milling corporation, to be capitalized at $60,000, at $100 a share. The Chinese newspapers carried the first news of the proposed corporation. American friends heard the news and asked if they could subscribe stock. John Auderkirk was our first subscriber, taking twenty shares. Sam McKay signed up for ten shares. William Mulch also became interested. Chinese friends then began to call. L. Ah Leong who had his store on Ward Street below Queen heard of the proposed corporation and called in person to subscribe ten shares. Ah Leong was known in Chinatown as a very shrewd and conservative business man, so the trust he showed in our corporation inspired me. . . . The first directors were: Wong Leong, first chairman of the board; Chung Muk-Heen, better known as H. A. Heen, father of Senator William H. Heen; Wong Chow; Pang Cheong; Ho Fong [Ho Fon]; and myself.

Within eight months, we had already collected sixty percent of our capital, and almost finished our new building when bubonic plague broke out in Chinatown. . . .

City Mill's loss amounted to $55,000, with another $25,000 due to our creditors. . . .

I then called on our creditors Allen and Robinson, Hackfeld and Company and others. I called first on Hackfeld's and asked if Hackfeld's would hold off collecting on our old bills until after the government had paid us off [for fire loss]. We proposed to continue to do business with Hackfeld's and would pay for whatever new purchases we should make from them. Hackfeld's agreed to do business with us on those terms. . . . Allen and Robinson also agreed on similar terms. We were not called upon to sign any written documents in those days, a man's word was as good as his signature. . . .

Five odd acres were only a lumber yard at first, and have now become the home of City Mill at 660 Nimitz Highway. . . .

In the story of my life during the past fifty years, I have already mentioned some of my experiments in Christlike living. I have given of myself and my possessions in community projects like the Wai Wah Chinese Hospital, the Palolo Old Men's Home, my church and the YMCA, the United Chinese Society; the Chinese and the Honolulu Chamber of Commerce, the Pan-Pacific Union, the Institute of Pacific Relations, and the Hawaiian Board of Missions. I have also tried joining political and other organizations devoted to the gaining of some measure of freedom and equality for the underprivileged of this world, such organizations sponsored by Dr. Sun Yat-Sen, Tseng Siu-Heng and Dr. James Y. C. Yen (in his Mass Education Movement) and such educational and religious organizations as the various mission schools, hospitals, mission stations, and their individual [students]. I have made visits in several parts of China hoping to set up homesteading as a means of enabling the Chinese farmer to derive more income from his farm—I have gone into experimental farming in southern

Kwangtung Province. . . . I have even invested in business projects in Hong Kong and elsewhere. . . . I have donated funds for scholarships: some of the scholars have turned out well. It is only after half a century of experimentation that I finally in August, 1953 set up the Chung Kun-Ai Foundation to carry on the Christian stewardship that has been my privilege to assume for so long. . . .

"It has always been natural for me to give rather than to receive."

Appendix A

Keoni Pake Sugar Agreement, 1839*

In 1839 an agreement was made whereby Kalauwalu, with the approval of King Kamehameha III, was to provide the land, cane, and labor, and Keoni Pake, sugar master and overseer, was responsible for the manufacture of sugar in the mill. Keoni Pake or John Chinaman was a brother of Atai, partner in the Hungtai Company that established a sugar mill at Wailuku in the 1820s.

TRANSLATION:

AGREEMENT between KALAUWALU and KEONI, PAKE (Chinese), a native of China. This is what they said, and which was agreed upon:

1. That Kalauwalu has taken Keoni as his man to make sugar for him, in Wailuku, permission is granted to Kalauwalu to plant one hundred acres, and that Keoni can stop the planting, and that Keoni shall be the overseer over all of the sugar-cane planters in Wailuku.

2. The division of the sugar has been agreed upon,—Keoni is to have four pounds in ten, and Kalauwalu and others, and the sugar-cane planters set apart for that purpose, to have six; the division to be only in that way until all of the sugar is finished, the division of the molasses to be in like manner, four gallons in ten.

* Foreign Office, 25 August 1839 (Archives of Hawaii).

3. Here is another matter which they have agreed upon, when the sugar-cane is fully matured, no day shall be left unworked, the Sabbath day is the only day to be omitted. If one day in the week should be omitted until the setting of the sun, and the mill lies idle, Kalauwalu et al, and those who plant the sugar-cane, shall pay to Keoni five pans of sugar, the penalty for a labor day not worked shall be paid in that manner only.

4. Here is another matter that they have agreed upon,— that Kalauwalu shall cut the trees and the boards, and that Keoni will do the building. This is what the King has to do,—build the sugar-mill, the sugar-boiling house, the house for making sugar, the house for storing sugar, the large warehouse down at Kahului.

5. It is agreed that there shall be sixteen laborers under Keoni to work in the sugar-making buildings, eight laborers for one week out of the sixteen, likewise as to the other eight, one week's work. It is for the sugar-cane planters to bring the sugar-cane on the cart to the sugar-mill, likewise also for going after the wood, to help Keoni with two carts, and Kalauwalu three.

6. In the first year of the maturity of the sugar-cane in Wailuku, Kalauwalu shall give Keoni assistance with his vessel, and at the end of the grinding of the first matured sugar-cane, then, Kalauwalu shall cease helping Keoni with his vessel.

7. Permission is granted to Keoni to withdraw within four years and five up to ten, he shall be released between those years. But, should Keoni desire to leave the work of making sugar during the second or third year, he will not be released.

8. The King will supply ten pair of sugar-cane working oxen for the heavy work of making sugar, and for hauling of such other material to the place for making sugar.

Appendixes

Kalauwalu agrees to a horse for Keoni, when acting as overseer in the planting of sugar-cane in Wailuku.
Honolulu, August 25, 1839.

Eyewitnesses:
J. Ii.
B. Mahune.
Kapule.

       KAMEHAMEHA III.
       KEKAULUOHI.
       KALAUWALU.
       KEONI PAKE.

Translated by
 E. H. Hart.

Appendix B

Chinese Sugar Plantation Inventory, 1848*

Ahsam and Ahmow were already manufacturing sugar before the arrival of contract laborers in 1852. When they died in 1848, an inventory was prepared of their estates. Achow signed his name in English while Ahin put his "X" mark as administrators. If they had signed in Chinese, the court clerk would have tried his best to draw the ideographs which really identified their Chinese surnames and/or given names.

* Probate File no. 4 (Archives of Hawaii).

Folio one

Inventory of the Property at Makahanaloa, District of Hilo, Island of Hawaii, belonging to the Estates of the late Ahsam and Ahmow who were in copartnership at that place as Sugar planters and manufacturers. viz

One Sugar Mill.
Five Iron Sugar Boilers.
One hundred and twelve Sugar Tubs.
Forty six Molasses Barrels
Seven Tubs (some good some bad)
One thousand seven hundred and thirty Mat Bags
One Sugar Sieve
Three tin Sugar Scoops
Two Sugar Vats
Twelve Molasses Spouts
One Musket
One half pound Powder
Five hundred feet Koa Lumber
One and one half Barrels Oil
Two Wooden Clocks.
Seven Old Barrels (with one head only)
One Straw House for boiling Sugar
One Straw House for Storing Sugar
One Straw House for Storing Rhine for fuel
Three Straw Dwelling Houses
Three Small Straw Houses for natives cooking and other work
Four Canoes
Cooking Utensils six pieces
Two Hoes
Seven new Axes
One Old Axe

Folio Two

Inventory continued
Four Axe hatchets (old)
Two Tables
Three Benches
Two Benches
Seven Fowls
One Dog
Sixty three acres new Cane just sprouted
Forty Acres of Cane on Daniel Castle's
   Land bought by Ahsam and Ahmow fit
   to cut in six months. (bought for one
   year only)
Thirteen Ox Yokes
Four Ox Chains
One new Ox Cart
Three Old Ox Carts
Three Bullock Hide Ox Chains
Three Lazos
Fifty one head of Bullocks (including
   Steers, Cows and Calves)
Nine Barrels Salmon
Twelve hundred and fifty pounds Rice
One half Barrel Onions
Eighty yards Blue Cotton
One thousand four hundred and sixteen and
   one half yards White Cotton
Fifty five yards Brown Cotton
Three hundred and ninety three yards

Folio three

Inventory Continued
Fifty Seven Yards Blue Drill
Thirty nine Check Shirts
One hundred and eight Yards Bed Ticking
Thirty Yards Denims
Forty eight Hooks and eyes
Nine Tumblers
Ninety pounds Cut Nails
One box Codfish containing eight pounds
Seventeen tin pots
Four red Silk Handkerchiefs
Two half Reams Paper
Eight Axe Handles
Thirty bars White Soap
Six Oo's
Eleven towels
One Small Bullock Hide
Nine pairs Common Suspenders
One Anchor Buoy
Twenty Fathoms Chain
One Spy Glass
Eight Acres of Kalo - more or less
Four Hammers (Blacksmiths)
Six Pincers
One Anvil
Seven Files

Folio four

Three Carpenters Hammers
Nine Chisels
Balance of Lease of the Land
to run thirteen months and three
days.

Island of Oahu ss. Achow administrator on the Estate of Ahsam, and Ahiu administrator on the Estate of Ahmow, both of Hilo, lately deceased, being duly sworn, do depose and say that the above inventory of the property of the joint Estate of Ah-sam and Ahmow is full and true according to the best of their knowledge.

Achow

Subscribed & sworn to before me this 8th day of Decr. A.D., 1848.

Ahiu ☓ His Mark

William L. Lee
Chief Justice of the Superior Court

Appendix C

Labor Recruitment Contract, 1865

On 23 June 1865, Dr. Wilhelm Hillebrand for the Royal Hawaiian Agricultural Society signed an agreement with Wohang Company of Hong Kong for the recruiting of laborers in Hong Kong.* Hillebrand, not familiar with conditions in Hong Kong and China, was glad to negotiate with an emigration broker to help him recruit the desired number of strong and healthy workers. Such brokers undertook to recruit emigrants for a fee, to provide food and lodging for them before departure, and to put them on board ships to sail to their waiting employers abroad.

> It has this day been agreed between the Hon. W. Hillebrand, acting as agent for the Hawaii Government on the one part and Wohang on the other part:
>
> That Wohang contracts for the supply of about 500 Chinese emigrants for Honolulu, Sandwich Islands, to be sent by two ships of about equal size, the first vessel has to be dispatched on or before 25th July next and the second ship on or before 20th August next.
>
> That the said emigrants must be strong and healthy able to perform field factory and domestic labour, none above 35 years of age, unless he belongs to a family to serve . . . under a contract drawn up by the Hon. W. Hillebrand in accordance with the regulations of the Hawaii Government. Families are preferable and Wohang engages to procure at least a proportion of Twenty to Twenty-five per cent married women of the whole number of emigrants. . . .

* Interior Dept., Misc.: Immigration—Chinese, 1864–June, 1865 (Archives of Hawaii).

That a present to the emigrants is given on embarkation at the rate of ($8) eight dollars to each male and ($20) twenty dollars to each female emigrant.

That the emigrant must be subject to inspection on embarkation, those found unfit for the purpose required to be rejected.

Wohang further agrees:

To fit out the ship for fifty six (56) days passage to the above named port of Honolulu—to erect berths, to provide water casks and water, firewood, wholesome provisions, ventilators and cooking utensils—to furnish the passengers each with two suits of clothing, one winter jacket, one pair shoes, one bamboo hat, a mat, pillow, and bed-covering.

To place medicines on board and every necessary article as required by the Hong Kong Emigration law, also to pay all fees for clearing the passengers from their port, bearing all the expenses to bring them from the interior, to victual them until their departure, to erect a hospital on deck and everything in accordance with the Hong Kong Law for the consideration of Twenty five Dollars ($25) payable as required, (balance to be settled before departure of the ship) for every passenger over 15 years of age and twelve dollars and a half ($12½) for every child under 15 years of age and over one year old, nothing being paid to babies under one year.

If an English doctor be engaged Wohang allows one dollar per head and the Hon. W. Hillebrand to find the necessary medicines.

Wohang agrees also to engage a competent interpreter and a Chinese doctor if required at the rate of twenty five dollars ($25) each per month.

On arrival in Honolulu the Hon. W. Hillebrand's agent to have the option of keeping the interpreter and doctor at the before named rate of wages or to dismiss them in paying them a present of ($50) fifty dollars each. . . .

Twenty of the passengers have to act as cooks as required by the local law . . . six have also to act as overseers and two as stewards on board during the passage. . . .

Appendixes

Wohang is bound to put up a rail partition to separate male and female passengers on board. . . .

In witness whereof . . . 3rd day of June, 1865.

W. Hillebrand

Wohang

Appendix D

Labor Contract, 1870*

Honolulu, Hawaiian Islands
_____ 1870

I _____ Party of the first part, a native of China, a free and voluntary Passenger to the Sandwich Islands, do bind myself to labor on any of the said Islands, at any work that may be assigned me, by the Party of the Second part, or their agents, upon the terms and in the manner within specified, for the term of Five Years from this date.

_____ Party of the second part, do agree and bind themselves, or agents, to conform fully to the within Agreement,

Witness _____ Signed _____
            Signed _____

MEMORANDUM OF AGREEMENT by the Agent of the Hawaiian Government.

No Contract can be made in Hongkong.

All Emigrants must go as Free Passengers.

Each Emigrant shall be given him, 1 heavy Jacket, 1 light Jacket, 1 Water-proof Jacket, 2 pair Pants, 1 pair Shoes, 1 pair Stockings, 1 Hat, 1 Mat, 1 Pillow, 1 Blanket.

A present of Ten Dollars to be paid the day before the ship sails. In no instance will any deduction from wages be made for Clothes or Money advanced in Hongkong.

A free passage to Sandwich Islands, with food, water, and Medical care, given each Emigrant.

The Master to pay all Government personal Taxes.

* Interior Dept., Misc.: Immigration—Chinese, 1870 (Archives of Hawaii).

All Children to be taught in the Public Schools, free of any expense to the Parents.

Each Man to receive $5 for each month labor performed of 26 days.

Each Woman to receive $5 for each month labor performed of 26 days.

The wages to be paid in Silver, upon the first Saturday after the end of the month.

No labor shall be exacted upon the Sabbath, only in case of emergency, when it shall be paid for extra.

All emigrants who are employed as House Servants, when their duties compel them to labor Sundays and evenings, shall receive for men 7 dollars per month, for women 6 dollars per month.

Three days Holiday shall be given each Emigrant at Chinese New Year and a present of $2.

These three days time to be counted the same as if employed.

In all cases, the Master to provide good and sufficient food and comfortable House Room.

In case of Sickness, Medical attendance and care free.

No wages during illness.

Each Emigrant to find his own Bed clothing.

Each Emigrant, upon arrival in the Sandwich Islands, to sign a contract (to work for such Master as may be chosen for him by the Government Agent) for the term of Five Years from the time of entering upon his duties, to work faithfully and cheerfully according to the laws of the Country, which compel both Master and Servant to fulfill their Contracts.

Families shall not be separated, the Government particularly desire that men will take their wives.

Every Emigrant shall have all the rights and protection under the law that are given to any Citizen of the Country.

At the expiration of the five years each Emigrant has a right to remain in the Country, or to leave it.

Saml. G. Wilder
H.H.M. Commissioner of
Immigration.

Appendix E

Labor Contract, 1890*

THIS MEMORANDUM OF AGREEMENT, Made and entered into at Honolulu,_____, by and between_____
hereinafter called the Employer, and _____
_____ hereinafter called the Laborer—

WITNESSETH THAT:

WHEREAS, the Laborer has arrived at the Hawaiian Islands, upon the understanding that he be there employed as an Agricultural Laborer, under the laws of the Republic of Hawaii; and in consideration of the sum of $54 in U.S. Gold Coin, advanced and lent to him by his said Employer for defraying passage money and expenses from his home in China to the Hawaiian Islands, and for clothes, receipt of which is hereby acknowledged, and for which sum the Laborer has signed a note; and in further consideration of the wages and other benefits to him moving, as hereinafter set forth:

THE FOLLOWING AGREEMENT HAS BEEN ENTERED INTO BETWEEN THE AFORESAID PARTIES HERETO:

THE SAID EMPLOYER, in consideration of the

* Interior Dept., Misc.: Immigration—Contract Forms (Archives of Hawaii).

stipulations hereinafter contained, to be kept and performed by the said Laborer, convenants and agrees as follows:

1. To procure for said Laborer proper lodgings and food at Honolulu while waiting for a steamer to go to _____plantation, and also proper transportation from Honolulu to the aforesaid plantation.

2. To give employment to said Laborer, as an agricultural laborer, for the full period of three years from the date such employment actually begins.

3. To pay or cause to be paid to said Laborer, during said 3 years, wages for each month of 26 day's labor actually performed at the rate of Twelve Dollars and Fifty Cents per month, and out of such wages earned to pay for said Laborer to the Hawaiian Government the sum of $1.50 per month for the first 24 months of this agreement, or in all $36.00, which sum the Government holds to the credit of the Laborer until such Laborer elects to return to China, when the said sum of $36.00, and accrued interest thereon, will be applied to the payment of his return passage, and the balance, if any, given to him in cash.

And after 3 year's faithful work not to collect his note for $54.00 for passage money and expenses, but the note of $54.00 shall be due and collectable of the Laborer, if the Laborer deserts his employment at any time before the expiration of this agreement.

4. Also that overtime work exceeding 30 minutes shall be paid for at the rate of 10 cents per hour to the Laborer.

5. During the continuance of this agreement the Employer guarantees to the Laborer the full and equal protection of the laws of the Hawaiian Islands, and to provide the Laborer with unfurnished lodgings, and with water and fuel for cooking purposes, medical attendance and medicines, but no rations, and to pay his personal taxes.

THE SAID LABORER, in consideration of the sum of $54.00 lent to him by his said Employer, and in consideration of the stipulations hereinbefore mentioned, to be kept and performed by the said Employer, covenants and agrees as follows:

1. After arrival at Honolulu to proceed to the _____ _____ plantation, there to perform such agricultural labor in the field, or in or about rice or sugar mills, or as domestic servant, as the Employer under this agreement, and under the herein contained terms and conditions, shall direct.

2. During the continuance of this agreement, being the full period of three years from the date such employment actually begins, to fulfill all the conditions of this agreement, and to diligently and faithfully perform all lawful and proper labor, and to obey all lawful commands of his employer, his agents or overseers, and to work during the night and rest during the day, if called upon to do so, and work on all days, but not on days which are holidays and as such recognized by the Hawaiian Government, or on Chinese New Year, the last mentioned holiday not to exceed two working days; but if the said Laborer should be employed in domestic service the usual and indispensable work shall be done on such holidays also.

3. A day's labor shall be 10 hours actual work in the fields, or 12 hours actual work in or about the sugar factory; the hours not being continuous, but allowing the necessary time for taking food and rest.

And 26 day's actual work as aforesaid shall constitute a month's labor.

4. If, at any time, during the continuance of this agreement, the Laborer shall desire to return to China, he shall be released from this agreement upon his departure from the Hawaiian Islands, and upon conditions that the Laborer shall refund to his employer the following portion of the costs of his passage from China to Hawaii, to wit: $1.50 for each month remaining of the term of this agreement.

FOR THE PROPER FULFILLMENT OF THIS AGREEMENT, the parties hereto bind themselves, one to

Appendixes

the other, as witnessed by their hands and seals hereto affixed, at Honolulu, _____

_____
_____
_____

WITNESS:

_____
_____

_____

ISLAND OF OAHU, } ss.   On _____
   HAWAIIAN ISLANDS.

personally appeared before me _____
Employer, and _____ Laborer, satisfactorily proved to me by the oath of _____
_____ to be the persons executing the foregoing agreement, and the same having been by me read, explained and interpreted to them, they severally acknowledged that they understood the same, and that they had executed the same voluntarily, and upon the terms and conditions therein set forth.

_____
Agent to take Acknowledgments to Contracts for Labor for the Island of Oahu.

$54.00.   HONOLULU, _____
On demand for value received I promise to pay to the _____ or order, the sum of Fifty-four Dollars _____. Payable at the office of the _____

此工約經工人照得該工人經由東家給出金錢銀伍拾四大元以備作舟資盤費衣服之需而該項經認收足並立揭單為據令該工人已由中國原鄉到來禮島自願按照禮山民主國例在禮先作田土之工役至論其工價或所沾諸般利益之處均由東主工人兩家訂明知如左

如該工人遵照約內所訂諸欵條例而行則該東主亦願照下列條欵而行

一該工人到漢拿喀爐畢之日起備足三年田土工夫之工價工逾限半點鐘之久經為額但凡操作二十六天即算一個月之工夫上歇曾有言明四當此工約三年未滿之日期每月計同銀壹元五毫繳遂該東主作為填補柴禮盤費等用以上各欵于一千八百九十

一該工人到漢拿喀爐畢之後即須赴工則日間歇息除禮山王家大日子及放假日期亦須開工家常服役係日中所必需者則一個月之內務須勤慎操作凡所做者不外合法之工夫及糖房米磨工夫或家常服役總要順從東家或代理人或管工之命而行倘該工人於此三年內新年之日準兩天做工在田土操作以十一點鐘為額做糖房或磨房做工則以十二點鐘為額接而計即用膳之時必須停息再計凡操作二十六天即算一個月之工夫上歇曾有言明

一到漢拿喀爐畢之後即須赴工按此約內所訂諸欵情節指揮二按此約內所訂諸欵情節或要做夜工如屬必要亦必遵從該工人亦願照下列約內所訂諸欵而行

茲因該東主廷前偹與工人銀五十四元兼依約內所訂諸欵情節而行則該工人亦願照下列約內所訂諸欵而行

工日起做足三年工夫應該工人於此三年內務須勤慎操作凡所做者不外合法之工夫及糖房米磨工夫或家常服役係日中所必需者則一個月之內務須勤慎操作凡所做者不外合法之工夫及糖房米磨工夫或家常服役總要順從東家或代理人或管工之命而行倘該工人於此三年內新年之日準兩天做工在田土操作以十一點鐘為額做糖房或磨房做工則以十二點鐘為額接而計即用膳之時必須停息再計凡操作二十六天即算一個月之工夫上歇曾有言明

茲立單實認收到銀五十四元正嗣後倘經支遂銀五十四元正

西一千八百九十 年　月　號

慈東主
見證人
工人

會同工人
在場見證人
在漢拿喀爐畢

發誓證明謂兩家確是立上
寫字樓
的筆
的筆
的筆
的筆

Appendix F

Labor Import Declaration, 1890*

> This is to certify that C. F. Hart, of Niulii has this day contracted Forty-three (43) Chinese Agricultural Laborers received under the provisions of the Act approved Nov. 14. 1890 "To authorize the introduction of Chinese Agricultural Laborers etc.", at the Port of Mahukona by the American Ship "Pactolus" for which number our Agents in Honolulu are bound to execute and deliver a bond in the sum of Seventy five ($75.00) dollars for each man, to His Excellency the Minister of Foreign Affairs, and the fee of one dollar ($1.00) for each Special Residence Permit issued by the said Minister of Foreign Affairs.
>
>   C. F. Hart
>
> Mahukona   Robt Hall
>   July 21. 1890.

*Hawaii Sugar Planters' Association Library.

Ninlie Mill

Name	No. of pleased	Height	Complexion	Description
Paw Chuo Tze	249	5ft 1½	Medium	Scar in front of left ear. Mole right side of nose.
Hoo Choo	250	5.3½	Light	Mole on left side of nose. Five scars on left cheek.
Hoo Sun	251	5.3½	Light	Cut over left eyebrow. Large scar back of right shoulder.
Hoo Chao	252	5.6½	Light	Mole right side of chin. Scar on left shoulder.
Hoo Hing	253	5.5	Light	Five moles on left shoulder. Six moles on back.
Chong Kim Sim	254	5.3	Medium	Slight cut left side of head. Teeth slightly red.
Cheng Heao	255	5.4	Light	Scar over right ear. Five parallel scars on right wrist.
Chong Pack	256	5.0	Light	Scar back of right ear. Large scar above left ear.
Pan Kin	257	5.6	Light	Mole above left ear. Five moles back of neck. Head shut.
Pan Sheng	258	5.6½	Light	Mole in front of right ear. Cut on back of neck. Scar on right shoulder blade.
Pan Mock	259	5.3½	Medium	Mole on edge of jaw right side. Scar down right shinbone. Blind.
Pan On	260	5.5½	Light	Scar over left eyebrow. Scar in middle of upper lip.
Soing Kwei	261	5.5½	Light	Three large moles on chest. Lower end of back scar crosswise on back of neck.
Hoo Yu	262	5.3½	Medium	Scar on left shoulder, one right side of head.
Hoo Seing	263	5.4½	Medium	Mole right side of nose. Scar on top of right shoulder.
Leong Wook	264	5.4¾	Medium	Scar left side of head, near hand. Red above right eye.
Cheng Chung Tha	265	5.6	Dark	Scar on each cheek. Large scar on right ear.
Chong Sheu	266	5.3½	Medium	Small scar with mole in cut on right eyebrow.
Ching Pack	267	5.4½	Light	Scar on both shoulders. Cut on back between shoulders. Cut on ...
Ching Ping Pong	268	4.11½	Light	Three moles closely on neck. Slight side of head badly scarred.
Weng Woo	269	5.2½	Medium	Large scar above and next to right of left ear. Gray hair.
Hoo Lem	270	5.3	Medium	Large scar on neck between shoulders. Mole on right shoulder.
Wee Yong	271	5.3	Medium	Scar near left corner of mouth. Prominent teeth.
Pien Yong	272	5.6½	Medium	Mole in front of right ear. Large three cornered scar on top of head.
Chong Yu	273	4.10½	Medium	Scar on right upper lip. Mole to left of nose.
Li Ping	274	5.4½	Medium	Mole right side of neck. Two scars on each shoulder.
Chu Heao	275	5.1½	Light	Two moles on right side of neck.
Chin Ing	276	5.5½	Medium	Tops of both shoulders scarred.
Lim Ciao	277	5.3	Light	Mole back of right eyebrow. Five large moles back of neck.
Wee Chuen	278	5.4½	Light	Three large scars running up left side of head.
Leong Wook	279	5.1½	Light	Large mole left side of nose. Slight cut on right eyebrow.
Wook Ing	280	5.8	Light	Round scar at right corner of mouth. Left ear lobe pierced.
Cop Heao	281	5.6	Light	Red mole above left edge of right eyebrow. Scar above right ear.
Leong Hai	282	5.1½	Light	Scar above left ear. Scar near right side of head.
Cheng Kim	283	5.4½	Medium	Large red hurt lips. Mole on right shoulder.
Chong Kee Yen	284	5.5½	Light	Large blunt mole on chest. Cut on left of lower lip.
Hoo Deat	285	5.5½	Medium	Slightly cross-eyed. Mole between shoulders on back. Five upper teeth mercury.
Chan Si Liam	286	5.2½	Medium	Mole on right side of neck. Three moles under left eye.
Chu Pan	287	5.4½	Light	Scar on left cheek bone. Small scar middle of forehead.
Chu Pok Yu	288	5.0½	Light	Scar above left ear. Indented mole on chest bone.
Chu Lu Chung	289	4.10½	Medium	Scar above and back of right ear. Slight cut front of left ear.
Chu Lu Ein	290	5.1½	Medium	Scar middle of chest. Scar 3 inches below right nipple.
Chin In Lan	20	5.¾	"	Black mole between eyebrows. Mole on right lower eyelid.

Appendix G

Chinese Mass Protest, 1894

The Revolution of 17 January 1893 succeeded in overthrowing the Hawaiian monarchy. The Chinese residents were disappointed with the provisional republic that was established because it excluded them from political participation. The proposed constitution did not grant them the franchise although the Chinese were eager to be a part of the new democracy. The object of the constitution-makers was to exclude Orientals from politics and to keep control of Hawaii in the hands of people favorable to annexation. The *Honolulu Advertiser*'s comment on 26 July 1894 undoubtedly presented the general attitude of most white people when it said that refusal to grant the vote to Chinese was justified because they were aliens to Hawaii. The new government did not need "ignorant voters who would sell their votes for ten cents of tea." *The Friend* (March 1894): 24 reported on a bill proposed February 1 that would require "all Chinamen to pay one dollar each for a license before engaging in any trading or mechanical occupation, and which forbids such licenses to be issued to any Chinaman not previously so employed."

It was against this background that the Chinese demonstrated their opposition to a proposed bill before the Advisory Council and Cabinet that would restrict laborers from engaging in business. The aroused Chinese voiced their protests—their "rice bowls" were at stake. The article from the *Hawaiian Star* of February 15 describing the event was read into Congressional records.*

---

* U.S., Congress, House, *Executive Document No. 47*, 53rd Cong., 2d sess., 1894, pp. 2068, 2070.

Appendixes

VOICE OF THE CHINESE COLONY DECLARES ITSELF IN A BIG MASS MEETING—POSITIVE EXPRESSIONS—WHAT THEY HAVE DONE FOR THE COUNTRY—THEIR RIGHTS—RESOLUTIONS

In no city of a State or Territory of the American Union could the Chinese have made such a demonstration as was held at the theater of the colony last night. Here the *Pakes* have been first tolerated, then encouraged, until they assume an attitude plainly defiant and close bordering on the dominant and dictatorial. From the weak and lowly field hand of the time of 1851 and the wage scale of $3 a month they have, by an unparalleled and alarming evolution, reached the station of an assertive element in the policy of the nation. The spectacle has not its counterpart elsewhere on the globe.

The Chinese theater here is a larger and better building than the colony of some 40,000 Asiatics in the city of San Francisco can boast. Last night the playhouse was jammed. It contained not less than 2,500 men, perhaps 500 more. Every particle of space was occupied. All Chinese business places, except the restaurants, closed at 4 o'clock. During the next two hours and a half Chinamen flocked to the theater from every direction. Hundreds of them rode in hacks. The tram cars were crowded and the rest walked in the heavy rain. The storm kept away those living at a distance. A weight was borne by the big gallery that it never had before. The throng extended well out into the street. As a mass meeting the event was in every way a success. The place is illy ventilated and scores were compelled to stand. The proceedings throughout riveted the attention of all. There were frequent outbursts of applause and positive expressions from the audience. Half a hundred of the leading Chinese had seats on the stage. A number of natives and a few whites were present. A squad of police was in attendance. It is said that nearly all the 800 vagrants of Chinatown were on hand.

The tenor of the meeting may be judged by the fact that the use of a man-of-war was more than hinted at. The statement the Chinese paid more taxes than any other class was made, also the claim that but for them Honolulu trade would die, and that they had only to unite and stand firm to gain their ends.

Kam Chim, editor of one of the Chinese newspapers, called the meeting to order. He named Lau Chung, of the Wing Wo Tai Company, as president. No one else was mentioned. Lau Chung designated Chang Kim and Chang Den-Sing as secretaries. Next Lau Chung announced the objects of the meeting at length and read and commented upon the license bill which has been placed before the councils by Attorney-General Smith. They were gathered, Chung said, to ascertain the views of the colony upon the proposed legislation. Chung had the act written on a sheet of paper about as large as a page of this paper and occupied about a quarter of an hour in placing it before the meeting.

Ing Chan, of the Tong On Jan Company, was presented as the first speaker, and was greeted with great cheering. He made a salaam and launched out into an impassioned tale of the wrongs [to] his race. When he asked: "Shall we put up with it?" a storm of noes came from all over the house. After suggesting that they communicate to the councils, he said: "If they will not listen to us, let us instruct our representative to communicate with the Chinese minister at Washington and ask him to write the home Government about our troubles." Chan said that up to ten years ago the Chinese on the islands had been treated as men and as the equals of all. They are law-abiding, but their treatment is getting worse all the time. They do not meddle with the politics. They are now over 20,000 strong, and in varied occupations do good for the country; and, like one big family, must unite their forces. The white people are dissatisfied and want to impose laws that other countries would not think of passing.

The next speaker was Wong Wah-Toy of the Wing Wo Tai Company, who said they were assembled to see if all were of one mind respecting the situation. Through their energy and industry they have made land more valuable. They have been oppressed long enough. The Government wants to tie their hands still more. Shall we allow it? (No,

Appendixes

no, from the audience.) "These foreigners do not remember their own scripture, which says 'Do unto others as you would they should do unto you.' They claim to be an enlightened people, but I say they are not if they act in this way. Unity is what we want and must have—unity in mind and action. If we unite we will gain our point. (Cheers.) We must unite, but in a peaceful way. There must be no talk yet of a man of war settling our troubles for us. That may come later."

"I have been in the country for fifteen years," said Ching Ling Him, a clerk for the Hawaiian Hardware Company, who says he hopes to become a merchant. "We are not a better nor a worse class than any other. (Cheers.) If this bill passes no man can do any business except the one allowed him by law. The Chinese pay most of the taxes, and were it not for us the white merchants of Honolulu would be ruined. I can not be a rich man if this law passes, and we are treated worse than dogs. We do not steal. Why do they want to make such laws against it? All we must do is to stick together and we will come out all right."

Chung [Chang] Kim, a lawyer's clerk, who brought his speech from C.W. Ashford's office, said that the meeting was occasioned by the purpose of the Government to place Chinese under the ban and favor Portuguese. The Chinese have been extremely patient. They have borne oppression which would from almost any other race have provoked revolution. The Government seems to have formed the opinion that no injustice heaped upon the Chinese will be opposed or resented. That is a mistake. Even a worm will turn when trodden upon, and so it may be with the despised Chinese should the oppression be carried too far. Are we not all members of one great family? Is there any reason why one of God's creatures should be trampled upon by his brothers?

By what right do our white-skinned brothers lord it over us to say that we shall do business and trade and live and breathe only by their consent? Is it only because our skins are brown and theirs are white? The Government is glad enough to collect taxes from the Chinese, but when it comes to finding a class upon whom the spite of all cranks shall be expended, they at once light upon the patient and long-suffering Chinaman. The Geary Act in the United States is bad enough, but this act proposed to be imposed upon us is even worse than that. The Hawaiian constitution declares that the Government established for the equal benefit of all men and all classes, but if the Chinese license act shall pass it will show that the Government intends to deny to us the equal benefit of the laws.

W.C. Achi, a practicing attorney, who calls himself a Chinaman without a queue, and who addressed the gathering as "countrymen of my father," spoke in the native tongue at length. "You have no representation in the councils to speak for you," wailed Mr. Achi, "but you have the right to make your wishes known to the councils by resolutions. If this law passes a laborer who may save his money can not engage in business. The law will put a rope around your necks; it will injure all the Chinese, rich and poor, high and low, strong and weak. To turn in our favor the tide that is setting against us we must take some intelligent action. (Very good.) The supreme court would decide that this law was wholly unconstitutional."

Another clerk of a lawyer was now heard. This was N. Monwor, of Paul Neumann's office. He believed that the good men at the head of the Government would refrain from passing an unjust law. Like Achi, he mentioned the supreme court, saying that it had protected the Chinese against the law of 1888.

Lee Chu, a carpenter, is a radical. Said he: "We are descended from great fathers. Why should we be treated differently from others? I say that if we do not do our best to overcome this law we will show that we have no blood in us."

A number of other addresses were made and this committee of thirteen was selected to place the resolutions given below: C. Winam, Wong Wah-Foy, Yun Quom, Chu Gem, Chang Kim, Ho Ton, Lau Chock, Chang Chick, N. Monwor, N. Chan, Chu Wing, I. Kat-Poo, Lau Chang. The resolutions read:

"Whereas there is now pending before the legislative body of the Provisional Government an act obliging Chinese residents of these islands to obtain a special license, not called for in the case of any other nationality, as a prerequisite to conducting business in this country; and

"Whereas such legislation is directed against the Chinese as a class, in violation of constitutional provisions and of the principles of equity and justice supposed to inhere in all civilized governments; and would, if enacted into law, prove an irritating oppression to a numerous and law-abiding class of residents who pay a large proportion of the taxes collected by the Government, and who are entitled to the protection of the laws, on terms of equality with other residents of these islands; now, therefore, be it

"*Resolved*, That we, the Chinese residents of Honolulu, in mass meeting assembled on the evening of Wednesday, the 14th day of February, 1894, do solmenly (sic) protest against the injustice, degradation, and insult threatened to be imposed upon us and our race by the legislation so, as aforesaid, pending and proposed to be enacted into law;

"*Resolved*, That we respectfully assert our right, under the principles of enlightened justice and the provisions of the Hawaiian constitution, to dwell in Hawaii and be accorded the protection of the law upon terms of equality with those of other nationalities here sojourning.

"*Resolved*, That the Chinese in Hawaii have been guilty of no act or course of action which should in justice subject them to the humiliation of being singled out as objects of legislative caprice, oppression, or hatred, such as the act herein protested against will, if passed into law, embody and express.

"*Resolved*, That while we ask for nothing more than equality with other residents of equally good behavior, we shall be satisfied with and shall support and respect nothing that accords to our race a lesser degree of consideration and injustice than residents of other nationalities enjoy.

"*Resolved*, That the chairman of this meeting do appoint a committee of 13 Chinese residents of this city to present these resolutions to his Excellency the Minister of Foreign Affairs at their earliest opportunity, and to urge upon his excellency the sentiments herein expressed."

Appendix H

Claim for Loss of Property, Chinatown Fire, 1901*

FIRE CLAIMS COMMISSION.

STATEMENT OF CLAIM.

The undersigned, claimant, respectfully represents that he is a resident of Honolulu, H. I.

That on the date of the loss hereinafter specified, he was the sole owner of the effects and property set forth in the schedules hereto attached, marked Exhibits A, B and C;* that the value of said property at its cost price is set forth upon said schedules opposite the items thereof; that said property and effects were lost by total destruction by fire on the 20 day of Jan. 1900 and that no part thereof was saved; that said fire occurred, as claimant is informed and believe, by order of the Board of Health in the suppression of Bubonic Plague; that the nature of the property lost is fully set forth in said schedules; that said property was situated at the time of said loss in Block 1 G aio 6 building, on Maunakea Street, in said Honolulu, Territory of Hawaii. Between Punahi and Beretania That said loss consisted in part of the destruction of the building more particularly described in Exhibit C; that the name of the owner of the land whereon said building stood is _____, and the nature of the interest of this claimant in said building is _____

That said property was insured for _____ Dollars in the name of _____ and _____ Dollars of said insurance has been paid by _____ Company, the insurer thereof.

That the foregoing statement of claim and schedules hereto attached do not include any claims for speculative or consequential damages, or for loss of rent, or for use of property, or for loss of profits through the interruption of business, nor any loss except the destruction of or direct damage to said property by fire or removal under the order or direction of the Board of Health as aforesaid.

TERRITORY OF HAWAII, } ss.
Island of Oahu,

謝四益 (Cha See Yick)

Cha See Yick being first duly sworn, says that he is the claimant above named; that he knows the contents of the foregoing statement of claim and of the schedules hereto attached, and that the same are true of his own knowledge, except such matters as are stated upon information and belief, and as to those he believes them to be true.

謝四益 (Cha See Yick)

Subscribed and sworn to before me this ____ day of June, A. D. 1901.

L. L. Kentwell
NOTARY PUBLIC.

* RULE XIV.—In order to facilitate business claimants are directed to present claims for losses of merchandise, goods, wares and stocks in trade in an itemized form, describing the kind and value thereof, upon a schedule to be marked "Exhibit A," and all claims for losses of personal belongings, jewelry, house furnishings and other chattels upon a schedule to be marked "Exhibit B," and for all losses appertaining to buildings or of building fixtures upon a schedule to be marked "Exhibit C."

* Claims to Commission on 1900 Fire Losses (Archives of Hawaii).

CHA SEE YICK

1 trunk	5.
1 " med size leather	5.
1 octagon clock	4.50
1 alarm clock	2.
3 tables	6.
3 chairs	6.
3 stools	3.
1 rocking chair	5.
1 bed stead	7.50
1 set bed planks	2.
2 picture frames	3.50
3 assorted looking glasses	1.50
1 pr. red blankets	8.
1 " white "	5.
1 mosq bar	5.
1 cott quilt	2.25
1 crepe silk counterpane	9.50
2 table lamps	3.
1 lantern	.60
2 umbrellas	4.50
2 assorted wash tubs	3.50
2 buckets	1.25
1 pan with cover	2.50
3 agate kettles	2.80
1 teapot with basket	.75
1 tea tray	.40
2 hats	1.25
1 cupboard	4.50
1 delicacy case	1.25
1 dish pan	.75
bowls, plates and chopsticks	3.50
1 hatchet	.75
2 woolen coats	12.
2 pr " pants	10.
1 reeled pongee coat	4.50
10 cott shirts Ch.	7.50
3 pr shoes	8.
2 " " Ch.	2.50

Appendixes

6 " socks	.75
2 straw hats	3.50
1 lady's silk gauze dress	9.50
1 do crepe robe	7.50
2 do gauze chemise	9.
1 do camlet dress	4.50
2 do blk pongee "	7.50
2 pr " crepe silk trousers	9.
2 do " chemise	11.
2 " " blk pongee trousers	5.50
3 " " shoes	4.50
2 woolen coats	4.50
2 pr " pants	4.50
2 " shoes	3.50
1 " " Ch.	.75
Total,	242.05

wife & 2 children

Appendix I

United Chinese Society Petition to Congress, 1916

The United Chinese Society, represented by attorney W. H. Hindle, presented a petition to a Congressional subcommittee meeting on 29 August 1916.* According to the petition, Chinese labor was needed for the rice industry but Chinese immigration was still restricted by the U.S. Chinese Exclusion Act of 1882. "All we ask is to be treated the same as people of other Oriental nations. Is it justice to single out the Chinese for exclusion?"

Letter presented by Mr. W. H. Hindle, Honolulu, Hawaii:

> Honolulu, Hawaii, August 5, 1916
>
> At a meeting of the United Chinese Society, held in Honolulu, at their hall, Friday, August 4, 1916, it was unanimously decided that a petition for the betterment of the conditions of the Chinese in Hawaii be presented to the administration at Washington, D. C. and C. K. Ai and Lee Let were appointed as the committee in this matter. These gentlemen then requested the president, Mr. Yee Yap, that Mr. W. H. Hindle represent them for all the Chinese of Hawaii.
>
> Therefore, Mr. W. H. Hindle is herein given full power to act on our behalf in all matters pertaining to this petition.
>
> (Signed)   C. K. Ai
>   Lee Let

---

* U.S., Congress, House, Committee on Territories, *Labor Conditions in Hawaii*, 64th Congress, 1st Sess., 29 August 1916.

Appendixes

Mr. Hindle. Now, I have the original petition signed by Mr. Yee Yap, the president of the United Chinese Society of the Territory of Hawaii. I gave several copies to the Hon. Mr. Houston, the chairman of the Committee on the Territories. This petition first gives a history of the coming of the Chinese to Hawaii. As far as we can trace them, we know that there came in 1789 on a very small sailing ship about 45 Chinese. While there is nothing authentic about the proposition that they remained there, yet in 1794, when Vancouver visited Hawaii, he found Chinese. . . .

That was the early days of Kamehameha. The Chinese opened the very first foreign market ever opened between Hawaii and another country. . . . Kamehameha the First sent one of his high chiefs over to China for the purpose of cementing the commercial relations between the two nations, as well as for procuring arms and ammunition for the further conquest of the other islands in the group. . . .

The Chairman. Mr. Hindle, if you will just leave off the historical conditions and deal with the present conditions in Hawaii, I think we can get nearer the real point of your statement, because we can get the historical matter afterwards anyhow. . . .

Mr. Brumbaugh. Now, as I understand, you want to modify our Chinese-exclusion laws———

Mr. Hindle. Yes, by a special agreement for the purpose of admitting Chinese labor to the Hawaiian Islands for work in the rice fields, without recourse to this country now or at any future period. The Chinese will be bound by this agreement, if any of them come to Hawaii for the purpose of labor, never, under any circumstances, to enter the United States of America.

Mr. Brumbaugh. You are acquainted, of course, with the difficulties arising in the western part of this country in connection with Asiatics?

Mr. Hindle. Yes.

The Chairman. What we want is the actual condition in Hawaii now—your need for Chinamen, why you need them, why you prefer them to the Japanese, and what the Japanese are going to do in the way of overrunning the country and furnishing all the labor unless you can get labor from some other source.

Mr. Hindle. All right. I have some figures and statistics here. For instance, there are 7,090 acres of abandoned land, a large part of which is only suitable for the cultivation of rice and taro, the native foods.

The Chairman. Why has that land been abandoned?

Mr. Hindle. Chiefly for want of labor. The higher cost of living has made the raising of rice a loss under any circumstances.

The Chairman. Well, if you had Chinese labor there, could you make it profitable?

Mr. Hindle. Yes.

The Chairman. That is the question we want to hear you on.

Mr. Brumbaugh. Just a question right on that point. If all the bars were let down and they could have all the Chinese labor they desired, would not 99 per cent of it go to the big plantations that are not run by Chinamen?

Mr. Hindle. No, sir; because the plantations do not go in for rice. They go in for sugar only.

Mr. Brumbaugh. Oh, you only want rice labor?

Mr. Hindle. Yes, sir.

Mr. Brumbaugh. But how can you keep the Chinamen from other lines of labor?

Mr. Hindle. Well, they will bring other lines of industry. They will bring trade to the storekeepers. They will want food and clothing, and that food and clothing will come from America, and not China.

Mr. Brumbaugh. Of course we have a Chinese problem in the United States that we have to look out for.

Mr. Hindle. Yes; but I have figures here to show the difference between the Chinese and the Japanese, and they will surely explain the necessity of importing Chinese labor against Japanse labor or any other oriental labor.

Mr. Brumbaugh. Do not the owners of these large plantations want Chinese labor, too.

Mr. Hindle. Yes.

Appendixes

The Chairman. I take it that every man who employs labor in Hawaii would welcome Chinese labor?

Mr. Hindle. Every man, wholesalers and retail storekeepers, clerks in the offices, salesmen for commission houses, or in any other branch of business, will prefer Chinese labor; and there is not a white man in Hawaii who will tell you differently.

The Chairman. Why is that?

Mr. Hindle. Because of their honesty, integrity, and everything that goes to making up a good servant to an employer. They never attempt to strike.

The Chairman. When the Chinaman gets there and goes to work what does he do with the earnings of his labor? Does he become a citizen? Does he make his home there?

Mr. Hindle. He makes his home there; he raises a family; he buys property and becomes a real-estate taxpayer. . . .

(The data and petition submitted by Mr. Hindle are as follows:)

CONSUMPTION [OF RICE] PER MONTH PER PERSON

Population, 1914:	Pounds
21,000 Chinese	50
15,000 Filipinos	60
91,000 Japanese	65
8,300 Koreans	60
...... All Others	5
135,300 Total	240
Rice grown in Hawaii, 1915	24,000,000
Imported from Japan, 1915	33,619,921
Exported to America	4,000,000

RICE LAND ABANDONED FOR WANT OF LABOR

	Acres		Acres
Pah On, Kauai	250	Kohala, Hawaii	250
C. Ako, Kauai	125	Waipio, Oahu	650
Hanalei, Kauai	500	Kailua, Hawaii	100
Ching Shai, Oahu	300	Wong Leong, Oahu	800

Wong Kwai, Oahu	50	Sing Chong Co., Oahu	1,923
Kahana, Oahu	200	Y. Ahin, Kahuku,	
Laie, Oahu	500	Mokuleia, Wailua,	
Mokoleia (Y. Ahin), Oahu	680	Waikealea, and	
Anahola, Kauai	50	Waikiki, Oahu	650
Kapaa, Kauai	70	Total	7,098

To cultivate this land needs 28,000 men, as labor required for every 100 acres is 40 men all the year round from the time of plowing to milling and sacking, cleaning and resacking.

The above figures do not comprise all the land that has been abandoned, as it has been impossible to obtain from smaller original planters, but the total could be conservatively estimated at 7,500 acres.

For many reasons rice is grown at a loss, chiefly for want of labor, higher cost of living, advance in price of fertilizer, conservation for consumption to the Chinese population, and decrease in export, which in all constitutes the reason for abandoning the land on expiration of leases. Abandoned land, 7,500 acres, and a large quantity of this is only suitable for the cultivation of rice or taro, the land being waste and swampy. The amount of these leased lands are a conservative estimate of $25 per annum, or $187,500, exclusive of loss of taxation to the Territory.

Should there unfortunately arise a conflict of any country with the United States of America and the Islands of Hawaii placed under siege there would not be sufficient conservation of food to withstand a siege but a short time, but if rice was grown on the islands as before annexation then there would be rice not alone in storage but in the field, rice crops are harvested three times in two years, and the climate of Hawaii is such that the harvesting of rice occurs every month.

PETITION TO THE ADMINISTRATION OF THE GOVERNMENT OF THE UNITED STATES OF AMERICA FOR THE BETTERMENT, CONDITIONS AND ADMISSION OF CHINESE LABORERS TO THE TERRITORY OF THE HAWAIIAN ISLANDS.

[6 November 1869]

To the President, Cabinet Officers, Members of the Senate and Congress and the Committee on Immigration and Labor.

Gentlemen: In presenting this petition for your perusal, argument, discussion, and disposition, we are offering for your consideration with the concurrence of the whole of the Chinese population of the Territory of Hawaii. . . .

Feeling assured of the spirit of Americanism for fair play, and equal rights for all men who obey the law, we now take this means to place before you the needs, requirements, and wants beneficial for our race, as well as the benefits which would accrue to the community at large, the Territory of Hawaii, and the Federal Government. . . .

The rice industry is still to a large extent controlled by Chinese, but owing to the nonadmission of Chinese labor since annexation this industry had deteriorated, and it is principally for this industry we desire labor necessary for its cultivation. . . .

From the years 1789 to 1852 the immigration of Chinese to these islands was not extensive, for we learn by an article in the *Polynesian,* a Hawaiian paper published in the early days, under date of August 24, 1850, that owing to the growing industry of sugar cane it was necessary that labor suitable for this work be encouraged from some other country. And after due deliberation China was the country selected in which to look for this class of labor. . . .

Until 1865 no assisted immigration had been made to Hawaii. In that year (1865), the sugar industry having passed to a large extent into the control of the Anglo-Saxon race, a dearth of labor was felt. As the sugar planters and the Hawaiian Government, from past years of experience, know the sterling worth of Chinese labor, we find that in

1865 Dr. William Hillebrand was appointed by the King royal Commissioner of immigration and sent to China to procure for the plantations; and up to the time of annexation Chinese labor had the preference in cane field work and as house servants, and at no time from the first introduction into these islands to the present date can an employer of labor of any kind show where there has been a strike of Chinese laborers for any cause or where a loss has been sustained by their employers and other laborers. . . .

Between 1852 and up to the time of annexation 37,817 Chinese arrived in Hawaii, and then not all by assisted immigration. Of this number 29,000 returned to their native land or died, which, being 50 per cent, should show conclusively that with the open door and unrestricted immigration to the islands they (the islands) would not be flooded with Chinese laborers. . . .

Under the monarchy, the provisional government, and the Republic of Hawaii the Chinese were well treated, enjoying the same freedom as all other nations, and many became citizens. . . . Hundreds of Chinese brought their wives and families to these islands with a view to permanent location, and many of the children born of Chinese parents are today filling important positions of trust and confidence in banks, wholesale and retail firms, and other branches of commercial life carried on in these islands.

The schools and colleges were never closed to, or segregation made of, any nation. Our race quick to perceive and seize opportunities for education and advancement, have risen to this occasion to such an extent that the highest honors have been divided with them in our schools and colleges. . . . That the young Hawaian-born Chinese, as well as those who have adopted Hawaii as their permanent home, are truly patriotic to America since annexation can be faithfully attested to in many ways: The love of the islands as their birthplace, the reverence for the Constitution and the flag of the United States of America, the national holidays, and the bulwark of America in times of trouble, "her militia." For, of their own volition there is to-day one company in the National Guard of Hawaii—Company H, which is composed (officers and men) entirely of Hawaiian-born Chinese young men who have sworn allegiance to the the Constitution and flag of the United States of America. This company is the largest in number of any company of the National Guard of Hawaii, and should occasion require there are in the islands hundreds of other Chinese who would respond to the call to uphold the independence of the United States.

In the public schools on these islands 60 young ladies of Chinese parentage are engaged as teachers and perform the same duties as their Anglo-Saxon sisters—instructing the young minds of a cosmopolitan gathering in the love of country and reverence of the flag so dear to the hearts of all Americans.

In no State, Territory, or possession, over which the jurisdiction of the United States of America exists are conditions of commerce and labor the same as in the Hawaiian Islands. For here there is no competition between Chinese and white labor, therefore there can be no conflict. Chinese labor is needed for rice industry, and for assistants in stores, markets, and offices of Chinese merchants.

In these islands, with the exception of the sugar industry, the greater part of the commercial life is oriental; divided between Chinese, Japanese, Koreans, and others of Asiatic birth.

Chinese as sugar planters, rice planters, and as merchants are the largest importers and taxpayers of any other nation in the islands per capita.

As realty taxpayers, while the number of Chinese for 1915, is but 889—the least of any nationality—the assessed value of their real property was $2,084,350. The assessed value of personal taxes paid by our race is $2,224,647, almost equal to the assessed value of the Anglo-Saxons who are greater in number than the Chinese, and far above that paid by any oriental nation, in proportion, which far exceed them in population.

Notwithstanding the fact that the population of the Chinese is less than a fourth of the population of the Japanese, hundreds of our Chinese residents own their own places of business, sugar fields, pineapple plantations, rice paddies, stores, and homes, the latter of which are in conformity with all American ideas.

As business men our race is highly regarded, not only locally among the wholesale houses here, but also by firms on the mainland whose business is transacted for them between merchants, occidental and oriental—by resident island representatives. Orders for American manufactured goods are eagerly sought for among Chinese merchants, because they know of the honesty, integrity, and faithfulness in meeting their obligations, as a majority, above that of all other oriental nations.

In the great conflagration of 1886, with a loss to our race of $1,500,000, and again in 1900, on an absolute loss by fire of $2,000,000 to Chinese merchants, with nothing to offer but their bare word that the obligations outstanding at those times would be met if given time, the wholesale and commission houses accepted these terms, and in no case was their confidence misplaced, notwithstanding the years of hard work, close economy, and privations of our merchants, every dollar and interest has been liquidated.

Instances can be cited where Chinese merchants have failed owing considerable sums, passed through bankruptcy, and been absolved by law. These men have uncomplainingly returned to menial labor, toiling for years to pay back their indebtedness, often with interest, to the last cent.

Comparing our imports from the United States in comparison to our race population and compared with that of other nations here, we are far in excess. However, if the Chinese had been accorded the same privileges as other oriental nations, both the imports and exports would to-day be the largest of any on these islands.

Our bank interest and dealings, deposits, exchanges, sight drafts, loans, letters of credit, and all that goes to make up finance are all made with banks doing business under the American Government.

The new Chinese-American Bank recently organized is incorporated under the laws of the Territory of Hawaii and is in every phase of its business truly an American institution.

Ninety per cent of goods handled by our Chinese merchants, both wholesale and retail, are of American production and manufacture—this being a marked difference with the majority of goods handled by wholesale (especially) and retail merchants of other Oriental nations, which are made and produced in the Far East, and for which millions of American-earned money is sent yearly for their purchase, the government here and the revenue of import receiving but a small percentage—thus demonstrating that the United States of America is vitally interested in merchandise offered for sale by Chinese merchants, wholesale and retail. Therefore, if the same conditions of labor were allowed the Chinese as other oriental nations on these islands the imports of American goods would be far in excess of these of the present day, by at least $10,000,000 a year to America, on purchase. And naturally would that amount be a benefit to white labor on the mainland; an increase of revenue to the manufacturer, railroads, steamship companies, taxes to the Territory, and revenues to the Federal Government.

This matter alone is worthy of your consideration from a standpoint of financial loss as an amelioration of the distinction now made between the Chinese and other residents here of oriental birth or parentage.

The Chinese of Hawaii have always been a law-abiding race, no matter under what government the Islands have been. Tong wars have never been nor do they exist in Hawaii. Our Tongs or societies are purely benevolent and eleemosynary institutions, for without ever seeking aid beyond our own race we take care of our sick, needy, and aged, never burdening or having recourse to the charities of other races.

We have always been willing contributors and subscribers to the great disasters of the world—earthquakes, floods, disasters at sea, war-relief and Red Cross fund, etc.—also lending our financial aid to the local charities of the islands as well as assisting in matters of promotion, pageantry, etc.

Morally we point with justifiable pride to our men and women, especially the latter, for we honestly say that 99 per cent are virtuous and conduct themselves as patterns of morality as wives, mothers, and daughters. And there can not be found in the haunts of vice, segregated or otherwise, in the whole of the Territory of Hawaii a Chinese woman who is an habitue, resident, frequenter, or servant in any place or district where prostitution is known to exist. This can not be said of the women of other nations on these islands. Recently a canvass was made of the known residents of the segregated district in Honolulu, and out of 107 of these unfortunate women 82 were of oriental birth, but not a single Chinese woman. The marriage law with our race is sacred, whether the ceremony is performed under the old Chinese custom of religion, the civil law of the Territory, or by those who have embraced Christianity, and only in very rare and extreme cases is the law of divorce sought or yet desertion of husband or wife.

As a strong and further reason for admission of Chinese labor to this Territory there recently appeared through our local press a communication to the effect that President Wilson appointed a commission to inquire into the means of food conservation in case of war with any other nation. In Hawaii 136,000 people consume on an average 60 pounds of rice per month per person. Is this commodity, in the vast quantity required, being grown on these islands to-day? No; hundreds of thousands of sacks are imported from Japan yearly. Why? No Chinese laborers are admitted under the exclusion laws. Rice to-day is raised at a loss. Hundreds of acres of rice land have been abandoned for want of labor and other races find it more profitable to secure labor in the cane fields than cultivate rice, thus making Japanese rice $1.75 a sack higher to the consumer than Hawaiian grown rice.

The foregoing statements are made with a view to endeavor, if possible, that the Government of the United States of America, and the Republic of China can enter into a special agreement for the Territory of Hawaii; that Chinese laborers may be admitted to the islands; that the same privileges be accorded to the Chinese race as to other nations of oriental race.

The Chinese are not the only Asiatic people here, there

are Koreans, Siamese, Burmese, Malays, and Japanese. The latter are the most numerous, having a population here of over 92,000. If none of these Orientals are interfered with, why should the Chinese be? We are law-abiding and have no desire to enter into or meddle with the affairs of the Government. All we ask is to be treated the same as people of other oriental nations. Is it justice to single out the Chinese for exclusion? We fear this has an effect of lowering China in the eyes of the world. We have endeavored to show that the Chinese are pioneers of the great industries of these islands; that it is not for the best interest of Hawaii to exclude Chinese from these islands where circumstances and all commercial life is totally different wherever the United States holds jurisdiction. And situated as these islands are, 2,000 miles from the American Continent there is not the slightest danger of competing or conflicting with white labor, and where there need not be any discrimination of nations of oriental birth or origin, but on the contrary by the admission of Chinese laborers the rice industry will again take its place of culture and progress. Land once under cultivation will again be put to its former use. Other lands now wastes and swamps will be acquired, and for this imports and exports beneficial to the Federal Government. Taxes in greater proportion to the Territory, as well as banking business and increase of sales, for commodities and necessities of life to the wholesale dealers and manufacturers agents in Hawaii.

These facts now placed before you are not intended as asking for privileges for the Chinese to the whole of the United States but for the benefit of the Territory of Hawaii only.

Trusting that American justice will be accorded to us. The Constitution and flag of the United States are ours to live under, respect, and obey; to you we look for protection; to the United States we give our loyalty.

That all men be equal under the law is the petition of all the Chinese of Hawaii.

THE UNITED CHINESE SOCIETY.
YEE YAP, President.

Appendix J

Chinese Population, 1853–1960*

Census Year	Number	Per cent of Total Population
1853	364	0.5
1860	816	1.2
1866	1,306	2.0
1872	2,038	3.6
1878	6,045	10.4
1884	18,254	22.6
1890	16,752	18.6
1896	21,616	19.8
1900	25,767	16.7
1910	21,674	11.3
1920	23,507	9.2
1930	27,179	7.4
1940	28,774	6.8
1950	32,376	6.5
1960	38,119	6.0

* Andrew W. Lind, *Hawaii's People,* 3rd ed. (Honolulu: University of Hawaii Press, 1967), p. 28.

Appendix K

Arrivals and Departures of Chinese, 1879–1898*

Year	Arrivals	Departures	Net
1879	3,812	337	+3,475
1880	2,505	828	+1,677
1881	3,924	984	+2,940
1882	1,362	1,076	+ 286
1883	4,243	1,056	+3,187
1884	2,708	1,417	+1,291
1885	3,108	1,618	+1,490
1886	1,766	1,571	+ 195
1887	1,546	1,494	+ 52
1888	1,526	1,529	− 3
1889	439	1,508	−1,069
1890	654	1,567	− 913
1891	1,386	1,982	− 596
1892	1,802	1,148	+ 654
1893	981	1,235	− 254
1894	1,459	1,268	+ 191
1895	2,734	1,136	+1,598
1896	5,280	1,589	+3,691
1897	4,481	1,614	+2,867
1898	3,100	1,784	+1,316
	[48,816]	[26,741]	[22,075]

* From Customhouse Reports (Archives of Hawaii).

The table includes figures for both contract laborers and free immigrants as well as merchants and their families traveling to and from China on permits. Re-entry figures for plantation laborers are included in arrivals.

Appendix L

Chinese Laborers on Sugar Plantations, 1882–1924*

Year	Chinese	Total
1882	5,037	10,243
1886	5,626	14,539
1888	5,727	15,578
1890	4,517	17,895
1892	2,616	20,536
1894	2,784	21,294
1896	6,289	23,280
1897	8,114	24,653
1898	7,200	28,579
1899	5,969	35,987
1901	4,976	39,587
1902	3,937	42,242
1904	3,738	45,820
1905	4,138	45,243
1906	3,684	41,525
1907	3,248	44,447
1908	2,916	46,918
1909	3,561	41,702
1910	2,761	43,917
1911	2,758	45,048
1912	2,741	47,345

* Figures extracted from Table 15, p. 26, Romanzo Adams, *The Peoples of Hawaii* (Honolulu: Institute of Pacific Relations, 1925).

Appendixes

Year	Chinese	Total
1913	2,561	45,600
1914	2,229	46,043
1915	2,208	45,704
1916	1,997	43,961
1917	2,129	45,000
1918	1,895	44,708
1919	1,908	45,231
1920	2,378	44,304
1921	1,639	38,593
1922	1,487	44,402
1923	1,517	46,648
1924	1,421	44,378

Appendix M

Age and Sex Distribution of Chinese in Hawaii, 1910, 1920, 1930*

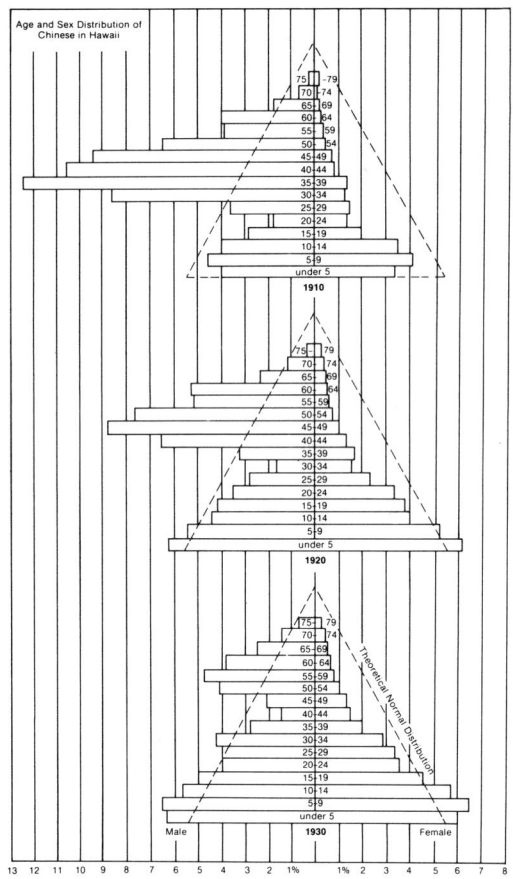

*Kum Pui Lai, "Occupational and Educational Adjustments of the Chinese," *Chinese of Hawaii* (Honolulu: Overseas Penman Club, 1936), p. 4.

Notes

Abbreviations
    AH   Archives of Hawaii
    HBC Hawaii Bureau of Conveyances
    JHKBRAS *Journal of the Hong Kong Branch of the Royal Asiatic Society*

CHAPTER 1

1. For a concise summary of China's history, see Chu and Winberg Ch'ai, *The Changing Society of China,* 2nd ed. rev. (New York: New American Library, 1962). See also Edwin O. Reischauer and John K. Fairbank, *East Asia: The Great Tradition,* 2nd ed. (Boston: Houghton Mifflin Co., 1960) for historical background.
2. Stuart C. Miller, *The Unwelcome Immigrant* (Berkeley and Los Angeles: University of California Press, 1969), p. 39.
3. U.S., Congress, House, *Executive Documents,* 27th Cong., 3rd sess., 1842–1843, no. 35, *Sandwich Islands and China.* It is noteworthy that King Kamehameha III sent commissioners Richards and Haalilio to Washington in 1842 to ask for formal treaty recognition of the Kingdom, which, in less than half a century, had made rapid advances from a primitive, feudal state to a constitutional monarchy under Anglo-American tutelage.
4. Foreigners from the West doing business in Hawaii in the same period also reacted to Chinese regulations on the Canton trade: "Now supposing the fanatical Emperor of China has kicked up a dust, or expelled the barbarians from China . . . petitions should be got up and forwarded to the nations whose flags are thus insulted, praying that a squadron of 4 ferry boats be sent to obtain satisfaction" (Ladd & Co. to Hooper, 5 June 1838, MS62-1082, unpublished "Hooper Letters," University of Hawaii, Sinclair Library).
5. Ta Chen, *Chinese Migrations, with Special Reference to Labor Conditions* (Washington: Government Printing Office, 1923), p. 6.
6. William Theodore de Bary, Wing-Tsit Chan, and Burton Watson, eds., *Sources of Chinese Tradition* (New York: Columbia University Press, 1963), pp. 680–704.
7. Ta Chen, *Chinese Migrations,* p. 6.
8. Ssu-yu Teng and John K. Fairbank et al., eds., *China's Response to the West: A Documentary Survey, 1839–1923* (Cambridge: Harvard University Press, 1954; paperback edition, New York: Atheneum, 1963), p. 1.
9. Carter to Cummins, 24 November 1890, "Report of Minister of Foreign Affairs," pp. 33–44, 101–103 (AH): "As to the Chinese treaty, the Chinese

minister told me privately that the Viceroy said that if they made a treaty with Hawaii, and then any trouble grew up, they would be obliged to enforce the rights of the Chinese and that might lead to trouble, that now if a Chinaman complained they could say well, you know we have no treaty there, and so avoid trouble. He said that the Chinese had better stay at home."

10. Ruhl J. Bartlett, ed., *The Record of American Diplomacy* (New York: Alfred A. Knopf, Inc., 1960), p. 423.
11. Chester G. Fuson, "The Geography of Kwangtung," *Lingnan Science Journal* 6:244. See also Hsu Ti-shan, *Research into the History of Hongkong-Kowloon Region* (Hong Kong: Society for the Advancement of Chinese Culture, 1941), text in Chinese.
12. "Dr. Sun Linked Closely With Hawaii," *Hawaii Chinese Journal,* November 1943 (Dr. Sun Yat-sen 77th birthday anniversary edition), p. 27.
13. Gravestones in Chinese cemeteries in Hawaii reveal that Hoklo men had come here. Earlier Chinese usually put the name and county of origin of the deceased on the gravestone. At Hook Chu cemetery in Honolulu, among other Hoklo and their families, there is the grave of a Hoklo named Akaka (Lee Shak) who died in 1920 at age ninety. He was the grandfather of the Reverend Abraham Akaka, present pastor of Kawaiahao Church of Honolulu. Because the Hawaiian language had no *s* or *sh* sounds, the name Shak became Kak, with the *a*'s added for euphony, thus Akaka.
14. Men of Shantung origin are identified on reburial gravestones in Puehuehue cemetery at Lahaina, Maui, and in the Chee Ying fraternal society cemetery in Honokaa, island of Hawaii. *Report of the Hawaiian Board of Evangelical Association,* 1898, p. 39: "At Waihee [Maui] there are 38 men from the Shantung Province, North China; they are interesting people and in many respects quite different from other Chinese in our midst."
15. Nancy Austin McLaren, "Russian Immigration: Hawaii" (M.A. thesis, University of Hawaii, 1951).
16. Francis William Damon (1852–1915) was better known as Frank Damon. He became superintendent of the Chinese Mission (Congregational) in Hawaii in 1881 (Albertine Loomis, *To All People* [Kingsport, Tenn.: Kingsport Press, 1970], pp. 189–190).
17. The Reverend Samuel C. Damon (1825–1885) was seamen's chaplain in Honolulu. His paper advocated temperance and politically held the "opposition" view. For a comprehensive view of Hawaii during the years 1778 to 1893, see Ralph S. Kuykendall, *The Hawaiian Kingdom,* 3 vols. (Honolulu: University of Hawaii Press, 1957–1967), 1:241.
18. "Coolie" was originally a Tamil term used in British India to mean "hired laborer." A coolie was a burden bearer, a porter, or a menial employed by Europeans. The word was used contemptuously in India to imply debased class. It is not a Chinese word, but in time it was translated into Chinese. In *Kuo Yu* ("national speech"), the characters used are *k'u-li* ("bitter strength"), and this was used by Gunther Paul Barth in *Bitter Strength: a History of the Chinese in the United States, 1850–1870* (Cambridge: Harvard University Press, 1964). The Cantonese translation is *goo-li* ("to hire a rough man"). Today in Hong Kong or Canton, the more polite terms of *gung-yan* ("working man") or *gung-yau* ("working friend") are used.

When Chinese were recruited under contract to work in Hawaii, British

Notes to Pages 25–36

North Borneo, South Africa, Cuba, British Guiana, and Peru, they were popularly identified as Chinese coolies. Contract laborers recruited from India to work in South Africa and India were called Indian coolies. By usage in the United States, coolie has been taken to mean "Chinese laborer" or "cheap labor." Stuart C. Miller made this observation: "In spite of the many public and private assurances to the contrary, the Chinese immigrant never lost his association with the coolie, an appellation readily bestowed upon him by friend or foe alike" (*The Unwelcome Immigrant*, p. 152).

19. Frank Damon meant Tin Hau ("heavenly queen") who was patron saint of seamen and fisherfolk. She was a Fukienese who kept a lighthouse, which saved many souls, and was officially canonized by the Imperial Board of Rites. She is one of the more popular folk deities worshiped in South China. See S. F. Balfour, "Hong Kong before the British," *JHKBRAS* 10:134–179.
20. The traditional Chinese family in China gained wide approval and respect if four generations lived together under one roof (*"See doi toong tong"*).
21. The chapter begins: "Let not your heart be troubled: ye believe in God, believe also in me.
 "In my Father's house are many mansions: if it were not so, I would have told you. I go to prepare a place for you.
 "And if I go and prepare a place for you, I will come again, and receive you unto myself; that where I am, there ye may be also" (John 14:1–3).
22. Henry V. Noyes. See Alexander Wylie, *Memorials of Protestant Missionaries to the Chinese* (1867; reprint ed., Taipei: Ch'eng-Wen Publishing Co., 1967), p. 277.

CHAPTER 2

1. Theodore Morgan, *Hawaii: A Century of Economic Change, 1778–1876* (Cambridge: Harvard University Press, 1948), pp. 61–68. The flow of traffic between Hawaii and China was greatly expanded in the nineteenth century. Three types of trade flourished: the fur trade from 1780 to 1830; sandalwood, 1790–1840; and whaling, 1820–1840.
 Long sea voyages were not unknown to the Chinese; overseas contacts had been made in the Earlier Han Dynasty (202 B.C.–A.D.9). There is an interesting account by a Chinese crewman who worked on a foreign sailing vessel for fourteen years (1783–1797), stopping at the principal ports of Europe, North and South America, and Asia. See Kenneth Ch'en, trans., "The Hai Lu: An Eighteenth-Century Seaman," *Monumenta Serica* 7:208–226; reprinted in Jeanette Mirsky, *The Great Chinese Travelers* (New York: Pantheon Books, 1964), pp. 263–272.
2. Joseph Feher, *The Pictorial History of Hawaii* (Honolulu: Bishop Museum Press, 1965), p. 145.
3. John Meares, *Voyages Made in 1788–1789 from China to the Northwest Coast of America* (1791; reprinted ed., New York: Da Capo Press, 1971); extracts in Bruce Cartwright, Jr., ed., *Hawaiian Historical Society Reprint No. 1*, p. 31 and Appendix.
4. F. W. Howay, "The Story of Winee," *Paradise of the Pacific*, March 1938, pp. 7–8.

5. William Dewitt Alexander, "Early Visitors for the Hawaiian Islands," *Hawaiian Annual,* 1890, p. 43.
6. Kuykendall, *Hawaiian Kingdom,* 1:23.
7. Ibid., 1:24–25.
8. *Honolulu Star-Bulletin,* 10 August 1939; Ah Jook Leong Ku, "First Chinese Came Before Vancouver," *The Chinese in Hawaii* (Honolulu: Chinese Chamber of Commerce, 50th anniversary edition, 1961), p. 21.
9. King Kamehameha I was attracted by the high profits of the sandalwood trade, and in 1816 he bought a foreign-built vessel, refitted and loaded it with a full cargo of sandalwood for Canton. Upon its return, the supercargo rendered his accounts of pilot fees, port charges, customs, stevedoring, and expenses of officers and crew while in China. Kamehameha lost money on this venture, but he learned a valuable lesson. From then on, he imposed pilotage dues and port charges on foreign goods brought in by foreign vessels to Hawaii (Joseph K. Goodrich, *The Coming Hawaii* [Chicago: McClurg Co., 1914], pp. 214–215).
10. George Vancouver (1757–1798), *Voyages of Discovery to the North Pacific Ocean and Round the World* (New York: Da Capo Press, 1968), 3:67.
11. Edward Bell, "Log of the Chatham," *Honolulu Mercury,* September 1929, pp. 7–26.

    Adelbert von Chamisso (1781–1838) wrote in 1818, "Commerce in the Sandwich Islands gathers the most motley pattern of people from all over the world. . . . Here for the first time I saw Chinese men. . . . (Chinese are frequently employed in this oceanic basin as seamen; they are obedient and easy to feed)" (Victor S. K. Houston, trans., "Chamisso in Hawaii," *Hawaiian Historical Society Annual Report* [Honolulu: 1939], p. 76). Chamisso was a German naturalist with the Russian Imperial Navy who visited Hawaii on two trips in 1817.
12. Carl T. Smith, "The Gillespie Brothers: Early Links between Hong Kong and China," *Chung Chi College Bulletin* (Chinese University of Hong Kong, December 1969).
13. Samuel S. Hill, *Travels in the Sandwich and Society Islands, 1849* (London: Chapman and Hall, 1856), pp. 306–307.
14. James W. Girvin, "Early Ones in the Islands," *Pacific Commercial Advertiser,* 1 January 1902; Lorrin A. Thurston, "Sugar—Its Status and Development," ibid. (50th anniversary edition), 2 July 1906.
15. Thomas G. Thrum, "Notes on the History of the Sugar Industry of the Hawaiian Islands," *Hawaiian Annual,* 1875, pp. 34–42.
16. Mary Clabaugh Wright, *The Last Stand of Chinese Conservatism* (Stanford: Stanford University Press, 1957), p. 76 and passim.

    In the closed shelves of the Library of Hawaii, Hawaiian and Pacific Room, is a copy of *Memoirs of Li Hung Chang* (Boston: Houghton Mifflin, 1923). It was a literary forgery with spurious evidences of authenticity. William Francis Mannix, the alleged editor, wrote the book while serving a sentence in Honolulu's county jail. His only experience in China was as a private in the United States Army during the Boxer Campaign in 1900.
17. Two of the steamers of the China Merchants' Steam Navigation Co., the *Ho-Chung* and the *Mei-Foo,* were used to transport contract laborers to Hawaii in 1879 and 1880. See "List of Arrivals of Immigrants," *Bureau of Immigration Reports, 1886,* pp. 266–277 (AH).

Notes to Pages 52–58

18. David Keawehaku was probably a brother of James Kiawehaku, but there is no explanation for the discrepancy in names.
19. James Hakuole, "My Impressions of Japan in 1882," *Pan-Pacific Magazine,* April–June 1937, pp. 23–24.
20. "Report of the Minister of Foreign Affairs to the Legislature of 1884," pp. 20–21 (AH).

CHAPTER 3

1. Robert C. Suggs, *The Island Civilizations of Polynesia* (New York: New American Library, 1906), p. 23.
2. Robert C. Schmitt, *Demographic Statistics of Hawaii: 1778–1965* (Honolulu: University of Hawaii Press, 1968), p. 75, Table 17.
3. Jacob Adler, *Claus Spreckels, the Sugar King in Hawaii* (Honolulu: University of Hawaii Press, 1966), p. 4.
4. Probate No. 3, First Circuit Court (AH); HBC, Book 2, p. 203.
5. Kuykendall, *Hawaiian Kingdom,* 1:175.
6. *Transactions of the Royal Hawaiian Agricultural Society* 1:50.
7. Hill, *Travels in the Sandwich Islands,* p. 305.
8. Aiko signed his name as Lum Jo in Chinese (HBC, Book 19, p. 220).
9. Charles Brewer & Co. had a freighting business between New England and various Pacific ports. It fitted out whaling vessels in Hawaii. By 1856, the company was involved in sugar, and the next year it was agency or sugar factor for four plantations and was later identified as one of the Big Five. See Josephine Sullivan, *History of C. Brewer & Co., 1826–1926* (Boston: Walton Co., 1926).
10. Samsing & Co., Tyhune, and Hungtai were three Chinese stores in Honolulu listed in the *Friend,* 11 August 1844, p. 72. Within the Samsing & Co. partnership were at various times, among others: Achi (Wong Chiu), Ahee (Mock Lee), Alum (Fung Look), Young Sheong, and Ahpong. At a later date, Ahpong signed documents as C. P. Samsing Co.
11. Kuykendall, *Hawaiian Kingdom,* 1:321. See also Laura Fish Judd, *Honolulu: Sketches of Life, Social, Political and Religious, in the Hawaiian Islands from 1828–1861* (Honolulu: Star-Bulletin, 1928), p. 149. She wrote that in the winter of 1849 "multitudes from California poured in upon us for food and shelter. . . . All the hotels, boarding houses, and untenanted buildings became full. Food grew scarce. Prices ran up exorbitantly high. . . . Spring came and the tide of humanity set back to the El Dorado."
12. A. D. Blue, "Chinese Emigration and Deck Passenger Trade," *JHKBRAS* 10:79–93. The greatest abuses in the emigrant trade involved South America and the West Indies. For example, a British ship left Hong Kong in 1856 with 332 emigrants for Cuba. The shipmaster reported losing 128 from suicide and disease during the voyage—38.2 percent. Losses up to 40 percent were not uncommon on such long voyages. It is not surprising then that the emigrant trade was called the "pig trade"—a reference to the Chinese custom of carrying pigs to market in round baskets. In Hawaii, some contract laborers used to say that they came as *mai chu dzai* ("sold as pigs"). While awaiting transportation from Macao, men were often locked in barracoons to prevent them from changing their minds and escaping. Some of them had been kidnapped or were losers at the gambling tables who had to honor their bets by selling themselves.

Notes to Pages 58–61

For a Chinese view of the coolie trade, see Ch'en Li-teh, *History of Chinese Emigration* (Shanghai: Chung Hua Publishing Co., 1946), p. 73.

13. The Chinese were not the only victims of vicious coolie traders. Norma McArthur (*Island Populations of the Pacific* [Honolulu: University of Hawaii Press, 1968], p. 184) wrote that "in 1862 and 1863 these Northern Cook Islands were amongst those raided by the vessels which had been chartered to engage 10,000 Polynesians to work in the copper mines of Peru and guano deposits in the Chincha Islands. Ostensibly, the natives were to be recruited under contract, but no such terms were honored by either the recruiters or the employers, and when the island chiefs proved reluctant to allow their people to leave their islands, the slavers used all sorts of ruses to entice the islanders to board their ships."
14. MacNair, *Chinese Abroad*, p. 218.
15. Schmitt, *Demographic Statistics*, pp. 4–6.
16. MacNair, *Chinese Abroad*, p. 219.

    The first attempt, in 1850, to bring in Chinese contract laborers failed. The Royal Hawaiian Agricultural Society had advanced $9,000 to $10,000 to G. F. Hubertson to import two hundred Chinese workers. After his ship, the *Amazon*, arrived in China, there was no further news of him (*Transactions of the Royal Hawaiian Agricultural Society* 1:91).
17. "Report of President of Bureau of Immigration to Legislative Assembly," *Bureau of Immigration Reports, 1886*, p. 23 (AH).
18. *Hawaiian Annual*, 1909, p. 129.
19. A complete list of Chinese surnames is found in *Po Chia Hsing* ("*Hundred Clan Names*"). Actually, there are 408 single surnames and 30 double surnames. The surname is always given first, whether in writing or orally. One may have a single given name or a double given name—Wong Hoon or Wong Ming-Hoon. In order to avoid the abruptness of calling this person only by his given name, Hoon, or the formality of Ming-Hoon, family and friends adopt the familiar style of calling him Ah-Hoon. "Ah" has no meaning. It is only used euphonically as a prefix, similar to English diminutives like Billie for Bill or Johnny for John. The difference is that the Chinese euphonic syllable is a prefix whereas the English one is a suffix.

    The early Chinese immigrants found it difficult to identify themselves by their full Chinese names because they did not know how to romanize them. Thus, on ships' manifests, their names appear as Ah Hoon, Ah Wai, Ah Ki, Ah Wan, etc. Their Hawaiian neighbors found it easier to call them Ahuna, Awai, Aki, Awana. In some cases, like Hew Len or Lee Loy, full Chinese names sounded good enough for Hawaii-born generations to use them as surnames. The Hawaiianization of Chinese names continues, and in some cases the correct surname is lost. Such is the interaction of different cultures.
20. "Naturalization Book B" (AH). For conversion before naturalization, see Hill, *Travels in Sandwich Islands*, pp. 305–317.

    Chinese and other foreigners became naturalized not only to marry Hawaiian women but also for business reasons. A notice was promulgated by the Home Office of the Hawaiian government on 16 June 1847 in the *Polynesian* that aliens had to be naturalized to become a co-partner in a mercantile and other business or to hold property. American missionaries who, after their support from the American Board of Foreign Missions ended, chose to

Notes to Pages 61–64

remain in the Islands found it necessary to apply for Hawaiian citizenship like other foreigners in order to go into business and enter into real estate transactions.
21. *Bureau of Immigration Report, 1882–1898,* 1:266–277 (AH).
22. Kuykendall, *Hawaiian Kingdom,* 1:330.
23. W. H. Wright, "Chinese Immigration," *Hawaiian Annual,* 1894, pp. 70–78.
24. *Laws, 1856–1800; Civil Code, 1859;* "Laws and Regulations Restricting Chinese Immigration to Hawaiian Islands," Chinese Bureau of Department of Foreign Affairs, 1896 (AH). See also Lawrence McCully, ed., *Statutes of the Hawaiian Kingdom* (Honolulu: Honolulu Advertiser, 1882), relating to apprentices and contract laborers, with a synopsis of the rulings and decisions of the Supreme Court of which McCully was justice. There is also a Chinese translation printed in Canton by order of the Hawaiian government in 1883.
25. William Speer, "Chinese in Sandwich Islands," *Friend,* May 1856, p. 36.
26. Andrew W. Lind, *An Island Community* (New York: Greenwood Press, 1968), p. 194.
27. "Report to Minister of Interior and President of Bureau of Immigration," Chinese Immigration File, Bureau of Immigration, 1 (1865): 22–23 (AH). See also *Bureau of Immigration Report, 1886,* p. 23.

The Reverend William Lobscheid's method of recruiting was simply by advertising. He wrote articles for Chinese newspapers in which he described the Sandwich Islands and dwelt on their close proximity to China, good climate, and good government. He stressed that the recruitment was conducted entirely by the Hawaiian Government through a specially appointed commissioner and was in no way a private speculation. All applicants were directed to the Wo Hang Co. Lobscheid was made Hawaiian vice-commissioner of immigration on the departure of Dr. William Hillebrand from China for Honolulu.

28. A dramatic exception was the murder of Jules Dudoit, French consul, by a mistreated Chinese servant. Dudoit was *persona non grata* to the Hawaiian government, "a continual thorn in the flesh" (Kuykendall, *Hawaiian Kingdom,* 1:388–389). Dudoit was probably a hard taskmaster demanding perfection from Ah See, the murderer, and his other servants to the point of cruel punishment and humiliation. Dr. Richard Hinds, a surgeon on board the British exploration ship *H.M.S. Sulphur* attended a dancing party given by Dudoit and made this comment, "The servants were all Chinese, here they are called Chinamen, a great many of the people are employed in this way, and they are not so slow or silly in appearance as we imagine at home. In dress they are neat and quiet and attentive to our wants" (E. Alison Kay, ed., "Journal of the Voyage of the *H.M.S. Sulphur,* 1836–1842," *Hawaiian Journal of History* 2:110). See also Alan Gavan Daws, "Honolulu, 1st Century to 1876" (Ph.D. diss., University of Hawaii, 1966), pp. 593–594, on Ah See.
29. Kuykendall, *Hawaiian Kingdom,* 3:119. Chulan & Co. and Afong and Achuck were prominent business firms, the former active in rice and the latter in sugar.

The Chinese remained a cohesive group in voicing their complaints and desires. Following the 1869 petitions, there were other occasions when they met collectively and voiced their opinions. See Appendix G on the mass

meeting of 14 February 1894 at the Chinese Theater to protest against proposed legislation by the Provisional Republic.
30. Lind, *An Island Community,* p. 193.
31. *Bureau of Immigration Reports, 1884–1886,* 1:162.
32. Reischauer and Fairbank, *East Asia,* pp. 355–356.
33. Göran Aijmer, "Expansion and Extension in Hakka Society" *JHKBRAS* 7:42–79. Ronald Ng, "Economic Life and the Family," *Weekend Symposium, Hong Kong Branch, Royal Asiatic Society,* 9–10 May 1964, pp. 32–35.
34. Kuykendall, *Hawaiian Kingdom,* 3:170. *Report of Minister of Foreign Affairs to Legislative Assembly of 1884,* p. 16 (AH), "But the influx of people from the vast and populous Empire of China has at times been in excess of the requirements of this country, or disproportioned to what may be termed a due equilibrium of races in a small State which is inviting people from all parts of the world. . . ."
35. Ta Chen, *Chinese Migrations,* p. 119.
36. R. C. Lydecker, "Memorandum on the Introduction of Foreign Laborers into the Hawaiian Islands," 1910 report prepared for the Secretary of Hawaii (AH).
37. *Bureau of Immigration Report, 1894,* p. 13 (AH).
38. Also called "Pake Camp." "Samsing Camp" at Puunene on the island of Maui was named after the Samsing Co. which had a sugar plantation on Maui and imported Chinese contract laborers. Pahon (Pak On) Camp of Kekaha Sugar Co. was named for Leong Pak On who was one of the largest rice producers on the island of Kauai (*Honolulu Star-Bulletin,* 11 March 1937).
39. George N. Wilcox (1839–1933), philanthropist prominent in business and political circles.
40. *Hawaiian Gazette,* 27 October 1869.
41. In reply to a complaint concerning the quarantine of the vessel *Madras* in 1883, the Hawaiian government wrote to James Wodehouse, British commissioner and consul general to Hawaii, and stated the problems it had encountered involving uninvited Chinese immigrants. The letter stated that tramp ships roving for freight business under unprincipled captains often ventured to take loads of labor passengers. The laborers on these vessels were unaccompanied by a licensed physician and suffered under substandard conditions such as poor sanitation and overloading of passengers. Mutinous passengers complained of having been shanghaied. Bills of health were counterfeited to hide cases of smallpox and other infectious diseases, or passengers jumped overboard while the ships waited for inspection or quarantine so that many sick cases escaped the quarantine guards. It was an unhappy situation for all except the labor speculators.

See *Report of Minister of Foreign Affairs to the Legislative Assembly of 1886,* pp. xlvi–xlix; cf. A. D. Blue, "Chinese Emigration and the Deck Passenger Trade," *JHKBRAS* 10:79–93.
42. "The Chinese Question in Hawaii," *Hawaiian Annual,* 1890, pp. 81–90.
43. As China did not have treaty relations with the Hawaiian Kingdom, the Chinese government appointed a community leader, Chun Afong, as commercial agent in 1879 instead of sending a consular representative. Instructions from the Chinese Embassy in Washington, D.C., to *Shang Tung*

Notes to Pages 83–88

("Commercial Agent") Chun Afong, are contained in Wu Shang-ying, *One Hundred Years of the Chinese in America* (Hong Kong: Carlo Press, 1965), pp. 461–462 (in Chinese). "Chinese Immigration Miscellaneous File, 1877–1890" (AH) has a copy of Commercial Agent Chun Afong's report on smallpox on the ship *Septima* upon its arrival in Honolulu. It was translated from the 18 July 1881 issue of the *Shun Wan Daily News* in Hong Kong. In 1882 Ching Alee and Goo Kim Fui (Goo Kim) served as commercial agents to represent Chinese interests. The first official consul, Yang Wei-Pin, was appointed by Peking in 1898 when Hawaii was annexed to the United States.

44. "Chinese Immigration," Interior Department Miscellaneous, 26 July 1865 (AH). Dr. Charles F. Guillou reported to the Board of Immigration on his inspection of new arrivals landed by the Chilean bark *Matador* at anchor outside Honolulu harbor: "The fifty men examined are all of the Chinese races: they are all able-bodied and in sound health, with the exception of the two men designated as No. 9 and No. 23. No. 9 has inguinal hernia of the right groin; he is however muscularly well developed and otherwise robust. No. 23 is laboring under pulmonary disease probably phthysis in its incipient stage. They all bear marks of having undergone smallpox." In "Contracts Assigned" (ibid., 28 October 1868), Haiku Sugar Co. of Maui reported that of contracted arrivals on the *Roscate* four had died on the plantation—No. 272 committed suicide by hanging, No. 162 died from bursting centrifugal machinery, No. 242 died from child delivery, and No. 259 died from inflammation of bowels.

45. John W. Vandercook, *King Cane: Story of Sugar in Hawaii* (New York: Harper, 1939), pp. 52–57, on labor relations: "Two factors have always been at work in the relationship of the island employers to the people employed by them. The majority of managers, there seems no doubt, have been to some extent ruled by a moral attitude. Even to pretend such a thing in a business relationship seems ingenuous. Laws of profit and of power and the law of supply and demand have more commonly been in force in fields and factories than moral laws. But in Hawaii, a by-the-book ethical attitude does appear to have been a reality. There were exceptions, surely. The blacksnake-wielding, heavy-fisted, damn-your-eyes type of planter in the early days was certainly not unknown—But, there were missionaries in Hawaii, rigid, intolerant men whose pious views came close to ruling the islands. Many of the planters were their sons and grandsons. Others were their friends and neighbors. There were few who did not live in awe of them. The missionaries' views were clear. They believed in work and there is no evidence they did not believe in profits. . . . But they did not believe in physical cruelty. A farmer who was brutal to his coolies was apt to find himself an outcast in the community—no trivial thing when a community is small."

Chapter 4

1. Francis A. Olmsted, *Incidents of a Whaling Voyage, 1841* (New York: C. E. Tuttle Co., 1969), p. 213. Sam and Mow became sugar planters on the island of Hawaii while Sam Sing Co. managed the bakery from 1843 to 1848 (Gorman D. Gilman, "Streets of Honolulu in the Forties," *Hawaiian*

Notes to Pages 88–90

Annual, 1904, pp. 74–101). Sam and Mow both drowned August 1848, while on a small boat which was trying to bring passengers into Honolulu harbor from a schooner off port by running through the surf in the dark (Richard A. Greer, "Honolulu in 1847," *Hawaiian Journal of History* 4:67).

2. When Chinese speak of themselves as being from Canton, they may mean from the province of Kwangtung and not necessarily from the city of Canton. The word *Cantonese* is used instead of *Kwangtungese*.
3. John Papa Ii, *Fragments of Hawaiian History, 1818–1832,* trans., Mary E. Pukui (Honolulu: Bishop Museum Press, 1963), p. 94.
4. The foreword to *Indices of the Board of Commissioners to Quiet Land Titles* (AH), explains the Great Mahele, the system of land divisions, grants, and titles; for "Principles . . ." see *Statute Laws* 2, pp. 81–94 or *Polynesia,* 19 June 1847.
5. Richard A. Greer, "I Remember Cunha's Alley," *Hawaiian Journal of History* 3:142–150.
6. First Circuit Court, Probate No. 3, Ahung (AH).
7. HBC, Book 7, p. 84 (HBC).
8. Interior Department Miscellaneous, September 1852; HBC, Book 1 (Miscell, Vessels), p. 2.
9. HBC, Book 9, pp. 283, 300.
10. W. D. Alexander, "A Brief History of Land Title in the Hawaiian Kingdom," *Hawaiian Annual,* 1891, pp. 106–124.
11. *Chinese of Hawaii* (Honolulu: Overseas Penman Club, 1929), Chinese section, p. 45.
12. *Naturalization Book D,* 2 June 1846 (AH). Aiina filed British Land Claims of 1843, No. 10 (AH) which included: (1) a sugar establishment at Piihonua, district of Hilo on the island of Hawaii; (2) a sugar establishment at nearby Makahanaloa; (3) fifty acres of land on lease for six years in Hilo; and (4) a residence in Honolulu.

Charles E. Peterson, "Pioneer Prefabs in Honolulu," *Hawaiian Journal of History* 5:25, 32–34. Prefabricated structures cut in China under the supervision of sea captains were brought here for reassembling. Aiina probably participated in putting up such buildings.

Stephen Reynolds' Journal, 1824–1845 (Cambridge: Harvard College Library Microfilms, no. 9258, Hawaiian Mission Children's Society) Monday, 23 February 1829: "The deputy Governor Kuanoa told Mr. French he must not let China carpenters work on Sunday."

Ethel M. Damon *(Koamalu: Story of Pioneers on Kauai* [Honolulu: private printing, 1931], pp. 8–10) tells of a beautifully constructed house with Chinese carved panels: "Its quaintly chiselled panels had been shaped by Chinese hands on Chinese soil, in days of the eighteen-forties. . . . Whole houses were shipped, cut, and fitted sometimes, it is said, of teak wood. And on voyages where only an insufficient return cargo lay ready to be had at the mouth of the teeming Canton river, the hold of the vessel was sometimes ballasted with hitching posts and millstones and paving slabs of white Chinese granite." Such slabs may be seen in downtown Honolulu on some sidewalk areas of Nuuanu, Smith, and Hotel streets. They are also in the Chinese courtyard of the Honolulu Academy of Arts.

13. Kauikeaouli was King Kamehameha III (1825–1854).

Notes to Pages 91–103

14. Alfons L. Korn, *The Victorian Visitors* (Honolulu: University of Hawaii Press, 1958), pp. 156–157. It is misleading to identify all Chinese in Hawaii at this time as contract laborers on sugar plantations. See Appendix L for figures on number of Chinese on Hawaii's sugar plantations.
15. Coulter and Chun, *Chinese Rice Farmers,* p. 63.
16. Dr. Coulter was professor of geography at the University of Hawaii. Hawaii-born Chun came from a rice planter's family. After graduation, he had been an agricultural economist in China and is presently with the Hua Chiao ("Overseas") Commercial Bank in Hong Kong.
17. The Lane McCandless mentioned by the writers was meant to be Lincoln Loy McCandless who arrived in Honolulu in 1882. His older brother James arrived in 1880, and another brother, John, in 1881.
18. Coulter noted that this information was from private conversations with W. L. Hopper, son of John Hopper, on 25 June 1936. The informant was then eighty years old having been born in 1856 (*Hawaiian Kingdom Statistical & Commercial Directory* [Honolulu: George Bowser & Co., 1880], p. 76).
19. *Pacific Commercial Advertiser,* 25 June 1892, as noted by Coulter and Chun.
20. Clifford B. Wood, M.D., "The Bubonic Plague," *Transactions of the Hawaii Medical Association Annual Meeting, 1926,* pp. 18–23.
21. *Chinese of Hawaii* (1929), Chinese section, pp. 8–10. Dr. Khai-Fai Li and his wife Dr. Kong Tai-Heong, both Western- (Rhenish Mission) trained physicians, had newly arrived in Honolulu. They took an active part in fighting the plague.

    At the Board of Health meeting, nearly all physicians of the city, including Chinese, were present. See *Pacific Commercial Advertiser,* 12 December 1899.

    Dr. Sun Chin has been identified as Chan Kok-Sun, Chinese herb physician at Wai Wa Hospital, a Chinese hospital from 1897 to about 1907 on King Street near Robello Lane, Honolulu.

    The Board of Health at its 14 February 1900 meeting approved the request of Chinese Consul Yang Wei-pin that Mrs. Li Khai-Fai (Dr. Kong), a Chinese physician, be allowed to be present when the Chinese women in the Kalihi Detention Camp took the final disinfecting bath before leaving quarantine. "Minutes of Board of Health Meetings, 1899–1900," p. 266 (AH).
22. Claims to Commission on 1900 Fire Losses (AH). For example, a fire loss to the household contents and personal effects of the Cha See Yick family that was inventoried at $242.05 was finally settled on 3 December 1901 for the reduced sum of $135. See Appendix H. See also Gavan Daws, *Shoal of Time* (Honolulu: University Press of Hawaii, 1974), p. 303.
23. Overseas Penman Club, *Chinese of Hawaii* (1929), Chinese section, p. 78. Mr. Chun came to Honolulu and opened a dry goods store at King and River streets. (He was so ashamed at seeing his fellow Chinese arrested for smoking opium and being marched to the police station with their pigtails tied one to the other that he joined others to start an Anti-Opium League and was its first president in 1907.) His son, Ellery Chun, took over the business and renamed it King-Smith Sportswear. He was the originator of Aloha Shirts and still holds the trademark, Aloha Shirts, registered on 15 July 1936.
24. See Honolulu Redevelopment Agency, *Chinatown* (Honolulu: 1972), for the

323

ongoing changes in the area. Chinese now form 19.9 percent of total Chinatown population. Filipinos form 46.6 percent of today's Chinatown population. See *Honolulu Star-Bulletin,* 25 February 1972, for census figures released by State Department of Planning and Economic Development. See also Andrew W. Lind, *Hawaii's People,* 3rd ed. (Honolulu: University of of Hawaii Press, 1967), pp. 55–56.

25. An official record in the *United Chinese Society 50th Anniversary Edition* ([Honolulu: 1934], p. 6), showed that the society called a special meeting on 19 February 1900 to solicit funds for the relief of 1,975 Chinese released from detention camps. Over $20,000 was raised. Beginning on February 28, each adult received one pound and each child half a pound of rice for daily relief until they were resettled.
26. For information on natural resources and people, see Kula County Extension Advisory Council, Honolulu Cooperative Extension Service, University of Hawaii, *Kula County Situation Report, 1959.*
27. Diane Mark, "Maui Safari Probes Old Chinese Community," *Honolulu Advertiser,* 29 August 1971.
28. The Reverend Shim Yin-Chin (1868–1918) graduated from the German Basel Theological Training School at Lilong in Pao On County, Kwangtung. He helped to establish the St. John's Episcopal Mission in Kula in 1900. For an account of his work and biographical materials on his wife, also a mission worker; his son, the Reverend Wai-On Shim of St. Elizabeth's Church of Honolulu; and the Reverend Kong Yin-Tet of St. Peter's Church of Honolulu, see *St. Peter's Church Anniversary Edition,* edited by the Reverend Yim-Sang Mark, 1936.
29. Kum Pui Lai, experienced social worker and researcher, produced in 1971 a much-needed "Index to *Social Process in Hawaii,* Vols. 1–26 (1935–1963)" (Sociology Dept., University of Hawaii).
30. Included in the curriculum of private tutors and of Hawaii's Chinese language schools was a course on Confucian ethics called *Sau Sun* ("Cultivation of Self"). This character training included stories of twenty-four examples of filial piety and of national heroes and classic personalities who conducted themselves in accordance with a strong moral code.
31. Founded in 1916 as the Chinese-American Bank. In 1935, the name was changed to American Security Bank.
32. In 1919, K. C. Ahana was elected treasurer of the County of Kauai. His brother K. M. Ahana started a long political career in 1924 as elected auditor of Kauai County. In 1926, Dr. Dai Yen Chang became the first Chinese elected to the Board of Supervisors of the City and County of Honolulu. In 1927, Yew Char became the first Chinese elected to the House of Representatives of the Territory of Hawaii. In 1929, Apau Paul Low from the island of Maui was elected a Senator in the Territorial Legislature.

On 7 July 1898, Congress had passed the Annexation Act, and Hawaii became a territory of the United States of America. Prior to this, a speech was made before the United States Congress in the House of Representatives on 11 June 1898 (in a debate on Joint Resolution 259 providing for the annexation of the Hawaiian Islands to the United States) by Missouri Congressman Champ Clark, "But how can we justify either to ourselves or to our posterity the act we are about to commit? How can we endure our shame when a Chinese Senator from Hawaii, with his pigtail hanging down his back, with his pagan joss in hand, shall rise from his curule chair and in pigeon English proceed to chop logic with George Frisbie Hoar or Henry Cabot Lodge?—A Chinaman never can be fit for American citizenship."

Later Champ Clark became Speaker of the House, and, in 1959, after statehood was granted, Hiram Leong Fong was elected the first senator from Hawaii.

33. *Report of the Hawaiian Evangelical Association,* 1886, pp. 31–34.
34. Japanese also use the local custom of calling the immigrant generation *issei* ("first generation") and the Hawaii-born generation as *nisei* ("second generation") with the rest following as third, fourth, fifth, etc.
35. Andrew W. Lind, *Hawaii's People,* p. 50.
36. Ch'en Kwong-Min, *Chinese in the Americas* (New York: Overseas Chinese Culture Publishing Co., 1950), p. 697.
37. *Chinese of Hawaii* (1936), p. 13.
38. Marion Wong and Richard Wong are not related. Marion is today Mrs. Samuel Lindley. Richard, then also a student, is the Reverend Richard Wong, author of *Prayers from an Island* (Richmond: John Knox Prints, 1968) and presently is pastor of Kaumakapili Church, Honolulu.
39. In China's male-oriented society, when a bride left her family, it was feared she would take away all the *fu* ("good fortune"). Hence, she walked beneath the trousers (also pronounced *fu* but written differently). Thus, the symbolic good fortune would remain with her older unmarried brother.
40. The plantations gave two or three days' holiday with pay for the Chinese laborers to celebrate. Students of Chinese ancestry in public schools in the 1910s were excused from classes. However, some fathers sent their children to school on these days, saying, "You are now Americans."

Chapter 5

1. Calvin Lee, *Chinatown, USA* (New York: Garden City Press, 1965), pp. 34–37, and "History of the Chinese Six Companies," *Chinese World* (San Francisco bilingual daily), 17 March 1956.
2. Wah Chan Thom, "A Study of Trade between China and Hawaii" (B.A. thesis, University of Hawaii, 1927), pp. 54–58. See also Thomas W. Chinn, "The *Wui* or Money Pool," in Chinn, ed., *History of Chinese in California* (San Francisco: Chinese Historical Society of America, 1969), p. 77.
3. Andrew W. Lind, *Hawaii, the Last of the Magic Isles* (London: Oxford University Press, 1969), pp. 95, 101, 120. See also Lucie Cheng Hirata, "Immigration Integration in a Polyethnic Society" (Ph.D. diss., University of Hawaii, 1971, no. 374).

Whenever a number of Chinese found themselves together in a strange land, they formed associations for the general welfare of each other. These associations assisted newcomers. They settled disputes between members, they carried on traditions and customs, and they provided respectable funerals for their members. This is a reflection of the *wah kiu* ("Chinese sojourner") idea of a temporary stay in a foreign country to earn enough money to retire in China to enjoy a higher economic and social status.
4. "Chinese Response to Anti-Chinese Agitation in Hawaii," in *Chinese of Hawaii* (1929), Chinese section, pp. 6–7. The United Chinese Society soon

Notes to Pages 148–160

assumed responsible leadership so that at times of anti-Chinese agitations, there was no need for armed defense. See Appendix I for a petition from the United Chinese Society, 29 August 1916, asking for (1) equal treatment with other Orientals instead of being singled out for exclusion, (2) admission of Chinese labor for rice and agricultural industries.

5. *Pan-Pacific Magazine* (October–December, 1937), pp. 45–55, has good photographs and articles about contemporary Chinese societies and the officers of the Chinese Chamber of Commerce, United Chinese Society, Chinese Civic Association, Ket On Society, and other Chinese organizations.

6. Its predecessor was the *Lung Kee Sun Bo* ("Hawaiian Chinese News")— "oldest Chinese language paper in Hawaii, 1881." Its 13 April 1889 copy (Bruce Cartwright, *Chinese Materials File M24* [AH], contains local and foreign news. It is filled with advertisements from the American business firms of Castle & Cooke, Spreckels Bank, Bishop Bank, Lewers & Cooke, Hollister Drug, and others. Chinese stores like Goo Kim's in Honolulu, Wing Wo Chan in Kohala, and Kwong Yick Lung in Kahului also put in their advertisements. Look Hop Wai Co. of Keanae, Maui, advertised that its rice plantation was for sale. Yee King Tong Cemetery Association in the Pauoa section of Honolulu put up a notice that those wishing to exhume or to bury could apply to Sun Gum Lung Store. There was also a list of 100 donors to the Chinese Protective League. Interpreters Ching On and Chang Kim advertised their services.

7. In 1928, the *United Chinese Press* became the official organ of the local Kuomintang. The paper carried a banner claiming to be the "outstanding Chinese newspaper in Hawaii." It gave preferential news coverage to Chung Shan Chinese language school, which had been started in 1912 to further Dr. Sun Yat-sen's program.

Chinese language papers had a small readership since most of the younger generation had a limited command of written Chinese. They obtained information on current events from the two metropolitan English dailies.

8. The *New China News* has been microfilmed by the University of Hawaii and the complete file is now available. The *New China News* (Sun Chung Kwock Bow) was established in 1900. It was a news organ started by the Bow Wong Wui (Protect Emperor Association or the Royal Protective Union of the Hawaiian Islands for the Support of Emperor Kuang-Hsu). It had been inspired by Chinese leaders of political thinking in China, K'ang Yu-Wei and Liang Chi-Chao. Their National Reform Movement had failed in China and both escaped abroad to avoid the wrath of the Empress Dowager. Liang spent some time in Hawaii in 1900.

The Reform party had a more conservative and Confucian approach to national reform than Dr. Sun Yat-sen's revolutionary program which succeeded with the establishment of the Republic of China in 1912. Members of the Reform party supported the Mun Lun Chinese language school. For a clear statement on reform vs. revolution in China, see Chai and Chai, *Changing Society of China*, pp. 204–221.

9. The clubhouse usually has wooden plaques adorning the doorways. Chinese words on them were painted in gold giving the society name. Door couplets have propitious sayings, dates, and names of donors. If it is a two-story building, the upper story will have a plaque over the lintel declaring it to be the Chung Yee Tong ("Hall of Loyalty and Righteousness"). The

initiation of new members into the brotherhood is conducted in this hall.
10. Two good sources on the Hoong Moon societies provide detailed information, especially translations of their secret initiation rites and other rituals. An early one was published in 1866 in Batavia. By Professor Gustave Schlegel, it was entitled *Thian Ti Wui*. The more recent publication is W. P. Morgan, *Triad Societies in Hong Kong* (Hong Kong: Government Press, 1960). Morgan's translation was used here because of its simplicity. Some members of Hoong Moon fraternal societies of Hawaii have photocopied Morgan's version to use as a handbook so that they can understand the Chinese language and traditions of the rituals and ceremonies of their lodge.
11. Clarence E. Glick, "Chinese Migrant in Hawaii" (Ph.D. diss., University of Chicago, 1938), p. 263. Professor Glick here quoted a case study: "When I first came here in the nineties, this (Hung Men) Society was very strong. There were hundreds of Chinese around here and most of them belonged to this Kung Si. When a Chinese got into trouble with another Chinese, it was a good thing to belong to this Society. If he belonged to no Society at all, there was no way of getting help. If he did belong to the Society, then he had the backing of the other men who were members. If both men or groups of men who got into trouble belonged to the Society, then they could bring up the matter before the headman to settle it. They would not think of going to the courts. The rest of the Chinese could get angry at any one who tried to do that."
12. Rose Hum Lee, "The *Hua-Chiao* in the United States of America," in Morton H. Fried, ed., *Colloquium on Overseas Chinese* (New York: Institute of Pacific Relations, 1958).
13. "Chinese Cemetery," *Paradise of Pacific Magazine*, July 1947, p. 21.
14. In a plantation camp there was no infirmary or health care facility for the sick and disabled. The seriously ill bachelor would go to his fraternal society house where lodging and cooking facilities were provided. Terminal cases received help from the society membership and from those ambulatory members who cooked and did daily chores. The sick and disabled did not die "lonely and neglected." At least, they were assured of health care and a decent burial. Today, convalescent and retirement homes, of course, provide better facilities and care and need not be called "death houses." In addition, the Social Security Act now provides funeral benefits.

CHAPTER 6

1. Kuykendall, (*Hawaiian Kingdom*, 1:116): "That no law shall be enacted which is at variance with the word of the Lord Jehovah, or at variance with the general spirit of His word. All laws of the Islands shall be in consistency with the general spirit of God's law."
2. Loren Fessler et al., *China* (New York: Life World Library, 1963), p. 78. See also Shao-Chang Lee, *Popular Buddhism in China* (Shanghai: Commercial Press, 1939).
3. Chai and Chai, *Changing Society in China*, pp. 150–155. See also E.T.C. Werner, *Dictionary of Chinese Mythology* (New York: Julian Press, 1961), pp. 225–227.
4. Dr. Min-Hin Li, a Western-trained physician and prominent civic leader, in

"Relation of Chinese Shrine Worship in Hawaii to Modern Medicine," (*Transactions of Hawaii Territorial Medical Association* [1926–1936], pp. 42–46) mentioned the competition of Chinese shrines with the practice of modern medicine. In cases where surgery was advised, the women in the family often postponed a decision until they had a chance to consult their shrine or temple.

5. Kuan Yin = Avalokitesvara (Arthur E. Wright, *Buddhism in Chinese History* [Stanford: Stanford University Press, 1959], p. 82).
6. The term *chim* as commonly used by local temple devotees represents the fortune sticks in the bamboo cylinder. It is here substituted for the author's *chi-chi* which is a hexagram used in the I-Ching (Book of Changes) system of divination.
7. For Chinese religious holidays, see Hartly H. Zeigler and Bernhard L. Hormann, "A Religious and Cultural Calendar for Hawaii," *Social Process in Hawaii* 16:59–67.
8. Ethel Damon in *Father Bond of Kohala* ([Honolulu: The Friend 1927], p. 269) touches upon this *esprit de corps* in telling about the church bell tower that needed repair, "Not a carpenter could be found in all Kohala who dared undertake to repair it. Only Ah Nee, the faithful Chinese workman at the Bond house, would venture it. And week after week he worked there by himself, creeping in gently and replacing one after another the rotten timbers with infinite care, until all was sound and firm." Children in the family were not stopped from learning to speak Hakka Chinese from domestic servants in the Bond household.
9. From unpublished notes on Basel-trained evangelists and missionaries in Hawaii by the Reverend Dennis A. Kastens of Our Savior Lutheran Church, Aiea, Oahu.
10. Samuel Couling, comp., *Encylopedia Sinica* (Shanghai: Kelly and Walsh, 1917), pp. 44–45, gave details of the various Hakka mission stations near Hong Kong, from which villages came most of Hawaii's Hakka Christians. See Tin-Yuke Char, "Chinese Christians among Early Immigrants Here," *Honolulu Advertiser*, 6 December 1970. Among those living in Hawaii today who read and write the Hakka colloquial are Mrs. Kong, widow of Pastor Kong Yin-Tet of St. Peter's Church and Mrs. Chong, widow of Pastor Chong How-Fo who had been pastor of Kula Chinese Church and the First Chinese Church of Honolulu.
11. In the biennial report for 1886–1888 (AH), the Department of Foreign Affairs of the Hawaiian Kingdom allotted $1,000 for the relief and return of indigent Hawaiians from abroad.
12. See Appendixes J and K for Chinese population figures and Table of Arrivals and Departures, respectively.
13. Loomis, *To All People*, pp. 181–193. Other mission leaders giving a helping hand to the Chinese Christians were the Reverend Norman C. Schenck as detailed in "Chinese Protestant Christian Life in Hawaii," (in *Chinese of Hawaii* [1929], pp. 21–24) and Bishop Henry B. Restarick who wrote of his experiences in *Hawaii from the Viewpoint of a Bishop* (Honolulu: Paradise of the Pacific, 1924) and other books.
14. Besides the YMCA of Honolulu, a Chinese YMCA was founded in 1877. In 1964, it changed its name to the Chinese Christian Association of Hawaii.

See "Chinese Christian Association Active for Three Generations," *Honolulu Advertiser*, 14 February 1972.
15. At Chaplain Lane near Nuuanu Street in Honolulu, where the Damon home stood for many years, the Christian Boarding School was established in 1892 to which many Chinese owed the English they mastered. Later it became Mills Institute and was moved to Manoa Valley next to the University of Hawaii. Oriental boys and girls from the outer islands as well as Oahu came to board there and to receive a Christian high-school education. Today it is called Mid-Pacific Institute.
16. Frank Damon used the term Chinese more often than Chinaman. The latter simply denoted a man from China. However, its feeling-tone could imply a derogatory usage. Chinese children in Hawaii used to join other racial groups in teasing the Chinese ice cream or confectionary vendor:
    Chink, Chink Chinaman, sitting on the fence,
    Trying to make a dollar out of fifteen cents.
    See also Harold R. Isaacs, *Images of Asia: American Views of China and India* (New York: Capricorn Books, 1962), p. 115.
17. One of the largest rice plantations of Hawaii was that of Leong Pak On, beyond Waimea on the island of Kauai, situated in the swamplands of Mana.
18. Clarice Taylor, "Chinese Veterans of Kekaha Find Happy Old Age Their Lot," *Honolulu Star-Bulletin*, 13 March 1937.
19. George Washington Akao Hapai, judge in the district court of Hilo for thirty-six years, son of Lau Fai (Hapai).
20. *St. Peter's Church Golden Jubilee Edition* (Honolulu: Ahana Printing, 1936). Yap See-Young in an address spoke of the Hakka Basel Christians emigrating to Demerara (in British Guiana, now Guyana) and British North Borneo as well as to Hawaii. Today, descendants of the three emigrant groups wholly agree that those brethren who migrated to Hawaii received the best treatment and enjoyed the most favorable advantages.
21. Some of the Lilong graduates served in Hawaii and were listed in the Chinese publication of Lok Yuk Thelogical Seminary (Hong Kong: 1959), edited by the Reverend Hung Tet-Yin, former pastor of the First Chinese Church in Honolulu.
22. The Chinese of Hawaii have a story about Mary Damon. She went to the fish market on Kekaulike and King streets in Honolulu to select her fish for dinner. The Chinese stallkeepers were impressed by her beauty and made admiring remarks in Chinese and wondered whether she was married. After making her purchases, Damon *See Nai* ("Mistress Damon") spoke in impeccable Chinese, *"How pang you* ("good friends"), work hard and someday you will meet someone much prettier." Thereafter, whenever she went to Chinatown to shop, she was greeted with respect and admiration and was sold the best of fish, poultry, and meat.

It may well be said that of all who helped the Chinese, none was as gracious as Mrs. Damon. She reached into the lives of many. For instance, the first Chinese nurse at Chinese Wai Wa hospital was Ruth Low (Mrs. Lum King, 1883–1957). She was sponsored by Mary Damon and the Gleaners Society. She received her training at Kawaiahao Seminary, first started as a boarding school for Hawaiian girls in the 1860s and now the girls' school of Mid-Pacific Institute (*Honolulu Advertiser,* 21 November 1954; *Hawaiian Evangelical Association Annual Report,* 1896, p. 30).

CHAPTER 7

1. Hsiang-lin Lo, "Chinese Genealogy and Its Place in Historical Scholarship," *The Eastern Miscellany* (Taiwan, publication in Chinese), November 1960, pp. 16–22.
2. One typical village is the Lo family village opposite the gate of Chung Chi College of the Chinese University of Hong Kong at Shatin, New Territories. This one-surname village was founded by two brothers and is made up of male members of the Lo clan and their mothers, wives, and unmarried daughters. Their wives came from the neighboring villages from families like Lee, Hew, Won, or Shim who had also migrated to this area during Ch'ien Lung's reign (1736–1795) of the Ch'ing dynasty.

    The Lo village is proud of one of its members, Lo Chong. He was born in Hawaii and married the daughter of K'ang Yu-wei, leader of the Hundred Days Reform in 1898. K'ang recruited young Lo from Hawaii and encouraged him to finish his education at Oxford University in England. Lo later became Chinese consul general in Singapore and served in other capacities in the Ministry of Foreign Affairs in Peking.

    The Lo clan records show migrations, in the late nineteenth century, of their members to Hawaii, Peru, and North Borneo. Today, the men still go overseas to London and other cities in Europe to work in restaurants to earn extra income. On the Chinese New Year holidays, chartered flights bring some back for family visits and marriages. Few take their families along to settle in the new places.

    Lo Chong's son, Jung-pang Lo, has edited and translated *K'ang Yu-wei: A Biography and a Symposium* (Tucson: University of Arizona for the Association of Asian Studies, 1967).
3. In Hawaii, the oldest grave in a Chinese cemetery was the popular choice to be designated as that of the *tai gung* or *chee tzu* ("founding ancestor") for the Chinese community of that area. In many other instances, however, a mass burial mound made of reburials from old graves would be dedicated to *sin yau* ("departed friends") and used as the "founding ancestors" grave. Such a grave mound would be surrounded by the traditional omega-shaped masonry structure. A ground-level platform before the marker would be used during the spring memorial ceremonies. This may be seen in Hanalei cemetery on Kauai, or Waiehu cemetery on Maui, or the new Chinese section in Hawaiian Memorial Park, Oahu, which has the reburials from Heeia Chinese cemetery moved because of a housing development.
4. Hong Kong dwellers reported destroying their genealogies and family records when the invading Japanese army occupied the area in World War II. Social organizations also reported destroying their records, especially membership registers, in order to avoid having members molested by Japanese intelligence units. Chinatown fires (1886 and 1900) in Honolulu and the 1906 earthquake in San Francisco also caused the loss of family records.
5. *Tung sing but fun* ("same surname must not marry"). Enlightened people in urban areas in more recent years tolerated marriages of the same surnames that did not involve blood relationship. When Chung Wing-Kwong, president of Lingnan University in Canton, married Chung Fan-

Ting, not related, it created only a mild sensation. In Hawaii today, there is no intolerance over marriage of the same Chinese surname as long as there is no close relationship. In Chinese villages, it was forbidden by the strictest of moral codes, based on the observation of genetic disasters from consanguineal marriages.

6. As already illustrated, the functions of welfare and care of the aged and needy, normally assumed by a Chinese clan, were assumed in Hawaii by employer-plantations or social organizations such as the United Chinese Society and fraternal and district or clan societies until these functions were taken over by government social welfare and social security programs. In the earlier days, Tung Wah Hospital in Hong Kong was the social agency to which overseas Chinese sent disinterred remains for transfer back to ancestral villages for reburial. Political upheavals in the last two decades interrupted these reburials. In many a Chinese cemetery in Hawaii, there are stone or concrete huts storing large white crockery urns of disinterred remains waiting for reburial in ancestral villages. One college-educated Chinese stranded in Hawaii arranged for cremation. When he died ten years ago, his ashes were scattered off Diamond Head on Oahu so that his spirit would forever flow across the Pacific to his beloved homeland.
7. Johanna M. Meskill, "The Chinese Genealogy as a Research Source," in Maurice Freedman, ed., *Family and Kinship in Chinese Society* (Stanford: Stanford University Press, 1970).
8. Mrs. Ernest K. Kai's probe into her husband's paternal and maternal Chinese ancestral roots to four generations has led to an as-yet-unpublished research study on the group of Chinese on the island of Hawaii who were among the earliest sugar planters and manufacturers in the Kingdom. They were here well before 1852, the year when the first contract laborers arrived.
9. Francis L. K. Hsu in *Under the Ancestors' Shadow* ([Stanford: Stanford University Press, 1971], pp. 232–237) discusses genealogy in north China, where strong lineages are less prevalent than in south and central China. Professor Hsu points out that as a part of genealogy a family included a biographic sketch of an important member of the family who had performed good deeds or received special honors.
10. Mary Roberts Coolidge, *Chinese Immigration* (New York: Holt, 1909), pp. 312–334: "The degree of irresponsible and directionary power vested in the inspectors and the absolute secrecy in which all the examinations and records gradually became enshrouded invited abuse. . . . To corruption was added oppression, prejudice, and intolerance." In Hawaii, there was an immigration bribery scandal which resulted in the demotion and suicide of an inspector (*Honolulu Adveriser,* 13 February, 27 April, 2 May, 15 May 1924).

On the other side of the picture were the Chinese frauds of "paper sons" and *chin sam* ("1,350"). These referred to the price of $1,350 paid for birth certificates of sons born to fathers visiting China. To make money, these legitimate birth certificates were sold to others wanting to bring boys to America. "Paper sons" were also substituted for unreported deaths. Imaginary "sons" were created to open slots by which some Chinese boys could conveniently enter the country.
11. Chiu Ying-Wing, ed., *A Brief History of the Chiu Clan* (San Francisco: Chiu Family Association, 1965). Like most Chinese genealogies, this

bilingual book tells of the beginnings when the clan was given its surname (spelled Chiu, Chew, Chu) during the Chou dynasty, 1001 B.C., in the northern region of Shansi. The foreword told of the migrations southward to Kwangtung during the Sung dynasty (A.D. 960–1127) and of the dispersions of the different branches into various counties.

In Hawaii, two family genealogies were privately printed in 1972: (1) *Ing Family Directories* by Harold C. Hill and (2) *The Char Family Genealogy Book* by Tin-Yuke Char.

12. Jack London: "Chun Ah Chun," *The House of Pride* (New York: Macmillan, 1912). For his fictional writing, Jack London disguised Chun Afong's name and changed his sophisticated and wealthy ancestry to that of a common laborer.
13. While fleeing an advancing Japanese army, Malulani was caught and almost shot as a guerrilla suspect. By a turn of fate, he was released and allowed to join other refugee students in Chengtu.
14. *Wo Chung (Ho Chung)* was operated by China Merchants' Steam Navigation Co. (Kuykendall, *Hawaiian Kingdom*, 3:208–211). It arrived 14 November 1879 from Canton with 452 passengers.
15. Long-time resident Kin-Moi Ching died in 1955 at age ninety-five.
16. Chinese, after leaving the Kakaako or Kalihi Quarantine Camps, where they had stayed following the Chinatown Fire of 1900 were sent to Wong Ga Kum ("government camp") off Vineyard Street above Buckle Lane until they found their own lodgings. This helped to move Asians from the central core of Chinatown to the intermediate residential areas of Palama, Liliha, Nuuanu, and Pauoa.
17. Albert Rebel in his *Survey of Hawaiian Industries* ([Honolulu: Chamber of Commerce, October 1930], p. 19): "There are several rice mills in the Territory, the most important one being the City Mill Co. of Honolulu. [It] does the milling work for independent rice growers with rice fields located on the island of Oahu. Last year a total of between 25,000 and 30,000 bags were milled from the island of Oahu alone. This year the company's plant is milling rice for rice growers on the island of Kauai."
18. Hung-Chin Ching of Honolulu who volunteered as a radio specialist with the rank of major in Dr. Sun Yat-sen's 1922 northern expedition to expel the warlords, values his *Three Character Classic (Sam Gee Keng)* which he had learned here at age five from teacher Ching Yi-Sun. Today in his retirement he enjoys passing out copies of this bilingual translation to his relatives and friends for their cultural enrichment.
19. Aona, surname Hew and given name Yin On. His son, Francis K. Aona (1893–1946) graduated from Kamehameha School in 1912 and served in the Territorial House of Representatives for twenty-four years.
20. As a revolutionist, Sun Yat-sen's life was in constant danger. Hawaii was his safest "typhoon shelter." He managed to obtain a Hawaiian birth certificate in order to gain entry into the mainland United States. Fluent in English and versed in Western political sciences, Sun did not seek help in these areas from the Chinese in Hawaii, but he did need their financial support and the help of individuals to be his bodyguards and aides. The kidnapping incident in London in 1896 highlighted the necessity for physical protection. Two of the Chinese from Hawaii who followed him and were given political titles were Tang Chung-sung and Chang Chau.

Glossary

Transliteration of Chinese terms, phrases, names of persons, places, and of Chinese and bilingual publications used in this work follows general local usage in Hawaii—the Cantonese dialect as spoken by the predominant group who migrated from Heung Shan county. Readers who understand Chinese can easily work out the Kuo Yu (national speech) romanization from the Chinese ideographs. Certain names are already in Kuo Yu from preferred or established use.

In Chinese usage the family name comes first before the given name as in Sun Yat-sen, the last two elements being a two-part given name. Some Chinese given names have only one element—Chock Lun. Names such as that of U.S. Senator Hiram Leong Fong that are in the Western style of given name first are inverted in alphabetizing: Fong, Hiram Leong.

Because the two parts of Chinese given names are both capitalized in local usage, such capitalization has been retained. A hyphen may be added to distinguish the given names from surnames, thus, Chung Kun-Ai.

The Hawaiian language has twelve letters in its alphabet—*a, e, i, o, u, h, k, l, m, n, p,* and *w.* Thus, some Chinese names changed—Achin became Akina, and Ah Fai became Hapai in Hawaiian, for lack of *ch* or *f* sounds.

Achu (Achi, Achiu, Achow) 黃朝
Afong and Achuck Co. 芳植記
Afong (Chun, Afong) 陳國芳
Afong, Malulani C. 陳熙橡
Afong, Tony 陳席儒
Ahana, K. C. 陳官祥
Ahana, K. M. 陳官明

Glossary

Ahana, W. W.　黃和興（棉鳳）
Ahee (Mock, Lee)　莫利（莫義）
Aheong, S. P.　蕭雄
Ahin (surname not recorded)　阿顯
Ahung　陳恆
Ah Ling (Ting Ling)　丁練
Ai, C. K.　鍾工宇
Aiina (Chee, In)　徐燕
Aiko (Lum, Jo)　林佐
Akaka (Lee, Shak)　李石
Alum (Fung, Look)　馮祿
American Security Bank　中美銀行
Amoy　廈門
Ah Nee　阿二
Ahpong (Apung, Ahu)　吳蓬
Aseu, Luke　鄭楊秀
Asing (Apokane; Hu, Pok Sing)　胡百勝
Atai (surname unknown)　恆泰股東
Atak (surname unknown)　阿德

Ba-Set Fui (Basel Church)　巴色會
bai san　清明拜山
Bak Sak Temple　白石廟
Bark Fook Tong (cemetery)　百福堂
Bark Yee Hong　白衣行
bee-mut say-wui　秘密社會
Bow Sin Tong　保善堂
Bow Wong Wui　保皇會
Bow Yee Tong　保義堂
Buck Toy Villagers' Club　北台同鄉會
Buddha's Hands　佛手
　　(fingered citron)

Canton　廣州
Cha, See-Yick　謝泗益
cha-siu　叉燒
Ch'ai, Ch'u　翟楚
Chai, James　蔡敬生
Chan, Wing-tsit　陳榮捷

334

Glossary

Chang, Chau　鄭照
Chang, Dai Yen　鄭帝恩
Chang, Fei　張飛
Chang, Kim　鄭金
Char Family Genealogy Book　謝氏家譜
Char, Yew　謝有
chee fa　字花
Chee Kung Fui Kon　致公會館
Chee Kung Tong　致公總堂
chee tzu　始祖
Chinese in America　美國華僑史　孫甄陶著　台北　正中書局　1962
Chee Yuen (Chee Ying)　致英會館
　　Association
Chen, Chin-nan　陳近南
Chen, Chiung-ming　陳烱明
Chen, Hsi-hsiang　陳熙橡
Chen, Ta　陳達
Cheng, Ch'eng-k'un　鄭成坤
Ch'eng, T'ien-fang　程天放
chi-chi　既濟（易經）
chia-pu (ka-pu)　家譜
Ch'ien Lung　乾隆
Chihli　直隸
chim　籤
Dr. Sun Chin (Chan, Kok-sun)　陳國臣中醫
chin sam　千三
Chinese in Hawaii Handbook　夏威夷華人手冊　美華文化服務社出版
　　(bilingual publication, 1950)
Chinese Buddhist Association　華僑佛教總會
　　of Hawaii
Chinese Chamber of Commerce　中華總商會
Chinese Chamber of Commerce　檀香山中華總商會　二十週年特刊
　　(Chinese publication, 1931)
Chinese Christian Association　華人基督教會
Chinese Educational Association　中華教育會
Chinese-English Debating Society　中西擴論會
Chinese-European Concordance　中西日曆合璧　上海徐滙書坊出版
　　(bilingual publication, 1904)

335

"Chinese Genealogy and its Place in Historical Scholarship" 羅香林：中國族譜學術地位 台北 東方雜誌出版 (Chinese publication, 1960)
Chinese in the Americas 美洲華僑通鑑 (Chinese publication, 1950) 紐約華僑文化社出版
Chinese Literary Association 華僑學會
Chinese Merchant Business Directory (bilingual publication, 1938) 檀島華僑商務指南 檀香山中華編印社出版
The Chinese of Hawaii (bilingual publication, 1929, 1936) 檀山華僑 第一集 第二集 華僑編印社出版
Chinese Reform Society 憲政會
Chinese Secret Societies (Chinese publication, 1911) 中國秘密社會史 上海商務印書館出版
Chinese Students' Alliance 華人學生聯合會
Chinese University Club 華人大學會
Chinese University Women's Club 華人大學婦女會
Chinese Women's Club 華人婦女會
Ching, Ah Fook 陳福
Ching (Tsing) dynasty 清朝
Ching, Alee 程利（汝楫）
Ching, Hung Chin 程慶全
Ching, Kin Moi 程建梅
Ching Ming (Tsing Ming) 清明節
Ching, Shai 程水
Ching, Yau Hong 程幼雄
Ching, Yi Sun 程雨臣
Chiu Clan History 趙族簡史 美國趙家公所出版 (bilingual publication, 1965)
Chock, Lun 卓麟
Chong Hang Kang 張坑徑
Chong, How Fo 張效和
Chong, How Kong 張效光
Chong, Sum Wing 張深榮 六十自述 1944
choy sun 財神
Chu, Gem 趙錦
Chu Kong (Pearl River) 珠江
Chulan and Co. 朝蘭公司

Glossary

Chun, Afong　陳國芳
Chun, Chee Kwon　陳致昆
Chun, Hoon　陳寬
Chun, Kam Chow (C. K. Chow)　陳金就
Chun, Mun Kai (C. M. Kai)　陳文啓
Chun, Quon (C. Q. Yee Hop)　陳滾先生壽集 1947
Chun Wing Chin Tong　陳穎川堂
Chun, Yee Han　陳宜侃
Chung Chi College　香港中文大學 崇基學院
Chung, Cho　鍾初
Chung, Fan-t'ing　鍾訓庭
Chung, Hoon　張寬
Chung, Hung Lum　鍾慶林
Chung, Kon You (C. Ah You)　鍾觀有
Chung, Kun Ai　鍾工宇
Chung Kuo (Middle Kingdom)　中國
Chung, Mook Heen　鍾木賢
Chung, Wing-kwong　鍾榮光
Chungshan　中山
Chungshan Tung Heung Hui　中山同鄉會
Chung Wah Seung Wui　中華商會
Chung Wah Wui Goon　中華會館
Chung Young Festival　九月重陽節
Confucius　孔子
C. Winam (Ching, Winam)　程蔚南
C. Q. Yee Hop Market　陳滾義合公司

dah dung mae　打燈謎
Damon See-nai　爹文師奶
Dai Goong (Tai Koong) School　大公學校
dong tin bai　當天拜
dou sup chai　鬥十仔
Dragon Boat Festival　五月龍舟節
Duck Doo Kee Loo　得都寄廬
Dun Wo Tong　敦和堂

Eight Great Spirits (Bart Dai Sin)　八大仙

Glossary

Fah Hsien (Fa Yuan)　花縣
fan-Ching *fook*-Ming　反清復明
fan-kwae Tong　番鬼東
fan-qui　番鬼
Fat Shan　佛山
Fat Sut Circle　法術團
Five Later Founding Fathers　後五祖
Flower Gardens　廣州花地
Fong, Hiram Leong　鄺友良
Foochow　福州
Fook On Tong (cemetery)　福安堂
fu (good fortune)　富
fu (trousers)　褲
Fukien province　福建省
Fut Mu　佛母
fun-ga　分家

Gee Hing (Chee Hing) Society　致興會館
Ghost Day　七月十四鬼節
gong　降
Goo, Kim (Goo, Kim Fui)　古今輝
Goo, Tet Tsin (Akina)　古德真
Gum Yee Hong　錦衣行
gung-gung　公公　阿公
Gut Hing Kung So　吉慶公所

Hakka　客家
Hakka *shuk-wa*　客家俗話
Han dynasty　漢朝
Hapai (Lau, Fai)　劉輝
Harbin, Manchuria　滿洲　哈爾濱
Hawaii Chinese Aero Club　檀山華人航空會
Hawaii Chinese Artists Association　檀華美術會
Hawaii Chinese Buddhist Society　夏威夷中華佛教總會
Hawaii Chinese Civic Association　華人土生會
Hawaii Chinese History Center　夏威夷華人歷史研究中心
Hawaiian Chinese Association　夏威仁華人公所

Glossary

Hee, Jack Sun 許直臣
Heen (Chung, Mook Heen) 鍾木賢
Heung Shan 香山
Heong San Chong Sau Co. 香山長壽公司
    (cemetery)
hing 興
Hing Chung Hui 興中會
Ho-Chung (ship) 和眾
Ho, Fon 何寬
Hoi Ping 開平
Hoklo 福佬
Hok San 鶴山
hong 行 洋行 十三行
Hong Kong 香港
Hoo Cho School 互助學校
Hook Chu Cemetery 福潮義地
Hookien-Chuchow (Chaochow) 福建—潮州
Hoong Moon (Hung Men) 洪門
Hop Hing Society 合興會館
How Wong Miu 侯王廟
Hsiao, Kung-chuan 蕭公權
Hsu, Ti-shan 許地山：香港與九龍租借地探略 中國文化
Hoy On Tong 海安堂   協進會刊行 1941
hui (*wui*) 會
Hung On Shch 洪安社
Hung, Siu-chuan 洪秀全
Hungtai 恆泰
Hung, Tet-Yin 洪德仁

Jack Shin Tong 積善堂
jah 姐
jai 齋
jang sai guy 爭世界
Jehol 熱河
Jing Sing Musicians Club 正聲音樂團
Jung Sun 忠臣
Jup Mun Say 習文社

ka heung 家鄉

Glossary

Ka Ying Chow 嘉應州
Kam Tin 錦田
K'ang, Yu-wei 康有爲
Kau-Tom Post 退伍軍人高譚分會
Kea King 嘉慶
Ket On (Kwock On) Society 國安會館
ket-tse 桔仔
Ki Ying 耆英
Kieh Yuen (Wat, Yuen) 屈原
Ko Lao Hui 哥老會
Kong Chau Society 岡州會館
Kong, Tai-Heong 江棣香醫生
Kong, Tet-Yin (Kontetyn) 江德仁
Kong, Yin-Tet 江仁德
Kowloon 九龍
kow tow 叩頭
Koxinga 國姓爺（鄭成功）
Kuang Hsu 光緒
kumquat 金橘
Kum Shan (California) 金山
kum-shan jong 金山庄
kung 公
K'ung, Ming 孔明
Kung Sheong Doo Society 恭常都會館
kung-si 公司
Kuomintang 國民黨
Kuo Yu 國語
Kwan Dai (Quan Dai, Kuan Ti) 關帝
Kwan Yin (Goon Yum) 觀音
Kwangchow 廣州
Kwangsi 廣西
Kwangtung 廣東
Kwangtung Tung-Chih 廣東通志
Kwangtung Wui Goon 廣東會館
kwe 鬼
Kwong Chong Lung 廣昌隆
Kwong Fook Tong 廣福堂
Kwong On Chan 廣安棧

Glossary

Kwong Sam Kee 廣三記
Kwong Yee Society 廣義會館

L. Ah Leong (Lau, Fat Leong) 劉佛良
Lai, Kum Pui 賴金佩
Lao-tze 老子
Lau, Yuk lin (Lew, Yu lin) 劉玉麟
Lee, Bung Chong 李炳昌
Lee, Han 李侃
Lee, Kai Chuck 李啓澤
Lee, Let 李烈
Lee, Loi 李來
Lee, Robert M. W. 李文華
Leong, Chew 梁照
Leong Doo Society 良都會館
Leong Ma (Niang Ma) 孃媽
Liang, Ch'i-ch'ao 梁啓超
Liberty News 自由新報
lichee 荔枝
Li, Hung-chang 李鴻章
Li, Khai Fai 李啓輝
Lilong 李朗
Lin, Tse-hsu 林則徐
Ling Hing (Luen Hing) Society, Hilo 聯興會館
li shee 利市 利是
Li, Sun 李孫
Liu, Pei 劉備
Lo, Chong 羅昌
Lo, Hsiang-lin 羅香林
Lo, Jung-pang 羅榮邦
Lo, Yuet Fu 勞日富
Lock Shin Tong 樂善堂
Lodge of Sorrow 倚廬
Lok Yuk Theological Seminary 樂育神學院
    (bilingual publication, 1959) 1959 畢業專號
longan 龍眼
Low, Paul Apau 羅新保

Luen Hing Club, Honolulu 聯興俱樂部
Luen Hing (Lin Hing) Society, 聯興公司
    Keanae
Luke, Chan 陸燦
Lum, King 林文京
Lum Sai Ho Tong 林西河堂
Lung Doo Chung Sin Tong 隆都從善堂
Lung Doo Benevolent Society 檀香山隆都從善堂
    (bilingual publication, 1966) 七十五週年特刊
Lung Kee Bo 隆記報
Lung Kong Society 龍岡公所（劉,關,張,趙）
Lungtauwan Villagers' Club 龍頭環同鄉會
lup dai tsang 笠底橙

maan-maan 慢慢
Macao 澳門
mai chu-dzai 賣猪仔
Manchu 滿洲
Man Hing Tong (cemetery) 萬興堂
Manoa Chinese Cemetery 萬那聯義會
Manoa *gung* 萬那公（劉澤公）
Mark, Y. Sang 麥蔭生
Mau Association 恭常都神前村毛氏同鄉會
Mei-Foo (ship) 美富
Min Chung Literary Society 民眾讀書會
Moh-tze (Meh-tzu) 墨子
Moo Hawk Club 務學俱樂部
Moon Festival 八月中秋節
mou 畝
Mow (Ahmow, surname not
    recorded) 阿茂
mui-tsai 妹仔
Mun Lun Chinese School 明倫學校

Nam Long 南朗
Nanking 南京
Nan Ling 南嶺
New Territories 新界

Glossary

Ngow Yuk Hong 牛肉行
Ningpo 寧波
noi keng 內荊

Ocean View Cemetery 位亞彊華人義地會
on 安
On Kai Say (On Ding Village) 安定村安溪社
on-kue lok-yip 安居樂業
On Tong Villagers' Club 安堂同鄉會
Oo Sack Kee Loo 谷都烏石寄廬
out-going, in-coming, peace! 出入平安
Overseas Chinese Emigration 中國海外移民史
　　(Chinese publication, 1946) 陳里特編著 上海 中華書局
Overseas Chinese and the Chinese 華僑與中國革命
　　Revolution, 1955 黃福鑾著 香港 亞洲出版社
Overseas Chinese in the United 美國華僑史
　　States and Canada 吳尚鷹著 香港 嘉羅印刷 1965

Pah On (Leong, Pak On) 梁百安
pailou 牌樓
paké 伯爺
Palolo Old Men's Home 華僑老人院
Pao, Chun 寶鋆
paper sons 假紙仔
Peach Garden Fraternity 桃園結義
Pearl River 珠江
Peiho (River) 北河
Peking 北京
Peng Hui 朋會
Po Chia Hsing 百家姓
pomelo 碌柚（波碌）
popo 婆婆 阿婆
Pun Yu 番禺
Punti 本地

Quan Dai (Kwan Ti) 關帝
Quon Chark Say 小隱羣策社

Quon On Kwock 羣安閣

Sai San 西山村
Sam (Ahsam, surname not recorded) 阿森
Sam Heung 三鄉
Sam Hop Wui 三合會
Samsing Co. 三盛公司
Sam Yup 三邑
sau mu 清明掃墓
sau sun 修身
See Dai Doo Society 四大都會館
see-doi toong-tong 四代同堂
See Yup Benevolent Society 四邑會館
senshaws 線紗
Seong Gah Hong 上架行
Seven Sisters Festival 七月七仙女節
Shameen 沙面
Shanghai 上海
shang tung 商董
Shantung 山東省
Shao Lin Temple 少林寺
Shatin 新界沙田
Shekki 石岐
Shim, Wai On 沈維安
Shim, Yin Jin (also Yin Chin) 沈榮貞
Si-Kiang 西江
"Silver River Festival" 七月七銀河節
Sin-on (now Pao On) county 新安縣（寶安縣）
sin yau 先友
Sing Chong Co. 昇昌公司
Sing Wong Miu 城隍廟
siu yee 七月十四燒衣節
Soong, Irma Tam 宋譚秀紅
Soong Yee Wui (cemetery) 崇義會
"Sui Chiang Lane" (Lincoln Loy McCandless) "水井連"
Sun Chung Kwock Bo 新中國報

Glossary

Sun Gum Shan 新金山
Sun, Mi 孫眉
Sun, Tai-cheong 孫帝象
Sun Wui 新會
Sun, Yat-sen 孫逸仙
Sun Yin Wo (restaurant) 新人和
sung choi 生菜 生財
Sung dynasty 宋朝
sup dung hu 十等胡
Swatow 汕頭

Ta-Tsing Leu-Lee 大清律例
tai gung 太公
Tai Ping 太平
Tai Po 大埔
Tai Sung Society 太盛公司
Tan, Commissioner 直隸總督譚廷襄
Tan Heung Shan 檀香山
Tan Sing Dramatic Club 檀聲劇社
Tan Wah Temple 檀華寺
Tang, Chung-sung 鄧松盛（三伯）
T'ang dynasty 唐朝
Tanka 蜑家
Tang (dong), (party) 黨
Tang (Teng), (lineage) 鄧族
Tang (Dang), Hung Sin 鄧行善
Tao Kuang 道光
tao t'ai 道台
Tartar 韃靼
Te Chih Sheh 德志社
Teng, Ssu-yu 鄧嗣禹
Thirty-Six Oaths 三十六誓
Thom, Wah Chan 譚華燦
Three religions are one 三教如一
Three Word Classic 三字經
Tientsin 天津
tin gau 天九
Tin Hau 天后

tin-joy yan-wo 天災人禍
Tin-Ti Wui (Tien-Ti Hui) 天地會
Ting Ling 丁練
tita 鐵笛
Toishan 台山
Tombs Day (Ching Ming
    Festival) 三月清明節
tong 堂
    lai tong 禮堂
    lai bai tong 禮拜堂
    miu tong 廟堂
    gau tong 教堂
    hawk tong 學堂
    chee tong 祠堂
    Chee Wo Tong 致和堂
    Chee Kung Tong 致公堂
    Man Fook Tong 萬福堂
Tong, Lao 唐榴
Tong, Shao-yi 唐紹儀
Tong, Phong 唐雄
Tong Sing Tong 同善堂
tong wars 堂鬥
Tong Wo Society 同和公司
Tong *yan* (Tang *jen*) 唐人
Tow Yee Kwock Society 桃義閣
Triad Society 三點會
tribute-bearing 朝貢
Triple C Club 三思會
Tsang, Kwai 曾貴
Tshi, Sak En 徐錫恩
tso-ho-yan, tso-sin-shee, mok tso 做好人 做善事
    kwai-sum shee 莫做虧心事
Tsoong Yee Society 叢義會館
tsu pu 族譜
tsung pu 宗譜
Tsung Tsin (Soong Jin) Society 崇正會館
Tsung Tsin Society 檀山崇正會
    (Chinese publication, 1958) 廿一週年紀念特刊
Tu Chiang Sheh 圖強社

Glossary

T'ung Chih 同治
Tungkun 東莞
Tung Ming Hui 同盟會
tung see (pronounced *tung shing*, for good luck) 通書（通勝）
tung-shih (interpreter) or *tung-che* 通事
tung-sing but fun 同姓不婚
Tyhune or Tyhoon (Wong Tai-Hoon) 黃帝桓

Utai Co. 裕泰公司（古鳳華）
United Chinese Labor Association 中華總工會
United Chinese Society 中華會館
United Chinese Society (Chinese publication, 1934) 檀香山中華會館五十週年特刊

Wahiawa Chinese Cemetery Association 位亞嘩華人義地會
Wah Hing Tong 華興堂
wah-kiu (*hua-ch'iao*) 華僑
Wah Mun School 華文學校
Wah Tow 華陀
Wai Bok Say 茶園惟博社
Waichow 惠州
Wai Wa Hospital 惠華醫院
Wan Yun-lung 萬雲龍
Whampoa (Whangpoo) 黃浦
White Lotus Sect 白蓮教
"Wind and Water Professor" 風水先生
Wing Lok Ngue Hong 永樂魚行
Wing Hong Yuen 永雄源
Wing Sing Wo 永生和
Wing Wo Tai 永和泰
Wo Hang Co. 和行
Wo Hing Society 和興會館
Wong-Ga Kum (Government Camp) 皇家"堪"
Wong Kong Ha Tong 黃江夏堂

Wong, Kwai　王貴
Wong, Leong　黃亮
Wong Leong Doo Kee Loo　黃良都寄廬
wongpee　黃皮
Wong, Wah Foy　黃華恢
Woo, Yee-Bew　胡爾標
Woo, Set-am　胡錫庵
wui-goon (*hui-kuan*)　會館
Wui On Sheong (Wai On Cheong)　維安祥

Y. Ahin (Young, Ah In)　楊然
yamen　衙門
yan mu sam-doi fu　人無三代富
Yan Ping　恩平
Yan Wo Co.　仁和公司
Yang Chung Hui　仰中會
Yang, Wei-pin　楊蔚彬
Yap, See Young　葉似雲
yat-poon sarn-sa　一盆散沙
Yee Hing Society　義興會館
Yee King Tong　餘慶堂
Yee, Yap　余揖
Yen, James Y. C.　晏陽初
Yenching University　燕京大學
Yi Yee Tong　以義堂
Yin Fo Society　人和會館
ying　英
yit jook . . . yee jook　一囑我郎去過番，
分離不過一時間；
總愛我郎時運好，
唔使三年轉唐山。
二囑我郎心莫野，
全心全意有顧家；
一月半月愛寄信，
三年兩載愛歸家。

Young, Kam Hoy　楊金海
Young People's Literary Club　少年學會

Glossary

Young People's Oratorical 少年演説社
    Association
Young Sheong (Yung Sheong) 容裏
Yuan, Shih-k'ai 袁世凱
Yuen Chong 源昌
Yuen Long 元朗
Yuk Wong Dai Dei 玉皇大帝
Yung, Wing 容閎
Yung Wo Tong 雍陌雍和堂

Index

Achu (Achi; Wong Chiu), 91, 317
Adams, Romanzo, 113, 138
Afong, Chun, 44, 90, 320–321, 332; family, 236–243
Afong, Malulani. *See* Ch'en Hsi-hsiang
Afong and Achuck Co., 64–65, 319
Ahana, K. C.; and K. M., 324
Ahana, W. W., 157, 264
Ahee (Mock Lee), 91, 317
Aheong, Samuel P., 193, 197, 198, 199
Ahia, 238
Ah Leong, L., 264–265
Ah Nee, 328
Ahung, 54, 89
Ai, C. K. *See* Chung, Kun-Ai
Aiina (Chee Inn), 89–90, 322
Aiko (Lum Jo), 56–57, 317
Akaka (Lee Shak); and Rev. Abraham, 314
Akina, Arthur; Clem; and Ernest, 233
Alexander, James, 216, 217
Allen, Elisha H., 62–63
Allen and Robinson Co., 265
Amoy, 5, 8, 11, 16, 60
Anahola, Kauai, 210
Angell, James B., 16
Apana Paké, 61
Armstrong, William, 44
Aseu, Luke (L. Ah Seu; Young Seu Chang), 75–80, 232, 234
Asing, 91
Atai, 54, 89
Atak, 91
Auderkirk, John, 264

Baker, Rev. Albert S., 215
Ball, Chinese, 90, 91, 147
Banks, 127, 131. Individual: American Security (Chinese-American), 117, 324; Liberty, 117; Hua Chiao Commercial, 323

Barbers Point, Oahu, 205
Beckley, Capt. George C.; Mary; and William Frederick M., 238
Bell, Edward, 37
Board of Health, 64, 101–110
Bond, Elias, 192–194, 215, 328
Bonk, William J., 176, 178
Boyd, Robert, 52
Brewer, Charles, 56, 57
Brewer, C., & Co., 317
Brown, Samuel, 11
Bubonic plague. *See* Chinatown Fire
Bulkeley-Johnson, F., 52
Burlingame, Anson, 14

Cass, John, 60, 62
Catalina, Antone, 56
California, 42, 43, 57, 70, 71, 91, 94, 229
Canton (city), 5, 6, 8, 16, 20, 21, 22, 23, 24, 33, 35, 36, 194, 218, 219, 221, 255, 259, 313, 316, 322
Cemeteries, 171–173, 175–176, 314; named, 169–171
Chai, Jimmy, 178
Chamisso, Adelbert von, 316
Chang Fei, 160
Chang Siu Hon, 116
Chang Yen Bau, 234
Chang Young Siu. *See* Aseu, Luke
Cha Yuen, 151
Chekiang, 10
Ch'en Chiung-Ming, 239
Ch'en Hsi-hsiang (Malulani C. Afong), 238, 240–241
Ch'ien Lung, Emperor, 1, 2, 38, 66
Chin Sam Fat, 112
Chin, Dr. Sun (Chan Kok-Sun), 103, 323
Ch'in Shih Huang, Emperor, 21
China (Middle Kingdom, Chung Kuo),

351

1, 3, 4, 5, 6, 36, 37, 38; disintegration of, 8–12; revolutions in, 12, 146, 156, 159, 161–162, 163
China Sea, 20
Chinatown, 117, 126–127, 183, 257, 265, 324. *See also* Chinatown Fire
Chinatown Fire, 101–110, 151, 154, 185, 251, 265, 323, 324, 330, 332; detention camps for victims of, 109, 251, 323, 324, 332; fire claims resulting from, 102, 293–295
Ching, Ah Fook, 178, 180
Ching, Harold W., 243
Ching, Kin Moi, 244–247
Ching Yau Hong, 116
Ching Ye Meng, 80
Chinn, Thomas, 227–228
Ch'i Ying (Kiying), 5
Chock Lun, 147
Chong Chuen, 80
Chong Chun, 80
Chong, Douglas, 179
Chong En Young, 112
Chong Hang Kang, 27
Chong Sum-Wing (C. S. Wing), 253
Chong, Mrs. Tai-Lai, 178–179
Chong, You, 103
Chou En-Lai, 240
Chulan & Co., 64, 94, 212, 319
Chun Afong. *See* Afong, Chun
Chun Ah Wing, 179
Chun, Chee-Kwon, 92
Chun Chik-Yee (Anthony Keawemaihili), 238–239
Chun Kam-Chow (C. K. Chow), 102
Chun Mun-Kai (C. M. Kai), 264
Chun Quon (C. Q. Yee Hop), 149, 253
Chunghoon (Cheung Hoon), 91
Chung, Hung Lum, 264
Chung Kun-Ai (C. K. Ai), 253–266
Chung Mook-Heen (H. A. Heen, Chung Muk-Heen), 157, 265
Chungshan (Heungshan), 16, 20, 23, 28, 65, 150, 152, 242, 254
Chung Yee Tailor Shop, 263
Churches: in Hawaii, 109, 116, 194, 202, 205, 206, 210, 212, 214, 215, 216, 232, 233, 234, 314. Individual: First Chinese, 328; Fort Street Chinese, 116, 232, 233; Kaumakapili, 66, 105, 106, 107, 108; Kawaiahao, 44, 102; Kula Chinese, 111, 328; St. Andrew's, 234, 235; St. Elizabeth's, 234, 235, 236, 324; St. John's, 111, 324; St. Paul's, 233, 234, 235; St. Peter's, 234, 235, 324, 328. *See also* Religion, Christian
City Mill, 254, 264–265
Clans: defined, 223–224, 225; government of, 226; purposes of, 226–227, 331. Individual: Au Young, 30; Ching, 152; Chun, 152; Lau, 152; Lo, 330; Lum, 152, 188; Mau, 152; Wong (Huang), 152. *See also* Genealogies
Clubs and organizations: civic, 68, 109, 111, 146–149, 158, 159, 265, 325; clan, 152; cultural, 154–155; educational, 154–155; extent of, 148; non-ethnic, 147; patriotic, 158, 163; political, 155–157; purposes of, 145–147, 148, 149, 150–160, 168, 325–326, 331; regional, 145–146, 149–152; religious, 161, 182, 183. *See also* Hoong Moon societies; Secret societies; Tongs
Coffee industry, 63
Coman, Katherine, 58
Confucius, 16, 21, 30, 181, 182
Cook, Capt. James, 33, 36, 39, 41, 55, 59
Cooper, Henry E., 103
Coulter, John W., 92
Cummins, Thomas, 52, 237
Cushing, Caleb, 3, 4, 5
Customs (Chinese), 119, 130–131, 132; burial, 26, 124–125, 131, 134–136, 150–151, 178; cemetery, 171–172, 314, 326, 331; childbirth, 133; intermarriage, 140–142, 214; family, 315; marriage, 97, 120–121, 133–134, 251–252, 264, 318, 325, 330–331

Damon, Ethel M., 192, 328
Damon, Frank W. (Francis), 314, 329; letters from, 23–32, 194, 199, 232; journal of, 200–217; recollections of, 218–222
Damon, Mary (Mrs. Frank), 52, 194, 218, 219, 220–222, 247, 329
Damon, Samuel C., 23, 192, 194, 195, 197, 221, 314
Dat Ming, 211
Davis, Isaac, 37
Day, Dr. F. R., 103
Dialects, 16, 20, 24, 61, 328. Individual: Hakka, 9, 16, 20, 22, 23, 24, 28, 66, 67, 124, 149, 179, 195, 328, 329; Hoklo, 16, 24, 314; Punti, 16,

Index

22, 23, 24, 29, 124, 179, 251; Sam Yup, 16; See Yup, 16, 149, 150
Dixon, Capt. George, 35
Dole, Edward, 80
Douglas, Capt. William, 36, 37
Dowsett, James I., 254, 263–264
Dudoit, Jules, 319
Duck Doo, 150–151
Dupont, Capt. Samuel, 13

Emigration from China, 9, 12–16, 26–27, 54, 58, 59, 127, 247–250, 254–260, 317, 330; and emigration broker contract, 275–277. *See also* Immigration; Labor
Emma, Queen, 91
Ewa, Oahu, 25, 82, 201, 202, 203

Fa Yuan (Fah Hsien), 9, 16
Fat San, 231
Fairbank, John K., 9
Festivals: birthday, 125; Chinese New Year, 121, 125, 136–137, 160, 178, 204, 256, 257, 261–262, 330; dragon boat, 137–138; memorial, 135; moon, 120, 121, 125, 137; other, 138, 147, 158
Field, Barnum, 90
Fong, Hiram Leong, 325
Foochow, 5, 8, 197
Franklin, Sir John; and Lady Jane, 90
Frear, Walter F., 111, 113
French, William, 55, 89, 322
Fukien, 11, 16, 22, 23, 161, 162, 231, 241
Fung, Quong, 81

Gambling, 200, 208
Genealogies, 227–230, 232, 331, 332. *See also* Clans
Geschwind, Norman, 3
Gibson, Walter Murray, 52–53
Gillespie family, 42, 43, 316
Gods and deities, 25, 160, 179, 183, 184, 185–188, 189, 210, 315. Individual: Fat Mu, 189; Hau Wong, 160; Kwan Dai (Kwan Ti, Kwan Kung), 160, 163, 179, 183, 184, 188, 210; Kwan Yin, 160, 179, 183–185; Tin Hau, 160, 315
Goo Kim, 81, 82, 232, 321
Goo Tet Tsin (Goo Akina), 232
Gook Doo, 150, 151
Gowan, H. H., 234
Great Britain, 8, 38, 197
Green, Jonathan, 198

Green, William L., 90
Grant, Ulysses S., 51
Guillou, Dr. Charles F., 321

Haalilio, 313
Hackfeld and Co., 265
Hakka, 9, 16, 20, 22, 23, 24, 28, 66, 67, 124, 149, 179, 195, 328, 329
Hakuole, Isaac; and James, 52, 317
Halai, L. K., 90
Halawa Valley, Hawaii, 176–178
Haleakala, Maui, 110
Hall, E. O., 202
Hamakua, Hawaii, 217
Hanalei, Kauai, 211, 330
Hanamaulu, Kauai, 208, 209
Hanapepe, Kauai, 213, 244, 245, 246
Hangchow, 10
Happer, Andrew, 52, 200, 201, 219
Harbin, Manchuria, 16
Hawaii Island, 39–40, 58
Hawaiians in China, 36, 52–53, 197–199, 219–222
Hawaiian Islands, 38–41, 42–44, 54, 57–58; annexation of, 68, 324–325; early relations with China of, 33–35
Hawi, Hawaii, 78
Hee Jack Sun, 116
Heeia, Oahu, 330
Heen, H. A. *See* Chung Mook-Heen
Heen, William H., 265
Herbert, Dr. G. H., 103
Heungshan. *See* Chungshan
Hikiau, Naukana, 197, 198–199
Hilea, Hawaii, 213
Hill, Samuel S., 42
Hillebrand, Dr. William, 64, 319
Hilo, Hawaii, 55, 57, 61, 82, 94, 102, 114, 196, 214–215, 217, 220, 221, 262, 322
Hinds, Dr. Richard, 319
Hitchcock, E. G., 76
Ho Ah Pui, 201, 206, 213
Hoffman, Edward, 90
Hoffman, Dr. W., 103
Ho Fon (Ho Fong), 265
Hoi Ping (Hoyping), 16
Hok San, 231
Hoklo, 16, 24, 314
Holidays. *See* Festivals
Honan, 7, 21
Honaunau, Hawaii, 261
Hong Kong, 8, 16, 23, 24, 29, 30, 42, 43, 60, 64, 66, 67, 127, 176, 177, 182, 195, 198, 199, 209, 223, 232, 236, 237, 238, 239, 241, 242, 243,

353

Index

248, 262, 264, 266, 314, 316, 317, 330
Honokaa, Hawaii, 314
Honolulu Iron Works, 107
Honolulu, Oahu, 29, 31, 32, 56, 92, 94, 97, 114, 167, 204, 219, 245, 250, 258, 261, 326
Honouliuli, Oahu, 204
Honuapo, Hawaii, 213, 262
Hoong Moon (Triad) societies, 25, 145, 146, 157–158, 159, 160–164, 167–168, 173–174, 176–180, 213, 327; thirty-six oaths of, 163–167
Hopei (Chihli), 13, 21
Hospitals, 327. Individual: Wai Wah, 265, 323, 329; Tung Wah, 331
Huha Kaha, 238
Hui (money pool), 146
Huleia, Kauai, 245
Hung Siu-chuan, 9
Hung Tai Co., 44, 54, 56, 89
Hupei, 162
Hwang-ho. *See* Yellow River

Ii, John Papa, 88
Immigration, 1, 62, 63, 118, 139, 200, 317–318, 319, 320; Bureau of, 60–61, 74–75, 76, 82, 196, 321, 331; Chinese protest restrictions on, 287–292; Japanese, 67, 68, 81, 109, 110; laws, 14–16, 60–61, 69, 74, 318–319; petition to U.S. Congress on, 297–300; quarantine, 320, 321; types of, 67–68, 140, 253, 314–315. *See also* Emigration; Labor
Io, Hannah Woo, 236
Iole, Hawaii, 56, 194
Iwamoto, Lana, 103

Japan, 11, 16, 44, 50, 61, 67, 68, 156
Jones, Peter C., 200
Judd, Charles S., 111, 113, 263

Ka'u, Hawaii, 32, 200, 213, 214, 217
Ka Ying Chow. *See* Meihsien
Kaahumanu, Queen, 238
Kaalaea, Oahu, 93
Kaauwaepaa, J. W., 90
Kahalehaka Valley, Kauai, 72
Kahana Valley, Oahu, 89
Kahului, Maui, 102, 216, 252, 326
Kaiana, 33–36
Kailua, Hawaii, 261
Kailua, Oahu, 93
Kaikioewa, Governor, 55
Kaimuki, Oahu, 117
Kaipu, 69, 71–74

Kakaako, Oahu, 106
Kalakaua, King, 30, 67, 171, 233, 244; visits China, 44–52
Kalihi, Oahu, detention camp, 109, 251, 323, 332
Kaliwai, Kauai, 211
Kamauoha, 52
Kamehameha I, 37, 38, 41, 316
Kamehameha III, 44, 90, 313, 322
Kamehameha IV, 63, 90–91
Kamokai, 90
Kanaina, 90
K'ang Yu-wei, 156, 326
Kapaa, 52
Kapaa, Kauai, 209
Kapaau, Hawaii, 79, 233
Kapena, John M., 199
Kau, Apau, 158
Kauai Island, 33, 34, 35, 36, 56, 57, 58, 70, 92, 206, 213
Kawananakoa, Prince, 52
Kealakekua Bay, Hawaii, 37
Kea-King (Chia Ching), Emperor, 6, 7
Kealia, Kauai, 209, 210
Keanae, Maui, 326
Keauhou, Hawaii, 262
Keawehaku, David, 52, 317
Kekaha, Hawaii, 320
Kekuanaoa, Governor, 44
Keswick, William, 199, 237
Kiawehaku, James, 52, 317
Kilauea, Kauai, 211
Kilauea, Hawaii, 214
Kohala, Hawaii, 75, 76, 80, 111, 192, 193, 194, 196, 215, 217, 233, 234, 235, 262, 326, 328
Koloa, Kauai, 56, 57, 58, 212, 213
Kong Tai-Heong, 323
Kong Tet-Yin, 192, 193, 215
Kong Yin-Tet, 112, 113, 192, 234, 236, 324
Kowloon, 66, 314
Koxinga, 66
Ku, Ah Jook Leong, 316
Kuakini, Governor, 56, 57
Kuang Hsu, Emperor, 156, 157
Kuck, Loraine, 38–42
Kui, 90
Kula, Maui, 110–113, 234, 324
K'ung Ming, 258
Kung Seong Doo, 150, 151, 152
Kwangsi, 9
Kwangtung, 4, 9, 16, 24, 145, 149, 150, 152, 192, 231, 239, 241, 254, 258, 266, 314, 322, 324; description of, 20–23

354

Index

Labor, 59, 62–65, 320, 323; camps, 70, 83, 84–85, 320; contracts, 60, 61, 66, 68–69, 70, 84, 279, 280–284, 285–286, 314–315, 316, 317, 318, 319; free, 69–70; living conditions of, 83–86, 97–101, 204–205, 208, 246, 250–251, 317, 318, 319, 320, 321; postal system for, 127, 128–129; recreation of, 98–100, 129, 179, 200, 208; treatment of, 70–74, 75–79, 81, 321; types of, 67–68, 69. *See also* Trades and occupations
Ladd & Co., 56, 58
Lahaina, Maui, 82, 89, 164, 193, 198, 314
Lai, Kum Pui, 114, 324
Lai Tet Sin, 195
Laie, Oahu, 93
Lanai Island, 44, 54, 55
Lao-tse, 21
Larm Doo, 150
Lau, T. Y., 240
Lau, Mary Woo (Mrs. W. W.), 236
Lau Yuk-lin, 240
Lavinia, 56
Lechler, Rudolf, 195–196, 197–198
Lee Han, 179–180
Lee Kai Chuck, 116
Lee Loi (Loy), 215
Lee, Rose Hum, 167
Lee, W. L., 62
Leleiohoku, W. P., 90
Leo Un, 80
Leong Doo, 145, 150, 151
Li Hung Chang, 30, 44, 48, 49, 50, 51, 314, 316
Li Hungtsao, 16
Li, Dr. Khai-Fai, 323
Li Sun, 48, 49, 50, 51, 314
Liang Chi'i-ch'ao, 156, 157, 326
Lihue, Kauai, 57, 81, 206, 207, 212
Lilong, 27, 66, 217, 324, 329
Lin Tse-hsu, 8
Liu Pei, 160
Lobscheid, Wilhelm, 64, 319
London, Jack, 237, 242, 332
Loo Sun, 156
Lovell, John, 52
Lunalilo, King, 241
Lung Doo, 150, 151; dialect, 20
Lungtauwan, 151
Lyons, Lorenzo, 217

Macartney, Earl, 1
Macao (Macau), 6, 7, 8, 22, 28, 30, 34, 223, 240, 254, 255; coolie trade, 29, 317
Magoon, Eaton, 238
Magoon, Marmion, 241
Mahoe, 210
Mahukona, Hawaii, 56, 78, 80, 85
Makahanaloa, Hawaii, 55, 322
Makalua, 52
Makanaila, 105
Makapala, Hawaii, 216, 233, 235
Makawao, Maui, 198, 216
Makee, James; and Charles, 263
Mana, Kauai, 93, 244, 329
Manchuria, 16, 68
Manoa Valley, Oahu, 102
Marin, Don Paulo, 56
Mark, Y. Sang, 235, 236
Maui Island, 37, 56, 57, 58, 81, 217
McCandless, Lane (Lincoln Loy), 93, 323
McKay, Sam, 264
Meares, John, 33, 34, 36, 38–40, 41, 42
Medicine, 10, 320, 321, 327, 328
Meihsien (Ka Ying Chow), 16, 24
Mencius, 30
Metcalf, Simon, 37
Mikaele, 90
Missions. *See* Religion, Christian; Churches
Mohaloa-a-Malulani, 238
Moh-tse, 21
Mulch, William, 264

Naalehu, Hawaii, 214
Nam Hoy (Nam Hoi), 16
Names and surnames, 318
Nan Ling Mountains, 20, 21, 22
Nanking, 9, 21, 236
Nawiliwili, Kauai, 207, 245
Newspapers and publications: *China Mail*, 196, 197, 198; *Chinese of Hawaii*, 114, 147; *Friend*, 23, 24, 101, 102, 195, 196, 200, 317; *Hawaii Chinese Annual*, 117; *Hon Mun Bo*, 158; *New China News*, 157, 326; *United Chinese Press*, 326; other, 43, 55, 75, 90, 108, 202, 238, 243, 253, 318
New Territories, 66–67, 223, 224, 226, 330
Niihau Island, 40
Ningpo, 5, 8
Nixon, Richard M., 2
Noyes, Henry V., 32

Oahu Island, 44, 70, 92, 94, 97, 213

355

Index

On Tong, 151
Oo Sack, 151
Opium: trade and use of, 8, 64, 86, 129, 179, 200, 208, 323; wars, 3, 8

Pahala, Hawaii, 213, 214, 262
Paia, Maui, 216–217
Palama, Oahu, 235
Pang Cheong, 265
Pao Chun, 16
Pao On, 16, 127, 194, 324. *See also* Sin-on
Pauoa, Oahu, 326
Payson, Adele M., 116
Pearl Harbor, Oahu, 74, 202
Pearl River (Chu Kiang), 16, 20, 58, 65, 260
Peiho River, 47
Peking, 1, 2, 3, 5, 10, 15, 16, 21, 46, 48, 102, 145, 221, 238, 239, 240, 243, 321
Pepeekeo, Hawaii, 44
Piianaia, St. Chad, 52
Piihonua, Hawaii, 322
Pikau, 70–71
Plants from China, 60
Political activities: China-related, 155–157; in Hawaii, 119, 147, 158, 324–325
Polulu, Hawaii, 233
Population, 54, 60, 74, 114, 118–119, 126, 127, 130, 139, 140, 141, 151–152, 324
Portlock, Nathaniel, 33–36
Pratt, Dr. J. S. B., 105
Prescott, Anne M., 235
Princeville, Kauai, 212
Puiki, 219–222
Pukak, 66
Pulaa, Charles H., 76–79
Punti, 16, 22, 23, 24, 29, 124, 179, 251
Pun Yu, 16
Punaluu, Oahu, 93
Puueo, Hawaii, 55
Puuloa, L. M., 90
Puunene, Maui, 320

Ranches, 111, 263
Reciprocity Treaty, 74, 94, 213. *See also* Sugar industry
Reed, William B., 13
Reiners, Gustav, 90
Religion, Chinese, 25–26, 124–125, 126, 181–191, 203, 204, 328; ceremonies of, 189–190, 191. *See also* Temples; Gods and deities

Religion, Christian, 32, 181, 192, 197–198; introduction of, into China, 231; missions and missionaries of, 10, 11, 24, 25, 26, 27, 30, 192, 194, 195, 197, 198, 200, 201, 202, 205, 212, 213, 214, 215, 216, 217, 232, 233, 324, 328. *See also* Churches
Restarick, Henry B., 111, 113, 235
Rice industry, 31, 61, 68, 91–95, 97, 127, 130, 201–202, 207, 208, 212, 213, 233, 244, 319, 320, 329; mills, 92, 94, 246, 264, 332; plantations, 95–96; clubhouse, 100–101
Richards, William, 313
Richards, Theodore, 218
Royal Hawaiian Agricultural Society, 16, 55, 62, 92, 318

Sai-San, 254, 256
Sam and Mow Bakery, 88, 321–322
Sam Sing, 42, 81
Samsing Co., 57, 89, 320
Sam Yup, 16
San Francisco, California, 42, 68, 92, 146, 147, 149, 177, 197, 209, 330
Sandalwood, 37, 54, 315, 316
Schools: attitude toward, 142, 261–262; Chinese language, 114, 115–116, 117, 130, 147, 155, 177, 182, 203; in China, 27, 200, 217; in Hawaii, 98, 105, 118–119, 155, 159, 210, 211, 218; outside Hawaii, 52, 205, 242. Individual: Bethel Chinese, 116; Chinese Children's, 116; Chung Shan, 117, 326; Dai Goong, 117; Fook Hing, 117; Hoo Cho, 117; Iolani, 235, 238, 254, 261; Kamehameha, 332; Kawaiahao Girls Seminary, 247, 329; Methodist Girls, 10; Mun Lun, 117, 182, 326; Punahou, 44, 72; Royal, 44; Mid-Pacific (Chinese Boarding; Mills), 329, 330; Wah Mun, 117; other, 11, 43, 48, 88, 142, 187, 232, 236, 238, 239, 241, 243, 329, 330
Secret societies, 25, 146, 149, 161–168, 174, 211, 213. *See also* Clubs and organizations
See-Dai Doo (Dai Doo; See Doo), 150, 151, 152
See Yup, 16, 149, 150
Seise, Maria, 42
Shanghai, 5, 8, 44, 46, 47, 209
Shansi, 21
Shantung, 16, 21, 314
Shatin, 66, 330

Index

Shekki, 20, 29–30
Shim, Rev. Wai On, 234
Shim Yin Jin (Shim Yin Chin), 112, 234, 236, 324
Ships, 315, 316, 317; whaling, 55, 57. Individual: *Amazon,* 318; *Amy Turner,* 197; *Auguste,* 195–196; *Billy Jack,* 250; *Chatham,* 37, 316; *Crusader,* 197, 199; *Eagle,* 42, 43; *Eleanora,* 37; *Eleu,* 107; *Felice,* 33, 36, 38, 40; *Grace,* 37; *Ho-Chung,* 316; *Iphigenia,* 33, 36, 40, 41; *Iroquois,* 107; *Likelike,* 262; *Madras,* 320; *Matador,* 321; *Mei Foo,* 316; *Milford,* 35; *Nootka,* 33, 42; *North West America,* 36, 40, 41; *Oceanic,* 264; *Pactolus,* 80; *Pautah,* 46, 50; *Peking,* 103; *Perusia,* 197; *Queen Charlotte,* 35; *Septima,* 200, 321; *Thetis,* 60, 62; *Wo Chung,* 244
Short, W. S., 112
Shun Tak, 16
Si-kiang River. *See* West River
Sin-on, 27. *See also* Pao On
Sit Moon, 216
Siu Yun, 151
Smith, Carl T., 42, 43
Soong, Irma Tam, 178, 239
Speer, William, 61
Spreckels, Claus, 217
Stores, Chinese, 89, 103, 126, 127, 145, 149, 262, 317, 326
Sugar industry, 54–59, 63, 64–65, 66, 70–74, 132, 206, 208, 212, 213–214, 270–273, 317, 331. Individual mills and plantations of: Ahsing, 55, 89; Ah Kina, 55; Aiina, 89–90; Amoi, 55; C. Brewer, 57; East Maui, 57; Eleele, 81, 213; Ewa, 82; Grove Farm, 69–74; Haiku, 321; Hakalau, 81; Hawaiian Sugar, 81; Hawi, 78; Hilea, 213; Hilo, 82; Honuapo, 213; Ka'u (Peter Jones), 200; Kekaha, 320; Kohala, 80, 85–87, 192–194, 215–216; Koloa (Ladd), 58, 72, 81, 212; Lanai, 54; Lihue, 81, 206; Makahanaloa, 322; Olowalu, 81, 82; Paauhau, 81; Pahala, 213; Pepeekeo (Chun Afong), 44, 239, 241; Piihonua, 322; Pioneer, 82; Ponoohawaii, 55; Princeville, 212; Samsing, 57, 320; Spreckelsville, 81, 217; Union, 78; Utai, 57; Waiakea, 82; Waialua, 205–206; Waianae, 205; Waikapu, 56; Wailuku (Hungtai), 44, 54, 56; Waimea (W. French), 55.

See also Sugar-making in China; Reciprocity Treaty
Sugar-making in China, 27–28
Sun Ah Mi, 261
Sun Chin, 152
Sun Fo, 155
Sun Wui, 16, 149, 150, 254
Sun Yat-sen (Chung-shan, Sun Tai-Cheong), 16, 150, 154, 155, 156, 159–160, 177, 239, 261, 262, 264, 265, 314, 326, 332
Swatow, 16, 24, 198
Swift, John F., 16

T'ai Tsung, Emperor, 163
Tang Peng Sum, 116
Tao Kuang, Emperor, 3, 4, 5
Taylor, Clarice B., 238, 253
Taylor, Wray, 82
Temples, 25, 161, 162, 181, 182–189; caretakers of, 187, 190; family shrine, 25. Individual: How Wong, 185–188; Kwan Dai, 183, 188; Kwan Yin, 25, 183–185; Leong Ma, 188. *See also* Religion, Chinese
Teng, Ssu-yu, 9
Ten-syan, Joseph, 195
Thrum, Thomas G., 55
Tientsin, 44, 46, 159
Ting, Mei-jung, 159
Toishan (Toyshan), 16, 149
Tom, George B., 158
Tong-Lao, T. S. Y., 242
Tong Phong, 262
Tong, Shao-Yi, 242
Tongs, 145. *See also* Clubs and organizations
Torbert, L. L., 55
Trade: in China, 8, 9, 10, 11, 22, 33, 38, 259–260, 313, 315, 316, 317; in Hawaii, 39, 57, 259–260, 315, 316
Trades and occupations, 88–89, 91, 94–95, 97, 108, 114–115, 117, 127, 132, 139, 205, 214, 215, 245, 250–251, 253, 262, 263, 316, 319, 322; carpentry, 40–41, 322; bakery, 88, 321–322; stores, 89, 126–131
Trescot, William Henry, 16
Triad Society. *See* Hoong Moon societies
Tsang Kwai, 200
Tseng Kuo-fan, 163
Tseng Siu-Heng, 265
Tshi, Sak En, 217
Tso Tsung-t'ang, 163
Tungkun, 16, 127

357

Tyler, John, 3, 4

Vancouver, George, 37
Van Deerlin, Hilda, 236
Vos, Hobart, 242

Waialua, Oahu, 93, 205, 206
Waianae, Oahu, 203, 205
Waichow, 16, 127
Waiehu, Maui, 330
Waiewa, Oahu, 202
Waihee, Maui, 314
Wailua Homesteads, Kauai, 244, 245, 246
Wailuku, Maui, 44, 54, 56, 112, 216, 251
Waimanalo, Oahu, 159
Waimea, Hawaii, 217
Waimea, Kauai, 55, 89, 213, 329
Waiohinu, Hawaii, 262
Waiole, Oahu, 203
Walker, James, 235
Ward, Frederick, 9
Wars, 12, 156, 159, 161–162, 163, 326, 332. Individual: Boxer, 11, 316; British 1860, 47; Opium, 3, 8; Sino-British, 255; Taiping, 9, 162; Tong, 145, 149
Waterman, C. C., 90
West River (Si-kiang), 20
Whalley, Herbert F. E., 233
Whampoa, 8, 35, 260
Wilcox, George, 70–74
Wilcox, Robert, 52
Williams, George H., 79
Willis, Alfred, 233, 234, 235, 261
Wing Wo Tai, 103

Wodehouse, James, 320
Women: in China, 26, 27, 32, 42–44, 67, 159, 330; in Hawaii, 42–44, 86–87, 97, 117, 141, 155, 159, 200, 329; and plural marriages, 120–122
Wong, Chow, 265
Wong, Clyde, 176
Wong, Elizabeth, 247–253
Wong Kim Shew, 80
Wong Leong, 265
Wong Leong Doo, 150, 151
Wong Min Tim, 116
Wong Tze Chun, 44, 54
Woo Set-Am, 231
Woo Yee-Bew, 230–236; children of, 230, 235, 236
Wood, Clifford B., 102
Woosung River, 46

Yan Ping (Yenping), 16, 149
Yangtze River, 20
Yang Wei-pin, 103, 321, 323
Yellow River (Hwang-ho), 20, 21
Yen, James Y. C., 265
Yellow Sea, 3, 47
Y.M.C.A., 116, 159, 201, 241, 265, 328
Young, John, 37
Young Kam Hoy, 116
Young-On (Aona), 261
Young, W. C., 232
Yun Doo, 150
Yung Sheong, 91
Yung Wing, 11
Yunnan, 20

Zen Len Fui, 234

About the Author

TIN-YUKE CHAR was born in Hawaii in 1905 and has had a colorful life combining business and education. A graduate of McKinley High School in Honolulu, he received his B.A. degree from Yenching University in Peking and his M.A. from the University of Hawaii, and pursued graduate studies at Columbia University. He then taught, both in Hawaii and in China. In 1938, Mr. Char and his family returned to Hawaii as refugees from the Japanese military invasion of Canton. He spent the next thirty years in the insurance business. In 1952, he became the first person in Hawaii to gain the national professional designation of CPCU (Chartered Property and Casualty Underwriter) in the field of insurance. Always active in community affairs, Mr. Char served on the boards of the Chinese Chamber of Commerce, the Hawaii Congress of Parents and Teachers, the Nuuanu YMCA, and the Board of Underwriters of Hawaii (insurance), among others, and is currently a member of a number of historical societies, including the Hawaii Chinese History Center. Upon retirement in 1969 as president of the Continental Insurance Agency of Hawaii, Mr. Char spent a year on the campus of Chung Chi College, a division of the Chinese University of Hong Kong, as a volunteer in student counseling and placement service. Since then, he has devoted his time to historical research and writing.

Mr. Char is also the author of *The Hakka Chinese: Their Origin and Folk Songs* and *Chinese Proverbs,* both published by the Jade Mountain Press of San Francisco in 1969, and *The Char Family Genealogy Book,* privately published in Honolulu in 1970.